The Making of a Class

THE MAKING OF A CLASS
Cadres in French Society

LUC BOLTANSKI

Translated by Arthur Goldhammer

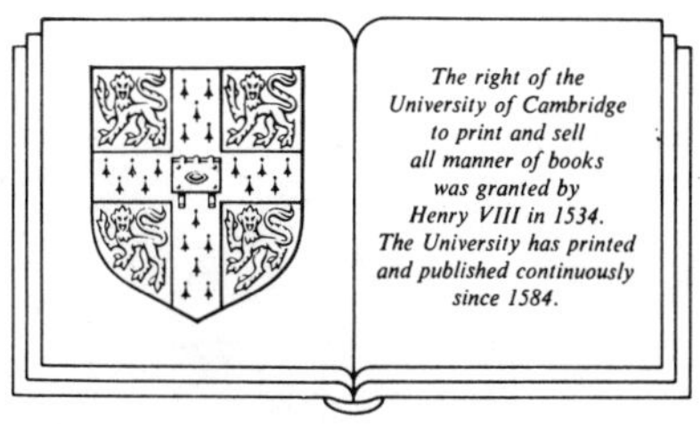

Cambridge University Press

Cambridge

New York New Rochelle Melbourne Sydney

Editions de la Maison des Sciences de L'Homme

Paris

Published by the Press Syndicate of the University of Cambridge
The Pitt Building, Trumpington Street, Cambridge CB2 2RP
32 East 57th Street, New York, NY 10022, USA
10 Stamford Road, Oakleigh, Melbourne 3166, Australia

Originally published in French as *Les cadres: La formation d'un groupe sociale* by Les éditions de minuit, Paris, 1982 and © Les éditions de minuit, 1982

First published in English in 1987 by the Cambridge University Press and the Maison des Sciences de l'Homme as
The Making of a Class: Cadres in French Society

Printed in Great Britain by
Redwood Burn Limited, Trowbridge, Wiltshire

British Library cataloguing in publication data

Boltanski, Luc
The making of a class: cadres in French society.
1. Middle classes – France – History
2. France – Social life and customs – 19th century
3. France – Social life and customs – 20th century
I. Title II. Les Cadres. *English*
944.08'0880622 DC33.6

Library of Congress cataloguing in publication data

Boltanski, Luc.
The making of a class.
Translation of: Les cadres.
Bibliography.
Includes index.
1. Social classes – France. I. Title.
HN440.S6B6513 1987 305.5'0944 87–5213

ISBN 0 521 32073 9
ISBN 2 7351 0200 9 (France only)

For Rosine

Contents

Abbreviations and acronyms

AFAP	Association française pour l'accroissement de la productivité
ANDCP	Association nationale des chefs du personnel
APEC	Association pour l'emploi des cadres
AO	Association ouvrière
BEP	Brevet d'études primaires
BEPC	Brevet d'études du premier cycle
BT	Brevet de technicien
BTE	Bureau des temps élémentaires
BTS	Brevet de technicien supérieur
CAP	Certificat d'aptitude professionelle
CCM	Confédération générale des syndicats de classes moyennes
CDS	Centre des démocrates sociaux
CEGOS	Commission d'études générales des organisations
CELSA	Centre d'études littéraires scientifiques appliquées
CEPH	Centre d'étude des problèmes humains
CEPI	Centre d'études des problèmes industriels
CFDT	Confédération française démocratique du travail
CFTC	Confédération française de travailleurs chrétiens
CGC	Confédération générale des cadres
CGCE	Confédération générale des cadres de l'économie
CGPF	Confédération générale du Patronat Français
CGPME	Confédération générale des petites et moyennes entreprises
CGT	Confédération générale du travail
CIPC	Caisse interprofessionnelle de prévoyance de cadres
CNAM	Conservatoire Nationale des Arts et Métiers
CNOF	Comité national de l'organisation française
CNOF	Commission nationale d'organisation française
CNPF	Confédération nationale du patronat français
CPA	Centre de préparation aux affaires
CRC	Centre de recherche et d'études des chefs d'entreprise

EDF	Electricité de France
EOST	Ecole d'organisation scientifique du travail
ESCAE	Ecoles supérieures de commerce et d'administration des entreprises
FASFID	Fédération des associations et sociétés françaises d'ingénieurs diplômés
FGEL	Fédération des groupes d'étude de lettres
FNEGE	Fondation nationale pour l'enseignement de la gestion des entreprises
FNSEA	Fédération nationale des syndicats d'exploitants agricoles
FNSI	Fédération nationale des syndicats d'ingénieurs
GIR	Groupements initiatives et responsabilité
HEC	Ecole des hautes études commerciales
INSEE	Institut national de statistiques et d'études économiques
ISST	Institut des Sciences Sociales du Travail
MCC	Mouvement des cadres, ingénieurs, et dirigeants chrétiens
MCE	Management Centre Europe
MRG	Mouvement des radicaux de gauche
MRP	Mouvement républician populaire
OCM	Organisation civile et militaire
OECE	Organization for European Economic Cooperation
PCF	Parti communiste français
PME	Petites et moyennes entreprises
PR	Parti républicain
PS	Parti socialiste
PSU	Parti socialiste unifié
RPF	Rassemblement pour la France
SEMA	Société d'économie et de mathématique appliquée
SIS	Syndicat des ingénieurs salariés
SNCF	Système national des chemins de fer français
SNECMA	Société Nationale d'étude et de construction de moteurs d'avion
SOFRES	Société française de recherche économiques et sociales
SPID	Syndicat professionel des ingénieurs diplômés français
SVRP	Syndicat des voyageurs, représentants, placiers
SYNTEC	Chambre syndicale des sociétés d'études et de conseil
TWI	Training Within Industry
UCB	Union de crédit pour le bâtiment
UCC	Union confédérale des ingénieurs et cadres
UCT	Union des cadres et techniciens
UDCA	Union pour la Défense des Commerçants et Artisans
UDF	Union pour la démocratie française
UF	Union fédérale
UGIC	Union générale des ingénieurs et cadres
UGICT	Union générale des ingénieurs, cadres et techniciens
UNC	Union nationale des combattants
UNEF	Union nationale d'étudiants français

USIC	Union sociale des ingénieurs catholiques
USIF	Union des syndicats d'ingénieurs français

Translator's introduction

This is a book about the social group that the French call *les cadres*. After much deliberation I decided that the best course was to leave this term untranslated. To have done otherwise would have been false to Luc Boltanski's whole approach, which is to show that the connotations of the word in French are historically derived and that the word itself has no single meaning. Boltanski cites Wittgenstein several times. One passage that he does not cite but that clarifies, I think, his attitude to social nomenclature is the following, from *The Blue Book*: "The idea that in order to get clear about the meaning of a general term one had to find the common element in all its applications has shackled philosophical investigation; for it has not only led to no result, but also made the philosopher dismiss as irrelevant the concrete cases, which alone could have helped him to understand the usage of the general term." What the reader will find in the pages that follow is a thorough examination of the concrete uses of the term "cadre," which I shall henceforth treat as though it were an English word. From this examination the meanings of the word will emerge more clearly than from any dictionary definition: "salaried staff" (Harrap's), "officials" (Larousse), "executives, managers, managerial staff" (Collins) are all misleading in one way or another, as the reader will discover. One point of this book is that terms of social classification are never natural or neutral and hence should always be approached as though taken from a foreign language; the impossibility of translation should drive this point home for English-speaking readers.

Certain secondary decisions followed from the primary decision not to translate "cadre." I have left bourgeoisie, petite bourgeoisie, grande bourgeoisie, haute bourgeoisie,and moyenne bourgeoisie as I found them. The reader may infer Boltanski's use of these vexed terms from the context. I have, however, translated *classes moyennes* as "middle class" or "middle classes," because it seemed too labored to do otherwise. This despite an explicit distinction between *classes moyennes* and "middle class in the American sense" that Boltanski raises at one point.

Free use is made here of a number of terms common in French sociological parlance and familiar to English readers of French sociology in translation. Readers unversed in this terminology may wish to consult the introduction to Charles C. Lemert (ed.), *French Sociology: Rupture and Renewal Since 1968* (New York: Columbia University Press, 1981), for an illuminating discussion.

Arthur Goldhammer

Preface

This work, or at any rate my interest in cadres [for more on the use of this term, see translator's introduction], came about partly by chance. In connection with a collaborative study of cultural diffusion I had occasion to study autodidacts (i.e., workers performing jobs for which they were not formally trained in school), a group that happens to include a fairly large number of low-level cadres and "in-house" engineers [i.e., engineers whose titles are bestowed upon them by their employers rather than by a formal diploma – trans.]. This work made me curious about the mechanisms of selection and promotion used by industrial firms. The literature was abundant enough – "selection," "evaluation," and "promotion" belonging as they do to that dubious realm where "management" meets the social sciences, where the personnel manager and the sociologist exchange ideas and reinforce one another's authority – but it did not provide satisfactory or adequate answers. It was the term "cadre" itself that puzzled me: peculiar to France, the word is used mainly inside industry. The more astute observers mentioned the uniqueness and ambiguity of the term but ended their questioning there. It soon became clear that I would never understand how cadres were selected until I understood how the social group denoted by the word "cadre" came to exist. The life stories of individual cadres, which I began collecting, all referred implicitly to the collective "biography" of the group in terms of which these individuals defined themselves and their social identities.

All this is a rather long-winded way of saying that while I found it necessary to cross disciplinary boundaries and borrow from history, sociology, social psychology, and so forth, my reasons for doing so had nothing to do with a priori judgment or intellectual fashion. The progress of my research was unplanned. It was the logic of the subject itself that took me from political history to individual biography, from social categories to mental ones, from statistical analysis to ethnomethodology, from institutions to individuals, and so on.

It would be tedious to list all the incidental research projects that I was obliged to undertake, particularly since there is no simple, one-to-one correspondence between my knowledge of any given topic and the surveys that I conducted. I deliberately set out to collect historical, sociological, economic, and psychological data simultaneously, and my daily schedule, not surprisingly, often seemed anarchic: I might easily go from reading forgotten works at the Bibliothèque Nationale to studying industrial monographs to plowing through recent statistical surveys to conducting lengthy interviews with real-life "cadres."

These interviews, incidentally, were conducted in ways of which most textbooks on methodology would no doubt disapprove. My relationship to my interviewees was comparable at times to that of a rather naive ethnographer to his native informants (in this realm I still had everything to learn). At other times I behaved more like a cognitive psychologist probing experimental subjects. And I should add, perhaps, that in the course of a long-term research project such as this, one inevitably forms friendships and relationships with the people whom one studies. Forewarned by my reading of the methodologically impeccable but often vacuous articles published in the official journals, I was particularly suspicious of the practice of conducting interviews at the workplace with the blessings of company and management. Even brief experience teaches that this kind of interview is not conducive to open and fruitful dialogue between sociologist and informant.

Industrial sociology, whose object of study is the firm, the place where class domination and the class struggle are most intense, most overt, and most difficult to hide, depends more than most types of sociology on its methods of investigation and, in particular, on the mediations between investigator and object of investigation. The internal approach, that is, the process of reconstructing the system of work relations within the firm and of isolating and identifying the objective mechanisms of domination and control – in principle the only way of studying what individuals say and do and how they react to behavior-determining collective processes – is in many cases distorted by the relationship between the observer and those plant officials who make his work possible. Much published work in this field exhibits theoretical orientations and interests quite unrelated to the experiences and concerns of the social actors themselves. This would be puzzling if one were unaware of the concessions that researchers often have to make to company officials in order to gain access to plants and conduct interviews with workers. In order to interpret what cadres reportedly say in these interviews, we must bear in mind that they are often held in formal settings, generally inside the plant, sometimes in group sessions; employees who expect to work for the company long after the interviewer has returned to his university meet with outsiders approved by management, who are sometimes difficult to distinguish from the "industrial engineers," "experts," and "advisors" of every ilk who are called in when a company is in crisis or about to be reorganized.

Accordingly, I felt it necessary to take a different approach, one that might seem utterly devoid of method if ethnographers had not taught us that the road to understanding a "native" culture is never straight and often surprisingly tortuous. Information is always costly, in terms of time and investment. I began by calling upon what few contacts I had among cadres. I asked people I knew to introduce me to their friends, to set up meetings and dinners at their homes, etc. Once the pump was primed, information began to flow, little by little.

I also approached the leaders of cadres' organizations on more formal terms. Every social group has its leaders – not always the members of the group best known to outsiders. On the whole I approached these cadre leaders without illusions: official spokesmen invariably speak, even in private conversation, in the name of the group they represent, and the sociologist rarely learns anything from interviews that he does not already know from reading their lectures, published interviews, political speeches, and the like. Yet I conducted many such interviews because, for complicated reasons that would take too long to analyze here, I felt that physical interaction, face-to-face familiarity with these spokesmen and actors would help me to understand their words and actions better than I otherwise could have done, even if the actual substance of the interviews added nothing new to my fund of knowledge.

Most of these interviews were tiresome affairs, but on occasion I met remarkable men whose experience, intimate knowledge of the milieu, and inexhaustible goodwill taught me a great deal. I am thinking especially of Pierre-Louis Marger of the UGICT, Pierre Beaudeux of the magazine *L'Expansion*, and Jean-Baptiste Eggens of the *Revue française de gestion*, as well as others too numerous to name.

Much of the time devoted to this work was spent gathering and analyzing statistical data. Lacking funding for large-scale research, I was unable to carry out a thorough statistical survey, and the time was not ripe, to say the least, for obtaining government financing from an agency such as CORDES or DGRST. Still, I tried to gather all available statistical data for later analysis. As is often the case, the financial handicap ultimately proved beneficial, for it forced me to reflect upon the fundamental questions raised by discrepancies in the statistical data, questions that I would most likely have evaded had I had the means initially to carry out a "rigorous" large-scale investigation, as I normally would have wished. Space does not permit me to list the names of all the individuals and agencies that made available statistical data, much of it quite interesting. In particular, I sorely tried the patience of Françoise de Turckheim of the Association pour l'emploi des cadres and, once again, Pierre Beaudeux, who provided me with *L'Expansion*'s survey on the "value of cadres." Both gave me the handsomest of gifts: several decks of punched cards. I also want to thank Alain Desrosières and Laurent Thévenot, who introduced me to the riches of the INSEE and who explained to me the mysteries of the 1970 survey of professions, skills, and training, computerized analysis of which (by Salah Bouhedja) proved especially useful.

All of this research was carried out under the auspices of the Centre de sociologie de l'éducation et de la culture at the Ecole des hautes études en sciences sociales. Again, space does not permit me to adequately acknowledge the debt I owe to the many friends who spent long hours typing, documenting, copying, and so forth, to say nothing of the most tiresome job of all, reading and rereading these pages.

I also benefited from the advice of Pierre Ansart, a man of unparalleled understanding, generosity, and consideration, to whom I am profoundly grateful, as well as from the suggestions and criticisms, invariably useful, of Pierre Fougeyrollas, Antoine Prost, and Jean-Daniel Reynaud (my memory of the afternoon of my "thesis defense" is more of a "working meeting" than of an academic grilling, for which I am also grateful). Finally, it seems rather strange to say what goes without saying in thanking Pierre Bourdieu, with whom many years of collaboration have immeasurably influenced the present work. I hope that in the few hundred pages that follow he will find what I might call a "homage in action," or, to borrow yet another of his concepts, a "homage in *practice*."

L.B.

Paris, November 1981

Introduction 1: one man's story

"I am a cadre"

I've been working fifteen years. My experience is unusual. For a while it was no joke. There was a time when things were pretty tense. I didn't let it show, didn't say anything, I'm an optimistic kind of guy, but inside I said to myself, "You're all washed up!" The book I'm writing – I plan to call it I AM A CADRE *– begins like this: "Where did you go to college?" I go, "I went to X." The interviewer says, "Oh, I see, a middle-class school." Then the guy says to me, "OK, but what did you do before that?" I tell him, "Sure, I went somewhere else," but I haven't got the nerve to tell him that it was the technical school at Champagne-sur-Oise. It would have been sort of like saying I went to Perros-Guirrec twenty-five years ago, or Morlaix. . . . After that I got hired as an on-the-job trainee. . . . I studied engineering and worked during vacation. I got a diploma as a general draftsman and a tool-and-die maker's certificate. . . . Ten or fifteen years ago the technical schools prepared you for a career as an engineer or technician. You could go on to one of the big engineering schools (Arts et Métiers or Polytechnique or Centrale), or you could drop out along the way. . . . They made you take exams, get your draftsman's certificate, your industrial technician's certificate, so in case you didn't get into one of the big schools you'd still have some kind of diploma and you could get a job somewhere as a draftsman or a machinist and go back to the shop floor or the assembly line and to hell with you. . . . One fine day I applied for a job as an engineer's assistant in this plant where I'd done on-the-job training. Engineer's assistant, see, because you had to go to one of the big schools to be considered an engineer. They told me, "Don't worry, in a few months you'll be promoted to engineer." In the department I got the jobs nobody else wanted. I was the only assistant, the only one who hadn't gone to one of the big schools. I worked hard, let me tell you. . . .*

One thing led to another. There was this guy I happened to know. . . . They called me in and said, "It seems you know Mr So-and-so." . . . There I was, me, an engineer's assistant, called in to see the big boss. You can imagine the stir that caused! So, anyway, I managed to have a word with this friend of mine . . . and the boss got the medal he wanted or whatever it was. So they called me back down to the front office: "How much do you want?" I said, "Look, all I want is to publish an article in a technical journal." . . . Well, let me tell you, it didn't take long. A few days after the article appeared, I had a whole army of vultures on my back. . . . "This won't do. . . . I'm your boss, I'm your superior." The whole mafia of graduate engineers had it in for me. I was called in to see the engineering supervisor, a graduate of Polytechnique. . . . After that they put me behind a desk for a year with nothing to do. Nothing, absolutely nothing: "technical documentation" they called it. . . . I asked for permission to go do a month's training in England: "No, out of the question, that's not for you." I went to England anyway, on my vacation, paid for it out of my own pocket. And I found out some interesting stuff, technical stuff. . . . When I got back, I still had nothing to do. I was still behind my desk, a little engineer's assistant nobody paid any attention to. One of the assistant department heads came to see me: "Look, how about writing up a little confidential report on what you saw in England." I said, "Sir, what you're asking me to do is called industrial espionage." He threatened to have me fired: "If that's the kind of guy you are, I think you'd do better in sales." . . . I picked up the ball and threw it right back: "If you get me a job in sales, I'll write your report." Tit for tat, no bones about it. The guy walks out and slams the door. A week later I'm called into the front office: "So, my friend, I hear you want to be in sales. OK, fine, we've got some small components to sell, little stuff, maybe that will suit you." So they put me with this guy, a retired officer, because you know in that kind of company that's all they've got, it's all a matter of contacts, their whole business is with the army. So I'm in a little office with this guy and I'm supposed to sell parts. It's a start. . . . After three months the orders start rolling in so fast I don't know what to do with them. . . . My boss left and I found myself head of the department, selling these parts. So there I was. I had everything I wanted. I was king of the castle, and for five years all outside orders went through me, I helped out with the quality-control testing, I tightened up the process internally, and my sales figure kept on climbing. . . . Then, one fine day, they tell me, "Look, we don't have time to deal with you, we're going to assign you to Mr So-and-so." He's a real English type, a business school graduate, a crackerjack manager but a jerk when it comes to sales and as for the technical end he didn't know beans. . . . And then the trouble started. . . . I was getting fed up. They gave me a hard time about expenses, details, little things. They treated me like a kid, corrected my correspondence because a comma was out of place, so sometimes when I wrote a client to confirm an order the letter arrived a month late. . . . I started losing custo-

mers. . . . One day this guy comes in: "Mr So-and-so sent me, I'm out of work, I have no job." I said to myself, "This guy doesn't look very smart. He'll act as a buffer between me and the boss." . . . I leave for a skiing trip, and when I come back what do I find: this guy behind my desk making a telephone call! . . . This bastard, no diploma, no nothing, somehow managed to get himself hired as an engineer. . . . I complained to the head office: "Before, two people ran this office. Now we've got three." "Well, look, you know, we think this new guy's not too bad." I said, "Fine, then, you keep him." I slammed the door. They put me in a different department and stuck me back behind a desk, another year of doing nothing. Nothing, nothing, nothing! I did a thesis at Arts et Métiers to get an official state diploma as an engineer and I waited. One day they took my lamp. I raised a stink. Then they took my telephone. Then, one morning, they called me in to the front office. "Look, we're unhappy. You know times are hard and your work hasn't been very satisfactory." After thirteen years, my work isn't satisfactory! "We think you'd make a good sales manager in a small firm." So I said, "In plain words, you're giving me the sack?" "No, no, but think it over, maybe you could find another job?" So I left on vacation, but things were starting to look bad. When I came back, they'd moved my office, they'd stuck me off in some corner with a guy who was a complete zero. Then they call me in again: "Have you found anything yet?" "No, nothing." "That's too bad, because we have no grounds for firing you." So I go, "I have no grounds for leaving." It went on like that for a while until finally I'd had it. I wound up leaving, with a little severance pay for a sweetener. . . .

That's a cadre for you. . . . We're not the ones who make the money. But be careful: there are cadres and cadres. Your executive is a cadre too. . . . I've looked around. . . . Right now your cadre is your pawn, your poor schmuck at the bottom of the heap. . . . Check out one of these big "interviews for cadres" sessions you read about in the newspapers. . . . The companies don't identify themselves in the ads. You don't know if you're applying for a job with the railroad or the subways or to make condoms or God knows what. They're looking for an engineer with fifteen years experience who speaks English, Russian, and German to do God knows what, and you're interviewed by people who don't know a thing about the profession. They don't know one technical field from another. They hire you on the basis of qualifications that don't really mean much. That's the tragedy. Letters, I've written plenty of letters, and I've been to dozens of employment agencies. . . . In one plant there were twenty-five candidates and it took all day. At six o'clock only two of us were left. The guy says to me: "OK, you're hired, but I forgot to tell you one thing. My son is in the service right now. He comes back in two years, and when he does you're out." . . . Another ad said to show up at such and such a place. There were seventy-five or eighty of us in a big hall. This guy there holds up a square: "What does this make you think of? . . . Good. Now I put a circle in the square. What does that look like?" I got up and said, "Listen, I'm sorry, I'm thirty-four years old. I'm through playing games. I'm leaving." Completely idiotic, those tests.... One middle-sized firm made me a totally fantastic offer: the impressive title of sales manager, a huge salary, the good life. I showed up for the appointment, the boss wasn't there. His secretary took me around to show me the plant, so it wouldn't be a wasted trip! There I was in my Ted Lapidus suit. By the time I left that night, I had stains like that. Incredible!... A week later the boss comes back. You know the type: argyle jacket, the golfer's look, snobbish, pretentious – everything about him said "I'm the boss." Everybody in that plant was a boss. "By the way, I forgot to mention, I can't pay you 7500 francs a month like I said, it's 5200." The bastard!... For that place it was peanuts. The car they gave me was all dented and scratched. Guys took me aside and let me have it: "You're coming in and taking the bread out of our mouths." Guys with the title of engineer, a lot of them self-taught. Guys who weren't capable of doing anything else, that was the tragedy.... Those guys, on their business cards, they wrote down "engineer." Once or twice I went with one of them to a client, and I asked myself, "Do I go in with them or not?" They wrote down "engineer" but they weren't engineers: your so-called sales engineer [INGÉNIEUR TECHNICO-COMMERCIAL] is a kind of half-baked cadre, nobody knows what the hell it means.... The atmosphere in that place was terrible! Dirty tricks galore, guys were stealing clients from one another. I suffered in that place. It was the pits!... Just because a guy's got a territory doesn't mean he's supposed to blow everybody else out of the water, not any more.... The company gave color TVs to buyers who were willing to accept them.... A whore's business.... I know plenty of buyers who'll send some business your way because you pay them off. It's highway robbery.... There's nothing wrong with a little gift, but some of the stuff that was going on was serious.... One buyer, twenty-seven years old, no training, bought himself a country house for 70,000 francs and the guy doesn't make more than 5000 francs a month. They say he gets fifty percent of every contract.... And the trips!... A weekend in Venice with the missus, or else she can order what she wants without leaving home.... Some like presents, some like fancy food, and then – I know plenty, OK – there are the ones who go for women. They've got 'em for every taste.... Everybody who worked in that plant had the attitude of that golfer, rotten, paternalistic.... One day somebody said to me, "Get a load of Mr So-and-so, dancing with the girls from the plant." That was the attitude in that place!... To top it all off, I was bound hand and foot to the company. I wasn't allowed to do anything without asking the boss. He was really the Boss, with a capital B. It was truly disgusting. I was a slave to the company. That's what your middle-sized company is like, and the small firms are something else again....

I had no clients. Wherever I went, they said to me, "Look, buddy, what's the *matter with you? What are you doing with that company anyway? Come look at these reports." In short, I didn't sell shit.... Then vacation came. I had practically no business when I was supposed to be "Mister Miracle" who was going to bring them 800 million in sales overnight. I tried to see the golfer so I could tell him, "Look, you hired me, something's not right in your company." I never could get in to see him. I saw him twice, when he hired me and when he fired me.... On 20 October he said, "Look, I haven't had a chance to evaluate your performance because of the vacation. Before I take you on permanently, I'm extending your notice." This wasn't legal, because my three months' notice had expired. But he handed me an extension form predated to 20 September: "If you don't sign, you're fired." In the middle of October this was no joke. I looked him in the eye and said, "I trust you. I'll sign. But first we're going to have a little talk about the products you've given me to sell." I explained things to him. I told him that the people I was trying to sell wanted something decent, that nobody was there just to run up sales figures, etc. "Perfect," he says to me. Three days later he calls me in and I'm fired. I was screwed, I'd signed the paper.... So I took a new job, because really I had no choice. It was with a personal friend who had a small company, sometimes fifteen employees, sometimes as many as sixty. I gave myself a year with him, since he'd done me a favor. He paid me well, but he paid me in three or four installments, so that in July I made 800 francs and in September 450.... There were women who worked in rubber boots. You have to wonder how their feet felt at the end of the day. Anyway, everybody who worked there, their hands were all eaten away by acid, they worked in dust and steam and for irregular pay and kept their mouths shut. They were the ones who really needed help.... The boss and his wife made three grand a month and bought everything – bidets for the country house, everything – at company expense. He bought himself a \$10,000 yacht. OK, that's unusual, some people are oblivious to what they're doing, to how it looks. But this nonsense kept up, and when I realized it wasn't going to stop I told him, "You can pay me more than you do. Your company's missing about 120 grand off the books. I'm sorry. I quit."*

So then I got a job through contacts, working for X again.... I sleep better at night. X ... is a great company, a really first-rate firm.... The working environment is tremendous.... It has to do with the intellectual level of the staff.... I have no worries. I don't worry about losing clients because the company's products hold up, they've been designed by competent people, by a large group, and there are no surprises in store for me.... It's steady, it's solid, and it's for real.... There's a better attitude here, no shady stuff like the guy with the argyle jacket.... A first-class employees' council (COMITÉ D'ENTREPRISE).... If I die the casket's paid for. Incredible benefits: vacations and everything. They pay my auto insurance. There are clubs, film clubs, sports clubs.... What's really interesting is the training program. They have a castle with a swimming pool and we go there for training courses, for two or three days. It's really nice.... I have no worries. I get my instructions, they tell me, "You're leaving on such-and-such a date." The company has a castle down there. For three days there are lectures about the company, what people do, what we make, it's fantastic. I get my instructions at the last minute. "You're leaving at such-and-such a time on such-and-such a train." They leave the choice up to me.... I could be sent to a factory overseas, in Japan, the United States, anywhere.... Hundreds of thousands of employees the world over: it's gigantic.... The company keeps a jet stationed at Roissy, and others in Zurich, Berlin, London.... When I travel for the company ... [I stay] in palaces ... they're not chintzy. After the courses at the castle there's a conference on sales. They may send us to Casablanca, to a hotel down there, for two days....

Love of work is a thing of the past in France. A guy doesn't give a damn because he says to himself, "For 2000 francs why should I work my butt off?" The man upstairs doesn't give a damn because he still gets his vacation and all he thinks about is going skiing or weekends at his country house. It's nothing like Japan, where people love their work and the company is part of every worker.... The French are lousy businessmen. You want to hear a story? In those days I had a [Peugeot] 404 sedan and I wanted to buy a [Citroën] D.S. I go down to the Citroën dealer, I open the door, naturally, and I nearly kill myself slipping on some kind of cigar butt on the floor. The place is done in this disgusting green linoleum and behind a crummy desk, made of wood, there's this girl typing. She looks up from her typewriter and says, "What can I do for you?" "I'd like to see a salesman about a car." "Sure, hold on." In a minute this guy comes out. It's about one-thirty, two o'clock in the afternoon, and this guy is buttoning up his jacket. "What can I do for you?" "I'd like to trade in my automobile." "Stay right there. Hey, Paulo, come here a second, will you? There's a guy out here wants to trade in his old tub." That was my reception at Citroën. So then Paulo comes in, wearing a white shirt that's not so white. "OK, look, here are the papers." He hands me a pack of dirty papers, covered with grease. "So you've got an old wreck, looks like." The guy takes my car and burns rubber down the avenue d'Italie, scaring the living daylights out of everybody on the street, and then he comes back fifteen minutes later with the car smoking. It was incredible. I said to myself, "These people can't really be serious about selling cars. What should I do?" So I went to Mercedes. Thick rug, soft music, guy impeccably dressed, wearing a tie: "Good afternoon, sir, would you care for an apéritif?" You could've knocked me over. "If you'd care to look over our range of models, you can make yourself comfortable over here. We won't praise our own automobiles. Study the catalogue at your leisure and judge for yourself." "OK, but I have a 404." "Of course, sir. No problem." And the French wonder why the Germans sell Mercedes....

The biggest scandal is the nationalized firms. You go to a nationalized firm at eight-thirty in the morning and you find people lined up in front of the coffee machine until nine o'clock. At nine they read their papers. At nine-thirty they make some personal calls, then they go to the bathroom, then they have a smoke until ten while waiting for lunch to be served at noon, and then at four the day's over: nobody works after that. It's a bloody mess, and you and I are the ones who pay for it. . . . Every person should be able to reach a level commensurate with his abilities. The important thing is what kind of stuff you're made of, how far you can go. If you hit your "Peter level" at customer service rep, you're finished. If you hit it at engineer, that's as far as you go. But if you get past that hurdle, the sky's the limit. You can be CEO. . . . It's a question of individual ability. . . . Personally, my life's dream would be to run a company. You've got to know what goes on from the top of the pyramid right down to the bottom: the guy who sweeps the floors has his own problems, and you can't neglect them in your company. But you've also got to know the financial end. I feel I'm capable of being sales manager for a small firm, but that doesn't mean I'm capable of managing sales for a firm that employs 20,000 people. . . . I think I might make sales manager some day. Sure. That is, I feel capable of doing the job. If you have the IQ and you catch the escalator on the way up, why not? . . . Here there are prospects for promotion. . . . An imbecile like me who's put in thirteen years in industry but who's still learning the ways of the company, he's got a chance in the next five years to land a job with major responsibilities. . . . You distinguish yourself through work. They set us a goal, it's up to us to follow through.

The meaning of the tale

The interview from which the foregoing excerpts were taken is unusual in that it records the product of a prior attempt at self-expression. M, who defines himself as a "cadre," has begun work on an autobiography to be entitled *I am a cadre*. He hopes to tell of his disappointments, to relate his experience, to share his life with his readers and thus to testify to the "condition" of the cadre in French society. In other words, the point of the interview, its focus, its themes, its representation of social identity are – partly prefabricated and partly improvised – the product of a quasisociological formalization that precedes any of the interviewer's questions. To understand what M says, therefore, one must take account of the social conditions under which the linguistic tools that make his discourse possible were fashioned. For like scientific discourse the report of an informant is not a mere accumulation of raw facts. The data are constructed. Introspection, especially when it becomes the occasion for public expression, makes some things explicit, others implicit: explicitly stating what had previously been an ambiguous part of everyday practice is tantamount to interpreting that practice in a way that brings out some meanings and suppresses others. The suppressed meanings survive as "implications" and might in turn be brought out by other kinds of guided introspection (i.e., introspection guided by other interlocutors in other circumstances). Hence what M says may be read as a parable in which features wrested from actual experience are reformulated, reinterpreted, and reordered in such a way as to form the stages of a developed argument.

In particular, there is no point trying to disguise the fact that the foregoing interview was shaped in part, and certainly in tone and style, by the conditions under which it was obtained: at a dinner party, in the evening, among friends, "in confidence," with a few bottles of good wine within easy reach. These circumstances define the speech situation. Whatever traditional methodologists may say, this speech situation does not violate norms of scientific objectivity, nor does it guarantee authenticity, as certain "naturalistic" social scientists would rather facilely maintain. Rather, it animates a particular dimension of the speaker's identity and evokes a particular kind of "language game": one of privacy, of relaxation, occasionally somewhat irresponsible in utterance because speech here is virtually without consequence – indeed, it is precisely this that distinguishes this particular speech situation from others in which language is used in more "official" ways. In order to interpret a specific utterance, however, it may not be enough to consider simply the speech setting and such attributes of the speaker as his language-defined social position (crudely measurable in terms of education) or what I shall call his "expressive interests." For the linguistic resources wielded by individual speakers are also the product of the collective process through which social groups create the symbols that enable them to cope with historical circumstances (*la conjoncture*). A fund of common stereotypes is both an instrument of knowledge (which individuals can use introspectively, to identify objects named by the group) and an instrument of legitimation, in the sense that the group is able to define its practice in terms of recognized models, thus enabling individual members to understand and cope with what is happening. We must grasp all the constraints affecting the speaker in order to determine the limits of the validity of what he says. This is perhaps not so much a matter of establishing the truth value of his utterances, which in any case are not all affirmations or statements of fact, as it is a question of establishing guidelines for the legitimate use of what he says. Interpreting the informant's account does not mean passively accepting the data as they are given, nor does it authorize us to erect our suspicions as a kind of symptomatology (limited only by the analyst's powers of imagination). The interpretation should be inspired, rather, by the way in which the informant's testimony is received in practice: a syncretic perception of what is said, of the way in which it is said, of the attributes of the speaker, of what he does, of what he says elsewhere and has said before, of what others say, and of what others say about him.

Recast in a more objective style, M's story is more or less as follows: the only son of a butcher from a small town near Paris, he studied technical subjects first at a technical high school and then at a small engineering school. Upon graduation he took a job as a technician in a small firm specializing in the manufacture of electronic components. For several years he "vegetated" before moving into sales in the same firm. In this new position he flourished, his status within the firm rose, and he was "king in his own castle." But he clashed with a new manager, a business school graduate, and his status plummeted. The firm first tried to get him to resign, then fired him. He thereupon took a job in a medium-sized firm with the title of sales manager and the promise of a high salary. But the title was eyewash and the promised salary was never paid. Unable to sell the "shit" manufactured by the firm, he lost customers, argued with the boss, and was abruptly dismissed. A friend who owned and ran a small electronics company agreed to take him on. But business was bad. M was paid irregularly. After a year he left. He then got a job, through contacts, as sales engineer with a major multinational corporation. After a year in this position and many disappointments, M says that he is completely satisfied. He can finally sleep easy. But this purely denotative version of the story clearly takes no account of the *intention* that motives it. These exemplary adventures and true-life tales are in fact a "polemic": cadres are not protected; they are exploited ("the cadre in our company is the poor schmuck at the bottom of the ladder"). One interpretation is all but ready-made: this "confession" reflects the crystallization of one cadre's self-awareness. A man becomes aware of his position within the relations of production and in solidarity with other wage-earners, other "exploited" men and women, disavows his former beliefs. But this interpretation leaves out what motivates and governs M's anger: namely, that the cadre is not appreciated at his just value or treated with the respect he deserves. Furthermore, his treatment, psychologically, financially, and otherwise, does not accord with the promises that have been made to him. There is a discrepancy between *de jure* status and *de facto* condition. Therein lies the ambiguity of the tale. In order to make himself understood, M is obliged to alternate between theoretical positions that have little in common: on the one hand the cadre and his insignia (the "suit by Pierre Cardin or Ted Lapidus," the "404 convertible," the "business trip," etc.), and on the other hand the "poor guy," the "dumb jerk," knocked around, humiliated, made a fool of, the guy who's been around and knows his way around yet is still cheated of his due. On the one hand the predator, sure of himself, a tough businessman, intelligent, ambitious; on the other hand the victim. Each of these images corresponds to a different "expressive interest," and while M cannot abandon either one, because each represents a fundamental aspect of his professional and social existence, neither can he make them work together, because the one neutralizes the other. Caught between two incompatible schemes, M adopts first one, then the other, and constructs his life in the manner of a picaresque novel, an unpredictable sequence of adventures and misadventures in a world of chance.

But this "speech strategy" also maps an identity. Lacking a self-image adequate to the position he occupies, and unsure of the nature and attributes of that position, M cannot define himself or exist socially without bringing into play vast regions of "social space" within which he is constantly on the move – at least symbolically. M's image is therefore structurally unstable, and, like one of those optical illusions that change their appearance drastically with a slight modification in the angle of view, he has only to forget himself for a moment, to lapse, no doubt deliberately in part, into momentary vulgarity, to bring out something in him more "common," less willing to be dominated, less complicitous with his employers: as, for example, when he stops defining himself as a "superior" supervising "inferiors" and sees himself as an "inferior" critical of his "bosses." The lexicological and syntactic controls are relaxed, and the tone becomes ironic and provocative. In these moments M's labile self-image touches bottom. Compared to the boss the cadre is "the poor schmuck," the fellow who is "kicked aroound," who lacks protection and security. To express the weight of the hierarchy, the distance between positions in the firm (*dans l'espace de l'entreprise*) and their associated symbolic attributes (*dans l'espace des propriétés symboliques*), M hits upon a military metaphor: the firm, he says, is "organized like the army: it's camouflaged, but it's the same." He is an object, a "slave of the company," of the "Boss with a capital B," always an instrument and never an actor, "called in to the front office," "called down by the big boss," hired on a whim, fired on a caprice, left to face the mystifying want ads, forced to take tests and to submit to interviews with employment agencies. Class relations are restored to the stark simplicity of pure economic relations. Money mediates all relations between agents at different levels of the hierarchy (thus one manager for whom he has done a personal favor has him "called in to the front office" and by way of thanks takes out his checkbook and asks, "How much do you want?"). M's changing fortunes similarly affect his attitude toward the trade unions. In good times he keeps aloof from the unions. All the cadres interviewed stressed the dangers of belonging to a union, even the Confédération Générale des Cadres [CGC], the only union acceptable to them: "Joining a union is the best way to get yourself fired." Yet when he has nothing to lose and his only reasonable strategy is to leave with the maximum severance pay, the union again seems valuable to him.

The "sales engineer"

"Sales engineer" is a relatively new position in the electronic components industry in which M works. As the name implies, the sales engineer uses technical competence to sell his company's product to other companies by extolling its technical virtues. He is also responsible for evaluating the "reliability" of products purchased from other firms. Sales engineers distinguish themselves in various ways[1] from ordinary salesmen: by the nature of the product they sell, by the magnitude of the deals in which they are involved, and by the nature of their clients – large companies, bureaucracies, etc. The job they do is important to the firm. Hence they enjoy a privileged but precarious position: admired and envied while their sales are on the rise, they risk a sudden downfall if business turns sour, if they have not by then quit the firm or risen in the hierarchy. Sales engineers therefore tend to be young men whose personal qualities are very important to their work, and whose rewards, chiefly symbolic, are not negligible: for example, the sales engineer often works outside the firm and is less subject to scrutiny of his working hours than other employees (ordinarily he does not punch a time-clock). In negotiating with a client he travels, entertains and is entertained, takes customers out to dinner or is taken out by them. He derives personal benefit from perquisites offered him as a representative of his firm, and the larger, more prestigious, and more ambitious the firm, the greater these perquisites are: the power of a firm can be judged in part by the standing of its cadre. For similar reasons, the sales engineer often derives a benefit through his title: the firm accords him the rank of cadre or engineer even though he is not necessarily an engineering school graduate. In this respect the relationship between a man's title within the firm and his formal schooling is relatively arbitrary. Furthermore, among sales engineers there is practically no difference between technicians and engineers, a distinction that is of great importance in most shops and research and development settings. The reason is that it would be insulting for a company to send a mere technician to deal with a client. Thus the sales engineer, whose job need not (although in some cases it may) require a high level of technical competence and who is usually not in charge of other workers, is granted a title that usually implies participation in the technical design of products and authority over subordinates.

There are still other reasons why the sales engineer commonly identifies with the firm that employs him. Since his job is to sell the firm's products, he is more likely to succeed if those products are better value for money than those of the competition. It is in his interest to believe, and to make others believe, that his firm is the best. All informants agreed that belief in one's firm is an important ingredient of success. Employers must fill these positions with honest and loyal employees, because sales representatives are in a sense the company's front line. They represent the firm to outsiders and negotiate important contracts. What is more, the men who occupy these positions are especially vulnerable to double-dealing and cheating. Many sales engineers admit to giving cases of wine as gifts; from there it is but a short step to outright bribery.

Similar remarks apply to buyers, as is shown by the following comments made by one buyer for a large department store, a man aged thirty-five and, like M, self-taught:

> People are constantly making me offers. I could have cash under the table every day of the week, since I have the power to make work and to stop work. Sometimes I'm handed envelopes – it breaks my heart to give them back – envelopes stuffed with 500-franc notes. There are some who do take them, which is fine until they're found out and the next day they're out on the street. The bosses talk to one another and they never get another job. You can't do it, in principle because it's dishonest, but you know, if it's

a question of whether my boss gets the money or I do, I'd rather it was me. If it's a moral question, my boss takes bribes, maybe not in the form of bribes, but it's all the same. When I make money for him, that's a bribe, it's money in his pocket that he doesn't pay me, but he's got nobody over him to raise a fuss. Still, morally, it's highly questionable.... We're always spending money for nothing. When you take somebody to dinner for the company, you order caviar, not sausages. If you take a fellow to Lasserre and you order *foie gras*, he'll be pleased and flattered. Anyway, he's got his receipt, it doesn't cost him anything, and he goes away happy. The company doesn't care because it can deduct the expense from its taxes. The restaurant is delighted. Everybody's happy, so you've got to spend the money.... A guy who thinks he's about to sign an important contract, what does he care about paying for a prostitute? So he spends a couple of thousand: the next day he's sure of getting his contract. You have to know people's weaknesses, their desires. As far as the expense account is concerned it makes no difference whether the guy takes you to Lasserre three times or pays three times for the same girl. What counts is the result. Some people you take out to dinner, others you pay for their women: what's the difference?

In order to make sure that its sales representatives walk the straight and narrow, a company must win their loyalty: symbolically, by appealing to their patriotism, their pride at working for the firm, etc., and materially, by offering stock, bonuses, supplements, etc. It must also maintain the morale of its sales force and be sure not to retain in these sensitive positions men out of step with the company and likely to voice resentment or criticism. For all these reasons, sales engineering positions are usually entry-level jobs where future executives are given a try-out. This is not always the case, however, and since the job description is still not very clear one often finds people of different educational attainment, social background, and career prospects in such posts. In addition to young engineers, graduates of the more prestigious engineering schools learning the business on the job before moving on to positions of power, one finds young salesmen graduated from business and law schools as well as men like M, former manufacturing technicians who can "stay in the game" only by constantly demonstrating their exceptional talent for sales, their loyalty, and their energy. Thus a position in sales, which for a future executive is merely on-the-job training, is for a former technician an achievement that sets him apart from his one-time peers.

The years of apprenticeship

For M it was by no means foreordained that he would become a cadre. Twenty years old in 1960, he left school just before the period of rapid expansion of higher education. As a young man he was drawn to professions that are difficult to enter (e.g., he dreamed of becoming an airline pilot) but obviously labored under no illusions as to his prospects. He followed a prudent strategy (as is common in families lacking social and cultural capital), securing diploma after diploma. The school he attended after completing technical high school is an ambiguous sort of institution: it grants an engineer's degree which is not universally recognized and which does not necessarily gain its holder access to positions bearing the title "engineer." The degree is one that can be read or interpreted in a variety of ways: it is a two-edged sword that can discredit its holder socially at the same time as it accredits him professionally (remember the insulting remark of M's first employer: "So you went to that middle-class school, did you?"). M did not in fact mention his alma mater by name until the end of the interview, by which time he had some notion of what the interviewer was after (not what he was used to). He also attended the more prestigious Ecole des Arts et Métiers for a year, apparently when, after several years on the job, he experienced his first career setback. His description of his educational career is impressionistic. Schools and degrees are not clearly specified. He alludes to both highly prestigious degrees and relatively undistinguished ones. This vagueness serves to obscure educational and social differences between him and other engineers in his branch of industry and to accentuate similarities in the nature of the work done (all are employed in "technical jobs"). The effect of this is to reduce life to one dimension, with education preceding career in a relationship of cause and effect (as in a textbook).

A similar vagueness shrouds M's professional debut. He goes to work (for a large French electronics firm that manufactures components for industry and the military) and is trained as an "engineer's assistant": an obsolete title, apparently more or less equivalent to senior technician and attractive precisely because of the promise implicit in the name – the prospect of advancement to engineer, the next rank in the hierarchy. Yet M remains in this position for five years, though he defines and describes it only in negative terms: He is not a real engineer and does the work that real engineers don't want to do. Finally, owing to a "combination of circumstances" (impossible to understand without knowing that M is a freemason), he is transferred to the sales department, a change of department which in this case implies a change of rank. The symbolism of technical labor (which with its uniform of gray coveralls and its tools in part overlaps the symbolism of factory labor) now gives way to the symbolism of business, the true mark of the cadre: chic clothes, well-cut suits, white shirts, automobiles, efficiency, meals, trips. Objectively, M's prospects for the future improve, but at the price of increased uncertainty and insecurity. Because M became a cadre in a period of economic growth and low inflation when the number of cadres (especially in the electronics industry in which he works) was on the rise, he tends to overestimate the value of the position. Similarly, he associates with the title images that reproduce, in a schematic, emblematic, and stylized form, a series of attributes, values, and expectations that do not necessarily correspond to his true position or to the material and symbolic resources at his disposal. M has some trouble locating his position within the firm and, even more, within the larger society, as if his whole system of reference, his internalized model of society, had been disrupted by his personal history, which has tended to distort his frame of reference. Indeed, M's professional adventures can be read as a series of attempts (and often failures) to ascertain the social attributes associated with the title that he has won for himself and is desperately trying to maintain. He does not really know what people expect of him or what he can expect of them. In particular, he does not know how far he can go: what his career chances are and how much authority he is allowed, how much freedom he has, or what his room for maneuver is, especially when it comes to relations with superiors. He slowly identifies his limits through unsuccessful attempts to overcome them and, more precisely, through interaction with others – cadres graduated from the elite schools, bosses – who raise his hopes of promotion, encourage his "energy," foster competition with his peers, and incite him to "outdo" himself, to "go beyond" his limits and yet keep him in his place, punish his transgressions, and knock him down when he attempts to rise too fast. These are the experiences that teach M the nature of the cadre's occupation – in the sense that he internalizes the values that govern the industrial order, values indispensable if he is to "dig a hole for himself" – and provide him with models of excellence that then become his own: he can no longer shake them, and it is too late to discover that he is not a cadre or at any rate that he is not a cadre to the same degree as some others.

In order to appreciate properly just how difficult an apprenticeship this was, one has to notice that it was the result of a conflict between lived experience and linguistic experience of the social world. It is as if the social actors' consciousness of their condition were mediated through a filter of words and images that delivers only a roughly approximate view of objective social space. M has difficulty using language to convey, in all its nuances, social experience for which no conventional name or image exists. Experience that cannot be articulated is for all practical purposes excluded from legitimate collective consciousness: either it is repressed, that is, relegated to the realm of the unsayable and private, or else it is expressed in a borrowed language that turns description into travesty. Anyone who falls into using this stylized, conventional language to describe the cadre's field of experience is in fact forced to describe that experience in terms appropriate only to certain privileged positions: for the words and images really only apply to those who are cadres in the full sense of the word, who hold degrees from prestigious institutions and who possess various other attributes characteristic of what was for a long time recognized as the "typical cadre." Attitudes and emblems associated with this stereotype may be internalized and exhibited without fear of ridicule, because they embody a collectively recognized pattern of social existence (associated in this instance with prestige and power).

Thus a distinction is to be made between, on the one hand, those "authentic" individuals who fit one of the subjectively recognized identities represented in language by a conventional noun, i.e., those who possess all the articulated attributes associated with their official, formal status, and, on the other hand, those whose relatively vague status makes them equivocal, ambiguous, opaque, difficult to assign to a recognized category, and "inauthentic" precisely because they seem to be attracted to two different identities at once. To put it another way, people who lack conceptual understanding of their objective status, who are, in a word, socially disoriented, are typically drawn toward various recognized, named, and "authentic" social identities. For actors situated on the dividing line between different social fields or classes, then, these authentic identities serve as magnetic poles or *attractors*. These attractors are perceived in many ways as desirable identities. They exhibit certain patterns of attributes that we expect to find together and also that we feel go well together or at any rate do not clash: in other words, these identities are somehow "right" in both a statistical and a sociological sense.

The state of uncertainty

In a confused and hazy situation, where everything from the job title to the job description itself is ambiguous and shrouded in uncertainty, even the smallest action becomes difficult and fraught with anxiety: the individual tends to see the outside world as an ordeal to which he must subject himself. The "self-taught cadre"[2] is constantly being put to the test: in order to get the most out of him, make him perform at peak efficiency, and justify the investment made in him (e.g., the cost of training at a company sales course), his superiors want "to know what he's made of." To find out, they confront him with new situations to which he must adjust, assigning him jobs for which he may not be prepared. M does not always have the information he needs to perform up to expectations. But conflicting expectations may be part of the definition of his position: explicitly he may be required to conform to an official job description (to be a dedicated employee, respectful toward superiors, punctual in his habits), and yet implicitly he may be expected to go beyond these official requirements and even to bend some rules (in order to prove himself a dynamic salesman ready to take the initiative, etc.). Finally, the skills required, partly technical (knowledge of the product line, familiarity with contracts, etc.) and partly social (manners, style, "class," etc.) are such that M is not always able to judge his ability to perform adequately, i.e., in a manner pleasing to his superiors, in his assigned tasks or tasks he may covet.

In this state of uncertainty, everything becomes a sign of election or dereliction; every move is watched and interpreted. The goal is not simply to look good, to please the boss, to be selected for promotion, to get ahead, and so on. At stake in the long run is the value of the job title itself and hence the self-image of the man who holds it. That value is called into question when reality fails to conform to underlying expectations: a case in point is M's story of starting work at a moderately large company with the "impressive-sounding title of sales manager," arriving the first day in his "Ted Lapidus suit," and going home that night disgusted, his suit covered with grease stains. His position with this firm can be interpreted in just two ways: either the title means "nothing" and M is just a "phoney" manager, or else, as he is more willing to believe at least initially, he is fully "entitled" to be called a manager, in which case the treatment he receives is outrageous because it is beneath his position and contradicts the expectations implicit in the title, which, however intangible, is the only reality that M can yet grasp. People who have worked hard to obtain a title and who have been rewarded mainly with words are thus likely to set aside that distrust of language which, in the working class, often governs attitudes toward symbolic goods and gratifications, and to accord to words an authority, a power, sufficient to repress any experience that threatens to contradict their assumed meaning.

When a man feels unsure of himself, he may view every challenge as a test of his mettle. Problematic situations abound, and he will seek to avoid them if he can. In such cases some people develop fear of such common inconveniences as riding the subway during rush hour: for example, a cadre may find that rubbing shoulders in the subway with ordinary workers deprives him of his feeling of superiority. His identity is too fragile to survive without the support of his environment or workplace setting [in French a pun, since one meaning of the word *cadre* is "setting" – Trans.]. Indeed, some real estate brochures take advantage of the psychological importance of the environment to the typical cadre: they advertise apartment buildings specially designed for cadres (M lives in a high-rise in Paris's fifteenth *arrondissement*), fortresses entered directly through underground parking garages, protected by electronic gates, doormen, and telephones to the street. There are also housing developments for cadres, vacation clubs for cadres (M met his wife at the Club Méditerranée), ski lodges for cadres, soundproof offices, carpeted hallways, "silent" automobiles (M and his wife both have cars and never use any other means of transportation), airplanes, "comfortable" and "quiet" hotel and restaurant chains, "integrated complexes" that cater to every need and eliminate the need to venture out of doors. Cadres are afraid of working-class suburbs, criminals (M and his wife are obsessed by fears of mugging), germs, insects (flies, lice, fleas, cockroaches, etc.), and filth. They are appalled by fleabag hotels and cheap restaurants like those that M was forced to use when he was on the road for the company run by the "man with the argyle jacket." But they are also afraid of "classy" and class-revealing occasions (cocktail parties, seminars, etc.), which are difficult to deal with unless one knows how to behave. And finally, they are afraid of tasks which they see as impossible precisely because they cannot imagine what someone who fully and legitimately embodies the "cadre identity" would do in similar circumstances.

M's investment in his company and his status uncertainty also explain his reactions to the ultimate trial: being laid off. M is in fact punished at several points in his career. Twice he is left for long periods of time with nothing to do, a way of putting him on notice and easing him out. The second punishment comes shortly before he is laid off: he is slowly humiliated, reduced to desperation, and then, some months later, invited to submit his resignation. At first he doesn't realize that the ax is about to fall. Then, by reacting violently (in the belief that the company still wants him), he helps to facilitate and legitimate his own firing. He resists and struggles until finally, tired of fighting, he is let go with severance pay (after thirteen years on the payroll).

The company

M is today a salesman with a large multinational firm. This corporation plays up the company spirit and the Protestant ethic. Still a family firm despite its size, it stresses a managerial approach and likes to see itself as a large family with an excellent working atmosphere (strikes are virtually unknown, according to the managers of the firm's French subsidiary). The company likes to offer its employees not just a job, not just regular paid employment, but a *position*, that is, a place within a frame of reference that the ambitious cadre can use to locate, define, and orient himself.

M likes the company and feels happy there. The somewhat forced enthusiasm with which he speaks of his new post may betray the effort he must make to reinvest his energies in a new job at a relatively advanced age. Hence he is probably suppressing anything of a nature to contradict the image that he requires of his new job in order to mobilize the energy necessary to survive professionally. Still, it must be said that the formal organization of the company encourages such self-reliant attitudes. The firm offers many benefits and above all "security" in various senses, all related in one way or another to its vast size and power as well as to the manipulative techniques it uses to encourage rationalization, standardization, and stabilization of the social environment. For one thing, the work of a salesman representing a huge company that enjoys a virtual monopoly of its market is objectively easier, less risky, and more attractive than that of a salesman representing a small or middle-sized firm. The assurance of being the best, of selling products that hold up, designed by competent people, together with pride at working for one of the largest corporations in the world and at having been chosen by that corporation, whose humblest employee shares in the corporate prestige and authority, tends to make company men self-confident and likely to accept the most respectable and flattering images of their own profession. The instructions in the sales manual that the company gives to each salesman advise against petty schemes, backbiting among colleagues, dirty tricks, dishonesty – the behaviour that so often turns this line of work into "a whore's racket" and those who practice it into "clowns" who "sully the title of engineer." Then, too, rationalization and formalization of relations within the firm, particularly hierarchical relations, must help to diminish the feelings of insecurity and arbitrariness commonly associated with employee–management relations in smaller firms. Many layers of oversight and decision-making coupled with formal equality among employees help to reduce resentment and to prevent the employee's loyalty from attaching to any particular individual. Instead, that loyalty is directed toward the firm, encouraged by the sort of fatherless paternalism typical of the social policy of large corporations.

To gauge the relative effectiveness of the modern methods of managing human potential employed by large American-style corporations, it is useful to compare M's remarks with those of a cadre employed by a medium-sized French firm which, despite rapid growth, is still run by its founder, today an elderly gentleman. The firm has grown too large for the owner to physically supervise all his cadres, yet no system of symbolic substitutes has been developed. The result is a mixture of fascination and dissatisfaction, admiration and resentment in employees' attitudes toward the boss:

The president, you know, the president is more awesome than God the Father. He is the invisible power. One day I actually got to shake his hand! The important people are the general managers, because they have direct access to the president. To see him you have to request an audience – it's like seeing the President of France. . . . You don't ask anything of the president: he's the hand that feeds you, so you leave him alone. But I think that the secret desire of 90% of the people who work here is to spend a day alone with him. I'd be the first in line. I'd love to say to him, "Good day, sir, what do you think of the situation?" He doesn't ignore us. Because he sends his orders down through intermediaries. You hear that the president said such and such or thinks such and such, and so it's in your interest to think the same way. For instance, there was a time when the boss expressed his desire that certain cadres join a union, the CGC of course. Anything else and you're out the door, no doubt about it. Immediately a whole bunch of people signed up to join the CGC.... Now and then we attend meetings where the president makes a speech. Everybody's there, it's like going to mass. That's the way they get you to think that these guys who own companies are exceptional people, the elite.... I'm not so much a socialist that I deny that the companies belong to them. But I'm in favor of not having businesses managed by the people who own them. It's enough that they have the money. They shouldn't have the power too. Because power has got to be earned. The guy with the power might be the owner's son, but not necessarily the owner. It might be people trained in the firm. It might even be me, when you get right down to it.

"Here," says M, contrasting his present employer with the small, paternalistic company in which he met with so many disappointments, "the guys in the golfing outfits have been replaced by the men in gray flannel suits." What better way of expressing unhesitating acceptance of the ideology of merit over inheritance, of legitimacy based on competence and success rather than money, of the authority of managers over the power of owners? The important point is that M's present employer is a company in which he does not feel out of place. The company is powerful enough to impose, at least in appearance, its own hierarchies in place of those that prevail in the outside world: the official company policy is that a diploma must never be regarded as a definitive possession and that individual value and true ability matter more than formal degrees. Now, true ability can be acquired in the company's own internal sales courses, at which the company trains, educates, and disciplines cadres formed in its own image, using modern methods of instruction and control. Frequently it wins the lifetime loyalty of its employees. Last but not least, the company is large enough to offer many opportunities for advancement. For example, many salesmen "come off the road" at age forty or so and are trained for other jobs that do not require the same dynamic qualities and youthful appearance as direct sales. Such an eventuality is explicitly provided for in the company's program, which makes the transition less tense that it often is in smaller firms, where the only alternatives are to rise in the hierarchy or move on to new employment.

Listen to one 34-year-old sales engineer with degrees in law and economics and a traditional upper-class background describe the salesmen employed by one large company:

I know the people at X.... I didn't go to work for X ... partly because of that. For a long time it used to be all blue suits and starched collars. It's not that way any more ... but ... In the company I work for, there's a somewhat puritanical side – respect the rules and traditions, certain traditions – but there is some opposition, I think, even if it's not openly admitted. But at X ... it's quite different: there are cases of people going to work for X ... and completely changing, becoming, really becoming. "X people" ... special people. It happened to a friend of mine. They're very sure of themselves: that's one of their strengths. People are always telling them they're the handsomest, they're the best: X ... relies on that a lot. The salesmen are convinced that they can't fail to sell, and that works in their favor.... It would be interesting to attend their sales training school. They have a school that eliminates people mainly on the basis of character. They get rid of the people they expect to have difficulty with because they're not docile enough.... They have no trouble recruiting: they pay well and they're better organized from the standpoint of promotion within the company. [In other companies] a fellow who goes into sales, if he doesn't make the jump to management by a certain point, he's through, he's out, all washed up, done for. Whereas at X ... they've found a solution to that problem, a way to hold on to salesmen and keep sales jobs attractive: after a certain number of years they move their salesmen into other departments and they keep both their image, if you like, and the benefits of their position in the hierarchy.

Since going to work for his present employer M is again looking forward to promotion. But the hopes that sustain him and keep him working are more reasonable than in the past. Here the manipulation of aspirations, supported by a whole apparatus, works more subtly and consistently than in other firms, with no abrupt ups or downs: this is accomplished by means of career planning, which, as the brochures that instruct cadres in managing their careers reveal, helps each individual to evaluate which jobs he qualifies for, given his unique skills, intelligence, and character. There are also profesional evaluation and advisory programs, which include interviews with department heads. The ideology of promotion in large firms usually involves a compound of competition and equal opportunity (appealing to the sporting instincts of cadres, a bit like the army), and this tends to reinforce meritocratic attitudes that most self-taught cadres acquire from their families and educational and post-educational experiences. The more successful they have been, the more likely they are to accept this ideology. One sales executive, whose rise had been relatively rapid despite modest origins and a start in engineering (he was a graduate of Arts et Métiers), suggested that it was a man's "competence ceiling" that determined how high he could go.

Finally, M's firm has the cash to offer him precisely those things that he wants but cannot buy on the salary it pays him, namely, the signs of a higher standard of living and the charm of a lifestyle befitting a cadre: specifically, these include goods and services appropriate to M's fantasy image of his position, things that the company provides and of course can also take away, such as comfortable, impeccable offices, first-class hotels, fancy castles with swimming pools for working seminars and relaxation, fashionable evenings with other couples, sporting clubs, bridge clubs, etc. And then there is travel. In large firms a stint at corporate headquarters, often with one's family, all expenses paid, is the ultimate reward, the high point of a man's working life. The time at headquarters helps to integrate the employee into the team and to reinforce his sense of belonging to the group: once you've been down to headquarters you're part of the team for real, one of those on whom the corporation relies, who take part in decisions or at least who rub shoulders with the decision-makers. The trip is put off until the cadre has become enough of a company man that he can no longer back out, and it finishes his "conversion," so to speak, while at the same time reinforcing the values by which large multinational corporations operate and fostering the employee's gratitude toward the company as the embodiment of those values.

By offering so many advantages and fringe benefits companies seem to be able to induce employees to place company interests ahead of career interests: the employee invests in the company, in what it is and what it represents, rather than in himself. He substitutes immediate gratifications for future hopes, for the deferred gratification that the competition for promotion so often requires. This is particularly true of cadres who lack economic, cultural, or social capital of their own. In return, the company expects its lower-ranking cadres to subscribe to what it is and represents, by adopting conservative attitudes in politics and a "Protestant ethic" in professional and private life (which is monitored in a variety of ways); by participating, actively and along with their families, in the life of the firm (in which wives also have their role to play); by exhibiting pride in and loyalty toward the company; and in short by demonstrating what some cadres call, derisively, a "good attitude."

One wife, given "bad grades" for her attitude and married to a cadre similar to M in terms of social and educational background and professional experience, describes private life in a large company in the following terms:

R [her husband] is washed up, the jig's up, poor guy. If he has a bad attitude, it's like in boarding school. You can't do anything about it. It's marked down and you're screwed. Inevitably it all comes out. I don't know how far it goes, maybe all the way to the front office. I don't know. I never set foot inside X . . . but I know that I've been given a bad grade. I'm not at all an "X wife." . . . Because X . . . is one big, happy family, and I'm expected to be part of the family. There are cocktail parties, people invite each other, you're supposed to invite other people. That's the attitude, and people know if Mr Smith is invited to dinner by Mrs Jones. I don't know how they know or who tells them, but they know. . . . R, in the end, you know, I think he's glad we're not too "X" . . . at home, but in another respect he's very involved in his work, so he has to be "X". You see! And to be "X" . . . is in a sense to put up with anything. . . . They have an image of the family! For example, it was bad that I didn't travel with my husband. A wife isn't supposed to leave her husband. . . . When he started working at X . . . he had a beard. Nowadays that's acceptable but at the time they let him know that if he wanted the job, he'd have to shave off the beard. So R said, "And what would I have to do if I were black?" And then, I don't know, there was a whole to-do. They found his response very interesting and that helped him get the job, and in the end he shaved off his beard. . . . All that bothers him a bit, but in the end he's happy because he likes his work. It got him out of a mess, and it was the company that got him out. What would he have done without X? . . . It's not easy, you know, to find a job. . . . At X . . . everybody punches in, everybody is on the same level, be it the janitor or the president, everybody gets the same benefits, insurance, sports, the whole thing. There are plenty of benefits: bonuses, vacation villages, clubs like you read about in the company newsletter. . . . Take, for example, something I didn't even know existed: R had an operation last year. He was out of work for three months, and at the end of that time he received a package from one of the big gourmet food stores, Fauchon or Hédiard, I can't remember which: a box of *foie gras*, a bottle of very good wine, OK? – a whole meal for two. The company sent it because of R's operation. Now, you'd get the same thing whether you were the janitor or the president. . . . When R went to the United States, they had a party for him in a restaurant, and somebody from the X Poets' Club . . . wrote a poem about him. He also writes in the company newsletter. . . . The newsletter prints the names of newborns, marriages, deaths. For deaths they write, "Mr Smith passed away at the plant on such-and-such a day, he started as such-and-such, he was such-and-such when he passed away." You get the point: they want to show how far he'd come.

By carefully selecting salesmen who might have been rejected under another system of selection, by giving them what they were denied elsewhere (or more than they received elsewhere), and by offering them rewards and values commensurate with their expectations, large companies secure the services of men with a reputation for steadfastness and loyalty. These men show a respect for order, obedience, and *esprit de corps* and exhibit in their work attitudes not unlike those that make a good soldier or noncommissioned officer. Like the army, the company sees itself as an organization that stands apart from the outside world, whose purpose is to foster a concern for both security and initiative and respect for both hierarchy and egalitarianism. In this modern firm, however, management models used by the US Army are increasingly replacing the somewhat obsolete authority models that more traditional firms (many of whose cadres, particularly in personnel departments, were military veterans) used to derive from the traditions of the French military.

Thus everything that M says about the company, about business, and perhaps about society as well must be interpreted in terms of large private corporations, especially multinationals, which are run according to the tenets of modern management, as opposed to both small family firms and firms in the public sector: on the one hand efficiency and reliability, with the job and the chance of success exactly suited to the talents of each individual; on the other hand injustice, arbitrary management, cronyism, castes ("graduates of Polytechnique, churchgoers, the whole gamut"), arrogant and incompetent technocrats, waste, incompetence, laziness, and scandal (at a maximum in the nationalized firms: "a mess, and you and I pay for it"). On the global level, you have on the one hand France, where love of one's work is a thing of the past owing to an absurd and unjust system, and on the other hand the United States and Japan (where the company is part of every worker) and above all West Germany, which in M's eyes is the company writ large, a nation in which comfort and order are the paramount values. M interprets everyday social experience in terms of this same fundamental set of distinctions, which are confirmed by such commonplace activities as buying a car: the contrast between the Citroën and Mercedes dealers as described by M reveals the same patterns of thought that we find in his life story.

In the mind of this sales engineer, the nationalism that provided the traditional *petite bourgeoisie* with an identity and a means of sublimating its class resentment has given way to a sort of multinationalism. To work for a multinational corporation is in itself a source of pride, just as nationality used to be; belonging to this cosmopolitan elite justifies acceptance of the company's values. For it is the company that sustains the individual, not just by paying his salary but also by affording him security in an insecure world. Through a subtle combination of signs of election and threats of exclusion, the company constantly reminds M that without it he would be nothing.

Introduction 2: a question of sociology

Provisional description

M's story is interesting chiefly for bringing together most of the questions that any analysis of the group commonly referred to as "cadres" would want to answer. It contains what Max Weber would call a "provisional description" of the difficulties that cadres face in obtaining promotions, of a typical career's ups and downs, of the crisis of isolation, of the competition between the formally educated and the self-taught, of the technologies of social manipulation used by large corporations (which can be used both to integrate and to exclude), of the dialectic of title and position, of nominal and real,[1] and of the uncertainty and anxiety with which the cadre must cope. We also find information about the differences between family and managerial firms and between the private and the public sector, about the fascination with America and American-style management, about the decline of nationalism and the rise of multinationalism, etc.

Above all, M's story raises, in an exemplary manner, a more fundamental question, a question that takes precedence over all others: namely, that of the existence of cadres qua group. M's uncertainty as to whether he is or is not a member of the group, and his acute awareness of the variety of concrete statuses (each with its own hierarchical rank) subsumed by the term "cadre," coupled with his almost fetishistic attachment to the title, which for him is an intangible symbol of promotion, of access to a closed elite, leave him in a state of constant anxiety, because he finds his own social identity an enigma. And it is precisely this enigma that the sociologist must penetrate if he is to describe the social group to which M claims to belong. The dilemma that has to be faced at the outset is this: one may speak of cadres as if they constituted a unified group, indeed, a collective subject with a will of its own and an ability to act (as when one says "cadres are such and such," "cadres do thus and so," "cadres want this and that," etc.), or else one may argue that cadres are so varied, so different from one another, that it is wrong to speak of them collectively as a social group at all. On the latter view, the notion that cadres form a group is a mere statistical artifact or, worse, an ideological smokescreen. But in that case how does one explain that real flesh-and-blood individuals claim to *be* cadres and to belong to this allegedly nonexistent group? And how does one account for the attitudes and behaviour of such people when these appear to be determined not by the market, with its aggregative logic, not by some sort of mechanical interaction of individual strategies and utilitarian calculations, but rather by belief in the existence of a concrete social group? These questions are in fact only the beginning. Many others crop up as one begins to collect data, especially when one tries to specify a statistical sample. There is practically no study of cadres that does not begin with a preamble, often embarrassed and confused, about the need to define the population under investigation and the difficulties of delineating what the object of study is "in this case." The difficulty does not diminish when one tries to use data collected by other researchers for other purposes: the figures are often wildly divergent because they are based on different definitions of the target group. Later (in Part 2, chapter 3) I will show how the problem of *definition* has obsessed sociological discussion of cadres to the point where it has been, for the past twenty years, the main topic of discussion among those who specialize in the study of what has been called, at one time or another, a group, an aggregate, a public, a category, a population, an elite, a class, a segment, a mass, a layer, and a stratum. Quite plainly, even choosing a word to designate this object, this "thing," is already a problem, indeed, the *major* problem with which any student of the subject must grapple.

The word and the thing

The only way to avoid the contradictions in which the theoretical debate concerning cadres often becomes bogged down is to acknowledge that the group exists (by what right do social scientists challenge the reality of a principle of identity in which the social actors themselves believe?) and to accept the all but insurmountable difficulties involved in any attempt to define it objectively (rather than dismiss those difficulties as inevitably troublesome yet ultimately superficial problems of method). These two requirements are not incompatible, provided one gives up the substantialist view of social groups that underlies so much of the sociological (and especially the industrial sociological) literature. Sociologists commonly attempt to delineate a social group they wish to study in two distinct but not incompatible ways: either they define it in terms of some formal typology tailored to the needs of their research, or they take it as a given, as defined by its conventional name and representations, and attempt to prove that these conventions have a rational basis in reality, in the way things are, most commonly by relating the existence of the group to technological progress and the technical division of labor. The procedure is intended to show that the group is a substantive entity with precise, well-defined outlines (which, as Wittgenstein says, is tantamount "to peering behind the word in search of the thing"[2]). It is a bit reminiscent of the way in which philosophers of law used to attempt to establish natural grounds for national unity and to demonstrate that historically determined frontiers were in fact inscribed in nature. To see the fallacy in this kind of reasoning, one has only to think of the naturalistic argument that what one eats is determined by one's "need" for energy. In fact, the needs that seem most closely associated with man's physical nature exist as social facts only when reinterpreted in cultural terms (as likes and dislikes).[3] Similarly, the naturalistic view of the relation of technology to society neglects the fact that the division of labor that comes to be embodied in the objectified form of technology exists as a social fact only through the mediation of symbolic systems that give explicit representation to class and group divisions. But the relation between technological (or economic) determinism and the symbolic phenomena whereby technical factors are reinterpreted linguistically as collective nouns, representations, emblems, or taxonomies is itself mediated through conflicts between social actors with various objective attributes of their own (partially shared, partially idiosyncratic) and through the strategies that these actors adopt, given their views of the issues and interests at stake. I do not deny that there is a connection between technological divisions and social divisions. To do so would be absurd. I merely wish to point out that technology is not external to society and that technological constraints still leave room for "strategies of social distinction" (*classement et déclassement*),[4] which a naturalistic view of social groups invariably obscures. The study of cadres is probably as good a place as any to examine why substantialism has proved so powerful and persuasive. It has turned out to be very difficult indeed to define the "cadre," which is a socially constructed object, in substantialist terms; nevertheless, theories that have nothing in common except for their substantialist presuppositions remain at odds over the problem of definition.

The foregoing remarks also apply, *mutatis mutandis*, to social history, a discipline in which attempts to study social groups diachronically generally follow one or the other of two contradictory approaches. Social historians sometimes pretend that a group in which they are interested has always existed objectively even though their sources never mention it, or, if they do, allude to it under some other name: for nomenclature, we are told, often lags behind reality. Quantitative historians in particular are likely to succumb to this temptation in their eagerness to obtain homogeneous time series, generally by subjecting the raw data to various manipulations. Other historians take a contradictory approach, pretending that a social group does not exist until it is named, that is, until there is some means of representing and quantifying its existence. Both approaches commonly neglect the social process by which the group was formed and, so to speak, made visible. The first approach lays stress on a group's social function, usually defined in some atemporal manner. Thus some scholars argue that cadres existed in the eighteenth and nineteenth centuries because the functions of cadres were then performed by engineers and stewards. The second approach tends to ascribe the emergence of a new social group to some sudden mutation in the technological and/or economic order. Presumably the social effects of such a mutation make themselves felt automatically.

To break out of the vicious circle in which the interminable and inconclusive debates on the class position of cadres remain trapped, one must begin by abandoning hope of defining the group a priori. And one must focus instead on the historical circumstances in which cadres first organized, as a group with a name, institutions, spokesmen, systems of representation, and values of its own. Rather than look for criteria in terms of which the group ought to be defined and the boundaries that one must ascribe to it in order to obtain a compact, well-defined object of study (generally, as I said a moment ago, by looking at the group in terms of pure technological determinism and the technical division of labor), one can investigate the organizational process (*travail de regroupement*), the process of inclusion and exclusion, that produced it. And one can look simultaneously at the associated social process of definition and delimitation. It is this latter process that gives the group the objective status that ultimately allows its existence to be taken for granted.

The "proper form" of a group

Cadres became a group in a two-stage process (which may well be a paradigm for a more general set of social processes). In the first stage, a group of engineers trained in similar institutions (the so-called Grandes Ecoles) and drawn together by common interests created a number of organizations. Some of these were religious (associated with Action catholique), others professional (most of the engineers involved worked in industry). The purpose of these organizations was to redefine, to create an image of, the social position of their members. The specific attributes characteristic of members were generalized and subsumed in a generic noun: *les cadres*. In the second stage of the process, after the initial steps of objectification and institutionalization were complete, these organizations developed a distinctive identity. Metaphorically speaking, they formed a distinct nucleus within the field of social forces. This nucleus became a "magnetic pole" toward which other social actors and groups were attracted – actors and groups objectively unlike the members of the primary organizations. But hitherto deprived of specific representative organs of their own, these new recruits found it expedient to recognize themselves in the official image of the cadre (and hence, inevitably, to neglect the objective differences between themselves and those who originally claimed the title).

Originally, my purpose in studying this concrete case, in which one magnetic group drew other groups into its orbit, was to contribute a partial answer to a question that had been left in a state of some neglect since the work of Durkheim and his followers: How do social groups form, and what holds them together? By any measure this has to be one of the fundamental problems of political sociology.[5] My plan was first to look at the social and political conditions that allowed the cadre group to form, as well as the political issues associated with its definition. These preliminaries out of the way, I then hoped to show that the group was itself the product, at least in part, of a process of social unification (which in many respects resembles a political mobilization).[6] For there is an obvious point that is nevertheless worth taking the time to state explicitly: Homogeneity is not a necessary and sufficient condition for cohesion. A group that manages to hold itself together, makes people believe in its existence, and establishes formal representative institutions is in some respects an objective entity. But this is partly illusory. What psychologists might call the group's "proper form" – its philosophy, purpose, and formal organization – is merely a reification of prior struggles about what the group is and should be, struggles that are often forgotten or repressed. In these struggles what is at stake is nothing other than the existence of the group qua group, as a distinct and visible entity. Think of the conflicts, inextricably social, political, and ideological, that accompanied the formation of the working class in the nineteenth century, conflicts that involved politicians, social philosophers, economic actors, and various inchoate social groups – artisans, industrial workers, master-craftsmen, and many others – all with conflicting aims and objectives. Those who took part in the debate also staked their lives and livelihoods on the outcome.

Pierre Ansart,[7] for example, has shown that the polemic between Marx and Proudhon cannot be understood by the usual procedures of the history of idea, i.e., in terms of internal textual analysis. In order to grasp the stakes in this political and theoretical controversy one must first understand early nineteenth-century social structure, and in particular the *classes populaires*. For the primary issue in the battle between Marx and Proudhon was the *definition* of the working class itself, its dominant representation and hence its destiny. Though both authors use the same collective noun, they do not use it to refer to the same groups: the philosophy of Proudhon can be understood only in relation to the practice of a specific stratum of workers, industrial master-craftsmen (*chefs d'atelier*) "involved in a very particular kind of socioeconomic structure. Unified in opposition to the power of the employer, they remained aloof from one another and relatively autonomous *vis-à-vis* other manufacturers and nearby shops. Unlike factory workers these master-craftsmen were not all reduced to the status of the lowest common denominator, but unlike traditional artisans they did not work in isolation. Still less can they be confounded with the 'petit bourgeois' typified by the civil servant dependent on the government and the small merchant intent on making a profit and outstripping his competitors" (p. 241). Proudhon "expressed the views of this particular segment of the working classes," of the "worker-created social movement known as 'mutualism.' ... This class segment is therefore neither defended for what it is nor described in terms of its actual problems and suffering but rather exalted for what it does and represented as the direct subject of its own action" (p. 243).

"One of Proudhon's intentions" was "to bring intellectual coherence to this class action," and his philosophy "responded to the ambitions of a class and to its certainty that it was called to serve as a universal class" (p. 245). It is clear how different this image of the working class is from that of Marx, who linked the rise of the proletariat and its potential for political organization to the decline of "manufacturing" (in his special sense) and the rise of large-scale industry.

These debates, though remote from us in time, are nevertheless close to our present concerns. Today, the fact that the process of objectification and institutionalization of the working class took place so long ago and with such intensity tends to mask the degree to which that class was internally heterogeneous. Those segments of the working class that did not succeed in durably institutionalizing their self-representations, much less in representing the class as a whole, have been forgotten. B. Zarca, in still unpublished work, has shown that craftsmen of various kinds, whose numbers have remained almost constant since the beginning of the twentieth century, today constitute a forgotten or neglected segment of the working class, whose specific attributes and interests are no longer represented.[8] This is also true of workers on the fringes of, or only recently integrated into, the working class. Edmond Maire [head of the CFDT, a leading French trade union – Trans.], an astute student of the subject, spontaneously sees the contrast between older and more recently unionized workers in metaphorical terms, as a question of center and periphery. He then uses this metaphor to criticize the inflexibility of the trade unions. His clear insight is the product not of scientific study but of a political strategy: Maire contrasts the openness of his own union, the CFDT (which he depicts as a relatively small, new union attentive to change), with the old-fashioned attitudes of its larger rival, the CGT. In other words, what we have here is yet another instance of altering the definition of the working class to suit the specific interests of one of several groups competing for a monopoly of class representation.[9]

In order to understand what present-day cadres owe to the process that created the objective entity with which they identify, I found it necessary to take two complementary approaches. The first was "deconstructive": by analyzing and criticizing the sources, especially the statistical sources, I tried to undermine the belief that cadres constitute some kind of quasinatural object. The chief virtue of statistical analysis in this first stage was to cast doubt on the definition of the group. This deconstruction was followed by an attempt at "reconstruction": in particular, I sought to uncover the history of the cadre, not for its own sake but in order to counter distortions of the cadre's image introduced in part by cadres themselves, in part by the group's institutionalization, and in part, too, by the simple passage of time. In order to treat the group not as a "thing" but as the objectified product of a practice, I found it necessary to analyze not only the organizational process that created it but also the concomitant symbolic process of group definition. For instance, in studying the development of cadres' unions, I found it more useful to consider the unions' beliefs and ideas about themselves than to look at internal organization and the details of negotiating positions (Part 1). Having done this, it became possible to interpret the structure of the group (with the help of abundant statistical data that would have been worthless without an understanding of how the data had been collected and why the numbers at times seemed so inconsistent) and to analyze its relation to other groups. I was then in a position to interpret the personal histories of individuals who claimed to be cadres, considering not only each individual's representation of himself but also his position in society (Part 2). Only then was it possible to assess the symbolic efficacy of the various competing definitions of the term "cadre" and to determine how the choice of one definition rather than another affected the relative power of the various rival subgroups and factions seeking to impose their own interests on the group as a whole (Conclusion).

Beyond pursuing my central goal, to analyze the processes of symbolic unification and representation of a social group, I found it useful to embark on several related discussions of history, macropolitics, and social and cognitive psychology. I use the term "representation" in a variety of ways. To begin with, there is the "representation" of the group. Initially nothing more than a mute aggregate of individuals, a social group must define what distinguishes it from other groups. It does this by naming itself, by forging a defining concept that in effect alters what I might call the "semantics of society" from top to bottom: the definitions of all other groups and classes, and their relations to one another, are altered in the process. "Representation" is also used in its more usual social psychological sense: in order to exist for itself and for others the group must create in the minds of its members, and in others through its spokesmen, a "representation" of what it stands for. Such a representation involves what Erving Goffman might call a dramatic enhancement of the group's defining characteristics, a stylized image that helps to establish the sort of collective belief in its existence that the group must command before it can claim social recognition.[10] Finally, a social group seeks to acquire "representation" in the political arena, where various groups and classes rehearse battles fought daily in other arenas but here played out according to the rules of the political game. Official agencies are authorized to act in the group's behalf, and authority is delegated to designated individuals to speak in its name.

I have tried in this work to avoid both the illusion of timelessness and the fascination with what is new. Sociologists are in the habit of using and abusing the term "new," as in the "new middle class" or "new working class." The main drawback of this is that the terminology begs too many questions: the birth of new social entities is presumably some kind of natural process. To judge by what many sociologists write, new groups invariably "emerge" from some obscure "mutation" or "shift." In other words they are created *ex nihilo*. Use of this kind of metaphor lends an "essentialist" cast to theories of social change. In fact, however, it is not often that social groups appear suddenly out of nowhere or disappear bag and baggage from the social scene, except perhaps in times of revolution or civil war.[11] Rather than focus on such infrequent and dramatic occurrences, I have chosen to study the more common case in which the emergence of a new group is the product of a lengthy restructuring that alters both social facts and the representations of those facts. Existing groups redefine themselves, perceive themselves in new ways, present new faces to the outside world, divide and fuse, and yet throughout this process of change preserve something of their old identity.

My purpose here is to examine the logic of this process, to understand why so many groups seek to forget their origins, as though by repressing in some sort of collective unconscious[12] the words and actions of their founders they might become part of the natural order or, what comes to the same thing, make themselves appear to be an ineluctable consequence of economic and technological development (which is nothing but a socially and politically acceptable substitute for the idea of natural necessity).

PART 1
The invention of cadres

1 *The crisis of the 1930s and the mobilization of the middle class*

The use of the term "cadre" as a unifying concept and the organization of cadre-based pressure groups seeking official recognition in the political arena are inseparable from the innumerable steps taken to restore calm and reestablish social order following the strikes of 1936.

In novels, plays, and other works prior to the 1930s cadres are never mentioned. They go unrepresented. Nor do they appear in census statistics until after the war.[1] Ignored by the right, cadres had no political organization that claimed to represent their interests. The key period in the evolution of the class structure and its associated representations was certainly the 1930s and 1940s, and the emergence of the term "cadre," along with "cadres' organizations" and related "middle-class groups," was but one aspect of a continuous process of ideological change affecting the *bourgeoisie* and *petite bourgeoisie*. This process culminated in roughly the period 1934–8, when consolidation of the workers' movement led to intensification of the class struggle. The result was a new representation of society as divided into not two but three distinct parts, paramount among which was the middle class, described as the "healthy," "stable" component of the nation. This representation was itself based on a new representation of the political sphere that was simultaneously developed by avant-garde thinkers of the new right, who discovered what they liked to call a third way between the two extremes of capitalism and collectivism. This ideology had some basis in social reality. The idea of a middle class (in itself not an invention of the 1930s[2]) took on new force in the interwar period. To understand why this was so, we must consider economic factors, specifically inflation and the crisis that affected broad segments of the bourgeoisie and petite bourgeoisie. An ideology calling for the unification and mobilization of the middle class would certainly not have received as attentive a hearing as this one did had it not found the ground prepared by objective contradictions that developed or came to a head in the same period (namely, contradictions between large and small employers, between the public and private sector, between independent and salaried segments of the bourgeoisie and petite bourgeoisie, etc.). Indeed, it is as though the primary function of the new ideology was to deny the objective forces that were tearing society apart.

Yet this new tripartite model of society was not developed *ex nihilo*. Its substance (philosophical precursors, vocabulary, emblems, etc.) was drawn from two main sources. The first of these was so-called Social Catholicism. Since the end of the nineteenth century the Social Catholics had been forced to do battle on two fronts: against socialism on the one hand and against the secular liberal bourgeoisie on the other. In seeking to find what Father Droulers[3] called "just passages" between these two perils, Social Catholics developed a ternary model that fitted the political domain as well as it did the social.[4] The appeal to the middle classes and the increased attention devoted to them cannot be understood unless one recalls that in Germany and especially in Italy fascism was intimately associated with a corporatist organization of society in which the middle classes were supposed to occupy a strategic position. In the writings of spokesmen for the middle-class and cadre movements, fascism is referred to constantly, in contradictory ways. The fascist state served two purposes: most often it was used implicitly as a model, but at times it was also invoked explicitly, as an instrument of pressure. Give the middle classes what they want, the message went, or you too will succumb, as other countries have done, to fascism. In other words, adopting new ideas and programs, many of which were borrowed from Italian fascism, was presented as a way, the only way, of warding off the "fascist threat."

Phase one: the middle-class movements

Two new social movements developed or were organized in the 1930s, particularly after the strikes of June 1936 (and more specifically, between the end of 1936 and the end of 1938). These movements maintained close organizational ties, and their leaders and spokesmen maintained intimate personal contact with one another. One was aimed at organizing and defending the middle classes. The other involved engineers and cadres (the latter term first came into use in this period but did not really catch on until later, under Vichy). After 1936 the engineers' movement led to the formation of engineers' "unions" (*syndicats*).

The leading engineers' unions were the Union des syndicats d'ingénieurs français (USIF), the Syndicat professionel des ingénieurs diplômés français (SPID), and the Syndicat des ingénieurs salariés (SIS). The latter group, the largest as well as the most active and influential of the three (with more than 10,000 member engineers), was originally set up by the Union sociale des ingénieurs catholiques (USIC), most of whose members joined the new group. But the USIC continued to exist as a legally separate entity from the SIS and indeed outlived its offspring.[5] The USIC since the turn of the century had not only championed the interests of engineers but also worked to "deepen understanding of the social doctrine of the Church" among Catholic engineers. It was led by priests associated with the group Action populaire. Most of its members were graduates of prestigious schools (the Grandes Ecoles, especially the Ecole centrale and the Ecole des mines) and of Jesuit preparatory schools.[6]

Syndicalism among engineers was directly related to strikes in the spring of 1936. The nowadays common refrain of the unpopular cadre, the cadre as scapegoat and victim, favorite target of workers and at the same time abandoned by employers, caught between "the anvil of plutocracy and the hammer of the proletariat," was first formulated by industrial engineers in 1936.[7]

Georges Lamirand, an engineer graduated from Centrale and a Social Catholic militant (a member of the USIC and of the *équipes sociales* of Garric), was the author of an oft-quoted document that helped fashion the image, later adopted by many cadres' unions and movements, of the humiliated and insulted engineer, victim of the struggle between proletariat and *patronat* (employers):

'In every firm, on the day the occupation began, workers' delegates headed straight for the owner's office. They submitted their grievances directly to the owner and discussed with him the terms of provisional settlements, and it was with him that they signed the first collective bargaining agreements. The engineer? He was out of the picture. The owners, caught unawares and overwhelmed by events, had but one idea: to reach a settlement as quickly as possible on the best possible terms, to turn back the tide that threatened to swamp them and everything they owned, and to cut their losses. Shuttling back and forth between board of directors, chamber of commerce, prefecture, police station, and strike committee, some owners completely forgot about their cadres and supervisory staff, who were left for days on end without the least word of support or even instruction. Abandoned by employers, engineers were also left in the lurch by employees, who took advantage of the opportunity to express long-smoldering resentments. In some plants engineers and foremen huddled together in sad, silent groups. In others, after braving hostile picket lines they were refused access to the factory or on occasion even prevented from leaving. Abandoned by both sides, engineers discovered that they were neither fish nor fowl, that they constituted a third party imperiled on two fronts, in the sad position of an iron caught between hammer and anvil.'[8]

Any number of first-hand reports paint the same picture of the engineers' awkward position in the events of 1936.[9] The highly stereotypical nature of these engineers' accounts shows that the eye-witness testimony of individual engineers was in fact shaped by collectively developed models (in the elaboration of which engineers belonging to the USIC seem to have played a leading role). Engineers sought to create a symbolic system with which they could comprehend and control this unprecedented and unthinkable turn of events – the occupation of the factories. Above all they hoped to restore the lost honor of their profession by blaming employers for the collapse of authority in the plants.

Spokesmen for the engineers' movement complained that "the legitimate rights and interests of middle-class engineers and supervisory personnel are being neglected" (*Echo de l'USIC*, January 1937). Here the characterization of engineers as middle-class is a symbolic affirmation. It establishes an explicit connection between the actions of the engineers' unions and the actions of organizations representing the distinct middle-class movement, which, like the engineers' unions themselves, proliferated after 1936 (and in fact close ties developed between the two sets of groups).

The years 1937–8 saw the development of a number of umbrella organizations aimed at regrouping some of the many independently organized middle-class associations, committees, and professional organizations. By the eve of World War II there were some sixteen middle-class organizations of one kind or another, including eight confederations, three committees, and various blocs, leagues, federations, and associations. The most important in terms of the number of unions and other groups gathered under its aegis seems to have been the Confédération générale des syndicats de classes moyennes (CCM), whose newsletter was the daily *Front économique*. This group claimed to represent "confederations, unions, and associations of professional organizations in agriculture, small and medium-sized commerce, small and medium-sized industry, the crafts, the liberal professions, and among supervisory personnel and cadres." Among the many diverse groups and federations that rallied to the defense of the middle class one should also mention the "Comité pour l'organisation et la confédération générale des classes moyennes" (known as the Comité de la rue Logenbach), which formed around Jacques Arthuys, Pierre Lefaurichon, and the banker Blocq-Mascart. Relatively inactive in 1938–9, it nevertheless became one of the agencies by which certain political themes associated with the defense of the middle class (most notably antiparliamentarianism) were perpetuated in the postwar period. Arthuys, a small industrialist who participated in the Faisceau de Valois and *Ordre nouveau*, Lefaurichon, and Blocq-Mascart were in fact the organizers of a resistance network known as Organisation civile et militaire (OCM), which played an important role in developing the political and social programs of the Resistance.[10]

What did these movements represent? It is quite difficult to say whether the development of so many associations and confederations reflects a spontaneous mobilization of the petite bourgeoisie against the "communist peril," or whether it was mainly the work of those who held positions of power in these various organizations, controlled their apparatus, and served as official spokesmen without necessarily belonging to the group or class they claimed to be defending. Among the presidents and board members of these middle-class groups we find no representatives of the lower strata of the petite bourgeoisie, such as shopkeepers, office workers, etc. All the leaders were either small industrialists representing various professional groups and employers' associations or else professionals such as physicians, lawyers, notaries, etc. Broadly speaking, a segment of the bourgeoisie that lived on inherited wealth assumed responsibility for the social and political representation of a less well-off segment, the petite bourgeoisie, whose power was mobilized and channeled through special interest groups. One of the social and political functions of these movements was in fact to reactivate the "natural" bonds among all those who possessed wealth, of whatever nature or magnitude. It is also quite difficult to say how many members these organizations managed to attract and what they actually accomplished. The CCM claimed to have as many as two and a half million members. But the federation, which did not accept individual memberships, claimed the members of all unions and professional groups that approved its purposes (so that many of its "members" may well have belonged to the confederation against their will or without their knowledge, as Henri Mougin has pointed out[11]). These organizations seem to have acted mainly through groups that lobbied parliament on behalf of small business and in defense of the middle classes (working, for example, for credit reform and overhaul of the tax system and against allowing foreigners to go into business or enter the skilled trades[12]).

No doubt one could show, more generally, that the presence of a bourgeois elite in predominantly petit bourgeois movements is a constant of political and social life: each segment of the petite bourgeoisie seeks out, to represent it politically and socially, the segment of the bourgeoisie most similar to itself.[13] In literature and film, for example and *a fortiori* in politics, the petite bourgeoisie seems doomed to be represented by another class.[14] It is an object about which one speaks, an object that can be defined and defended only from outside, and only to serve the interests of some other group. In other words, conflicts over middle-class issues (especially intense in the 1930s) must be viewed largely in terms of attempts by other groups and agents to mobilize and co-opt the middle classes for reasons of their own, and only secondarily in terms of the relatively divergent interests of the various segments of the middle class itself.

The importance of the middle-class issue in 1935–8 was a direct consequence of the social and political situation.[15] Indeed, it is a commonplace of political science to say that the 1930s saw a crisis of the middle class (especially after the abrupt deflation of 1935) and to view this crisis as a potential factor in political change. During this period most political parties pledged to defend middle-class interests, either to preserve their electorate or to attract voters unhappy with the other parties.[16] This was true, for instance, of the Communist Party, which after abandoning its "class against class" line called for an alliance of the "proletariat," the "peasantry," and the "middle classes"[17] (while denying that the middle classes had any autonomous existence apart from the "two fundamental classes"[18]). It was also true of the Socialist Party. The Socialists' interest in the middle class was relatively new. As Alain Bergounioux has shown, the majority of the party had hitherto shared "a vision of society in which two principal classes, the bourgeoisie and the proletariat, confronted each other, leading to inevitable polarization of intermediate categories on either side." The "steady concentration of property in the bourgeoisie" was supposed to lead to "increasing proletarization of the rest of the population."[19] As early as 1900 Jean Jaurès invoked these beliefs in his critique of Bernstein: the existence of "intermediate gradations," argued Jaurès, must not be allowed to obscure the "opposition of contraries"[20] (although this did not prevent the Socialists from seeking electoral alliances – "republican discipline" – with groups such as the Radicals, defined by their affinities with the "middle class" of small businessmen, craftsmen, etc.). It was not until the 1930s that a faction of the French Socialists, the so-called Neo-Socialists led by Marcel Déat, raised the issue of the middle classes as such, both to respond to the "fascist threat" and to pave the way for a rapprochement with the Radical Party (while competing with it on its home ground). By abandoning the ideas of proletarization and polarization and accepting the analyses of Bernstein and his follower de Man, the Neo-Socialists were able to call for a "rallying of the national collectivity" against a "minority of owners,"[21] which contributed to the Neo-Socialists' rapprochement with the nationalist right. Winning the middle classes was a fundamental goal of the right as well, especially the Catholic right, which saw the crisis as an opportunity to recapture some of the voters it had lost to the Radicals.

Thus the allegiance of the middle classes was one of the main stakes in the elections of 1936 (and the ensuing Popular Front period). The vote remained fairly stable between 1932 and 1936, with right-wing losses (35.88% of the vote in 1936 compared with 37.35% in 1932) amounting to less than 1.5% of registered voters. In the circumstances even minor voting shifts become major stakes in the political battle. Now, the middle classes (a term used by all parties but not necessarily to refer to the same groups) were considered by most political observers of both right and left to be especially volatile. More specifically, the middle-class question was linked to the fate of the Radical Party, whose fortunes had taken a turn for the worse in the period 1932–6. Having presented itself traditionally as the party of the middle classes, the Radical Party lost 4 percentage points, from 20.7% of the vote in 1932 to 16.57% in 1936. The defectors went in two directions: some, especially small peasants, voted Socialist, while others, especially craftsmen, businessmen, and small entrepreneurs, moved to the right.[22]

The middle-class movement and the syndicalism of engineers and cadres were also associated with the right-wing, and especially the Social Catholic, counteroffensive against the workers' movement. The aim was to woo the petite bourgeoisie away from the parties of the left and to mobilize those segments of the middle class most hostile to the Popular Front. Thus, for example, engineers joined unions in part in reaction to the fact that large numbers of office workers and technicians had joined the CGT: in June 1936 the CGT's Federation of Technicians, Draftsmen, and Industrial Craftsmen swelled from 500 to 79,000 members in the space of just a few weeks.[23] In the early days of the Popular Front, when the first engineers' unions were formed, militant opposition to the actions of the CGT and to the rise of the workers' movement was never stated explicitly: the unions presented themselves as champions of the engineer, not as weapons in the war against the CGT and Communism. Quite frequently, in fact, even as USIC engineers denounced the factory occupations as contrary to property rights and as the work of agitators seeking to use the strike weapon for revolutionary ends, they also recognized, in a spirit of conciliation, the legitimate character of the workers' demands.[24] Only later, under Vichy, was the cat let out of the bag. Then, for example, M. Liouville, president of the USIC, declared openly that "the year 1936 was a year of anguish for France. Aided by the Popular Front, Communism threatened to impose its tyranny upon all social and syndical activity among technicians as well as workers. The USIC decided to react by creating an engineers' union" (*Echo de l'USIC*, June 1941).

Numerous signs suggest that middle-class groups and at least some of the engineers' and cadres' unions organized in 1936–7 were encouraged by major employers, despite the fact that these groups often expressed hostility (not necessarily ungenuine) to large-scale capitalism. For example, late in 1936 Louis Renault envisioned setting up a league, one of whose objectives would be to encourage the development of middle-class groups.[25] The CGPF was concerned about progress by the CGT in organizing office workers and technicians. A CGPF bulletin dated February 1936 expresses concern about "discontent with employers among engineers and technicians." According to several informants questioned about their participation in the cadres' movements of 1936, the Syndicat professionel des ingénieurs diplômés, which was formed at the behest of the FASSFI (see below), was supported by big industrialists. The same seems to have been true of the Confédération générale des cadres de l'économie (CGCE), set up in April 1937 on the initiative of independent unions in the Nord region of France (where the first strike of cadres erupted in January 1937) for the purpose of organizing supervisory personnel. The Confederation saw itself as "the mother cell of the Third Party and the key to establishing an organization of the middle classes."[26] A circular issued by the CGPF's Comité de prévoyance et d'action sociales in April 1937 expressed "delight at the formation of this new group," to be "numbered among the many reactions against the dictatorship of the CGT."[27]

The formation of engineers' and cadres' unions and leagues of the middle class was in the first place a response to the semi-official status bestowed upon the CGT by the Matignon Accords. The conditions of the class struggle were in some respects altered by the establishment of three-way discussions among the CGPF, the CGT, and the government, the development of collective bargaining agreements,[28] and the proliferation of councils and professional groups of all sorts, such as the National Economic Council, the Superior Labor Council, The Superior Council of Technical Instruction, etc. (precursors of the neutral forums that developed in the 1950s in conjunction with the state economic planning commission). Henceforth, social conflicts were no longer confined to civil society, to the private sector, to individual firms. Strikes were no longer battles between owners enjoying the full protection of the law and workers, private individuals, whose organizations were not legally recognized. They became affairs of state and entered the public realm. Legally protected, strikes were henceforth to be settled through official negotiations (and this same period saw extensive elaboration of labor law). In this new arena all players wished to be present and represented. The middle-class organizations and new unions were formed initially to represent the middle class on various arbitration boards under whose auspices representatives of government, workers, and industry were already meeting. Here, the class struggle was continued by other means, and one explicitly stated purpose of the middle-class groups was to counter the influence of both the CGT and the Popular Front government, which was seen as the ally and "accomplice" of the working class. During this period, which engineers and cadres unhesitatingly characterized as "revolutionary," the counterrevolution was obliged to adopt the outward forms (and terminology) of revolutionary action: trade unionism, political agitation, public demonstration, and even strikes, no matter how contrary to the good manners, the reserved and discreet ethos of the Catholic engineers and small businessmen who formed the spearhead of the movement. This shows how wrong it would be to view the mobilization of some engineers and the formation of engineers' and cadres' unions as the result of a sudden mutation brought on by the crisis that somehow made bourgeois workers suddenly aware of the growing power of big employers and showed them that, exploited themselves, they shared common interests with other workers. The groups that claimed middle-class affiliation allied primarily against the working class and the Popular Front government and only secondarily against big employers accused of cowardice and complicity with the government.

But the paramount need was to carry on the class struggle in the new circumstances resulting from the changed relationship between state and civil society. *Dirigiste* radicals in the Socialist Party and among new right intellectuals proposed that the state serve as supreme social arbiter and economic planner. As a result, groups that had previously been able to protect their interests through economic maneuvering in the private sphere were now forced to seek political representation. As workers had already done, these groups became conscious of their common class interests and began to define themselves accordingly.

One of the main demands of the middle-class and engineers' groups was for political representation. "The CCM," declared its spokesman, "intends to give the middle classes the role that the working class and employer class have had in France since the Matignon accords. The CCM is therefore asking that the middle classes be represented to the same extent as the nation's other classes in all government councils, bureaus, and administrations. Simply stated, the CCM is asking for a post wherever the CGT now has one" (CCM, *Déclaration confédérale sur le syndicalisme des classes moyennes*, 1938). The engineers, for their part, did not unite solely to defend their material interests (through collective bargaining) or to form antiworker self-defense groups ("A group of colleagues met to discuss mutual support in case their plants, neighbors of one another, should again succumb to disturbances," reports the *Echo de l'USIC* for March 1937) but primarily to ensure that

> a place would be made for them in the great national and international councils and participatory committees.... The moment has come to observe once and for all that, when it comes to making laws, the category of "producers" includes not only the owners and workers but also the engineers and other cadres.... We who have always favored conciliatory methods, we who have steadfastly manifested our instinctive aversion to violence, we say to the authorities, Beware, take care not to try the patience of this third estate any longer. We want to be counted, and our cup runneth over. There are already enough occasions for social unrest without creating new ones by exasperating the very people without whose cooperation production would grind to a halt – people who have hitherto shown themselves to be bulwarks of order and progress. (*Echo de l'USIC*, January 1937)

The threats were not only verbal. In January 1937 engineers and cadres in the Nord region, supported by the USIC, went on strike during the course of a conflict between workers and employers, partly to protest "infringements of the right to work" allegedly perpetrated by the workers' unions ("with the knowledge and complicity of the government") and partly to protest the fact that employers had drawn up an arbitration agreement with "the CGT alone as if there existed no intermediary group, namely, the engineers and supervisory cadres" (*Echo de l'USIC*, January 1937). Lamirand recounts the details of the episode as follows:

> Bad habits quickly took hold and when new strikes broke out early in 1937, engineers suffered yet another blow: openly this time they were asked to leave many factories by revolutionary agitators, and in the Lille region extremely serious acts of violence were unfortunately committed against several of them. Worse still, after being physically abused engineers were taken to court by workers' organizations, and since the arbitration mechanisms established by the government did not provide for representatives of supervisory personnel to sit alongside representatives of workers and owners, it seemed that the accused would be found guilty without being allowed to mount a defense. This was the moment at which engineers' unions decided not to return to work on the date set by the arbitrators. Without cadres plants remained closed until the minister of labor gave his solemn promise that supervisory personnel would have the place they sought in the arbitration process.... This was the beginning of ongoing union action to make sure that the law would give engineers a fair shake. For previous legislation had afforded engineers no place on major national councils, most notably the so-called representative committees (*Commissions paritaires*). The door to the National Economic Council had been left slightly ajar, but the Superior Labor Council and the Superior Council of Technical Instruction shut out engineers entirely, as did even the relatively unimportant labor conciliation board (*conseil des prud'hommes*). (op. cit., pp. 265–6)

To understand why this line appealed not only to engineers but also to a still nebulously defined but much larger group of foremen, technicians, office workers, and other "collaborators" (as they were called at the time), one must bear in mind the state of labor relations in many factories following the strikes, i.e., in late 1936 and early 1937. Working conditions in large firms had seriously deteriorated during the Depression as employers attempted to cut costs and speed up production. As a result, after June 1936 the workers' revolt often focused on cadres, especially lower-level cadres such as foremen, shop supervisors, and even inspectors and checkers (*contrôleurs, vérificateurs*): in short, all personnel who in one way or another were responsible for enforcing factory discipline, sometimes by very harsh means. As Simone Weil pointed out in her 1937 report to the CGT on "the lessons to be drawn from industrial conflict in the Nord," the success of the 1936 strikes, whose primary targets were the "regime of terror" in the factories, "the speed-up of production," and, more generally, the "organization of work," forced employers to "in effect eliminate sanctions" without in any way altering "settled habits." The employers' reaction, compounded as it was of conservatism and fear, introduced "some play in the mechanism of industrial authority and a certan slack in the production process." The "relaxation of discipline" brought about a return to "natural work rhythms" and, "in certain plants," a "decrease in the quality of the work":

Inspectors and checkers, no longer as vulnerable as in the past to management pressure and more sensitive to pressure from their comrades, have begun to pass defective parts. As for discipline, workers have experienced the possibility of disobedience and occasionally taken advantage of it. They tend, in particular, not to follow the orders of foremen who do not belong to the CGT. In some places, particularly at Maubeuge, foremen have almost lost the power to transfer workers. There have been several instances of refusal to obey orders in which supervisors have been forced to back down.... Foremen, used to giving orders brusquely and until June seldom if ever obliged to resort to persuasion, found themselves totally disoriented. Caught between workers and management, to which they were responsible but from which they received no support, their moral position eventually became untenable. Accordingly, they slipped gradually into the antiworker camp, especially at Lille, including those who retained their CGT cards.... Disaffection with the workers' movement on the part of technicians has been one of the main factors in restoring employers' confidence in their own strength. This growing disaffection, signs of which were evident as early as June and which could not have been avoided altogether, has reached proportions disastrous for the trade union movement. Employers are no longer afraid, as they were in June, that the factories can run without them. The experiment was tried in Lille. In one plant employing 450 workers, the owner, having decided on a lockout because the workers would not allow the chief union delegate to be fired, abandoned the plant. The technicians and office personnel, all CGT members, followed him, and the workers, after trying for two days to keep the plant running on their own, were forced to give up. Such an experience shifts the balance of power in a decisive way.

The panic of low-level cadres forced to confront workers' delegates who "hounded supervisory and management personnel ... and provoked intolerable nervous stress in plant officials already heavily burdened with purely technical concerns"[29] would be exploited some years later by engineers to encourage low-level collaborators to join organizations they controlled.

Third party and third way

The problem, then, was to fashion a middle-class movement in the image of, but in opposition to, the workers' movement. This movement was to rally the middle strata of society by establishing principles of identity and creating unified representative bodies. In this way an inert, vaguely defined mass was to be transformed into a *class* large enough and powerful enough to counter the working class, halt its forward progress, and eventually vanquish it. Paradoxically, it was in reaction to the workers' movement that some of Marxism's most implacable adversaries adopted the vocabulary of "class," which they had once fought tooth and nail. Middle-class theoreticians, especially those associated with Social Catholicism and Action populaire, were apparently forced by the mobilization of the working class to learn the lesson of Marxism, to reconsider a doctrine that on the whole had proved its efficacy. Fortunately for them, the teachings of Marx had recently been made available to Catholic social thinkers by Henri de Man, a socialist converted to Catholicism, who had translated Marxist ideas into spiritualist language. Catholics were drawn to de Man in part because he predicted that Marxism was dying and would soon be replaced by a new and yet to be discovered alternative.[30] Father Desqueyrat, a Jesuit member of Action populaire who exerted considerable influence on the middle-class and engineers' movements and whose book, published in 1939, summed up efforts to unify the middle classes in the years since 1936, wrote that "every social class stands at the confluence of a 'mystique' and an economic structure. The middle classes are no exception to this general rule." The mystique that was supposed to play the same formative role for the middle classes that Marxism played for the working class was, according to Father Desqueyrat, none other than "personalism." For "the only 'mystique' adapted to the social role of the middle classes and capable of saving them from ruin is beyond a shadow of a doubt [personalism], whose alpha and omega is the cult of the person. Apart from the person, apart from personalism, there is no salvation for the middle class."[31]

What, then, was this "personalism" that was destined to play so important a role? From roughly 1936 on, we find, in the writings of priests associated with Action populaire and in the publications of Catholic engineers' group, watered-down popular versions of many ideas first put forward some years earlier by the Catholic avant-garde, *Ordre nouveau*, and the "young right." (Similar themes were discussed, though in less forthright terms, in the well-known review *Esprit*, which in Catholic circles was often deemed too "bold," that is, too left-wing[32].) These new ideas helped to create a new alignment of forces in the ideological field. To put it simply, the aim was to outflank established positions by creating a new image of the center: neither right nor left, this third force condemned both the power of money (plutocracy) and the power of the masses (the parliamentary regime) and heaped invective on both capitalism and Bolshevism. Spiritual revolution was to take the place of socialist revolution. More than that, class was to be defined in terms of spiritual principles rather than mutual interest. Personalism rejected both collectivism and individualism (which was associated with liberal capitalism) and located the basis of class in what was called a "natural intermediate community"[33] between the state and the individual. Class became a feature of the *corporatist order* that many engineers and middle-class activists applauded.

> Corporative organization is necessary. Everything requires it: the failure of liberalism and the no less grave failure of socialism.... Liberalism has led to anarchy of production and to the utopia of unlimited consumption.... That socialism has little by little discredited itself the world over is a proposition that hardly seems debatable. It has evolved "beyond Marxism," to borrow the title of the celebrated work by the Belgian socialist de Man. Dwelling within the bosom of capitalism, socialism has had to bear capitalism's discredit. It has left the masses to wallow in materialism and has itself fallen victim to the perils of statism. (*Echo de l'USIC*, April 1935)

Celebrated anew in almost every monthly issue of the *Echo de l'USIC*, corporatism was seen as a clever strategy for ending the class struggle by carrying the fight into the enemy's territory: by recognizing the existence of classes (as socialists did but liberals did not), corporatists hoped to shift the balance in their favor.

The Jesuits associated with Action populaire, in a review published in *Cahiers d'action religieuse et sociale* of the 1939 special issue of *Semaine sociale de Bordeaux*[34] devoted to the "Problem of classes in the national community and the human order," acknowledged that "the existence of social classes is an observable fact, attested by history. This fact is reflected in such phenomena as class spirit, class solidarity, and class dynamics, whose tangible manifestations have a powerful effect on the life of the social body as a whole," so that "to deny the existence of classes is a purely negative and hence dangerous way of resolving a serious problem: the problem of class relations within the human community." Recognizing the existence of classes is a powerful means of neutralizing the working class and combatting socialism, in several respects. For one thing, it is a prerequisite for the construction of a "natural order" in which the various classes, treated as natural objects ("class arises from biological, psychological, and social affinities") and arranged in a natural hierarchy (according to the "inequality of gifts"), are said to occupy "complementary" positions: "Every class is essentially incomplete. It can achieve only a part of the common good that society brings within the reach of individuals. Part of a whole, a class cannot pretend to become the whole. Each class must therefore join other classes in subordinating itself to the national community, which, because its ends overshadow all others, has the power to establish order among its constituent groups."[35] It follows, moreover, that classes must be acknowledged to exist in order to prevent the working class and its socialist spokesmen from acquiring a *de facto* monopoly of class definition. The only way to halt the advance of the workers' movement was to create a middle class organized like the working class and able to hold its own in the class wars. According to Albert Gortais, writing on the social role of the middle classes in the *Semaine sociale de Bordeaux*, "the middle classes have an 'indispensable mission': that of keeping the individual human being uppermost in our minds, and hence, in a society threatened by the anonymity of collectivization and the steamroller of totalitarianism, of insisting upon that authentic reign of liberty without which the preeminence of the human person is but a fiction."[36]

The ideological literature on the middle classes, particularly that stemming from Catholic and/or corporatist writers, drew heavily on Belgian sources.[37] The corporatist view of social classes was stated in the clearest, sharpest, least euphemistic terms by a Belgian priest, abbé Octave Mélon, spokesman for the powerful "Belgian Association for the Development of the Middle Classes" (his brother, Corneille Mélon, was chairman of the board of the Banque des classes moyennes in Liège). Like all the products of Belgian Social Catholicism, abbé Mélon's work, *L'ordre social et les classes moyennes*, had a tremendous influence on the thought of Action populaire.[38] Abbé Mélon did not mince his words. The middle classes, he said, are a weapon against Bolshevism: "Our only dike against the rising Bolshevist tide is surely a strong social organization of the middle classes" (p. 82). But to achieve this goal one must first recognize that classes exist. Paradoxically, the virtue of socialism is that by organizing the working class it forces the middle class to organize in turn:

> Socialism was first to create a class-based party in our parliamentary democracies. By doing so it reminded us that classes exist, that they are by nature part of every human society, and that it is absolutely pointless to deny this fact. This is the fundamental reason for the power of socialism that we see before our eyes. Socialism cannot be defeated at the ballot box. It can be stopped only by organizing the social classes and by refusing to allow them to be wiped out or reduced to the level of the lowest common denominator. For as soon as one class becomes conscious that it exists, as the working class has now done, it forces all the others to do the same. Classes that had lost consciousness of their existence, classes plunged into disarray by the machinations of others, can now regain control of their destinies, and the first thing that a reinvigorated class does is to demand its rights and privileges – in a word, it proclaims its charter. (pp. 20–1)

But no sooner is class recognized as a fact than it is said to be inscribed in the natural order and thereby neutralized. Class is a product of "the order in which people rank themselves according to social condition" (p. 13). It is therefore a "natural grouping" (p. 14), that

> grows spontaneously from seeds sown by nature herself . . . the result of heredity, i.e., of nature. . . . Owing to heredity men are born unequal in intelligence, health, and morality; moreover, owing to heredity of property, men are born unequal in fortune. Now, inequality is a natural, providential law. Inequality is not in itself an injustice, contrary to what many people think. Men are naturally unequal, as are all created beings, because they have different roles to fill. (p. 14)

In the coming corporatist order, the social world is supposed to be institutionally divided into three parts: in the words of Father Desqueyrat, "a country in which the ideologies and interests of two antagonistic, rival classes clash constantly and in which no third social class is in a position to impose arbitration is in a latent state of civil war, a state that always ends with the dictatorship of one or the other of the two adversaries."[39] What happened, then, can be summarized as follows: certain individuals and groups created a new range of social symbols based on the tripartite scheme first tried out in the political realm (i.e., the left, the right, and the third way). In politics, the primary enemy was Communism, but the anti-Communist forces strengthened their hand by designating a mirror-image enemy on the right (plutocracy or whatever), empty though this designation may have been. Once this was done, it became possible to define a third estate, third party, or middle class by contrast not only with the working class but also – and this was relatively new – with capitalism, big capital, oligarchy, or plutocracy. Symbolically, this realignment of forces divided the bourgeoisie, which had previously been a coherent, represented entity – a master-stroke. Thus began a series of denials, as the bourgeoisie ceased to represent itself as such, and the old image of the bourgeois was replaced by new stereotypes, denoted by such euphemistic terms as "cadre," "intellectual,"[40] etc. According to the *Echo de l'USIC*, for instance, "Catholic engineers" were part of the "middle-class elite" (January 1938). What better euphemism could one invent for the bourgeoisie? On the one hand engineers belong to the middle classes and hence not to the bourgeoisie. But on the other hand they are not middle-class but elite, and as the conclusion to the issue of *Semaine sociale* devoted to the question of classes put it, the elite is *hors classe*: elites "may be born, may develop within each class" but their "intrinsic vocation" precludes their indulging in "any class particularism."[41] The invention of the middle class – i.e., of a group strong enough and vigorous enough to halt the rise of the working class – symbolically unified a whole range of social groups. This middle class incorporated broad segments of society that had previously been recognized as belonging to the bourgeoisie. But the middle class could not simply absorb the bourgeoisie and then deny that any such class existed. A second pole, formally symmetric to the working class, was also required, by definition. To that end, a very narrow segment of the bourgeoisie was granted a measure of autonomy: these "two hundred families" (as the well-known slogan would have it) were said to control the largest banks and corporations.[42] Thus taxonomic surgery created a new class: the plutocratic oligarchy. Though all-powerful, its numbers were negligible, since practically the entire population now belonged to either the working class or the middle class. This oligarchy was also excluded from the nation. For did it not consist mainly of Jews and "men without a country," local representatives of international capital and foreign interests? The tripartite model is of course inextricably associated with what Zeev Sternhell has called "nationalization of the masses," which was the response of the "revolutionary right" to Marxist-backed "socialization of the masses."[43] In this effort of nationalization, the mobilization of the middle classes, the invention of the middle class as a specific social entity, played a central role.

Historically, the appeal to the middle classes, particularly when made by the left in times of crisis, seems to have been linked quite frequently to nationalism. This is quite clear when one follows the trajectories of those who moved in the 1930s from communism (like Doriot), socialism (like Déat or de Man), or left-wing radicalism (like de Jouvenel) to fascism, particularly if one focuses on the moment in their ideological development when they shifted from left to right, the moment when, still claiming to belong officially to the traditional left, they became dissidents seeking to transform the left "from within." Space does not permit examining these cases in full detail here. But comparative study of de Man's *Au-delà du marxisme* (published in 1927[44]), Bertrand de Jouvenel's *L'Economie dirigée* (published in 1928[45]), and above all Marcel Déat's *Perspectives socialistes* (published in 1930[46]) would probably reveal a common pattern based on renunciation of the class struggle and especially of the notion that the proletariat has a preeminent role to play in that struggle. The opposition between "capitalism and the worker" gives way to a somewhat different opposition, between "capitalism and the community as a whole."[47] The notion of a "general" interest,[48] which leads to that of the "national" interest, is set against the notion of "class interest."[49] The primary unit of mobilization is no longer the class but the nation. These themes are usually intertwined: the middle classes, according to Déat, henceforth constitute the "decisive factor" in the struggle; "spiritual interests," according to de Man, take precedence over "material interests"; "rationalization of the economy" and the "organization of labor" are, according to de Jouvenel, the common goals toward which the various classes must work together.

What is the middle class?

Since unification of the middle class was a weapon in the war against the workers' movement, it is easy to understand why the size of that class was a hotly debated topic. Far from being a purely scientific, sociological, or statistical question, the size of the middle class was in fact a major issue in the ideological class struggle. If it could be shown that the middle class was at least as large as the working class, then by the logic of sheer numbers (and hence on democratic grounds) it should be the nation's leading collective actor. Factoring in the superior economic and social importance of the middle class only magnified this result. Pierre Frédérix,[50] a journalist who wrote for *Tableau des forces en France* and agitated in favor of recognition for the middle classes, managed by scraping the bottom of the barrel to prove that the middle class was larger and hence potentially more powerful than the working class: counting not only employed persons but also their families (and including 5,000,000 farmers and 200,000 domestic servants), he put the size of the middle class at 20 million, compared with 19 million for the working class.[51] But the desire to make the middle-class population as large as possible conflicted with the political and logical need to show that the class was reasonably homogeneous socially and to define its unifying principle. This contradiction emerged clearly when groups included to increase the size of the middle class (such as civil servants) were excluded from explicit definitions and lists of constituent groups; indeed, some of these manipulations came close to outright deception, as for example when the same group was counted sometimes as working class, sometimes as middle class.[52] The problem was that the statistics merely summed up numbers without reference to their social context. When it came to using language to describe the groups that actually belonged to the middle class, it turned out that words inevitably conveyed ideas and connotations governed by rules quite different from the rules of statistical analysis. With statistics one had only to count. When it came to *representing* the middle class, however, it was a matter of "standing up and being counted," i.e., of determining who might potentially be mobilized or induced to join the new social movement while at the same time *rationalizing* (and thereby consolidating) what had been only a loose tactical alliance. One way to do this was to develop principles that could be used to show that the middle class was in some sense an inevitable natural phenomenon – no easy task. CCM spokesmen described it in these terms: "What the writer [C. F.] Ramuz said of the Swiss cantons is also true of the middle classes: 'We are communities linked together by a destiny. We must either perish together or confront life together.' No words can better express the sense of unity that links the members of the middle-class professions."[53] The analogy with Switzerland, a nation objectively divided but ideologically united, is no accident. In seeking to develop a principle that could be used to unify a heterogeneous group and transform a mere tactical alliance into a class, the members of the CCM's Executive Board spontaneously hit upon the device of employing nationalist rhetoric, which represented the unity of the nation as the product of a national purpose and will, a destiny and an image, irreducible to the sum of its parts.[54]

How is one to conceptualize the unity of a group that has no solid consistency? The first problem that theoreticians had to confront was that the groups to be united under the aegis of the middle class were actually quite disparate in terms of wealth. The solution to this problem was to posit a distinction between patrimony and capital homologous to the distinction between the middle class and the dominant plutocratic class. In the 1930s and 1940s the middle class was still most commonly defined in terms of inherited individual or family wealth (called patrimony). Hence there was no essential difference between, say, a *rentier* (who might, in addition to clipping coupons, also practice a profession to earn additional income) and an individual whose patrimony consisted entirely of his means of earning a living, such as a craftsman, small merchant, small industrialist, etc. Quantitative differences of wealth and income could be ignored: anyone possessed of a spirit of thrift and a respect for inherited wealth was naturally a member of the middle class, regardless of the size of his fortune. Possession of a personal patrimony distinguished the member of the middle class from the oligarch or plutocrat, who possessed not patrimony but mere shares of capital, anonymous capital, collective, disembodied capital, capital without roots, cut off from the individual, the family, and the nation – in other words, capital in the great joint stock companies, the large soulless corporations, the giant "trusts." Patrimony was wealth that had economic value only because it had moral value, derived from its association with a person. Thus the concept of patrimony established an ideological link between disparate economic groups whose unity could only be based on some mystique such as personalism. The presence or absence of patrimony defined the boundaries of the middle class. This was true at the top: it was not the amount of wealth that distinguished the capitalist from the middle-class entrepreneur but the way in which that wealth was held, personally or anonymously. It was also true at the bottom: "The middle classes begin at the economic level where saving becomes possible," said Pierre-Henri Simon in the *Semaine sociale*.[55]

Patrimony is to capital as personal is to anonymous, as productive is to unproductive, human to inhuman, national to international, thrift to credit, or, again, as legitimate enjoyment of the fruits of past labor is to reckless anticipation of future profits. CCM spokesmen accordingly distinguished between "speculative capitalism, unfortunately international," and the "capitalism of thrift," the only capitalism "productive of true national wealth" ("Sur l'union des classes moyennes," *Front économique*, 4 January 1938). Similarly, Father Desqueyrat distinguished between large-scale capitalism, based according to him on "bank credit" and hence on "future savings, on tomorrow," and the "capitalism of thrift," based on "preexisting savings" and hence on the past. The "capitalism of thrift," Father Desqueyrat tells us, is the "economic foundation on which the middle classes rest." It is characterized by the "predominance of personal or family capital over anonymous or collective capital" and hence by a practical combination of capital and labor: the head of the firm is both "manager" and "worker" (op. cit., p. 23). As Albert Gertais put it (in *Semaine sociale* for 1939),

> the real difference is not, despite appearances, between the small firm and the large firm but between the personally owned firm and the publicly owned corporation. The large privately owned firm whose head is at once the owner, manager, and source of invested capital differs from the middle-class firm by a difference of degree, not of kind. By contrast, in the corporation we do not find the same total responsibility, the same unlimited personal commitment, moral as well as material. Scattered, *anonymous* capital is assembled in search of profit, but the means by which this profit is earned, which is to say the branch of industry in which the firm operates (metallurgy, textiles, coal, etc.), is of only secondary importance. The separation between the ownership of capital and effective management means that a business organized in this manner is no longer fully human in nature: capital sees the company primarily as an opportunity for investment or speculation" (*Le problème des classes*, p. 538).

Once one has defined the middle class in terms of patrimony, it becomes perfectly plausible (given the universalizing tendencies of all ideology) to assert that possession of a patrimony is a general attribute of class in the abstract and hence to argue that the working class is not a class because its members possess no inherited wealth. Lacking property, history, and roots, the working class on this view scarcely deserves to be called a class: in the absence of inherited wealth, it is a mere mass, a vague, inert grouping composed not of persons but of interchangeable individuals.[56]

Consider, in particular, one text that offers a particularly good example of certain common clichés in wide popular use before being adapted by new right intellectuals for high-brow consumption. In February 1939, after the fall of the Popular Front and the failure of the general strike of 30 November 1938 against the abolition of the 40-hour week (the warhorse of the middle-class, engineers', and cadres' movements), during a period of reaction and repression, a schoolteacher from an industrial suburb with an interest in social issues (and a follower of de Man, whom she cites frequently) lectured engineers of the USIC on the "Psychology of the Working

Class" (*Echo de l'USIC*, February 1939). The working class, she argued, is a mere mass. It exists only in a negative sense, lacking precisely those qualities of mind that make the middle class a class. It is "a class that has no memory of having been one, a class without a past." The worker is rootless. He is "detached from his native soil, his family, his social origins ... in some cases a foreigner.... The worker lacks traditions ... [he] has inherited nothing and will bequeath nothing to his children." His home is a mere lodging composed of anonymous rooms to which he has no sentimental attachment. Having no family or history he of course has no "humble museum of family heirlooms of the sort that even the corner grocer builds with his first profits." Without hearth or home, lacking roots, he is individual man sunk in the anonymity of the collectivity, lost in gray uniformity: he is absorbed into his surroundings, standardized. Lacking not only a past but also a future he sacrifices everything for the sake of immediate pleasures, shows no inclination to save, and can only live for the present moment. Workers, who form an inert mass that cannot provide for its own needs, are manipulated by demagogues and must live by begging from society. "Workers nowadays believe that society owes them a living." They demand, in a presumptuous manner, that "society ... bear all the burdens once borne by the family patriarch."

Patrimony also became the criterion used to justify the exclusion of civil servants from the middle class: 'Their situation is too protected and provides too little opportunity for responsible initiative."[57] Civil service is to private enterprise as security is to risk, as cowardice to courage, as sloth to energy, as routine to innovation, as submissiveness to freedom, as blind, mechanical bureaucracy to "personal responsibility." The civil servant is a parasite on society who holds a kind of tenure in the bureaucracy; he does not stake his personal or family patrimony in his work. Beneath the language of moral indignation we detect traces of a social and political conflict that largely determined the structure of the petite bourgeoisie. Civil servants were to be excluded from the middle class, it was argued, in part because they excluded themselves by supporting the CGT. Desqueyrat tells us that schoolteachers in particular were guilty of this offense. In the corporatist social order the middle class (defined in terms of patrimony and paternalism) had no room for those segments of the petite bourgeoisie aligned with the left, meaning not only those who supported the revolutionary forces – the CGT, the working class, and the Popular Front – but also, more generally, those who aligned themselves with secularism (*laïcité*), republicanism, and the public sector: in other words, to use a term of late nineteenth-century political taxonomy, the "radical-socialist" segment of the petite bourgeoisie.

In the 1930s the opposition between, on the one hand, this republican and secular element, which tended to favor the Popular Front (and which by the end of the interwar period had moved at least part of the way from radicalism to socialism)[58], and, on the other hand, the Catholic (or "re-Christianizing"), antiparliamentarist, and corporatist element tended increasingly to overlap the opposition between public and the private sector. On one side we find the civil servants, who formed a highly distinctive group (in this connection it is worth noting that most taxonomies produced by economists and sociologists in the interwar years distinguished between civil service employees and objectively similar groups such as white-collar office workers; this ceased to be true after World War II). Teachers played an important role in this group. On the other side we find all those who made common cause with private enterprise: merchants, industrialists, physicians, "high-level industrial support staff" (*employés supérieurs*), etc. Clearly, the middle-class and cadre movements developed in the private sector and against the public sector.[59]

Clearly, however, the "patrimony criterion," one of whose functions was to ensure the symbolic unification of the middle class by quelling conflict between small rentiers and large property owners, between the poor and the rich, was also the main obstacle to eliminating another, more troublesome impediment to the unification of the middle class: namely, the opposition between the "independents," such as merchants and small industrialists, and those who "worked for a living," many of whom possessed some sort of technical skill and, quite often, formal educational credentials. During the 1930s, when possession and exploitation of inherited wealth remained the principal criterion for membership in the middle class, corporatists were at a loss when it came to explaining *in theory* why engineers and cadres should be included, though it was recognized in practice that they did indeed belong to the middle class. In the corporatist conception the position of engineers and cadres within the middle class is at once marginal and central. Central, because no group was objectively in a better position to represent and embody the ideological fantasy of a third force or third party, an intermediary and arbitrator standing between employers and the working class: for what was the "engineer" if not a mediator between "general management" and "the lower operational echelons," an "artisan of social collaboration?" (*Echo de l'USIC*, June 1935). Yet also marginal and ambiguous, because those who wished to base middle-class unity on a rational principle (or, to use a Marxist term, on "objective" criteria) were unable to free themselves from the traditional representation of the middle classes, in which the hard-working, independent, thrifty small businessman remained the central figure. Now, in the fundamental structural dichotomy – capital versus patrimony – cadres, many of whom worked for large firms, seemed to belong on the side of capital. This dilemma was overcome, symbolically, by ringing a series of changes on the word "patrimony."

An ideological rebus: How to integrate the cadres into the middle class when "middle class" has been defined in terms of patrimony? Solutions to this problem put forward by the Jesuits of Action populaire are impressive for their ingenuity. Consider, for example, the views of Father Desqueyrat: "Cadres," he writes, "except for subalterns and a few high-level cadres ... generally" belong to the "middle classes." The evidence for this is that they "look favorably on middle-class unionism, while they refuse to join both workers' unions and employers' associations." How can "this anomaly be explained," asks Desqueyrat, given the fact that "cadres are salaried workers whose very existence depends on large-scale capitalism?" The answer, he says, is that cadres "owe their position to constant personal effort" and "believe in saving when it comes to the family budget." They represent "the revenge of the capitalism of thrift within the capitalism of credit" (*Classes moyennes françaises*, pp. 28–9).

A similar argument was made by Albert Gortais, who assigned the middle classes the "mission" of maintaining personal rights in the face of the anonymity associated with big capitalism and collectivism. The large corporation is the exact opposite of the middle-class firm. In the satanic world of big capital, however, cadres are the personal element, and it is because they exercise personal responsibility that they belong to the middle classes: "The role of cadres is thus marked by personal responsibility, to some extent comparable with the responsibility of an owner, and it is this that gives cadres a position within the middle class whose importance is increasing along with that of the firms in which they are such active participants" (A. Gortais, "Le rôle social des classes moyennes," in *Le problème*, p. 538).

Because of the need to bring cadres into the middle class without abandoning the patrimony criterion, the reverend fathers of Social

Catholicism were forced to become unconscious but prodigious ideological innovators. They extended the definition of patrimony to include "social" and "cultural" as well as "economic" wealth. For example, Father Mélon, for whom "the middle class is the social and political Order in which are grouped, within the corporatively organized Nation, those citizens who exert control over both labor and capital," tailored his definition to make room for cadres alongside the owners of small businesses: "Here, labor is to be understood as referring to intellectual as well as manual labor, and capital may take the form of a diploma, a job, or a situation as well as a sum of money" (*L'ordre sociale*, p. 45). Ten years later Desqueyrat's disciple, abbé Lecordier, is still trying to resolve the same contradiction, magically, by ringing yet another change on the meaning of the word patrimony: what characterizes the middle classes, he says, is first of all the possession of a patrimony that enables them to reconcile capital and labor. Cadres, however, are workers who have in common with the "independent laboring classes" a "*patrimony of values* that goes beyond their sometimes opposing interests: this may take the form of ownership of the instruments of labor, autonomy, or risks and perils on the job; always we find the spirit of initiative, thrift, respect for the past, modest wealth, a sober way of life, and social esteem."[60]

It is as if no symbol could, in the 1930s, encompass the notion of "cadre," as if the concept remained elusive because no one could quite imagine what a cadre was without referring to some kind of patrimony, even though it proved quite difficult to say just what the nature of the cadre's patrimony was. More generally, the discourse of this period seems haunted by an objective need to draw together and conflate categories and groups that, in the wake of postwar social developments, especially after 1960, became polar opposites: independents and workers, economic patrimony and cultural patrimony, past and future, etc. The social milieu best summed up as "corporatist" is perhaps most aptly characterized by its refusal to conceive of society in terms of internal divisions, coupled with an objective intention to reconcile the irreconcilable: on the one hand, the small businessman with his patriarchal virtues, the personal responsibility born of direct involvement in the work, control over both capital and labor, and paternalistic employer–employee relations; on the other hand, organization of production by the state, mass production, *dirigisme*, and rationalization of the labor process. Characteristic of both Ordre nouveau and personalism, and, along with them, of one form of fascism, is the marriage of spiritualism and rationalism, which in practice took the form not only of an openly avowed objective of "class collaboration" but also, at a more profound level, of an alliance within each class between declining segments and rising segments: between peasants and workers on the one side and old-fashioned small businessmen and new-style cadres on the other.

Rising and declining segments

One aspect of the process by which cadres acquired official status seems, *in retrospect* at least, paradoxical. Decades after the fact, all analysts – scholars as well as political spokesmen – agree that cadres were a "new" group, as distinct from, say, small industrialists, who had long been recognized as a distinct segment of society. Yet this new group first formed (and developed consciousness of its existence *qua* group) in the context of a political and ideological process in which no distinction was made between "rising" and "declining" segments of the industrial sector. The same set of conceptual categories was used to treat both.

During the interwar years owners of business accounted for a considerable proportion of the total working population (approximately 38% in 1931). Yet there was a slow decline in the number of very small firms (continuing a trend that began around the turn of the century): specifically, the fraction of the working population employed by firms with 1–4 employees declined from 20% in 1926 to 16% in 1936. The percentage of artisans declined up to the Depression (from 14% in 1926 to 12% in 1931) but rose to 17% in 1936, a development related to growing unemployment in industry.[61]

It is impossible to demonstrate the rise of the cadre statistically, because the group was not yet defined as such and the relevant statistics cannot be isolated. Many signs suggest, however, that the number of people for whom the term "cadre" served as unifying symbol increased during this period. First, the number of people classified, according to the old census categories, as *employés* (including *employés supérieurs*), rose from 11.5% of the working population in 1926 to 15.1% in 1946.[62] Second, there was clear growth in the service sector, especially in the period 1926–36.[63] Third, there was an increase in the number of people classified as working in the "liberal professions" (a census category which in 1946 did not mean, as it does today, "independent" but rather "performing a highly skilled task requiring intellectual competence"[64]), from 657,000 in

1926 to 821,000 in 1936.[65] Finally, within the liberal professions category, there was an increase in the number of experts and technicians from 76,138 in 1926 to 126,414 in 1936.[66]

Since most engineers and cadres were employed by large firms, the fact that an alliance developed between owners of small firms and cadres may seem surprising. One must be careful, however, not to reify the differences between groups that were neither clearly differentiated in "objective social space" (and I shall show in Part 2 that this is still the case today) nor generally perceived as antagonistic (at least until the crisis of 1936). For example, if some engineers owned the firms they managed, others were *employés supérieurs*, high-level staff personnel. No sharp dividing line separated the two groups: between full ownership and total dependence there were many intermediate positions. Hence the difference between the two groups was neither clearly established nor fully incorporated into people's thinking. Until 1936 individuals from both groups belonged to the same organizations, and the differences in their respective positions did not prevent them from developing a common line. "Salaried bourgeois" had worked in private industry since long before the 1930s. But until 1936 conflict within the bourgeoisie between those who earned salaries and those who did not was irrelevant or at any rate unimportant. Salary was rarely the only or even the principal source of income for most bourgeois employees at least until the late 1920s. Furthermore, French lacks a word that fully encompasses the distinction in English between "salary" and "wages." The money that bourgeois employees were paid for their work in a firm was not regarded as *salaire*. Until quite recently the words *salaire* and *salariés* were in fact associated exclusively with workers [and generally translated as "wages" and "wage-earners," respectively – Trans.].

In attempting to come up with a positive definition of *salaire* and, in particular, to analyze the social uses of the term, François Simiand deliberately avoided looking at

> managers, executives, department heads, and engineers, even though they are in no way the owners or suppliers of raw materials, means of production, capital, etc., and hence have only their labor to contribute.

Simiand goes on to say that

> their compensation, though it has nothing in common with the ordinary profits of the owner, is generally referred to as *appointements, traitements, émoluments, indemnités*, etc. but not as *salaire*.... In common usage it seems to me that the term *salaire* applies both generally and specifically to the cat-

egory of workers.... It is apparently only by extension or assimilation (more verbal than real, moreover, and generally after the fact and more often in scholarly discourse than in common parlance) that the term *salaire* is used in conjunction with other categories of labor.[67]

In this connection, it is worth pointing out that until World War II the courts treated contracts between cadres and employers no differently from contracts between other professionals and those whom they served. So it is revealing that in a 1937 case involving a claim for workman's compensation by the chief physician of a mental hospital the appeals court refused to recognize a "labor contract between a physician and the public hospital that employs him." The court said that this doctor could not be regarded as a "wage-earner" (*salarié*), and hence that the accident in which he was involved on the job could not be termed a "work accident". The reason for this was that there was no "relationship of subordination" between the "director" of the hospital and the "man of art."[68]

It was the 1936 strikes that accentuated the distinction between bourgeois employees and owners by inducing "salaried" engineers to define themselves explicitly as "employees" in opposition to the "owners." In order to claim the same rights to representation and arbitration as the workers' unions, the engineers had to carry out nothing less than a purge of their ranks, eliminating the owners and retaining only salaried employees. This was part of the difficult (but ultimately successful) strategy of contesting the trade unions on their own turf while taking advantage of all the concessions that the unions managed to extract from employers (for example, engineers and cadres were the first to benefit from the new right-to-work law that was passed just before World War II).[69] Without such a purge, the cadres' claim to constitute a specific and autonomous group, a middle class standing between the working class and the owners, would not have been credible.

For example, the Syndicat des ingénieurs salariés (SIS), which was created by the USIC on 13 June 1936, one week after the creation of the Technicians' Federation of the CGT, had, unlike the USIC, no official religious affiliation in its name and included no "owners" among its members. Indeed, what was called the "mixed character" of the USIC, which

grouped together in one organization engineers occupying very different positions in the business hierarchy, facilitated some kinds of contacts but in many circumstances hampered the organization's work. An example of this arose in connection with participation in the work of one legislative committee, when it was necessary to act either as an employers' organization or as a workers' organization (in the broad sense of the term) but not as both (*Echo de l'USIC*, March 1937)

Yet the CGT Technicians' Federation accused the new organization of being "dominated by owners and in the majority made up of owners." M. Liouville, the president of the USIC, replied that 80% of his group consisted of workers (*salariés*):

Our comrades the engineer-owners, who belong to the USIC as engineers and as such have interests in common with all engineers, have never in any way hampered the actions of this union on behalf of salaried engineers. On the contrary, they have often helped to overcome the intransigence of other owners when the opportunity arose. But you will never understand this type of action, because your methods rely on threat and on the class struggle.... The SIS, for its part, is made up 100% of salaried engineers ... and is as free and independent as the USIC, as its consistent attitude, with which you are quite familiar, makes clear. (*Echo de l'USIC*, Sept.–Oct. 1936)

But the formal division between owners and salaried bourgeois employees established by the first engineers' and cadres' unions should not be allowed to conceal the fact that the interests, and in particular the economic interests, of the new segments (which gained autonomy from the division) and the old segments (which the division in part constituted as such) continued to overlap substantially. Until the 1920s and 1930s members of the "liberal professions," "salaried partners," etc. (whose professional incomes seem in many cases to have been relatively modest) derived a variable proportion of their income from investments. Income on inherited wealth was practically indispensable if one wished to "maintain one's station" and live "in a bourgeois manner." This inherited wealth consisted mainly of real estate but also (to a growing extent in the interwar years) of government and fixed-income giltedge bonds and to a lesser extent of stocks and other securities.[70] Now, the rising cost of living and declining value of money tended in the 1920s[71] to diminish the value of income from fixed-rate securities, whereas the profits of large industrial firms increased, and this in turn meant that the interests of *rentiers* and those of big industry tended to diverge.[72] By the same token, the interests of people with inherited wealth (even if they also earned salaries) tended to converge with those of small industrialists threatened by competition from large firms.[73] For example, people living on fixed income, and especially those holding fixed-interest securities, stood to benefit from revaluation of the currency. But the segment of the bourgeoisie associated with big business stood to benefit from devaluation, which would have made French products more competitive on the international market. Between 1930 and 1938 the value of an average share of stock declined 40%. Most affected were small shareholders who, "not being involved in business," lacked the necessary competence to manage their portfolios.[74] The decrease in income from inherited wealth and the increase in the share of total income derived from the practice of a profession also affected engineers, whose salaries, and especially starting salaries, were relatively low. Engineers, and with them a growing segment of the bourgeoise, joined the ranks of "income earners" ("la sphère du salariat"[75]) in the 1930s. This change in the composition of income, in conjunction with various other phenomena, including, in particular, the increased importance of education as an instrument of social reproduction (as shown by rising rates of secondary and especially higher education), proved to be a powerful factor in changing habits of consumption, use of leisure time, savings, and credit and hence in altering the whole style of life of this segment of the bourgeoisie, especially after the mid-1950s.

Rates of secondary and higher education began to rise rapidly in 1925 with what Jean-Claude Toutain has called the "acceleration of schooling" that led to the "educational explosion" of the 1960s and 1970s. The percentage of those completing secondary school rose from 6.8% in 1925–26 to 12.4% in 1935–36, and the figures for higher education went from 0.68% to 1.21% in the same period.[76] Despite the importance of private schools (which accounted for about 44% of those in secondary school in 1935–36), it seems that the growing availability in the interwar years of free public secondary schools contributed greatly to these developments, especially after 1932. At first this favored the bourgeoisie, as Marguerite Perrot has shown: in studying bourgeois family budgets in the nineteenth and first half of the twentieth centuries she found that the portion of the budget devoted to education declined substantially, from 20–25% before 1914 to around 4.5% between 1920 and 1939.[77] But this comparative gain was compensated, Perrot goes on to show, by the increased burden of taxes, which suggests that the relation between household economy and state economy, between private and public, began to change in the 1930s. The bourgeoisie and especially salaried bourgeois no doubt paid more taxes than in the past, but they were also the first beneficiaries of the system of redistribution that developed at the same time. French government expenditures increased considerably during and after the Depression, and this increase was due largely (though to a lesser degree than in the United States) to the growth in the share of the budget devoted to infrastructural expenses (roads, schools, etc.) and to social purposes.[78]

Between 1930 and 1940, however, bourgeois families increasingly found that the old budget-keeping habits inherited from the nineteenth century no longer served, while the new equilibrium between earned and unearned income, private expenditure and access to public services, etc., was not yet firmly established. In short, it appears as though a portion of the bourgeoisie found in this period of change that its economic position was deteriorating; it was caught between two "modes of reappropriation" of profit: the decrease in income from inherited wealth was not yet compensated by a corresponding increase in the share of profits distributed in the form of salaries.

In an article published in the *Echo de l'USIC* in January 1935 under the title "Some Notes on the Situation of the Engineer," we read the following:

> The most profound difference between that period [i.e., the years prior to World War I] and the present is that then most families had some private wealth, generally modest but enough to cope with unforeseen expenses and provide a feeling of security. . . . Engineers not involved in business and finance and for the most part absorbed in their work generally did not take steps to protect themselves against the fall of the franc or the subsequent fall in the value of securities (1931–1933).

It is difficult to determine how much engineers and *employés supérieurs* in private firms earned in the interwar years.[79] In 1936–37 the base starting salary of a graduate engineer was about 25,000 francs per year. The base salary of a low-level civil servant in the same period was around 9,000 francs. A middle-level civil servant earned 30,000 francs, and a high-ranking functionary 100,000 francs. But given the virtual absence of a "market price" for engineers, actual salaries varied widely depending not only on the branch of industry but also on individual factors. Even more than today an engineer's salary depended on his connections, especially family connections with the owner of the firm. "French engineers and chemists earn very low starting salaries," according to a report of the Bureau international du travail, which condemned what is called anarchy in this regard.[80] Some evidence suggests that the standard of living of engineers was often quite low: for example, the repeated counsels of thrift that G. Lamirand (and most others who addressed salaried bourgeois in this period) offered to the wives of engineers. Furthermore, the note of asceticism that is so powerful in Catholic engineers' attitudes towards society (which condemned "the consumer mentality," materialistic "idolatry," frivolous luxuries, and corrupt tastes and praised thrift and such "healthy" – and free – pleasures as outdoor exercise) was based in part on objective realities made bearable by transfiguration into spiritualist terms. In 1936 the Caisse d'entraide (Mutual Aid Fund) of the USIC offered "the wives of our colleagues ... three commonly used items ... at below-market prices": "Large five-kilo packages of pasta," "bicycles of excellent quality selected by our Saint-Etienne section," and "folding bridge tables covered with your choice of green fabric or stained wood." Here we read a whole way of life: cheap, nutritious food for large families, Sunday constitutionals, and decorous evenings with one's colleagues.

Until 1936 the bourgeoisie was identified mainly with the private sector and the petite bourgeoisie with the public sector. Conflict did exist, between owners and employees, for example, or, again, between those for whom wealth was primarily economic and those for whom it was primarily cultural, but private and public remained distinct. In 1936, however, the center of social conflict shifted to the new official negotiating bodies, and this led to the emergence of a new dividing line: within the industrial sector bourgeois employees gained new autonomy relative to the owners or, as they were sometimes called to distinguish them from "pure" capitalists, the "engineer–owners" or "owner–operators" of small firms. Thus the emergence of this new category, the cadres, and with it the formation of a *salariat bourgeois*, i.e., a group claiming to be part of two hitherto conceptually distinct social entities, on the one hand the "elite" or "bourgeoisie" and on the other hand the *salariés* or sellers of labor power, formally identical with "the workers" (*ouvriers*), was the product of objective changes within industry (and in associated classes and class segments) coupled with a collective process of redefinition whose roots can be traced in part to the class struggle: in order to defend their own interests against attacks by workers, cadres were forced to distinguish themselves from employers. But it was also the class struggle and the need to stand united against the working class that precluded explicit recognition of this new division, requiring instead collective mobilization and symbolic unification of the "middle class" around the traditional shibboleth of "patrimony," the only available symbol of unity. Thus mobilization against the working class helped to maintain unity among the various segments of the bourgeoisie and petite bourgeoisie. Paradoxically, this occurred at precisely the point in the evolution of the economy when those segments associated with an earlier stage in the process (characterized, to put it simply, by competition between independent, family-owned firms) saw their interests diverge more and more sharply from the interests of those who were objectively bound up with the newly emergent economic structure (characterized by complex financial relationships among formally distinct firms, by the dominance of large corporations and holding companies, and by increasing bureaucratization of economic relations).[81] In short, it is as though the class struggle had the paradoxical effect of camouflaging or quelling potential conflicts between class segments associated with different stages of economic development, whose interests tended to diverge as the economy evolved. The result, as many observers have noted,[82] was that "French corporatism" and "French fascism" had a paradoxical nature, in part based on religious themes and looking backward to a mythical time when economic relations were direct and personal, in part looking forward to a futurist utopia of rationality and technology in which economic relations would be mediated through the state. This paradox may merely reflect the sweeping denial of reality whose function was to make acceptable – and hence possible – the establishment of a relatively new mode of domination.

Two meanings of the opposition to capitalism

The effort to symbolically unify the middle classes was powerless, however, to prevent internal divisions from developing (and indeed from erupting into the open in the postwar period), even though diagnoses of the situation by small employers and engineers seemed on the surface to be quite similar. In particular, the two groups attached different meanings to the terms "collectivism," "capitalism," and "third force." One thing remained constant: "collectivism" or "Bolshevism," the great evil upon which everyone agreed. But engineers' complaints against capitalism were of a different nature from employers' complaints. Criticisms ranged between two extremes. Some critics, arguing on behalf of people with small amounts of inherited property, attacked "trusts," "concentrations of wealth," and what they called "the abuses of capitalist centralization" (*Front économique*, 13 January 1937). Other critics emphasized "economic disorder," which they blamed on "liberal capitalism" and accused of causing "unemployment" and "depression." The meaning of the "third way" depended on which points the critic emphasized: the evils of "big capital" and the defense of owners of "small capital" on the one hand, or, on the other hand, the evils of "capitalist anarchy" and "established disorder" (to borrow Mounier's phrase), coupled with the presumed virtues of an efficient economic order and (secondarily) public relief for the worst-off. "Artisans, small merchants, small industrialists, and professionals" – the groups which, according to the *Front économique* (14 January 1937), made up the "middle class" – were said to be opposed to *dirigisme* and "attached to the ideas of freedom and property" associated with economic liberalism. They accused the "masters of capital" of seeking deliberately to put an end to small enterprise by restricting competition through mergers, cartels, and monopolies and by failing to take a sufficiently adamant stand against new social legislation that imposed allegedly intolerable burdens on small business.

Small business was in fact severely affected by the Depression. In 1935 there were 10,000–11,000 bankruptcies compared with 5,000–6,000 in 1929, and the number of court-ordered liquidations also doubled.[83] Comparison of the purchasing power of various income groups between 1930 and 1935 reveals that while income from pure capital and labor was fairly well protected (declines in workers' income being due mainly to unemployment, with some 800,000 persons out of work in 1936), the purchasing power of businessmen in agriculture, industry, and commerce declined sharply.[84] What is more, throughout the 1930s and especially after 1936 numerous conflicts erupted over social legislation, pitting small employers against both workers and big business. Henri Hatzfeld has shown, for example, that opposition to social insurance proposals was a major factor in mobilizing small businessmen (and, more generally, small property owners and the traditional middle class) in opposition to both the CGT and big business, which was less hostile to social legislation than small business. In this battle owners of small businesses were guided in part by self-interest (which dictated opposition to "employer contributions" to social insurance funds) but in a more profound sense by the need to defend the values of their class: they felt that "social insurance dealt a mortal blow not only to their private firms but also to the social system of which those firms were the component parts."[85] The signing of the Matignon Accords aggravated the smoldering conflict between big and small business.

The owners of small and medium-sized firms challenged the representativeness of the CGPF, the only employers' organization to sign the accords. Their first charge was that the CGPF represented only big business (and hence the sectors in which big business operated, such as steel, mining, railroads, etc.[86]). Big business had not been "firm enough in collective bargaining." Wage increases and especially the 40-hour week encountered hostility from small businessmen. Finally, the strikes, the holiday, the "psychoanalytic cure of June '36" (as Jean Coutrot baptized the crisis, in language rare for the time) were all repugnant to small businessmen and threatened both their privileged position and their social identity.

At the opposite end of the spectrum were the movements associated with the avant-garde of Social Catholicism (which I suspect included more professionals and other experts whose value derived partly or totally from cultural capital than it did small businessmen – this hypothesis remains to be proven, however). As is well known, these Catholic movements favored a moderate form of *dirigisme*. Borrowing (while at the same time toning down) ideas common in left-wing and trade-union circles, Catholic activists believed that it should be possible to stabilize the "free sector" of the economy by establishing a "planned sector,"[87] provided that this "planism" (as it was termed by Arnaud Dandieu and Ordre Nouveau[88]) went hand in hand with the institution of a "communal order" (Perroux). The engineers of the USIC, though ostensibly devoted "to certain principles of liberalism" whose "essential workings must be preserved" ("L'organisation de la profession," *Echo de l'USIC*, Oct.–Nov. 1939), hoped to "mitigate the inhuman harshness" of capitalism and above all to stabilize "its unruly operations" which were "a cause of social disorder."

The *Echo de l'USIC* for February 1935 states that

> the fate of engineers, perhaps more than any other social group, is intimately connected with industrial prosperity. To revive the prosperity of industry we must do everything possible in a country that suffers above all from the absence of the basic social and economic discipline without which enterprise is impossible.

In the July–August 1934 issue of the same journal we read that

> the disorder revealed by the crisis [proves that] the hoped-for economic recovery depends essentially on a revival of moral discipline coupled with a social organization that would encourage the development of a spirit of collaboration in all workers.

Between 1933 and 1939 engineers alluded constantly to a new corporatist order that would ostensibly reduce the risks of liberalism by instituting a moderate, limited form of *dirigisme* and that would diminish social conflict by encouraging class collaboration. Corporative organization "establishes order, economic and social order," by "allowing all interested parties to discuss their problems and adjust their interests in light of what there is to be divided up" (*Echo de l'USIC*, January 1937). It "integrates the various economic forces into the state" (*ibid.*, Oct.–Nov. 1939). The USIC favored the establishment of a "corporative council" responsible for settling disputes over wages and working conditions and for protecting "the future of the human race" by encouraging "mothers to return to the home" (Oct.–Nov. 1939). Fascist Italy was constantly celebrated in these panegyrics, and not just by engineers. The economist Maurice Bouvier-Ajam wrote in the introduction to one of many books he published on corporatism in the years before World War II that

> for the past two years we in France have been witnessing an extraordinary vogue for corporatism. Periods of crisis are propitious for the elaboration of social and economic theories. . . . There are, however, deeper reasons for the revival of corporatism: France has been intrigued by the fact that several nearby countries have modified their constitutions so as to move their economies toward a corporative form of organization. The French, with their usual skepticism, refused at first to believe that the Mussolini and Hitler experiments would last. Today they see that these systems have not only altered the economies of the countries that adopted them but as a result have changed the face of the world.[89]

In subscribing to corporatism engineers were not merely expressing their predilection for order. They may also have been putting forth a relatively new demand that first surfaced in the prewar years and eventually drove a wedge between them and small employers: namely, the demand by technicians and managers that power be based on competence rather than inherited position. Generally speaking, no one in France had yet clearly formulated the principle of a separation between owners and managers that was introduced into social science parlance in the United States by Bearl and Means as early as 1932. The conditions for such a separation had not yet been fully realized in France. Still, the Catholic engineers' groups never missed an opportunity to point out that it was engineers who actually ran things in the factories, mines, and construction trades; engineers were the true leaders of men and in many cases the sole practitioners of the "management function."

Jean Coutrot, a graduate of the Ecole Polytechnique, manager of his family's firm, founder of BICRA, the first French engineering organization, leader of the group "X-crise," and personally associated with the Catholic avant-garde, especially Teilhard de Chardin and the Dominicans of *Sept*, probably went as far as it was *possible* to go in imagining his own version of utopia: a world organized entirely according to the principles of rationality first introduced into big business in the 1920s. An extraordinary precursor of things to come, he was a man who could write about the "modern technology of revolution" and in the space of a single page touch on such diverse subjects as the marvelous new "sciences of man" (especially "group psychology" and "psychoanalysis"), "advertising" (about which no one, he said, knew more than the "professors of the Sorbonne"), "technologies of suggestion" (which would nowadays be called the mass media), "worker delegates" in the shop as "factors promoting psychological equilibrium within the firm," and "concentration camps designed as temporary sanatoriums with teachers and nurses."[90] Yet even Coutrot could not entirely free himself from the idea of patrimony. In a chapter of his *Humanisme économique* entitled "The Personalist Reaction" he refers to Ordre nouveau and, as was customary, simultaneously disparages both capitalism and Marxism. He proposes "limitation of private ownership of the means of production" (p. 44), arguing that competence, too, has its rights: in the new economic order that must be instituted the "captains of production" will be recruited half from the ranks ("as in the army," says Coutrot) and half from "engineers graduated from the greater and lesser institutions (such as Saint-Cyr and Polytechnique)" (p. 64). He goes on to say that "ownership of the means of production, limited as it should be, will no longer entitle a man to manage a business unless he comes up through one of the two channels just mentioned." For "inheritance" in the absence of "competence" must no longer grant "an unlimited right to manage a business" (p. 100). The competence of industrial managers should be certified by an "Order" and a corps of "inspectors" having "no personal involvement in any of the firms they inspect" (p. 79). Nevertheless, even in this proposal, which it is tempting to call, somewhat anachronistically, "technocratic" and which is based on the notions of competence and the separation of ownership from management, we still find the traditional small industrialist, the very incarnation of inherited wealth. Large firms, says Coutrot, should be organized along the lines of the Czech firm Bata, in such a way that "a giant company becomes a federation of small businessmen" (p. 65). Later, he sings the praises of the "hard-working" small businessman (pp. 97–8).

In a "Note on the Training of Engineers" published in the November 1934 issue of the *Echo de l'USIC* we read that

> nowadays industrial capitalism is obliged to rely more and more on the engineer. Workers no longer respect the financiers who own firms, but they still respect the engineer who has knowledge that they lack and whose effects they see every day and consequently cannot deny. The engineer respected for his knowhow becomes the indispensable link between capital and labor. To be a leader today one needs more than gold braid: one must earn that braid and be recognized as a superior person by those whom one is called upon to lead.

This remarkable text (which predates the social crisis of 1936 by two years) clearly reverses the usual principles of legitimacy: authority must be based on knowledge and not solely on ownership. These were relatively unusual sentiments among engineers in the 1930s. Prestigious diplomas were often mentioned, but seldom in order to challenge the rights of property. What is more, knowledge was not the defining criterion of the "cadre." Indeed, it is as though the diploma issue impeded the definition and symbolic unification of cadres as a group. The diploma divided more than it united.

A magnetic pole: the engineers

In order to understand the debate over educational credentials that developed among engineers and cadres, we must first recall briefly the nature of those credentials and the way in which the economic crisis affected those who held them. The crisis was in fact responsible for a deterioration in the status of engineers, and not just in a material sense: it has been said that the situation affected not only engineers' income but also, more profoundly, their position and career prospects and hence their prestige, their self-image, and their "honor." Bankruptcies and the slowing of production[91] effectively decreased the number of engineering jobs, and even those who had attended prestigious schools sometimes experienced difficulty finding work. The effects of the crisis were especially severe because the preceding years had seen a rapid increase in the number of engineering schools and hence graduates seeking employment.[92] Unemployment, lack of advancement opportunities, and devaluation of the title "engineer" (which forced some engineers to accept jobs not requiring advanced degrees) are repeatedly mentioned in engineering publications in the period 1933–35.

In 1934 the USIC's employment bureau counted 464 unsatisfied job-seekers, half of whom were totally unemployed, or twice as many as the previous year (*Echo de l'USIC*, Feb. 1935). In addition, the tight job market forced many graduate engineers to accept positions incommensurate with their educational background, working, for example, as draftsmen or technicians. Early in 1935 the *Echo de l'USIC* published a large number of letters deploring the devaluation of the title "engineer." Some samples: "Many engineers have fallen beneath their station in life." "Some graduate engineers are now finding it necessary to accept very low-level positions" (Feb. 1935).

> Young engineers complain that they erred in choosing a career, because they find that their current positions do not generally correspond to the high level of technical competence acquired in the course of what is almost always a highly competitive and difficult period of training.... Many of them hold jobs once filled by supervisors and foremen.... It is neither reasonable nor just to subject a student to rigorous examination only to award him a meaningless diploma, a degree that may have genuine value one year and yet be worthless the next.[93]

Engineers graduated from the most prestigious schools, who dominated most professional groups, were fairly supportive of the law of 10 July 1934 "concerning criteria for, and use of, the degree of graduate engineer," which they hoped would limit the "unfair competition" to which they believed they had been subjected. Very quickly, however, they charged that the new law had been too generous: it protected the use of the title "engineer" by employees who were "not true engineers" and "placed the official seal of approval on engineering degrees from eighty-eight different schools" whose graduates did not all share "the general culture and technical training characteristic of a true industrial engineer" (*Echo de l'USIC*, Jan. 1934). In order to "halt this veritable inflation of engineers," M. Liouville, president of the USIC and a graduate of the Ecole Centrale, proposed setting "stricter quotas on the size of entering classes" and restricting the use of the title "engineer" by "foreign technicians" (*Echo de l'USIC*, Feb. 1935). The USIC saw to it that a special committee composed solely of engineers was set up to review all requests to the ministry of labor by foreign engineers for work permits and contract extensions, and proposed that at most 5% of engineering jobs be awarded to foreigners. It is against this background that we must view the desire, often expressed in the 1930s and forcefully reiterated under Vichy, to establish an "order of engineers" (*Echo de l'USIC*, Jan. 1934), as well as the interest on the part of many engineers graduated from prestigious institutions in the proposal by the Sindicato nazionale fascista ingenieri to form a European Federation of Graduate Engineers, "i.e., engineers holding selected diplomas, whose headquarters would be in Rome." Professional groups were purged of undesirables: in response to the attacks of the FASSFI (and through it of big business, represented in the FASSFI by Baron Petiet of the CGPF), whose spokesman charged the SIS with being "made up of second-class engineers," Liouville set forth stringent conditions to be met by engineers applying for admission to the SIS. The union's council "reserved the right to examine each individual case" so as to reject not only engineers without degrees but also engineers with degrees granted by schools deemed insufficiently prestigious. All in all, only 1%, or 90 members out of more than 9000, had no official degree and were accepted on the basis of testimony as to their competence as engineers.... We therefore have the right," Liouville concluded, "to say that the SIS is a homogeneous organization consisting exclusively of true engineers" (*Echo de l'USIC*, Jan. 1937).

The devaluation of the franc and with it the erosion of inherited wealth and the failure of many businesses did not damage engineers to the same degree or in the same way as the devaluation of their cultural capital and the collapse of "noble" and "sublime" career hopes encouraged by educational success. Bankruptcies could be ascribed entirely to external causes and agencies (such as the "trusts"), and the ruined property owner could be painted as a mere innocent victim. This kind of failure could in a sense be objectified. But the devaluation of cultural capital – embodied capital felt to be acquired on the basis of talent and merit – affected a man's identity in a more fundamental way. Cultural capital underutilized in low-level jobs not only failed to reap the expected returns but actually deteriorated for want of maintenance. Here especially the engineer's "loss of station" was felt to be a waste of human potential and an outrage.[94]

The constant criticism of luxury and money, of lucre and pleasure, which regularly accompanied Catholic engineers' attacks on plutocracy, may also express social resentment on the part of a group that felt that in a presumed meritocracy there ought not to exist such a scandalous gap between, on the one hand, its competence, the result of long years of study, its great virtues, and the eminent social role it was called upon to play and, on the other hand, its mediocre social status and economic position. This resentment and these ascetic tendencies can no doubt also be ascribed in large part to the social background of some of the engineers who graduated from universities established or developed in the first half of the twentieth century.

As Terry Shinn has shown, *industrial engineers* in the late nineteenth century came to occupy a new social position between the so-called *gadzarts* (often of lower-class background and responsible for direct supervision of workers) and the elite engineers who belonged to various official government corps of engineers (graduates of the Ecole Polytechnique, etc.), many of whom stemmed from the upper reaches of the bourgeoisie. This elite group established the image of the engineering profession as a whole up to the twentieth century. The emergence of a new category of "industrial engineers" was related to the creation of new engineering schools, such as the Ecole supérieure d'électricité or the Ecole supérieure de physique et chimie, where technical training was paramount, and the Ecole centrale, where leadership training predominated. According to Shinn, these engineering schools, whose graduates were employed for the most part in private industry,

> drew their students from the middle and lower strata of the French middle class (*moyenne bourgeoisie*). The majority of these future engineers came from the families of middle-level cadres and low-level civil servants and even from the petite bourgeoisie, for whom engineering training and an engineering career represented a sure way of rising in the social hierarchy.[95]

Engineers, whose patrimony had already dwindled and now depended chiefly on holding a once rare and prestigious degree, could think of no way to halt the devaluation of that degree other than to resort to restrictive and elitist measures. The educational system with its many hierarchies was capable of generating virtually limitless distinctions, and engineers tended to emphasize these rather than attempt to influence the labor market through collective action. Those who joined the various engineers' associations, societies, and unions whose purpose was in part to defend the profession frequently pointed to the dignity of their position and the many qualities and high levels of culture acquired through long years of training. Diplomas were used to divide rather than to unite. The idea that competence or technical skill might serve as a rallying-point for cadres of one kind or another seems not to have occurred to anyone. Diplomas were used to deny this or that group the right to be called "cadres" or to indicate the distance between cadres with engineering degrees and those without (especially those without any kind of college education).

The diploma issue was also at the center of a debate that was carried on between 1937 (when a number of engineers' unions joined together to form the Fédération nationale des syndicats d'ingénieurs with about 20,000 members) and 1939, concerning the extent to which engineers should take the lead in organizing what was then referred to as the "sound segment" of the industrial work force, meaning all who were prepared to fight the workers' unions and who wielded some authority: foremen, technicians, salesmen, sales managers, bookkeepers, etc. – in short, all those who, even though they were not engineers and held no degrees in engineering, were nevertheless inclined, because of the jobs they held, to support positions taken by the engineers. It was precisely this scattered, disparate, disorganized group, lacking any identity of its own and previously lacking even a name, that people began to denote by the vague term "cadre," counting on the ambiguity of the word to avoid the question of who should and who should not be included in the movement (*champ de mobilisation*) of which the engineers formed the center.

In some respects engineers favored admitting as many people as possible into organizations they were destined to lead: in these "unions" engineers would "be in a position to take the greatest possible advantage of their moral ascendancy over their fellow workers," for it was "only natural, especially in view of the engineer's culture, that he should become the backbone, the very soul" of the movement. "Nonhomogeneous in their recruitment," these "cadres' unions" (like the Confédération générale des cadres de l'économie, or CGCE, which was formed in 1937 of an amalgamation of small groups of "collaborators," mainly from the insurance, aeronautical, and petroleum industries, and predominantly composed of foremen and other relatively low-level "cadres") "seem to some better suited to the needs of the day, since their numbers are large and they tend to create useful alliances, especially in times of social unrest" (*Echo de l'USIC*, March 1939). The new unions made it possible for cadres to defend themselves "against the attacks and demands of certain revolutionary elements" (*ibid.*, May 1937). But the engineers' unions were not only mass organizations whose power depended on the number of engineers they could mobilize but also, like the prestigious schools from which many of their members had graduated, "clubs," or, if you will, partnerships in which each member held a share in the group's symbolic capital. Hence there was a risk involved if engineers' unions whose members held high-level degrees merged with other groups whose members held no degrees at all: engineers might lose their distinctive position, and their organizations might be thrown into disarray. To be sure, engineers filled leadership positions in the cadres' unions. But it was feared that "in many cases they could be swamped by sheer numbers" (*Echo de l'USIC*, Feb. 1937). The same argument recurs constantly: "There are already examples of unions with nonhomogeneous recruitment, led initially by engineers, that evolved so rapidly that the founders were soon forced to resign" (March 1939).

> We ask [wrote Liouville in February 1937] our readers to contemplate the construction of a modern building, in which the entire framework from foundation to roof is constructed first. After that, masons gradually attach to this sturdy skeleton the materials that will form the walls. At present, we engineers have established a framework in the form of our federated unions, and more than half the brickwork is already in.

Engineers might take the lead in the reorganization of cadres, but it was essential that certain conditions be met. First, engineers must play the leading role in industry, in corporative organizations, and in social life. Second, the values they upheld must be universally recognized. And third, the social role that engineers had carved out for themselves must be powerful enough so that the lower-level cadres, the *petits patrons*, would be forced to model their social identity on that of the engineers. These conditions were satisfied under the Vichy government, and Liouville's prophecy was then borne out. Despite the doubts of graduate engineers about the wisdom of accepting lower-level cadres into their ranks, engineers did indeed constitute the backbone of the new cadres' organizations, which though objectively heterogeneous were unified enough to establish the existence of "cadres" as a specific social group. The engineers became the core element around which a number of other social groups organized.

The Vichy government

It was the Vichy government that created the conditions that led to objectification of the cadre group, if only by officially recognizing its existence. The Charte du travail took official notice of the term "cadre" (borrowed from the military) and provided cadres with an institutional role (in keeping with "third way" ideology) in various industrial committees (*comités sociaux*). The *comités sociaux* were made up of representatives of employers, workers, and cadres (meaning technicians, foremen, engineers, administrative personnel, and so forth), and cadres thus held the deciding vote. Through these committees cadres of all kinds were integrated into professional societies. In addition, Vichy created a National Committee of Cadres. Under Vichy, ideology became effective practice. In trilateral committees like the *comités sociaux* the one working-class vote was of course outweighed by the two votes cast by the cadres and employers.[96] From 1941 on, the term "cadre" was almost always linked to the term "engineer" in the notes that the *Echo de l'USIC* published regularly on the newly formed corporate institutions (such as the Comités d'organisations professionels in 1941, the Charte du travail, etc.). It became common to speak of "engineers and cadres." Together they formed 'a sort of middle class of production." Even more significant, the term "cadre" was increasingly used by engineers to describe themselves.

The literature of combat – against the working class and the liberal republic, against international plutocracy (read Jews) and foreigners – was eventually replaced by a hagiographic literature that picked up where certain writers of the thirties, notably Lamirand (who had meanwhile become Vichy's Secretary General for Youth), had left off. This literature firmly established the image of the "engineer" or "cadre" as a skilled and disciplined leader, an officer in the army of labor. Indeed, it was to the traditions of the military (which had, of course, shaped the organization of industry in many ways, particularly in regard to discipline) that Catholic engineers had looked for role models. Then they reworked those models to suit the needs and interests of their profession.

A considerable volume of such hagiographic literature was published in Vichy France (and in Belgium during the same period). Following Lamirand's lead, the virtues of the engineers were celebrated and made known to a large audience. The titles of these works are no less repetitious than their contents: e.g. (translating the titles into English) P. Haidant, *The Social Role of the Engineer* (Brussels, 1940); F. de Bois, *The Social Formation of the Engineer*, with a preface by François Perroux (Paris, 1941); E. Huc, *The Engineer in France* (Bordeaux, 1941); H. Marre, *The Engineer in the Communal Order* (Paris, 1941); M. O. Peters, *The Leading Professions and their Social Role: The Engineer* (Paris, 1943); L. Bekaert, *The Social Formation of the Engineer* (Brussels, 1943); and so on.

Consider, for example, Lamirand, the model for all these writers, whose book, first published in 1932, was itself based in large part on

Lyautey's *Social Role of the Officer.* The engineer, writes Lamirand, is a leader: he must "serve and command – therein, in two verbs that trumpet the clarion call of duty, lie the strength and grandeur of the leader" (p. 40). The engineer must "gain the sympathy of his men by his manner" (p. 50). He must never "be caught not knowing the name of one of his men" (p. 53). He must "look his men directly in the eye" (p. 55) and "impress them (in the true sense of the word) with the force of his mind and will" (p. 68). He must "give the impression of physical superiority" (p. 55), which can be achieved through gymnastics and sports, and in short he must possess the virile qualities that make an officer:[97] frankness, a firm sense of reality, courage, tenacity, and dedication to his work (he is "the first to arrive and the last to leave," p. 49). Finally, the engineer must "know how to punish" (pp. 56–7). Everything, even his dress, to which Lamirand devotes a paragraph, must contribute to his mission as a leader: "Dress has an importance that is not always sufficiently taken into account. High fashion and sloppiness are both to be avoided. Being too careful about one's dress makes it difficult to get close to the men. . . . One practical solution, always popular, is to wear riding pants, gaiters, and rugged boots" (p. 51). Finally, routine work is described in terms of a battle for "productivity," and the analogy with the battlefield recurs constantly: "The shop floor is like a battlefield. Those who command must produce quick results" (p. 139). Elsewhere Lamirand compares the "responsibility" of the engineer with that of a "general commanding troops in battle" (p. 147). And so on. The factory is the front. The picture of the engineer is based largely on the role of a department manager in heavy industry: steel, mining, cement, or the like (where the analogy with the military officer is, in part for technical reasons, most apt). The engineer's role is still relatively undifferentiated. He is called upon to take a hand wherever trouble arises: in technical matters, personnel management, direct supervision, customer relations, etc. This image of the engineer's job seems to indicate a less extensive division of the labor of domination than exists today (e.g., Lamirand speaks of personnel managers as newcomers to industry who are beginning to encroach on the engineer's domain, p. 116).

In this fight ("engineers are fighters by principle," p. 201), the engineers' natural allies are "foremen" and "cadres" (here compared quite bluntly to noncommissioned officers in the military).

But an engineer is not simply an officer, because in addition to the virtues of the "man of action" and the "leader of men" he has the qualities of the "technician" and of the man of learning and "culture" whose concerns are also "intellectual." Consider the "engineer's office," that "little room free of all disturbance where he composes his thoughts." To be sure, this is in part a "pillbox" with "a helmet, a sword, an epaulet and other decorations over the door." But the "simple rustic table" in the center is "covered with books and papers," and the shelves, too, are "full of books." Sketches on the walls, "evoke memories of school and university," and next to a "crucifix" and a "head of Christ" are "engraved reproductions of some of the finest masterpieces of French painting" (pp. 189–90).

Obituaries of engineers in this period commonly found these contradictory virtues epitomized in a single individual. In 1941, for example, we read of the death of Joseph Mille, one of "the key men in the USIC" and the founder, along with Delacommune, of the SIS. Liouville, writing in the *Echo* in June of that year, praised this graduate of the Ecole supérieure d'électricité: a "distinguished engineer" with "solid qualities as a professional," he also had a "sense of social responsibility" and was an "ardent, devout Christian," a man "loyal to his flag and his oath" who "never compromised with his conscience," and a "wonderful father and family man." In short, Liouville went on, "he was the perfect model of the Catholic engineer."

At a more profound level, the innovating segment of the dominant class, which came to power under Vichy, institutionalized many of the themes championed by Catholic engineers and the middle-class movement in the 1930s and made them an official part of the regime's ideology. To see this, one has only to compare the *Echo de l'USIC* for 1936–39 with the same magazine in the period 1941–43, following a brief interruption of publication due to the "exodus." By 1941 the ideological gush of the thirties had come to an end. Silence had taken its place, silence interrupted only to celebrate and comment on the statements of Marshal Pétain. This silence had a dual nature. For opponents of the regime (such as the militants of OCM) it was the enforced silence of censorship or self-censorship. But for others, for the many who joined Vichy's official organizations, it was the silence of power. There was nothing more to defend, nothing more to demand, nothing more to *say*, because the revolts that had led to angry words were over: the utopias conceived by engineers devoted to corporatism and tempted by fascism were now realities. Society now had to endure what previously it had only imagined. All that remained was to consolidate the new order and live according to its dictates.

The CGC and nostalgia for corporatism

The Confédération générale des cadres (CGC), which was formed immediately after the Liberation in late 1944 and which claimed the mantle of the old CGCE, was the direct heir of the middle-class and engineers' movements of the late 1930s. Organized by the Fédération nationale des syndicats d'ingénieurs (or FNSI, which had not been dismantled by Vichy) and dominated by industrial engineers, the CGC continued the work begun during the Vichy period: to organize cadres with engineers in the leadership roles.

Members of the FNSI became the founders and spokesmen of the new Confederation. They were joined by a wide range of organizations, including the Syndicat des voyageurs, représentants, placiers (SVRP, representing salesmen) and a large number of independent unions (some of which had belonged to the old CGCE), such as the Syndicat national des cadres du verre (representing engineers as well as administrative and supervisory personnel from the glass industry), which joined the CGC in January 1945 (see the *Circulaire d'information de la Confédération générale des cadres*, Feb. 1945). We do, however, find one sign that the amalgamation of cadres belonging to different job categories did not go without a hitch: the CGC as initially set up consisted of three sections. The first was reserved for "management cadres" (in engineering, administration, and sales), and the bulletin cited above specified that "the functions of this first section are now being discharged by the FNSI." The second section was for "supervisory personnel (technicians and, again, administrative and sales personnel)." And the third section was for ordinary salesmen. The official lines between these three sections blurred with time and eventually disappeared (though the same distinction has been perpetuated in the division between *cadres supérieurs* and *cadres moyens*). The masses of low-level cadres, and especially salesmen, for whom affiliation with the CGC represented a kind of patent of nobility, functioned objectively as shock troops in the service of the engineers. At the same time the CGC developed membership criteria consistent with a broadened definition of the term "cadre": the cadre was any employee of a firm who exercised "responsibility," whatever the nature of that responsibility might be (and no matter how insignificant).[98] People who had no obvious grounds to call themselves "cadres" joined cadres' unions and thereby reaped the essentially symbolic rewards associated with the title, in exchange for agreeing to serve as a soldiers of the union. Without the support of these troops the elite of engineers and executives who also called themselves cadres could never have done battle with the trade unions.

By 1945 the CGC claimed to have 80,000–100,000 members, "engineers and other, similar employees," and sought to win government recognition as a "representative" body – a prerequisite for recognition of the cadres as a bona fide social group.

The legitimacy of a representative body depends on its ability to claim the allegiance of group members in preference to other bodies claiming to represent the same group. Since the collective bargaining law of June 1936 labor law has been based on the notion of "the most representative union." The law was designed to answer questions such as which unions were authorized to send representatives to such official bodies as the Conseil économique et social, how many representatives each union could send, and above all who had the authority to establish the answers to these questions, and by what procedures. Between 1945 and 1950 the CGC constantly challenged the government's ability to determine which unions were representative and demanded that an "objective criterion" be established, either "by convention, by legislation, or by decision of the courts."[99] Also at stake in the battle over representativity was the CGC's definition of what a cadre was. In effect, when the "objective criterion" called for was a democratic vote, as was most often the case, the troublesome issue of who was eligible to vote and hence what defined membership in this or that group somehow had to be resolved.

After the Liberation the CGC mobilized its members against the government and especially against the Communist Party and Communist ministers (in particular, Marcel Paul, the Minister of Industrial Production). The CGC worked out its program and staged several strikes, street demonstrations, and rallies at Mutualité and the Salle Wagram in Paris (on 24 June 1945 and 25 March 1946) to display its hostility to the government. But now it was impossible for its spokesmen to adopt the language of counterrevolution or of the "corporatist revolution." The change in mood that can be detected in the cadres' movement and its organizations is not necessarily a sign of changes in the leadership or in the cadres themselves. It is perhaps most of all a sign of passive adaptation to the new political situation: the symbolism surrounding the title "cadre," the issues behind which cadres had hitherto mobilized, and the term "cadre" itself had changed meaning, or, if you will, value. For engineers and cadres whose participation in political and social struggles before the war had been associated with corporatism or with one form or another of Social Catholicism, the political crisis and its associated realignments and scissions exacerbated an already confused political situation. The old "third way" – "neither right nor left" – was now strongly polarized on the left and right: the Christian Democratic party that emerged from the Resistance was forced to differentiate itself from the Christian Democratic party under Vichy by formally repudiating corporatism. Catholic members of the Resistance, many of whom had worked with secular and anticlerical socialists and were tolerant even of Marxists, claimed, as though by some sort of collective amnesia, to have nothing more in common with the ideologues of corporatism and Social Catholicism who had taken an active role in Vichy's "National Revolution." The crisis drove a wedge between individuals who only a few years earlier had shared the same nebulous ideology and found sufficient common ground to warrant debate over their differences.

Any crisis situation forces people to adopt extreme positions, to choose sides unequivocally. Thus crisis leads to discontinuity, as unifying ambiguity gives way to divisive clarity. In ordinary situations social actors generally perceive other social actors in different and contradictory ways. It is hard to say exactly what they see, in fact, because in the absence of any need to focus on some decisive criterion each actor will see a variety of qualities in the others. People often behave in uncharacteristic ways. They may be friendly to the enemy, to the boss, say, who claims to be "on the left."[100] Hence exclusion in ordinary times is never definitive or total: a person who ought to belong to the other side, who is not truly "one of us," is, in other respects, on a more "personal" level, still deemed "all right." If this were not so, it would be hard to understand the ways in which perceptions change following a crisis. Those who emerge as mortal enemies find it incomprehensible that they were once allies, or even scandalous and shameful. Consider, for example, some of the men who played leading roles in the 1930s but who, when it comes to writing their memoirs in the 1970s, find it difficult to explain how it was "possible," "conceivable" or even "natural" that they should have written Pétain's first speech[101] or supported Doriot[102] or "chosen the wrong side." Crises are reductionist: they reduce social actors to a single, fundamental property (papist or red). They are also determinist: they demand commitment and foreclose alternatives. In such catastrophic situations the choice of one side or the other may be determined by a quality that had seemed of only secondary importance, a difference that would ordinarily have seemed insignificant (like being of Jewish descent[103]). In the end, people with much in common can easily end up on opposite sides of the barricades.

Between 1944 and 1947 many cadres joined the CGC in order to defend themselves not against their employers but against the forces that had grown out of the Resistance, and in particular the CGT. But to declare oneself a cadre and hence an employee rather than an employer was also (much as it had been in 1936) to claim some of the social benefits that had been won by the workers' movement. This of course did not preclude defending established privileges and developing weapons for use in the fight against workers and Communists when the time came, as it did in 1947.

It is against this background that one must interpret the intrinsically ambiguous attitudes of cadres and of their principal organization in the period 1944–47. The only ideological tools available for defining cadres as a group were those that had been forged in the 1930s, but in the postwar climate one had to be careful about using such tools. Cadres' organizations were still heavily influenced by the spirit of Vichy. The CGC, for example, was frequently accused of collaboration by its adversaries, especially the CGT.[104] To defend themselves against such charges, as they had to do in order to remain effective in the fight against the postwar order, the cadres' organizations were forced to listen to new ideas and to adopt a modernist outlook while joining those who sang the praises of increased productivity (this was in one sense economic blackmail: the message was that without support from cadres modernization was doomed).

From 1944 to 1946 the CGC avoided any frontal assault on the new institutions, though it did criticize many of them, including the new works councils (*comités d'entreprise*). In the postwar climate it was of course impossible to ask for abolition of the councils. But the CGC constantly argued in favor of its own definition – namely, that the councils were "an expression of the good of the firm as a whole" – and against that proposed by the CGT, which according to spokesmen for the CGC "made the works council subordinate to the union" (*Le Creuset*, January 1947). More generally, the cadres saw their main enemies as the unions and the government. For example, in a report on a study published in the *Echo de l'USIC* in 1947 on "malaise among cadres" (a phrase that first appeared after the war and that would recur frequently thereafter), we read that

> union delegates intervene all too often without recognizing the responsibility of middle managers. Company owners, who may manage their firms but who often cannot make decisions without orders from the government or the unions, also find it difficult to take their subordinates' views into account. Subordinate managers are therefore reduced to simply following orders and lose all sense of responsibility.... The works councils consider questions about which the cadres in charge have little or no information other than what they may learn from subordinates.

The CGC's opposition to the Resistance-born government, muffled and toned down in the period 1944–46,[105] erupted in full force in the "restoration" atmosphere of 1947, when CGC spokesmen launched violent campaigns against postwar innovation and the CGT. In March 1947 the CGC held direct discussions with employers: the April 1947 issue of *Le Creuset* stated that "we have never understood what the government had to do with collective bargaining." In July of the same year Messrs Fournis and Ducros, both engineers and, respectively, secretary-general and president of the CGC, attacked the new regime with hitherto unprecedented violence in two front-page editorials in *Le Creuset* that touched on many of the themes developed by the CGC since the war but dropped the paper's usual euphemisms and reserve. Attacks on the MRP and the Socalist Party accused the parties of "giving in to pressure by the masses of workers and peasants" and of wanting "to restrict the range of salaries," reviving some of the leitmotifs of the fascist-influenced right wing of the 1930s: antiparliamentarism ("the deputies who champion the 'little guy' and defend the 'weak' in Parliament and who are so quick to sponsor measures against cadres are paid more than any cadre but are clever enough on the whole to exempt themselves from paying taxes"), antigovernment ("No need for the government to make it possible for people all of whom are supposed to be motivated by love of their country to sit down together around a table and talk"), antibureaucracy ("Another turn of the fiscal screw and each cadre will be feeding a bureaucrat in addition to his family"), and antiunion ("Strike after strike, French production is dwindling.... Down with strikes!"). But the bulk of the cadres' invective was directed against nationalized firms.

Nationalization was "state dictatorship with all its consequences: elimination of freedom and stifling of the individual."[106] Ownership was "anonymous," and the structure of the state-run firm was not "conducive to human development." "Managed by bureaucracy," nationalized firms suffered from "reduced production," "excessive costs," and "chronic deficits." "In order to please the masses ... the principles of hierarchy have in some cases been seriously undermined," leading to bad management: "It is sheer demagogy, for example, to invite manual laborers to sit on plant modernization committees."[107] In order to interpret the CGC's attitude toward nationalized industry one must remember that engineers and cadres employed in firms eventually taken over by the government – men who had staunchly defended the status quo and the establishment hierarchy – were dismayed to find themselves forced to deal with new managers, many of whom were former Resistance fighters with left-wing connections, sometimes trade-unionists who had participated in the Popular Front government or led strikes in 1936 and former enemies of the very cadres they now supervised. A prime example of the new generation that came to power after the war was Pierre Dreyfus. Born into a bourgeois Jewish family, he had been a Socialist Party militant, worked after the collapse of the Blum government along with Jean Coutrot and Alfred Sauvy as an advisor to Georges Bonnet in the Ministry of Finance,[108] participated in the Resistance, helped to found the State Planning Commission, where he was "in constant contact with Jean Monnet," and served as managing director of the Houillères du Nord before succeeding M. Lefaucheux as head of Renault in 1955. In his memoirs he says that when Lefaucheux, a veteran of the OCM, took the helm at Renault after the war, he named as personnel manager a man who had been a union activist in 1936, a Resistance leader, and, representing the CGT, secretary of the postwar purge committee: "The union's stewards did as much as traditional management to help in the resumption of production." Lefaucheux had promised them that the Renault plants would "become the showpiece of trade unionism."[109] A world turned upside down: Jews and even Communists were now hailed as "good Frenchmen," and church and army leaders sang the praises of the working class. To cadres these changes were all the more disturbing in that they doused any lingering hope of rebellion, for the battle was now being waged in the name of "the national interest" rather than of class struggle. This was precisely the change that the classes favorably disposed to Vichy's National Revolution had attempted to bring about in the 1930s and 1940s.

The resurrection and death of "the middle class"

The period 1947–50 also saw a revival of the "Confederation of Middle Classes." Leaders of the CGC associated themselves with this movement.[110] The exclusion of Communists from the government, the strikes of 1947, the beginnings of the Cold War, and economic troubles all seemed to augur well for the reunification of the middle class. The strategy was the same as in 1936: to create a broad-based movement large enough to hold the workers' movement at bay. "We understand the need for unity, because the only criterion recognized by government today is that of sheer numbers," wrote Fournis in an editorial entitled "The Crusade of the Middle Classes" and published in *Le Creuset* of 15 April 1947.

> The unification of the middle classes proves that the masses [of the CGT] can be counterbalanced by other masses, just as numerous and better organized.... People sometimes smile at the threat of a strike by cadres. But no one would dare smile today at the threat of a strike by the middle classes, which would lead to the closing of factories and businesses and bring agricultural production to a halt. The middle classes today are conscious of their strength. Now it is up to the government to recognize that strength in order to prevent it from being used.

In 1947 as in the 1930s, the leaders of the middle-class and cadres' movements were quite close. They knew one another, met frequently, savored a common past, engaged in joint actions, shared the same ideology and the same nostalgia for corporatism, and recognized that they had "common interests." Léon Gingembre, who created the Confédération générale des petites et moyennes entreprises (CGPME) in October 1944, knew Ducrot, the engineer who became the first president of the CGC, as a prisoner of war. Together they worked out the doctrine that shaped the programs of their respective organizations. Roger Millot, who along with Gingembre was one of the leaders of the Mouvement des classes moyennes in the 1950s, was an engineer, a graduate of the Ecole centrale, a Catholic, and a personal friend of André Malterre, who became president of the CGC in 1955.[111] Vice-president of the USIC after the war, Millot became secretary of the CGC in the late fifties.

To judge by what leaders of the movement wrote, little had changed since the thirties. Abbé Gaston Lecordier published in 1950 a book entitled *The Middle Classes on the March*,[112] a carbon copy of the book published in 1939 by Father Desqueyrat, to whom Roger Millot paid "heartfelt homage" in his preface. In 1950, in a long article on the middle classes Roger Millot took up the old themes of Social Catholicism more or less where the collapse of Vichy had left them. The only novelty, and not an insignificant one, was the inclusion of allusions to writers like Colin Clark and Jean Fourastié and to the notion of "development of tertiary production," which it was claimed gave the middle classes a *raison d'être* as the "social expression of an economic reality" (a precursor of the theme of "economic rationalization" that was a topic of much discussion in the 1960s).[113] Nor was there any change in the workings of the organization. In keeping with the tried and true formula, the Mouvement des classes moyennes was primarily a lobbying group that worked through a "coalition for the defense of the middle classes" in the National Assembly. But with the passage of time and the establishment of the new postwar mode of economic and political "regulation," it became less and less credible, less and less probable, that all segments of the middle class – "independents" and "employees," "petty bosses" and "managers" – could be mobilized simultaneously and unified under the aegis of a single group. There was less and less of an impulse toward unity, as if the historical failure of corporatism and fascism had also destroyed belief in the possibility of reconciling and unifying the diverse interests of all these different categories.

Another reason why the cadres' and middle-class movements faded in the early fifties was the rise of the RPF, as though the RPF at its peak occupied the entirety of the political and social space freed by the collapse of the pro-Vichy right. The demographic structure of the RPF's membership was roughly comparable to that of the middle-class movement: businessmen, industrialists, and artisans accounted for 34% of all members in 1954, even though they accounted for only 17% of the nonfarm working population.[114] The party was "characterized by the predominance of the traditional petite bourgeoisie of merchants and artisans, led by the industrial and especially the financial bourgeoisie and by high-level civil servants and diplomats."[115] But it also contained, particularly in its affiliate Association ouvrière (or AO, which was founded by Capitant and Wallon – a graduate of Polytechnique and former member of X-crise – and which developed the idea of a "capital–labor association"), a high proportion of engineers and cadres (who accounted for 5.3% of the membership of AO compared with 3.9% of the population as a whole) as well as technicians (15.9% compared with 8.1% in the population as a whole). Similarly, among the "worker" members of AO, foremen accounted for a disproportionate share (three times their share in the total population).[116] The figures suggest that there was considerable overlap between the RPF's base of support and the CGC's. The RPF's base contained within itself the seeds of potential conflict. The party was built on militant opposition to both Communism and parliamentary democracy and included representatives of the traditional bourgeoisie and petite bourgeoisie, bourgeois employees, and technocrats. The issues that mobilized its troops derived from traditional corporatist thinking. In these respects the RPF had a great deal in common with the middle-class movements of the 1930s, and like them it was based on a system of alliances that until 1944 had seemed capable of preserving social order and maintaining "national unity." This outdated structure is surely part of the reason why the movement collapsed so quickly.

There was one final, abortive attempt to unify the middle classes in 1975–77 (in anticipation of the legislative elections of 1978, which the left seemed likely to win). Beginning in 1975 several organizations were formed whose avowed purpose was to unify the middle classes: the Syndicat national des classes moyennes (created in 1975), the Syndicat national de coopération interprofessionnelle (created in 1976), and above all the Groupements initiatives et responsabilité (GIR), created in 1977 by Michel Debatisse, president of the FNSEA, with the support of Jacques Chirac. Among those who joined these groups were Francis Combe, president of the Chambre des métiers, Dr Monier, president of the Confédération des syndicats médicaux français, and Léon Gingembre, secretary general of the CGPME. Leaders of these groups, especially the GIR, revived the language of 1936, condemning "a France undermined by ideological bipolarization," "cut in two," caught between "revolutionary pressure and conservatism," between the "employers' bloc" and the "national trade unions" (*Le Monde*, 3 Nov., 1976). Their aim was to "put an end to the confrontation between MM. Séguy and Maire [leaders, respectively, of the CGT and CFDT – Trans.] on one side and M. Ceyrac [leader of the CNPF] on the other" (*Le Monde*, 2 March 1977). A sign of the times: Yvon Charpentié, president of the CGC, who joined the movement on behalf of his organization, was immediately disavowed by a large number of its members.

As the failure of these final attempts at unification shows, the middle class vanished in the 1960s without having been able to develop a stable and durable system of representation. The utopian visions of the 1930s had not found suitable social moorings. The segments of society that the proponents of these visions had claimed to represent and attempted to unify turned out to be too heterogeneous, too susceptible to the appeals of rival groups already organized and institutionalized, to achieve unity in practice or even to enunciate a formal principle that would have defined the shape and contours of the middle class, whose "common interests" were few and difficult to identify. The middle class failed to achieve unity because its members derived their value from too many different "kinds of capital."[117]

Toward a new bourgeois household economy

Nostalgic for an outmoded order, in the opposition and on the defensive, the heirs to the cadres' movements of 1936–40, particularly the CGC, did not take part in the postwar modernization of French society, even though such participation was essential if cadres were to obtain a central place in the dominant social representation. Political changes in the wake of the Liberation, coupled with the rise of a new generation of political leaders, transformed the vanguard of the 1930s into a rear guard. Still imbued with corporatist ideas, cadres' organizations continued to define themselves in terms of patrimony and middle-class affiliation, shunning the new managerial ideologies. Still, the CGC's actions, aimed mainly at short-term political and professional goals and more interested in restoring the past than in shaping the future, did much to alter the economic and social condition of large segments of the bourgeoisie.

To begin with, the CGC succeeded in obtaining legal recognition of cadres as a group. The group was officially named in the Accords Parodi (and, somewhat later, in standard INSEE nomenclature, most notably in the "code of socioprofessional categories" established by Jean Porte in the 1950s).[118] This helped to create the impression that the diverse assortment of job categories represented by the CGC did indeed constitute a new and homogeneous social group.

With the decline of the "patrimonial economy," however, the CGC's actions focused mainly on questions of salary and profit-sharing. The major themes of the CGC's 1945–7 campaign were as follows: to increase the range of salaries, to obtain special clauses covering cadres in collective bargaining agreements, and above all to secure special social security and retirement programs for cadres only.[119] Indeed, the retirement issue has been a CGC warhorse from 1945 to the present day.

What held the CGC together was its refusal to allow cadres to be included in the regular social security and retirement system and thus to be lumped together with other employees. It is impossible to understand the importance of the retirement issue[120] in the CGC's ideology, not only in the past but even today, unless one recognizes that this issue (along with tax breaks for cadres and an expanded salary range) was the primary means of mobilizing the group's fairly heterogeneous membership[121] and, further, that support of the cadres' retirement plan was, and to a certain extent still is, the major bond uniting a rather diverse assortment of people and organizations. Participation in a cadres' retirement plan is still the most general criterion for determining whether an employee is or is not a cadre.[122] It is the criterion that yields the broadest definition of the group (thus reflecting the interests of lower-level cadres). This broad definition must compete with other, narrower definitions, based, for example, on cultural capital (see part 2, chapter 4), which are favored by some higher-level cadres. Promotion to the rank of cadre, which is formally indicated by eligibility to participate in a cadres' retirement program, is therefore an important symbolic benefit. In practice, this is often used by employers as a means of manipulating low-level staff and supervisory personnel. Such a promotion has intrinsic value and need not be accompanied by a change in job description or even salary level. Here we see the specific efficacy of the law: by rationalizing and according official status to practical systems of classification, the law helps to define the boundaries between groups, selecting certain discrete social units from the rather confused and multifarious hierarchies of ordinary social practice. The new retirement program had more than just symbolic value, however. In addition to encouraging social unification, the program also played an important economic role. Rampant inflation from 1935 on had reduced income from fixed-rate securities, forcing many members of the bourgeoisie to take a greater interest in their work and careers and in questions of salary, bonuses, and retirement. In the CGC's Information Bulletin for July 1945 we read that "a series of devaluations since 1924 has undercut efforts by many cadres to put aside a sum of money for their retirement, frustrating the sacrifices they had made to protect themselves in their old age." From now on, "retirement income" must be sufficient to allow people to live decently, i.e., in a bourgeois manner, and for those without inherent wealth it must be sufficient by itself, i.e., without any other source of income.

"Our attitudes and our rules are not those of ordinary retired workers (*petits retraités*)," declared M. Fournis, secretary-general of the CGC, speaking before that organization's national convention on 24 June 1945.

What we are proposing is not some paltry pension after years of loyal service, just enough to retire to the country or to take a new job to supplement your retirement income. That is no ambition for any cadre worthy of the name.... We are saying that it is unfair, as soon as a cadre becomes too old to work, to put him in a position where he can no longer maintain his rank and must flee to some remote province to hide his poverty. Cadres must have a decent, dignified pension, enough to maintain a standard of living comparable to that of their working years.... Capitalization systems must therefore be immediately abandoned. We know what the advantages of such systems are. We know that the money deposited earns interest and grows accordingly. But we also know the sad experience of recent years, we have seen devaluation on top of devaluation, we have seen the value of money decrease day by day to the point where a person who had once dreamt of retiring on 20,000 francs now finds that sum scarcely enough to keep him alive for a month. Thus it is absolutely essential that this plan be replaced by profit-sharing, which is a means of distributing real resources to all participants. The CGC is probably the first organization to have carried out an in-depth study of such a plan, examining it from every angle, with the result that we are now ready to propose the following: a deduction of 16% of our salary will entitle you to retire on 60% of your average income or 50% of your income in the final years of your career.... In any case, what I want to say is that once again we must join together to oppose any steps that the government might take to introduce a uniform retirement program for all Frenchmen.... It is in our view inappropriate that everyone should receive the same pension. Again, each person's individual effort must be taken into account. If one foreman has worked harder than another, he should receive a greater pension, and the same holds true for everyone. Uniformity is to be avoided: this is a view that we cadres in particular must champion, because with legitimate pride we maintain that we are not part of an indistinct mass. We are an elite that must rise above the mass. It is therefore legitimate that the members of this elite receive special treatment (*Cadres de France*, August 1945).

The establishment of the "cadres' retirement program" was of fundamental importance because it inaugurated a series of profound changes in the household economy of the bourgeoisie and hence in the economy in general. The status of inherited wealth was altered, as were attitudes toward consumption, material goods, and especially time. Among bourgeois employees, individual savings and direct access to profits were replaced by collective savings and indirect (as well as camouflaged) profit-sharing: salary increases and broadening of the salary spectrum; private retirement funds based on profit-sharing rather than capitalization; changes in labor law won by the trade unions, which guaranteed job and salary security;[123] income stabilization as a result of institutionalized procedures for salary review in the light of changes in the consumer price index, etc.[124] All of these changes were related in complex ways to changes in the cadres' value system: asceticism was out, at least in private life, and consumption was in. Strategies of social reproduction also changed: the educational system became increasingly important, and economic wealth was in part converted into educational capital.

This process widened the gulf between independents and bourgeois employees and made people increasingly aware of the differences between them. Scholarly perceptions of the social structure also changed. Between the 1930s and the 1950s the relative position of "genuine employers" (as spokesmen for small business are wont to call business owners[125]) and salaried employees was reversed: cadres, who had gone almost unnoticed until the 1930s, by the 1950s had become a leading social model or, if you will, a "magnetic pole" (*attracteur*) around which other groups arrayed themselves in ever-widening circles.

There is something contradictory in the fate of the cadres both as collective individual and as social representation. When the cadres formed as an explicit group shortly before World War II, their movement was closely linked to attempts to unify the middle classes, a category that subsumed both independent employers and their salaried employees. Spokesmen for the cadres looked to corporatism for the ideological principles which they claimed justified the existence of this new group, whose institutionalization was encouraged by the government of Vichy. In the 1960s cadres, especially young cadres, were the very embodiment of modernity, of the new bourgeoisie, and hence of the life style and "mode of economic regulation and political domination" characteristic of the "postwar regime of accumulation."[126]

In the space of twenty years the social representation of the cadre, the principles of excellence that define the group, had changed profoundly. The image, so often described in the 1960s, of the "forward-looking young cadre," "embodiment of a new bourgeoisie without blinkers,"[127] apparently differed in every possible way from the model engineer as defined by, say, Georges Lamirand: explicit references to the army, the church, the authority of the commander, the virile, ascetic values of the leader, and even the factory as the battlefield of production have all but disappeared, replaced by celebration of the cadre's intelligence, education, achievement (as distinct from inherited position), dynamism, openness, feeling for human relations, and economic and technical competence deployed in a futuristic office or laboratory.

When questioned about these changes in the cadre's social image, old engineers, now in retirement, who took part in the cadres' movements before the war, under Vichy, or in the late 1940s and early 1950s (in the USIC, CGCE, CGC, and so forth), often allude to the "pernicious effects of publicity," "consumer society" (especially if they are Catholics), and, still more often, to "fashions imported from America." The critique of the "Americanization of French society," commonly associated in the postwar period with the extreme left, is here based on nostalgic regret for another possible social order: that promised by corporatism, which provided the ideological underpinnings of the original cadres' and engineers' movements.

2 *The fascination with the United States and the importation of management*

One cannot hope to understand the changes in the social representation of cadres in the postwar period without understanding what those changes owed to the importation of value systems, social technologies, and standards of excellence from the United States, in conjunction with (or even in some cases prior to) the Marshall Plan. More precisely, one must understand how the image of the cadre was affected by political and social conflicts within the bourgeoisie and petite bourgeoisie over the "Americanization of French society." The debate over Americanization in France has always been highly political and filled with acrid polemic. This was particularly true in the mid-1960s, when France quit the NATO alliance and de Gaulle opposed the purchase of certain French firms by American corporations, and later, during the events of May 1968 and the Vietnam War. Attitudes toward America are like a social Rorschach test. Each social group takes its own partial view (in both senses of the word "partial"), defining the United States in terms of the group's own interests and position in French society. In these confused debates, the period from the Liberation up to 1960 seems to have been forgotten or repressed.[1]

Yet America has in one way or another dominated French social and intellectual life since 1945, and military and economic issues have not been the only ones on the agenda. Indeed, another question has always been regarded, quite explicitly, as more fundamental: What is the "nature" of French society as compared with American society? In other words, how do the political regimes and social structures of the two countries compare? How do management techniques differ? What forms of social control are used, and how are social conflicts resolved? How can American dominance be explained? What can one learn from the United States? Which aspects of American society should be rejected, and which imported or adopted? Central to all these questions is a social issue that gained prominence after the war: What kinds of people should become managers and supervisors in industrial firms? Who should manage? How should supervisors be recruited, trained, and monitored in order to achieve "efficient" management that workers will accept? It was primarily in order to reform management methods and to train middle management personnel that the French imported from the United States new management technologies such as group psychology. As these technologies spread to other areas of collective life (such as social work and even the parochial school system), they helped to establish new forms of social control.

In this chapter I shall try to recreate the intellectual climate of the period 1945–55, during which a new industrial ideology and a new representation of "social space" (which became dominant in the 1960s) were first constituted. To do this I shall be looking at a rather diverse range of sources, from the management press to "role-playing seminars." I am not unaware of the risks involved in trying to cover so much ground, the gravest, surely, being that of suggesting that some "invisible hand" was at work: "the hand of the foreigner." Although I found it necessary to point out the obvious relationship between, say, the actions of various international agencies established under the auspices of the Marshall Plan and certain ideological changes in France in the 1950s, it goes without saying that official programs and policies would have accomplished nothing had they not met with the right historical and social circumstances. It is a matter for endless debate, in any case, whether the social changes that occurred after World War II would have been different in nature or magnitude had there been no concerted and orchestrated effort to influence them.

The "productivity missions" to the United States

American-style "human engineering" and "management" practices were introduced into France in conjunction with economic changes begun under the first Monnet plan (and even earlier, under the Economic and Social Program of the National Resistance Committee). These changes continued under the Marshall Plan in the late 1940s and early 1950s, which saw the reorganization and restructuring of French industry followed by the formation of the European Coal and Steel Community.[2] Modernization of the economy meant more than just technological modernization. It affected more than just blast furnaces and rolling mills. One condition of American economic aid was that France should train "managers" who would be economically knowledgeable and politically reliable.[3] More generally, the Americans wanted a stable French society that would halt the rise of the PCF, particularly worrisome after a wave of strikes hit France in 1947.[4] Economic modernization was explicitly intended to bring about a wholesale transformation of French society. To that end, social action had to focus on men and their "attitudes" and also on "social structures," on social relations between groups and classes.

In 1948 a Working Group on Productivity was set up at the Commissariat général au Plan under the chairmanship of Jean Fourastié. This group set forth a "French productivity plan," whose points included "establishing records and statistics concerning productivity, sending experienced people to the United States for instruction, and training teachers in new, productivity enhancing techniques." Later came the establishment in 1949 of the Comité provisoire de la productivité, followed in 1950 by the creation of the Association française pour l'accroissement de la productivité (AFAP) and in 1953 by the Commissariat général de la productivité, headed by Gabriel Ardant (who was a close associate of Pierre Mendès France). One of the principal tasks of the AFAP, which was set up with the help of a large American grant, was to organize "productivity missions" to the United States. In 1949 the chief of the Office of Technology and Productivity of the United States Department of Labor was sent to France to investigate practices in 120 firms and to assist in the development of a French productivity plan. Between 1950 and 1953 the AFAP sponsored more than 450 productivity missions to the United States, involving more than 4,000 employers, engineers, cadres (who accounted for 45% of all *missionaires*), union delegates (around 25%, and including no representatives of the CGT, which refused to work with the AFAP), top civil servants, economists, psychologists, and sociologists (around 30%), etc.[5] The rationalization of industry, which the productivity missions were intended to assist, was not limited to such areas as technology or the organization of work. As one early group of *missionaires* noted, "France's productivity lag" was not "the result of a technological lag," since industrial technologies in France were "similar to, and in some cases better than, technologies used in the

United States": "Broadly speaking, American machinery held no surprises for French technical experts."[6] Thus France's economic lag was not due to technological inadequacy or engineering incompetence. According to one important OECE report, which summed up steps taken to improve productivity and suggested various additional measures, "the Americans clearly stated that there is no difference in technology between Europe and the United States. In fact, they had had the opportunity to observe many cases in which European industrial technology was ahead of American technology." But, the report added, the French are not "aware of the direct relationship that exists between a high level of productivity and the use of sound methods in the area of human relations."[7]

Many of the reports repeat the same refrain, telling of French amazement at the discovery of the "American productive spirit" and of the importance of "psychological factors," of a "new conception of human factors in industry."[8] For those who sponsored the productivity missions, the primary goal was to "reshape the minds" of the major economic actors, to change their ways of thinking and acting. Even a cursory glance at the reports of the various missions is enough to show that the importance of social technologies far outweighed that of material technologies.[9] The first priority was to import new "scientific" methods of organizing work and "rational" methods of industrial management in order to establish in French firms a climate similar to that found in American firms: this climate was indeed the product of a technology, but a new technology, one that required knowledge not only of engineering but also, even more, of the human sciences, psychology and sociology.

A report of the European Productivity Agency states the following:

> The growing complexity of industrial life points up the need for cooperation between employers and workers in the common interest and for the sake of economic growth. But real cooperation is in many cases still difficult to achieve, owing to the emotional climate and various traditional fears, which stand in opposition to the general interest, rightly understood. Scientific research, which by its very essence is neutral and impartial, provides a unique opportunity to identify common ground and prepare the way for a measure of cooperation. Research in the human sciences therefore turns out to be both scientifically fruitful and socially beneficial.[10]

Talk of productivity was regularly accompanied by an appeal for "cooperation among all employees." Through the establishment of a "productive climate" and "productive attitudes" some in France hoped to achieve what corporatism had never been able to accomplish, but by other means. Where corporatism had failed they hoped to succeed, at the cost of some sacrifice: the price of conservation was change. The Americans could instruct the French in the use of gentle persuasion as opposed to strong-arm methods, of "communication" as opposed to secrecy, of "dialogue" as opposed to authoritarianism, and of "generosity" (that most fruitful of investments) as opposed to avarice.

> Technological progress must not be imposed on employees but should be planned with the cooperation of all concerned: employers, cadres, and workers. Trilateral committees should be formed in every firm to plan, for example, for the retraining of employees made redundant by technological progress in one branch of industry. If such precautions are not taken, it is to be feared that a segment of the working class may oppose improvements in productivity that, in its view, would impose immediate costs on individuals without offering any obvious collective benefits as future compensation.[11]

A first priority was to improve relations with the trade unions, "which seem to play an increasingly important role in the modern American organization." Unions should be granted recognition and induced to "participate" and "cooperate."[12] This was attempted with the "free trade-union confederations," representatives of which were sent to the United States and in 1951 formed the Centre intersyndical d'études et de recherches de productivité.

Once a climate of confidence had been established, redistribution of increased profits due to enhanced productivity through wage and salary increases (a major innovation compared with the 1920s and 1930s, when major productivity gains had virtually no effect on wages, thus helping to trigger the Depression and making recovery quite difficult) would help to maintain "cooperation between employers and workers."[13] The same theme recurs again and again:

> Employees will not help to increase productivity unless they are the first to reap the benefits of what they accomplish. This sharing of the fruits of productivity is legitimate, even if the enhanced profits result solely from the introduction of new machinery or investment of additional capital.... Employees deserve rewards for adapting to changed working conditions. In any case, capital in the form of machinery will not earn a profit unless the machinery is run by intelligent and diligent workers.[14]

Again it is the American example that must be followed, for American productivity is "in part the result of American workers' being broadly aware of the influence of productivity on their standard of living and on the standard of living of the nation as a whole."[15]

The American "experts" sent to France under the auspices of the Marshall Plan concentrated their criticisms on French executives and plant owners.[16] After pointing out that the "constructive attitudes of workers" in the United States were due primarily to the "constructive attitudes of management," they charged French industrial leaders with "opposing all constructive change," "failing to plan for the future," "failing to delegate adequate responsibility and authority to subordinates," and failing to recognize "the importance of human factors" and "respect for the dignity of workers." French managers were called upon to "adopt a realistically optimistic attitude, to display enthusiasm and confidence in themselves, in their subordinates, and in the future of their businesses," to "improve communication in both directions between management and workers," to "employ sound methods in the area of human relations," and finally to "give workers the sense that they have a part in the enterprise" (which, it is added, does not necessarily mean giving them a "share in the profits or management of the firm"). The most urgent need, according to the experts, was to train loyal and efficient "middle managers": "The Americans were greatly surprised to discover that no industrial managers were university trained." In particular, there was a lack of instruction in management and business administration, without which "Europeans will never accept the idea that industrial management is a profession." Nor was there sales training, and many firms that "employed highly competent engineers in their production departments showed little concern as to the abilities and training of sales representatives." Besides "improving the selection and training of sales personnel," firms should encourage "the dynamic and methodical search for new markets" by "strengthening market research." Basic tasks, then, were to train new cadres, establish schools of management, and "upgrade the skills of existing cadres." To these ends, businessmen should organize "meetings, lectures and planning groups," "publish in their own languages a greater number of books, manuals, and magazines on industrial management," expand existing "study groups, lecture courses, night and weekend classes," and bring in outside "lecturers and teachers on a regular basis," especially "American experts who have come to Europe to participate in this kind of effort." In addition each country should send "groups to the United States to participate in a program of study of about a year's duration." They should "encourage the formation of specialist groups" in order to "promote progress in various areas of scientific organization of labor," etc. Finally, "management attitudes must be changed": "The most delicate task is to perfect techniques and methods that will make it possible to bring about this change."[17]

The campaign to increase European productivity, with its "productivity actions" and "productivity missions" to the United States, was promoted by the United States under the Marshall Plan. It affected countries other than France: orchestrated by the OECE, missions were sent to America from all over western Europe.[18] Still, one cannot understand how the missions worked in terms of mechanical, diffusionist theories; some account must be taken of the mediations involved in spreading the influence of American methods and ideas. Some observers, who believed in economic and technological determinism, held that new management techniques were inevitable (this theory appealed, in particular, to the industrial engineers who introduced American techniques into France). Others alleged that "imperialist violence" was at work. It is important, however, to understand how the American model linked up with older French ideas and how the French bourgeoisie was divided over the issue. In this controversy cadres occupied a central position in more than one respect: they were among the principal participants in the debate (primarily through their representative organizations), while at the same time their allegiance was hotly contested. Indeed, one of the primary objectives of the productivity missions was to convert cadres to belief in the new economic ideology.

"America, youth, success, beauty, the future"*

If we want to watch the image of the modern cadre, the versatile new manager, come into being in the postwar period, we must paradoxically turn our attention away from the cadres' organizations and focus instead on those who at the time counted among the adversaries of the cadre: high-ranking civil servants (both Catholics and socialists), veterans of the Resistance, and salaried heads of nationalized firms with their retinue of planners, economists, organizers, sociologists, psychologists, etc. Employed by the state, dedicated to the common good, hostile to industrialists and, more

*"It was natural to identify with John Kennedy, who embodied the leading ideas of my generation: America, youth, success, beauty, the future." Jean-Louis Servan-Schreiber, *A mi-vie: l'entrée en quarantaine* (Paris: Stock, 1977), p. 137

generally, to the private sector (suspect as always on grounds of individualism and selfishness), and sensitive to the "poverty and exploitation of the worker," these men were the primary architects and proponents of the modernization of French society, which they extolled in the name of both progressivism and nationalism. In other words, modernization was necessary not only to shut the door against "totalitarianism" (i.e., to stem the Communist tide and prevent any revival of fascism) but also to restore French power *vis-à-vis* other countries, especially the United States. The modernization of economy and society was part of a political program that could not be carried out until two potentially dangerous classes had somehow been eliminated or altered, namely, the "reds," or working class, and the "blacks," or traditional petite bourgeoisie, the class that had provided the staunchest supporters of various forms of fascism.

American models would never have caught on so quickly had the actions taken by Marshall Plan administrators not coincided with the interests of this reformist avant-garde. The reformers did not identify themselves with any organization or political party. They had no formal organization, no means of representation, no clearly delineated contours or symbols. What they did have was a network of personal contacts that first developed in the Resistance.[19] When one looks at who cites whom (in conversation or in writing) and traces these networks of friendship, ideological affinity, and political loyalty and allegiance, one finds two men at the center: Jean Monnet, who orchestrated the productivity campaign,[20] and Pierre Mendès France, whom enlightened, economically literate, progressive civil servants at the time saw, according to abundant evidence,[21] as the only politician capable of accomplishing the modernization and democratization of French society. Mendès France maintained close relations with Pierre Dreyfus, Georges Boris, and Alfred Sauvy; with young, progressive economists at the planning commission, such as Hirsch, Marjolin, Ripert, Massé, Dumontier, and especially Pierre Uri; with Gabriel Ardant, commissioner for productivity; with François Bloch-Lainé and the economists of the SEEF, who established national accounts bookkeeping in France for the first time; with Claude Gruson (whom Bloch-Lainé had selected to organize the SEEF[22]); and with Gruson's collaborator Simon Nora. Mendès was also linked to Nora via another route, since Nora was, according to several informants, the best friend of Jean-Jacques Servan-Schreiber, who mobilized his family, his protégés, and his magazine (*L'Express*) behind Mendès France. According to Françoise Giroud (*op. cit.*, p. 138), the story of

L'Express was the "story of a group of people who fervently hoped to see France take off: the goal was to put Mendès France and his ideas in power, in action, for the good of France" (p. 151).

The strategic position of the Servan-Schreiber family in the progressive, modernist avant-garde of the 1950s has to do not so much with the stands that family members took on the issues or with their direct political actions as with their talent for bringing together individuals and groups that had previously been separate or even hostile (civil servants, intellectuals, employers, etc.) and for appropriating the sometimes contradictory values of those they assembled. In this way the Servan-Schreiber clan helped to shape and to popularize a relatively new cultural model. The Servan-Schreibers, who as a family combined many characteristic features of the political and economic avant-garde, were no doubt well suited to serve as a paradigm for the new bourgeoisie. Their wealth had been acquired fairly recently. They were half-Jewish and, as is often the case in Jewish families (and, to a lesser degree in Protestant families) in which a "minority effect" tends to maintain group cohesiveness by attenuating internal conflict, stood at the intersection of a number of different milieux: the press, business, the civil service, politics, the university, etc. The Jewish bourgeoisie, or at any rate what was left of it after the war, was strongly represented in the 1950s avant-garde. Bourgeois Jews were ahead of their times, but not because of anything inherent in Jewish culture or religion as such (most had been brought up to believe in republican values of a radical or socialist cast). Their "lucidity" was, rather, a result of their exclusion as a group during the 1930s and the Occupation, owing to the virtually unanimous antisemitism of the dominant segments of the dominant class in France. Antisemitism drove Jews toward the left, estranged them from Vichy, and kept them from succumbing to the illusions of fascism or corporatist utopias. At the same time it brought them closer to England and the United States, where some French Jews had sought refuge. Many were nationalists, often ardent nationalists, who had fought in the Resistance. In 1945 the survivors acceded to positions of power at an age when a young bourgeois of the previous generation would have been making his first entry into society. They were predisposed to represent youth, not only because they were young but also because the war had cut their ties to the past, to their roots, and to their class. With the Liberation they acquired a future, thanks to their battle ribbons and university degrees. In opposition to the established bourgeoisie, to the old values of the old families whose aging had been accelerated by Vichy's collapse, they stood for new values and could in all good faith deny that they belonged to the dominant class, with which they had their own score to settle.[23]

The new bourgeoisie differed from the old not only in its personal values (intelligence, efficiency, competence, and professionalism in contrast to the amateurism of the dilettante) but also in its manners, a mixture of the asceticism of the partisan fighter and easy-going, "American-style" simplicity. The new bourgeois turned up his nose at French gastronomy: *L'Express* was renowned for its disconcertingly simple lunches, consisting of a sandwich or an airline-style meal on a tray. The new bourgeois also disdained alcohol, high society, bourgeois manners, hypocrisy (in matters of sexuality), traditional education, etc. The new bourgeoisie joined the feminist vanguard, and Françoise Giroud especially was in the forefront of the family planning movement.[24] When Giroud coined the phrase "new wave" in 1955 to characterize the readers of *L'Express*, it was all of these things that she had in mind: a new, relaxed way of being bourgeois, a new way of life that had not yet become a rigid style derived from American stereotypes, and a new system of values. The latter combined, in a way that was, for France at any rate, relatively new, the idea of achievement that lies at the root of capitalist enterprise with the spirit of public service. It incorporated both the qualities of the entrepreneur (the willingness to take risks, the work ethic, the ideal of efficient management) and the virtues of the compleat civil servant (the ideal of service, dedication to democracy, and social responsibility as opposed to profit for profit's sake and dedication to self-interest to the exclusion of all else).

The second "third way": from corporatism to the New Deal

The postwar avant-garde's fascination with America went hand in hand with its critique of the traditional right wing – employers bent on defending their "caste interests" and "bourgeois elites" that had "failed in their mission."[25] Meanwhile, in the eyes of the reformers, the America of the 1950s, of the Cold War and McCarthyism, remained the America of the New Deal, economic planning, and the struggle against fascism.

In order to understand the reformers' attitudes toward America (and particularly the attitudes of those who had taken part in the Resistance), we must first briefly review the image of the United States that was current in France during the 1930s, when most of the members of the reform group acquired their political views. In the late 1920s and early 1930s anti-Americanism became quite common among the dominant class and especially among intellectuals in France. Works critical of the United States, theoretical essays, and accounts of American travels were published in large numbers throughout the 1930s. Few of these works were written by Marxists, Socialists, or Communists, because the attention of left-wing writers was directed mainly to the evolution of Soviet Russia, and, as proponents of internationalism, leftists were little moved by the argument that the growth of American power posed a threat to Europe and to France.[26] Even before the New Deal leftist writers tended to judge the evolution of American capitalism (described by most observers between the wars in terms of concentration of wealth, mechanization, and mass production) as a "positive development."

Thus anti-Americanism developed mainly on the right, more precisely among young right intellectuals associated with Ordre nouveau and among Catholic fundamentalists who, since the late nineteenth century, had seen a link between "liberal Catholicism" and American Catholicism.[27] Many who criticized American society in the most vehement terms later joined fascist movements or became active supporters of the Vichy regime (e.g., Lucien Romier,[28] one of the most widely heeded commentators on American "materialism," Alfred Fabre-Luce,[29] Paul Morand, and Henri Massis, to name a few). For these writers anti-Americanism was not simply a consequence of diplomatic disputes between France and the United States over such issues as reparations and disarmament after World War I.[30] Nor was it simply a product of nationalism, which inspired the first attacks on American "financial imperialism"[31] (described as different from, but no less dangerous than, military imperialism) and early debates over American investment in Europe, which expanded greatly between the wars, especially in the electrical industry (with ITT's move into Europe) and the petroleum industry.[32] At a deeper level, anti-American sentiment was directed against what America symbolized: mass production, Taylorism, the assembly line, mass consumption of standardized commodities, advertising that "raped" the minds of consumers – in short, mass society and what had been considered since the nineteenth century as the archetypal democracy. Consider, for example, the assembly line. Writers who visited the United States in the early 1920s had looked rather favorably upon what they considered at the time a symbol of efficiency and progress. But within ten years the assembly line had become the symbol of something else: American materialism, mass society, indeed, a novel form of collectivism that the most radical commentators, such as Fabre-Luce and Romier,[33] likened to Bolshevism. Their slogan was "Neither Ford nor Lenin." Here we recognize some of the familiar themes of personalism (especially as interpreted by Ordre nouveau[34]), which drew upon a series of dichotomies: between the material and the spiritual, the individual and the person, public opinion and private conscience, etc. Writers associated with the young right (and with Social Catholicism) contrasted what they called America's "standardized mass man" (or Babbitt: there was much talk in the thirties of "Babbittization") with the peasant, the artisan, the individual entrepreneur, the responsible industrialist, the man of private means, the man in whom capital and labor were joined, who both managed and worked in his own business.

Corporatists opposed not only Soviet Bolshevism but also the mass society they saw embodied in the United States.[35] "Third-way" rhetoric is scarcely intelligible until one understands the way in which it confounds political regimes (communism/liberal democracy) with social classes (proletariat/plutocratic oligarchy) and national cultures (American materialism/Soviet materialism). If the United States and the Soviet Union were the extremes, then the European middle class was the happy medium. Anti-Americanism and pro-Europeanism developed in parallel until shortly before World War II. Corporatism, Europe, the middle class – all three shared the same fundamental qualities (which differentiated Europe from the United States and the Soviet Union): deep historical roots, a spiritual outlook, subtlety and culture, respect for the person and for the riches of personal relations. Europe has its civilization; the East and the West had only their masses or hordes.[36] In certain respects third-way rhetoric was merely a reworking of the same masses versus elites dichotomy that had governed conservative thinking since at least the middle of the nineteenth century.[37]

In contrast to the apocalyptic images of America put forward by the prefascist right, "modernists", including both liberal reformers and socialists, often saw America in a fairly favorable light. Liberals like Hyacinthe Dubreuil[38] and Emile Schreiber[39] saw mechanization and rational organization of labor as means of increasing the general wealth and in the long run of achieving worker emancipation. Like such socialists[40] as Georges Boris[41] and Robert Marjolin,[42] they had a passionate interest in the New Deal. Interpretations of the New Deal depended strongly on the political views and social position of the observer. For liberals close to business circles like Emile Schreiber, the aim of the New Deal was to establish a solid basis for free enterprise. Socialists, on the other hand, hoped that it would give birth to a novel form of socialism.

Even though Emile Schreiber's America – the America of Taylorism and rationalization of the labor process – was not the presocialist America of Georges Boris or Pierre Mendès France, "progressive democrats" of every stripe agreed at least that the New Deal was an alternative not only to capitalism and Bolshevism but also to corporatism and fascism (which defined themselves in terms of the same dichotomy): the New Deal was a median solution between the old private capitalism and state socialism. Unlike fascism, the New Deal respected democracy.[43] After the historic failure of fascism (which had presented itself as an "original" response to the Depression), this alternative vision of the third way, derived from the New Deal, was left as the only ideology that offered a way out of the crisis. When the fascist solution to the class question (and especially to the question of the middle class) was finally rejected, and the collapse of the Vichy regime had altered the domestic balance of power, it became possible, and necessary, to create or import a new representation of society and politics based on a combination of planning, reformism, and liberalism – rather like the New Deal, or at any rate rather like the image that French progressives had formed of the New Deal. In this new representation "political space" became circular: the extreme right joined up with the extreme left. Society, meanwhile, was represented in terms of its rising and declining sectors: the traditional middle classes were now seen as outmoded and reactionary, while the working bourgeoisie, cadres in the van, represented the wave of the future.[44]

This new version of the third way was able to dispense with the old authoritarian hierarchy, because steady economic growth held out the prospect of a gradual diminution of class divisions. After the discovery of America the ideological project of searching for common ground between cadres and employers, for a unifying principle capable of rallying the middle class, was not abandoned but stood on its head. Henceforth, cadres and the new middle class they typified were defined by contrast with the traditional small businessman and the traditional, old-fashioned, Malthusian, Poujadist, and reactionary middle class, a group presumably destined to disappear altogether. The new middle class became the only group capable of sustaining the fantasy of a third way and a third party. The rise of the cadres heralded the birth of a new social order, in which the antithesis between employers and proletariat was ostensibly *superseded* (and not merely mediated, as in the corporatist representation of the middle classes): superseded in part because the category of ownership was dissolved (managers were also employees, so that the fundamental Marxist criterion, "position within the relations of production," became obsolete) and in part because advances in automation would ultimately eliminate the antithesis between manual and intellectual labor.

Corporatists had imagined a society composed of solid blocs. But the reformers conceived of society as a liquid through which various "currents" flowed, some stronger than others, or again, as a gas, a statistical ensemble of independent molecules (top civil servants educated at various elite engineering schools frequently used and abused such images, borrowed from thermodynamics). To be sure, one could always distinguish various layers or strata, but these were unstable and tended to mingle with one another and lose their identity. All converged toward a new focal point, a new social center of gravity: the middle class. But this designation no longer had the same meaning as it had under corporatism (family/patrimony). Instead, it was understood in terms of the American middle class, that vast group of people leading comfortable lives, sharing similar values, and employed by large organizations – individualists governed by the competitive spirit and the drive to achieve. The transformation of the "*classe moyenne*" into the "middle class" would, it was thought, permit the most turbulent countries of western Europe (Germany and the Latin countries) to achieve political stability.[45] In a well-known article, Seymour Martin Lipset reviewed the "changes in European political life" and the "reasons for the decline of ideology" and saw these changes as converging toward the creation of a new middle class of cadres and technicians. The new class "alleviated class tensions" by "rewarding moderate parties and penalizing extreme parties." It encouraged "the politics of collective negotiation." It favored "increased productivity," which, "by permitting a more equitable distribution of consumer goods and education, reduced intrasocietal tensions" and thus discouraged "recourse to total ideologies." It "recognized scientific thought" and "the professionalism and authority of experts" in areas "that are at the heart of political controversy." For all these reasons the cadres and technicians are the most representative group of "postindustrial" or "postbourgeois" society, in which "achievement" takes precedence over "ascription" and "universalism" over "particularism." The consummate form of this postindustrial society is to be found in the United States, "technologically the most advanced society" in the world and a "harbinger of things to come for western Europe."[46]

The phrase "new middle classes" came into vogue in the 1950s and 1960s to denote that segment of the population that worked for a living, usually for a large corporation, that held advanced degrees and had competence in some technical area, and so on: in other words, technicians and cadres, as opposed to artisans, small merchants, and entrepreneurs, who were categorized as belonging to the "traditional middle classes."[47] Pierre Bleton's book, *Les hommes des temps qui viennent, essai sur les classes moyennes* (1956), an attempt to revive Social Catholic thinking on these issues, clearly marks the moment at which employees for the first time eclipsed independents as the more prominent component in the social representation of the middle class. For example, Bleton repeatedly remarks upon "the importance that supervisory personnel have taken on" within the middle class while noting that "farmers and others associated with agriculture play almost no part." Conversely, "to eliminate cadres and the bulk of the civil service from the middle class would be to reduce that class to a caricature of the bourgeoisie."[48] Another milestone was the publication in 1965 of a special issue of the Catholic magazine *Chronique sociale de France* devoted to the "new middle classes," reviving, after a lapse of twenty-five years, the theme of the 1939 *Semaine sociale de Bordeaux* (which is cited, along with Michel Crozier, Raymond Aron, and even Gilbert Mury in the introductory bibliography). An article in this issue treated of cadres: it was entitled "Cadres: New Middle Class or New Aspect of the Working Class?"

L'Express: "the magazine for cadres"

It would be wrong to suppose that the new representation of society took hold at once, without opposition or conflict. In fact, much of the traditional right mobilized against it. In the 1950s opposition to both fascism and Communism was not, or at any rate not solely, a mere flourish of partisan rhetoric. It reflected the objective position that the Mendésists occupied in the political arena, between the Communist Party and the Pétainist or fascist-inspired right wing, represented on the one hand by Maurice Gingembre and the CGPME (which, in alliance with the CGC, supported Pinay and Laniel)[49] and on the other hand, from 1954 on, by Pierre Poujade's UDCA, whose standard-bearers shared with their opponent Gingembre the idea that Mendès and his clique constituted the main enemy and employed the slogan "Mendès to Jerusalem."[50]

The contest between Pierre Mendès France and Antoine Pinay had symbolic value for the fascist right. It was the incarnation of an archetype (the image of France, common sense, and the soil of the fatherland versus that of the Jew without a country, the intellectual, the demagogue, etc.), expressed in paradigmatic form in the book *Mendès ou Pinay* by Alfred Fabre-Luce (published under the pseudonym Sapiens).

Pinay: Behind the politics of Antoine Pinay stands a personal philosophy and a way of life with roots in France's long history. "Honesty," "liberalism," and "thrift" are for him not shopworn words to be used or not used as parliamentary fashion dictates. One feels that he is more intimately involved in his actions than politicians usually are. His calm, serious face, which seems to guarantee his sincerity, makes him an invaluable intermediary between "legal France" and "real France." (p. 47)

Mendès: Mendès, the man of tomorrow, arouses considerable curiosity. He prepares his audience like a playwright at a dress rehearsal. His little Jewish brain-trust, led by Georges Boris, stands behind him on the floor of the chamber. Other fervent supporters are scattered through the galleries. Whispers are heard: "What courage! What talent! Léon would have been pleased." Although he is now forty-seven years old, Mendès still looks a bit like a child prodigy. This child is doted on. He is Jesus amid the wise. What accounts for his prestige? Like Pinay, Mendès is a man who does not seek power for himself. No doubt his election as deputy at age twenty-six in a *département* selected at random on the map was the first fruit of diligent effort and a precocious sign of ambition.... The left is proud to possess such a man. When accused of habitual demagogy, it points to this severe financier as proof of its innocence.... Another plus: Mendès is a doctor of law. For that reason he is reassuring to the Republic of Schoolteachers. Bureaucrats and *dirigiste* intellectuals nod their heads approvingly. (pp. 50–4)

The forces of reaction, among which the CGC occupied an important place, were fighting for the survival of the traditional small factory, farm, and shop, for the short-term interests of cadres in private enterprise (such as preserving the salary hierarchy, alleviating the tax burden, reinforcing the authority structure, etc.), and for continued colonial occupation of Indo-China and North Africa – goals that were regarded as inseparable. Jean-Jacques Servan-Schreiber, for his part, repeatedly stated that decolonization and economic modernization were inextricably intertwined, and that the former took precedence only because without decolonization modernization was impossible. To charges that he altered the line of *L'Express* after the Algerian War, when he transformed what had been a political magazine into an American-style news magazine, Servan-Schreiber (as well as Françoise Giroud[52] responded that *L'Express* had not changed: the weekly in 1964 was what it had been intended to be from the outset, and the original plans had only been delayed by the colonial wars ("so much wasted time," Servan-Schreiber said, in 1968, to Roger Priouret). As early as 1954, *L'Express*, which would later style itself the "magazine for cadres," was calling for many of the changes that have since come to typify the 1960s, such as economic concentration, industrial rationalization, enhanced productivity, higher wages, increased consumption, and modernization of the educational system. *L'Express* also contributed to the formation of a group of skilled managers, to the education of cadres, and, more generally, to improving the public's knowledge of economics.

The pioneers of "management science" shared with enlightened economic planners and Finance Ministry officials a faith in the virtues of economics. France's economic backwardness, they believed, was due in large part to the secrecy in which industrial operations were shrouded. "Preconceived ideas," "a priori views," and "prejudices" were "all obstacles to smooth economic development.... Modern democracy requires that people understand economics." For instance, the "only way to make an incomes policy work" is to "educate public opinion."[53] "Rational" management of the economy requires educated, and therefore rational, producers and consumers, whose economic behavior will then conform to the laws of "economic science" and who must at least be willing to recognize the wisdom of decisions taken in their name by "experts."[54]

The Schreiber family was also responsible for creating a whole series of publications for cadres, whose growing influence after 1965 helped to shape and publicize the new image of the group that began to develop in the 1960s. The Schreiber publishing interests have a long history. Emile Schreiber started *Les Echos* early in the century, originally as a journal of classified advertisements. In the period 1950–70 this became the family's financial bastion and the basis of its political influence. *L'Express* commenced publication in 1953, for the first few months as a weekly supplement to *Les Echos*. Finally, *L'Expansion* was launched in 1967 by Jean-Jacques Servan-Schreiber's younger brother Jean-Louis. The new magazine epitomized the evolution of business publishing in general: from financial news for industrialists and investors to general-interest magazines for cadres. *Les Echos*, which claimed some 40,000 subscribers in the 1950s, was addressed mainly to industrialists. Immediately after World War II the business press consisted mainly of stock market newsletters like *Côte Desfossés* and *La Vie française*, a weekly founded in 1945 with about 15,000 subscribers, mainly investors. The financial press was for the most part tightly controlled by the business community (one journalist maintains that a telephone call from the CNPF was all it took to have an article changed or killed).

In the late 1950s a new type of business magazine appeared on the scene. *Direction, L'Economie, Economie contemporaine, La France industrielle*, and *Entreprise* averaged fewer than 25,000 readers. *Entreprise* was the largest, with 40,000 readers, and its editor, Michel Drancourt, was a respected spokesman for enlightened industralists and "modern managers."[55] Publications for cadres emerged mainly in the mid-1960s. *L'Expansion*, mentioned above, was edited by Jean Boissonnat, whose thinking had been shaped by the progressive Catholic review *Esprit*. Modeled on the American magazine *Fortune, L'Expansion* was explicitly designed to reach a broad audience of cadres and had a circulation of more than 150,000. It offered its readers information on how to manage their careers (publishing each year the results of a survey of cadres' pay). It published news about the operations of large firms and interviews with top managers and more generally served as a kind of guide, helping young cadres find their way through the industrial thicket. Like *L'Express*, it was also used as a manual of *savoir-vivre*: the portraits of top managers, the advertising, the career analyses, and the interviews provided the run-of-the-mill cadre with an identity and role models (note that *Le Nouvel Observateur* performed a similar function for a different readership, introducing secondary-school teachers, provincial intellectuals, and the like to the glittering spectacle of the Parisian intelligentsia). With *L'Expansion* it was part of the magazine's explicit policy to set the tone for all cadres: according to one editor, the magazine was "a mirror that shows them their own image and encourages them to contemplate their navels." Today, Jean-Louis Servan-Schreiber is himself one of the most successful examples of the American-style manager, the man of the future of whom his older brothers once dreamed. From his many descriptions of himself and of the group he served as a leading spokesman one can form some idea of how far cadres have come since the early 1950s.

By comparing the finished product, Jean-Louis Servan-

Schreiber, to his prestigious elder brother Jean-Jacques (the inventor of a life style that was at once novel, hard-to-define, all-embracing, and yet somehow ineffable – as the spontaneous products of what Bourdieu calls a "habitus"* invariably are), we see how a new life style comes to be taken for granted. Eventually it is stylized and packaged for easier transmission to a broad group and can be adopted by individuals who may not have shared the experiences or internalized the ways of seeing that shaped the original style. A graduate of the Ecole des Sciences Politique and managing editor of *L'Expansion*, Jean-Louis Servan-Schreiber presents his vision of the world along with his self-portrait in his book, *A mi-vie* (*At Midlife*), which is perhaps the quintessential statement of the new values and life style that the new Parisian bourgeoisie offered as a model to the mass of cadres. Jean-Louis, who easily assumed a position of power in the mid-1960s, had no personal experience of either the Resistance or the colonial wars and found it unnecessary to swing to the left in order to make the "world's stupidest right wing" aware of its own true interests; his relationship to his brother is that of continuator to producer. The perfect representative of the enlightened grande bourgeoisie, Jean-Louis is also a model manager, as Claude Glayman points out in his introduction: "Jean-Louis Servan-Schreiber runs a magazine whose readers fit a certain description. To simplify, perhaps too much, I shall refer to them as cadres. This group has played a significant part in the evolution of French society over the past two decades" (p. 10). Jean-Louis Servan-Schreiber's book contains most of the clichés of neo-bourgeois rhetoric. Consider the following:

The agitated life of the overworked manager: "I led a hectic life" (p. 36). "A harassed manager" (p. 138). "A decision-maker" (p. 45). "My position as a top manager" (p. 74). "Twelve-hour days were followed by working weekends, business trips, and nighttime conferences" (p. 36). "The official intoxicated by his fast pace finds it physcially impossible to provide for quiet moments in his day and his week during which he can tranquilly reflect upon events" (p. 42). "My appointment book has become a part of me" (p. 42). "My secretary" (p. 43). "A man in his thirties, in a position of responsibility" (p. 208). "Do you really think you'r enjoying your home on weekends when you sit yourself down in your arm chair, your accursed attaché case on your stomach, and you proceed to chew on paperwork until Sunday night?" (p. 207).

The dizziness of success: "A top manager on the way up" (p. 207). "At the age

*Habitus: a term coined by Pierre Bourdieu to refer to a set of enduring dispositions and responses acquired by social agents through their interactions with social structure. – Trans.

when the manager of an organization builds his career" (p. 36). "To build. to rise as high as possible" (p. 80).

The power of competence (as opposed to the inherited power of family and money): "Today's establishment is the product of a changing society. Money is no longer enough to gain entry" (p. 170).

Note that although Servan-Schreiber praises college-educated managers and criticizes dynastic family businesses, at the same time he nonetheless extols the virtues of "family." His own family, the Servan-Schreiber clan, is a group who, notwithstanding their kinship, seem to have chosen one another of their own free will. Each member of the family must prove by personal success that he is worthy of his birth. Only then can he join his "likeminded clan" and discover that "working with one's family is more efficient and more fun because confidence and partnership come more readily" (p. 31).

Management: "As the manager of a business, I studied in the school of efficiency" (p. 114). "My début as an adult coincided with the rush to enter business in France" (p. 45). "A revelation on the road to New York: my eyes opened and I discovered 'management'" (p. 147). "Stanford, California" (p. 138).

The cult of the waistline and devotion to the physique: "Daumier's bourgeois were recognizable more by their waistlines than by their dress' (p. 87). "I owe it to my body to take care of it" (p. 91). "My indispensable daily workout" (p. 91). "I've tried all the diets and I've read all the books ... on dieting. I've learned all about calories and carbohydrates. I dreamed of nouvelle cuisine before anyone ever heard of Michel Guérard" (p. 93).

Feminism, and Marriage as Brain-trust: "It is obviously easier to be on the left on Chile than in your own bed" (p. 190). "In favor of the legislation on abortion" (p. 212). "Our marriage is based on sharing" (p. 50). "How many thousands of hours of dialogue have we shared in our life together?" (p. 50). "On vacation ... we can be more philosophical" (p. 51). "Our briefing" (p. 50). "Communicate" (p. 52).

The new psychology: "When I taught at Stanford, in California, in 1971, we wanted to spend some time at Esalen.... Many people joined a group and were initiated by an instructor in the latest introspective techniques: T-groups, Gestalt therapy, and rolfing, along with a good dose of Abraham Maslow, the pope of the new humanist psychology. On the advice of Mike Murphy, the founder of Esalen, we decided to try psychosynthesis" (p. 198).

Distance from one's role, and the sense of humor (young, open, relaxed): "Distancing" (p. 123). "Don't take yourself too seriously" (p. 131). "I love humor" (p. 131).

Liberalism and obstruction: "As the head of a firm, my freedom of decision was limited at times by the law, at times by pressure from the employees. With this I had little quarrel.... I had no intention of waging a rear-guard action against those consequences that affected me personally" (p. 74).

"When an entire nation rapidly acquires economic liberty, the liberty of each individual is reduced.... The pressure affected the freedom of those with cars in two ways: the volume of traffic imposed physical limitations, and the government was forced to impose rules and regulations to stem the slaughter" (p. 76).

Undesirables: "The owner–manager, or as we say in France, the 'small' businessman" (p. 147). "When I was a child, French industry was not in favor" (p. 145). "Nationalism" (p. 130). "Colonialism" (p. 116). "Fascism" (p. 110).

The industry of management

The cadres' press would never have been able to standardize values and life styles had its development not been preceded by the creation of a system of institutions intended to reform the industrial bourgeoisie and petite bourgeoisie by inculcating the stereotypical values of the American middle class. In order to understand how, as Michel Beaud puts it, "intensive concentration and accumulation of capital in the hands of monopolistic conglomerates" could have taken place "without intense opposition from the classes and class segments faced with bankruptcy and defeat,"[56] one must look at institutional developments in the postwar period, the function of which was to encourage industrial restructuring. These institutional changes, designed primarily to organize and train the "new" group of cadres, also served to retrain many individuals belonging to the traditional petite bourgeoisie of industry, individuals who increasingly defined themselves as cadres even when they possessed only the title and none of the benefits or attributes implicit in the paradigmatic image of the cadre.

It would be impossible to list all the schools, training courses, seminars, and study groups that were established not only for cadres but also for their employers in the period 1945–65, often under the auspices of the AFAP, which urged consulting firms, unions, professional organizations, and other groups to set up courses of training in management, human relations, sales, marketing, etc. For example, the Commission nationale d'organisation française (CNOF) created the Ecole d'organisation scientifique du travail (EOST) and established various other management training programs.[57] The Paris Chamber of Commerce set up the Centre de préparation aux affaires (CPA). At around the same time the Lille Chamber of Commerce created the Centre d'études des problèmes industriels (CEPI). The Centre de formation et de perfectionnement, in conjunction with the Association nationale des chefs du personnel (ANDCP), established a "system of in-plant study circles," described as a French adaptation of the American method known as "Training Within Industry" (TWI); it also staged regular dinner-debates and invited various noted personalities who had "thought about labor-relations issues," such as Hyacinthe Dubreuil, André Siegfried, and others to speak. The Centre français du patronat chrétien (CFPC) established a "school for executives and top managers." In 1950 the Centre des jeunes patrons (subsequently renamed the Centre des jeunes dirigeants d'entreprise) staged three-day meetings on the problems of industrial management. CEGOS, which was the largest French industrial consulting firm until the arrival of even larger American-based firms in the late 1960s, ran a very active training program (including on-the-job practice, seminars, etc.). Finally, in 1954 the CNPF established the Centre de recherche et d'études des chefs d'entreprises (CRC), which among other things organized ten training sessions annually to teach "executives and top managers modern management methods" (attended by about 2,500 people between 1955 and 1963).[58] By 1960 there were some 150 institutions specializing in the training of cadres, twenty-five of which offered "comprehensive training in management methods."[59]

The development of so-called schools of management designed to educate not working managers but students came later, as did the introduction of courses in business administration into the universities and courses in the human sciences and human relations into the Grandes Ecoles. In 1953 the Institute of Economic Research at Lille's Catholic University led the way by offering "courses in human relations." Earlier, in 1951–52, the Ministry of Labor established the Institut des Sciences Sociales du Travail (ISST), which later became part of the University of Paris. The ISST was not a school of management in the strict sense, in that it was designed primarily to train workers and leaders of the trade-union movement. But it helped to spread the gospel of the social sciences and human relations, notably in firms where ISST graduates were employed in social services, particularly as labor counselors attached to the works' councils.[60] It was not until 1955 that a certificate of aptitude in business administration was offered by the Instituts d'administration des affaires (IAA), which were associated with the law and economics faculties of various universities.

Some years later, Guillebeau organized a lecture series on "Humanism and Enterprise" at the Faculty of Letters of the University of Paris (which later developed into the Centre d'études littéraires scientifiques appliquées, or CELSA). Speakers in this series included many figures typical of the new culture that was developing around the schools for cadres: they came from the planning commission (Albou), from banking (Amar), from the economic analysis departments of the trade unions (Barjonnet), from big business (Calan, Chenevier, etc.), from advertising (Bleustein-Blanchet), from psychology (Max Pagès), from marketing (Agostini), etc. The lectures dealt with economic questions (such as financing for industry), social questions (such as, the political philosophy of worker syndicalism), and above all with human and psychological problems connected with personnel management, especially with the management of cadres (e.g., the hiring and selection of cadres, communication, information, and the social climate within the firm, concrete application of human relations in industry, problems of training cadres and improving their performance, socioanalysis, the role of cadres in modern industry, industry and adult education, psychological methods and testing, psychological and cultural factors, the human sciences in industry (taught by two major industrialists, Huvelin and Landucci), psychology and sociology applied to industry, the psychology of sales, industrial sociotherapy, the human sciences and life, etc.). In the preface to the printed texts of these lectures (published in 1963), Dean Aymard called upon firms to recruit cadres, and especially personnel managers, from the faculties of letters and described the recent establishment of Masters' degrees in psychology and sociology, which "do not lead to any university position," as a first step by universities toward a role in the world of business and industry:[61] "How will cadres be trained tomorrow and in the future?... Our universities have not been unresponsive to the demand."[62] But university teaching of management by departments of economics and law did not really take off until the late 1960s (and even later in the major engineering schools, at the instigation of Bertrand Schwartz, director of the Ecole des Mines of Nancy).[63] Starting in 1968, the Fondation nationale pour l'enseignment de la gestion des entreprises (or FNEGE, created by the CNPF), the Assembly of Chambers of Commerce, and the Ministry of Industry coordinated the teaching of management in a variety of institutions, ranging from the universities and technical schools to such leading business schools as HEC and the Ecole supérieures de commerce and to other, less prestigious schools of business administration (the Ecoles supérieures de commerce et d'administration des entreprises, or ESCAE, an association of eighteen middle-ranked business schools that was formed in the mid-1960s). Furthermore, the period 1950–70 saw the creation of a large number of private schools specializing in the training of cadres and management: of thirty private schools of management in the Paris region in 1972, twenty-five were established after 1950 (nine between 1950 and 1960 and sixteen between 1960 and 1970). The most prestigious of these, the Institut européen d'administration des affaires, was founded in 1959.[64]

The founding of the first schools of management was supported by the European Productivity Agency, which in 1956 began sending future professors of management to American universities for a year's training (between 1956 and 1958 some 225 students took part). It also offered summer courses to professors interested in "familiarizing themselves with the content and teaching methods of management courses" in the United States. In addition, the Ford Foundation placed American professors at the disposal of French business schools.

The 1950s also saw rapid development of management consulting firms, which retrained cadres already employed in industry and helped set up management training programs. Management consultants and "organization theorists" were known in France before the productivity missions. Taylor's work found its first adepts before World War I and gained popularity as a result of the war, particularly in the armaments industry, even as the seeds of economic planning were first being sown.[65] But the number of management consultants remained quite small until the productivity enhancement programs opened up a new market for them.

Henry Le Chatelier, a mining engineer and professor at the Ecole des Mines, introduced Taylorian ideas into France around 1907. The first applications of those ideas were made by Charles de Fréminville, a metallurgical engineer and personal friend of Le Chatelier, who was engineering director for Panhard and Levassor and the first to present the new Taylorian methods to the French Society of Civil Engineers. But little use was made of those methods until World War I. Many industrialists resisted the idea of scientific management, seeing the costs of technical studies, additional foremen, and so forth as added overhead and unproductive investments. The first management consultants, who were inspired by native traditions (Fayol) as much as by Taylorism,[66] appeared in the interwar years. Big business encouraged the establishment of the Commission d'études générales des organisations (CEGOS) under Auguste Detoeuf[67] (which did not really become active until 1945), the Comité national de l'organisation française (CNOF),[68] and the Bureau des temps élémentaires (BTE) under Bedeau, who rigorously and systematically applied time-and-motion study techniques. But it was probably Jean Coutrot's BICRA, established in the late 1930s, that most clearly prefigured the modern management consulting firm. Set up in conjunction with two organization specialists, Hernst Hysman of the Netherlands and Heinz Oppenheimer of Germany, BICRA was unusual in that it used not only rationalization techniques similar to those employed earlier by Bedeau and Paul Planus but also new management methods based on work in the human sciences. Coutrot was probably one of the first French industrialists to realize how psychology and sociology (disciplines in which he took an active interest) might prove useful in industry. One who followed Coutrot's lead was his friend Gérard Bardet, an adept of corporatist thinking (in 1936, in the factory he ran, he established a system of "shop delegates" and "corporative committees ... consisting, for each corporation, of the manager, the shop steward, the foreman, and the corresponding delegate"). After Coutrot's death, Bardet established his own consulting firm, COFROR, in 1942, and hired two former employees of BICRA.

Earlier, in 1934, Jean Coutrot organized a meeting at Paul Desjardins's Abbey of Pontigny, the purpose of which was to "extend to man's problems – individual and social – our sure knowledge of the world of things." To that end, he invited "specialists in the human sciences and human endeavors: biology, physiology, medicine, psychotechnology, philosophy, sociology, industry, and political economy." In the same spirit Coutrot established in 1936 the Centre d'étude des problèmes humains (CEPH) in conjunction with the writer Aldous Huxley, the archeologist Robert Francillon, and the economist George Guillaume. Hyacinthe Dubreuil, Jean Ullmo, Alfred Sauvy, Teilhard de Chardin (a personal friend of Coutrot), Chakotin, and others took part in meetings of the CEPH, which sponsored eight commissions in economic humanism, applied psychology, rational and humane limitation of inequality, propaganda, industrial deconcentration, psychobiology, history, and the study of Marxism. The work of these commissions was published in the center's review, *Humanisme économique*.

In a paper read in 1935 to the Congrès d'organisation scientifique du travail, Jean Coutrot criticized the blind application of Taylorian precepts (which he called "static analysis") and proposed instead a new approach, "dynamic analysis," which "requires the collaboration of the worker and involves him in a joint project of creative research with his leaders," for "in the factory of the future the worker will supervise the inanimate producer, and his job will require not physical effort but precision, painstaking care, general understanding, and mechanical intuition. The pace of production will no longer be determined by the worker's motions and will require him to intervene only when something goes wrong." Jean Coutrot was the principal teacher of the organizational specialists who popularized the new American management techniques and social psychology in the 1950s. Many senior specialists had worked for Coutrot's BICRA. Their experiences prepared them to travel the road that led from corporatism to "human relations."[69]

In the 1950s the AFAP supported the activities of consulting firms like Bedeau's that had survived the war, but not without second thoughts. These old-line firms were criticized for neglecting the "human factor." The celebration of American productivity in the 1950s was often associated with criticism of French management consultants. The new generation of consulting engineers that came of age in the 1950s, led by a core group of graduates of the Ecole Centrale who worked for CEGOS and who had been associated with BICRA, like Noël Pouderoux and Gilbert Bloch, repudiated, verbally at least, the rigid and authoritarian instrumentalism that had previously guided most management consultants: an organization, they argued, should not be thought of in narrow technicist or oversimplified Taylorian terms. Mere rationalization of the physical production process through decomposition and rearrangement of manual tasks is not enough to increase productivity and yield. What had to be done, they believed, was to bring together the two main schools of thought in organizational science, namely, the technicist tradition centered on the mechanical organization of the labor process and the more recent tradition associated with the human relations movement and group dynamics.[70] These new management consultants took an interest in psychology and even psychiatry[71] and sociology, and many were readers of sociologist Michel Crozier's work from the 1960s, which they interpreted as a plea on behalf of the human relations approach.[72] They proposed to deal with the "human factor" in management and to analyze the underlying motivations of the organization man. They believed they could plumb the depths of the "capitalist spirit" extolled by Octave Gélinier, director of CEGOS in the 1960s and a Pouderoux-trained graduate of the Ecole Centrale, who proved to be one of the leading importers of American management techniques over a period of some twenty years.

After the war, management consultants were no longer interested solely or even primarily in the rationalization of manual labor and the physical layout of the shop floor. Much of their work was devoted to the selection, socialization, and training of management, technical, sales, and white-collar personnel. The change of object was the primary determinant of the change in method: the authoritarian methods that had been used for the management of workers were no longer suitable now that the problem was to retrain engineers and even self-taught cadres, who were less tolerant of high-handed management techniques and who had to be handled carefully since they themselves held positions of some authority.

The "crisis-of-authority" theme figures prominently in the rhetoric of organization theorists of the 1950s. It was necessary, they said, not only to repudiate the "myth of the leader" promoted by Catholic engineers at the height of the Occupation but also to establish new principles of legitimacy as the basis of all power relations. "Relatively new problems of leadership are cropping up today in all areas. In the family as well as in the schools, industry, and politics, a crisis of authority is evident," according to a report of one CEGOS study session in 1958, devoted to "cadres and the exercise of leadership."

> What entitles one man to a position of leadership, i.e., to the exercise of a certain power over other men? How can leadership qualities be recognized, taught, and put to the test? It is reasonable to ask whether the traditional justifications of authority are still valid today.... In a transitional era like our own, there is a certain time lag between technological development and development of the human sciences. Human problems are often approached in outmoded ways, particularly in a country with ancient institutions. That is why we are obsessed by a certain "myth of the leader."... To begin with, one must admit that there is no absolute distinction between the leader and the non-leader.... Depending on circumstances and opportunities, men have varying likelihoods of filling leadership positions, which in any case are invariably positions subordinate to other leaders. There is no such thing as a pure leader, a leader isolated from the network of human relations that makes him a leader.[73]

It would be impossible to think of a better justification for the new modes of control that developed in this "period of transition" and economic concentration following the opening of the Common Market. The "myth of the leader" actually captured fairly accurately the experience of an engineer or even a foreman in the 1930s or the immediate postwar period, when the division of the labor of domination among those who were referred to at the time as "collaborators" (with the plant owner, of course) was determined by the fragmented nature of concrete production units (the shop, the plant, the department, etc.) rather than by specialization of tasks, and when an "engineer" was often involved not only in technical aspects of production and research and equipment maintenance but also in worker discipline, in what were called "social responsibilities" that had not yet been assigned to an autonomous personnel department. This division of labor, coupled with the fact that the instruments of self-definition available to cadres were still fairly rudimentary and various other factors (such as the nature of the training offered by engineering schools, especially the Ecole Centrale), helped to shape the social identity of those who held positions of some power in industry: for role models they chose sometimes the military officer conscious of his "social role" (this was especially true of Catholic engineers from bourgeois families who had attended the Grandes Ecoles and chosen careers in the military or the civil service), sometimes the "individual" industrialist, the absolute and strict master of an isolated production unit, an independent and sovereign autocrat responsible for both the "quality of his product" and "reduction of production costs."

These representations were no longer appropriate to the new situation in industry as the pace of change accelerated in the early 1960s.[74] The outmoded image of a one-dimensional, unequivocal, hierarchical relationship was replaced by the new image of the "network": the "network of human relations" that miraculously adjusted itself to the structure of industry, with its financial interlocks and complex systems of domination through which the power of vaguely defined "groups" was exercised. Thus the invention of the new mode of social control and the new industrial petite bourgeoisie seems to have been closely associated with the increasing bureaucratization of industry and the gradual integration of smaller production units into larger organizations.

The "managerial avant-garde" valued the new psychosocial technologies at least in part because they seemed capable of reconciling requirements that had previously been seen as contradictory (because they derived from different realms of practice and different ideologies and, ultimately, from different social groups): on the one hand efficiency, rationalization, discipline, and respect for hierarchy, and on the other hand imagination, intelligence, initiative, and above all flexibility in relations with both superiors and subordinates (a controlled form of "permissiveness" that repudiated both "blind obedience" and overt conflict, a permissiveness associated in many people's minds with "intellectuals" and other "creative" individuals). The new psychology was supposed to make cadres "more flexible in their professional relations" as well as encourage them to accept company discipline (though not too rigidly) and let them know that the authority they exercised was relative and delegated (they were not pure leaders). At the same time, it was meant to encourage cadres to devote themselves to their work and keep a close eye on the performance of subordinates. The new psychology was supposed to make cadres "happy": another way of recognizing them as belonging to the bourgeoisie and of dissuading them from joining workers' unions. In contrast to the rigid and indeed military methods of control that had hitherto been employed in industry, these new techniques of gentle persuasion respected bourgeois notions of propriety,[75] and this helped to maintain a good understanding between cadres and top managers (*dirigeants*) and to encourage internalization of the new values on which the smooth operation of the plant would depend. Under the old system of posted labor, authoritarian methods could work because the application of Taylorian principles of division of labor made it possible to transfer much of the workers' knowhow to the organizational system; workers became interchangeable parts. But those employees whose job it was to manage the firm and supervise other employees had to be dealt with in another way. Not only did they have to learn specific rules; they also had to internalize role models and develop proper attitudes.

The restructuring of industry and the need for cadre reeducation and training helped to make "organizational consulting" a flourishing industry in this period. CEGOS, which employed about forty people in the 1950s when Octave Gélinier became its director, grew subsequently at a rate of 20% per year, adding new departments in marketing, personnel management, administrative organization, fiscal control, general management, data processing, management development, etc. CEGOS specialized in mergers and buy-outs and established subsidiaries throughout Europe. By the mid-1960s CEGOS employed 600 people in countries such as Spain, Holland, Italy, Belgium, etc. Its board of directors included academics (like Dean Capelle), financiers (from the Banque Nationale de Paris, the Banque d'Indochine, etc.), big businessmen (like M. Chenevier, head of British Petroleum in France), and others. Also associated with CEGOS was Jean Stoetzel, professor of social psychology at the Sorbonne and head of the Institut français d'opinion publique and of the market-research organization ETMAR,[76] which provided CEGOS with "antennae" in the new area of market research and public-opinion polling. This was the strong suit of its principal rival in the 1960s, the Société d'économie et de mathématique appliquée (SEMA), the parent organization of the well-known polling firm, SOFRES.[77] SEMA, associated with the Banque de Paris et des Pays-Bas, was founded in the late 1950s by Jacques Lesourne, a graduate of the Ecole Polytechnique, together with a handful of other engineers. It employed 120 people in 1960, prior to its expansion into the major countries of the Common Market; by 1969 it employed 2,000. The firm specializes in the most "modern management methods," such as "decision support," "comprehensive consulting," "applied economics," and above all "operations research" (based on "systems theory"), as well as the "softer" sciences, including "psychosociological studies," "personnel selection, evaluation, and training,"[78] etc. All of this has contributed to the rapid expansion of this "gray matter industry," which has "opened up a quaternary sector beyond the tertiary."[79]

After 1960 the number of management consulting firms grew rapidly: the Chambre syndicale des sociétés d'études et de conseil (SYNTEC), formed in 1969, counted more than thirty large consulting firms in its "organization and training" section alone, nearly all with headquarters in Paris.[80] Growth was particularly rapid in the areas of commercial organization, sales promotion, sales training, and cadre recruitment: by the late 1960s there were some 200 cadre recruitment firms, 80 in the Paris region, including the 10 largest, accounting for 80% of all business in the field.[81]

Group dynamics versus totalitarianism

Again, it is the bureacratization of industry that explains the interest of enlightened employers and modern managers in the human sciences, and especially in techniques derived from industrial psychology, which was invented in the United States in the 1930s and spread rapidly in France in the 1950s. Group techniques, psychosociology, brainstorming, creativity stimulation, T-groups, and role playing were all used with cadres, particularly lower-level cadres.[82] These methods constituted a kind of "social orthopedics," a way of enabling employees "to know themselves in relation to others." By experiencing conflict in limited group settings, people learned a relaxed and effective "relational style," which was supposed to be of service in their relationships with both superiors and subordinates in the workplace.

The major nationalized firms such as Renault, Electricité de France, etc., which were run by progressive managers in the forefront of the fight for increased productivity, economic modernization, and elimination of business "reactionaries," were also the first to pay serious attention to the human relations movement, to add psychologists to their staff, to create personnel departments that relied on the new methods, and to open their doors to labor sociologists. In the mid-1950s they were followed by other enlightened managers in charge of modern, highly bureaucratized firms (such as Télémécanique, Alsthom, Péchiney, Ciments Lafarge, etc.). Many belonged to ACADI (which in 1947 had set up a study group on industrial relations[83]) and to the Catholic movements. As one Catholic executive put it: "The Americans share our philosophical and moral views, because they believe that a worker who does not have a sense of freedom, who feels frustrated, and who is forced to work in unpleasant surroundings will not contribute all that he can to the company."[84]

It is as though the avant-garde of industrial innovators (many of whom had ties with Social Catholicism) decided in the mid-1950s to transfer hopes once invested in corporatism to the American model, and especially to human relations, the human sciences, and the techniques of social and industrial psychology. A mixed discourse evolved, combining the spiritualist vocabulary of personalism (typified by words such as community, person, man, liberty, and dialogue[85]) with the rhetoric of technological efficiency and psychoanalysis. The conversion of the heirs of Catholic social thought to human relations and the human sciences following the demise of corporatism did much to facilitate the creation of disciplined cadres' organizations. Like any new church, this system of retraining and correction needed texts to convey its catechism, reproduce its clergy, and routinize its educational methods. Hence there developed a vast literature with a wide readership consisting of growing numbers of "specialists" in organization theory, personnel managers, and old-fashioned employers and cadres anxious not to be left behind. The new literature taught such readers all they needed to know about cadres, with endless discussion of the cadre's psychology, contradictions, problems, conflicts, feelings, fantasies, desires, personality, identity, motivations, and drives. As management schools proliferated (each with its anointed "master," who naturally assigned his own books as required reading) and the numbers of management consulting firms, industrial counseling offices, and the like grew, the market for "organizational cookbooks" also grew. The content of these manuals for managers was largely similar, though subtle differences marked out the various "schools" (here, too, something like a *field* [*champ*] developed). "Leaders" could read about ideal leadership styles and learn how to train men, how to integrate cadres into the firm, how to evaluate job requirements, how to create participative structures, how to handle cooperation, how to reconcile the man and the organization, how to recognize the new psychological needs of workers, how to adapt the man to the organization, how to construct personality tests, how to evaluate performance, how to manage by integration and self-control, how to profile subordinates, how to develop a training program, how to understand individual aspirations, how to establish an orderly flow of information, how to manage using forecasting models, how to cope with conflict, and how to animate, incite, communicate, personalize, get the message across, test, and evaluate. For those interested in depth psychology, there was information about how to overcome inhibitions, neutralize defenses, free blockages, channel aggression, avoid countertransference, stimulate insight, feedback, and guided introspection, and conduct a focused nondirective interview, as well as such matters as follow-up, looking away, two-step flow, tutoring, shaping, and reinforcement.

Industrial psychology and group techniques[86] were popularized in France largely thanks to the efforts of the Mission psychotechnique française to the United States, which was organized by the AFAP in 1952. The mission was headed by Paul Fraisse,[87] and included Jean Bonnaire, head of the psychotechnical department at Renault Motors, Jean-Marie Faverge, who worked for the Ministry of Labor's Centre d'études et de recherches psychotechniques, and Suzanne Pacaud, a principal researcher at the CNRS and head of the SNCF's psychotechnical laboratory. The mission's report was the subject of a special issue of the *Revue de psychologie appliquée* (vol. 4, no. 1, January 1953), which devoted considerable space to cadres, their selection (which, according to Jean Bonnaire, pp. 38–54, should be based on experimental studies of "leadership"), their promotion (which it was said should be "organized rationally" and based on "grading systems" and "training periods"), and above all their "psychological formation" (Suzanne Pacaud, pp. 98–128). Suzanne Pacaud's contribution is especially noteworthy, because it enables us to see how a progressive psychologist, who had worked before the war with Dr Lahy[88] and was also an antifascist activist, could have seen human relations techniques as a means of combatting authoritarianism, reinforcing the democratic spirit and community (or group) values, and overcoming selfish devotion to individual pleasures. After pointing out that the "science of human relations" was developed in America by a "small group of German refugees led by Kurt Lewin," who had "fled not only the racial views of the Nazis but also the social theories of pro-Nazi psychologists" (p. 105), Pacaud draws a distinction between "democratic leadership" and "authoritarian leadership" (p. 107). The switch from the latter to the former requires nothing less than a "conversion," "for unless each individual sincerely desires to change his behavior both as individual and as member of the group, this program can accomplish nothing."

> I emphasize this point [wrote Pacaud], because I have a clear impression that European interpreters of the goals set for the training of American managers have perhaps unconsciously focused exclusively on (1) intellectual preparation for positions of leadership and (2) teaching future leaders about psychology. But in fact something else is involved, something far more difficult: one must bring about a change in the natural behavior of leaders who may be highly qualified professionals. (p. 123)

The purpose of role-playing is to "modify behavior" and thereby to achieve the "emotional and moral well-being that comes from richer human contact." This was to be done by "developing sensitivity to the feelings of others" and greater "tolerance" of other people's views (pp. 122–3). "Group discussion of carefully chosen cases" should "develop the cadre's spirit of relativity through the clash of opinions and through comparison of diverse human qualities in a specific situation and of specific qualities in diverse situations." This "should help the cadre to overcome his stubbornness, his contempt for opinions other than his own, and his undue confidence in the correctness of his own reasoning" (pp. 125–6).

A new generation of psychosociologists bestowed legitimacy upon these imported American group techniques by introducing them into industry and the universities. Claude Faucheux, Jacques Ardoino, Guy Palmade, Max Pagès, Robert Pagès, Didier Anzieu, Jean Maisonneuve, and Roger Muchielli, all of whom were born between 1920 and 1925 and several of whom took postgraduate training in the United States with the leading lights in American social psychology (most notably Carl Rogers), not only taught in universities or did research for the CNRS but also served as management, hiring, and training consultants to industry in the 1950s. Some even formed their own "non-profit consulting firms." For example, Guy

Serraf, who in 1960 became the chief consultant to Bernard Krief, owner of one of the largest employment agencies in France, founded the Association nationale pour le développement des sciences humaines, or ANSHA, in conjunction with Didier Anzieu and Jacques Ardoino. ANSHA was, according to Krief, "a small group of academics with consulting experience. Thanks to this group I discovered, back in 1959, techniques for leading groups, dispensing information, understanding human relations, and so on, techniques that were not employed in industry until several years later."[89]

In a rural setting (the Hôtel du Grand Veneur at Rambouillet[90]), ANSHA held its first "national seminar in industrial psychology" under the direction of Didier Anzieu, Jacques Ardoino, and Guy Serraf. Besides the organizers the seminar included consulting psychologists (like Raymond Fichelet), academics (Claude Faucheux), physicians (Jacques-Martin, a neurologist and head of the medical department at SNECMA), military officers, welfare workers, personnel managers, training directors, etc. The seminar followed the procedures of a diagnostic group, but its purpose was mainly one of demonstration and training. Informal notes of panel discussions prepared by one of the organizers were distributed to participants. These were later collected in a sort of catalogue of psychosociological services that ANSHA offered to potential clients. The presence of abundant psychoanalytic jargon (flight into anxiety, dependency reaction) and of frequent references to the powers of the unconscious serves as a reminder of the "scientific character" of the enterprise and of the academic credentials of its promoters.

Industrial psychosociologists occupied the middle ground between the universities, industry, and government (specialists in the human sciences worked in various ministerial departments and with the planning commission).[91] As a result, they were the ideal paradigm for the new model intellectual, the intellectual–cadre directly involved in "action" in the world of affairs, which developed in the 1960s. More generally, the interest that top civil servants and leading employers took in psychology and sociology played a large part in the development of the human sciences in the 1950s and 1960s.

A special issue of the *Bulletin de psychologie* (vol. 12. nos. 6–9, 1958) was devoted to social psychology. Contributors included most of the psychosociologists who helped to introduce group techniques into industry (such as J. Stoetzel, D. Anzieu, J. and M. Van Bocstaele, R. Pagès, M. Pagès, C. Faucheux, J. Maisonneuve, G. Palmade, and P. Bize). One article, by P. Albou (an official of the planning commission), entitled "Recherche sociale dans l'industrie" (pp. 290–9), was entirely devoted to a celebration of the new ties that had developed in the 1950s between the universities and industry. After reminding readers of the contribution of the European Productivity Agency to the development of the "human sciences of labor," Albou extolled the recent "contacts" between "scientific research and industrial, agricultural, and commercial practice," which in his view had

> helped to enrich both research and practice and to improve the training of academics, technicians, and specialists. [These contacts] have helped to dispel the suspicions of some and the doubts of others. They have brought the traditional disciplines closer to the realities of working life. They have expanded and transformed the range of administrative concerns.

Fostering closer ties between the universities and industries was one of the constant concerns of the agencies created by the Marshall Plan. To cite again from the OECE report mentioned above:

> In certain areas, specifically, industrial psychology and sociology and market research, it seemed appropriate that the work of industry be complemented and supported by genuine scientific endeavor. In many countries work of this kind is done in universities, but only in a few does one see the kind of close and confident cooperation between universities and industry that made such a great impression on all the visitors to the United States.

"The conversion of the entire world"

The introduction of management, human relations, group dynamics, and marketing, together with the underlying representation of the economic agent as a free subject driven by a desire to achieve and consume, also helped to persuade many people, especially cadres, of the superiority of commodities, norms, and forms of knowledge associated, rightly or wrongly, with the United States (this development accompanied the opening of European financial markets to American capital[92]). Many people also came to believe that society would inevitably evolve toward a new order, the most fully developed example of which was, again, the United States.

One of the most ardent apostles of the new creed, Octave Gélinier, wrote in 1965 that

> today we can see things more clearly. To begin with, the economic and pol-

itical system of traditional Europe has proved to be bankrupt. That strange amalgam of medieval concepts and modern technologies was able to hold the spotlight for three centuries, owing to its initial lead and to the weakness of its rivals, but its collapse, about which there was nothing fortuitous, is final. . . . The American model, imperfect though it may be, offers industrial civilization its unifying principle. It has demonstrated its effectiveness at creating wealth and power and proven its flexibility and its capacity to adapt. Those who intelligently adapt this model to their own particular situations will soon reap the same benefits; many have already done so, and more are jumping on the bandwagon every day. It is reasonable to think that this trend will continue. . . . The Protestant ethic, reborn as the science of management, has renewed its strength. It is no longer taught in catechism classes but in business schools. To spread the faith throughout the world, missionaries have been replaced by "productivity institutes" that have been established in each country with American subsidies and expert assistance. Every year, leaders from all over the world come to the United States on pilgrimages (called "productivity missions") to see and hear the latest revelations. The Protestant ethic as management science is today sweeping the entire world, including France and the USSR.[93]

The management industry was to some degree responsible for a partial homogenization of value systems and styles of behavior. This explains a remarkable feature of multinational corporations, namely, their ability to recruit, in countries with fairly different social structures and cultural traditions, workers, and especially supervisory personnel, who are sufficiently alike to allow top management to exert central control over internal policies, personnel management rules, and more generally what I shall call the "professional habitus."[94] (This remains true even now, despite the increase in the power of corporate headquarters over national subsidiaries, whose autonomy has decreased steadily in the current period of crisis.) Analysis of cultural dependency effects[95] induced by economic dependency should enable one to determine the extent to which multinationalization (which in practice means Americanization) of the model cadre (the standard of reference for other cadres, including relatively low-level employees whose objective arena is national or even provincial) has been one of the causes of social and political conflict among rising segments of the middle classes.[96]

Praise for the American model was in fact quite commonplace (and often couched in clichéd language). Indeed, the dominant class in the early 1950s was nearly unanimous in its belief that the American way of doing things was the best. T. A. Wilson was not wrong when he remarked that although "it later became quite fashionable in Europe to make fun of those who imitated American cultural models and the American 'business' style, and to accuse the United States of practicing 'Coca-Cola imperialism,' it remains true that during the years of the Marshall Plan the United States was widely acknowledged as a model: most Europeans were passionately attracted by everything America stood for" (*op. cit.*, p. 43). And what America stood for was first of all scientific management, technical competence, and industrial might. The American landing in Europe, the Liberation, and the victory over Germany brought an influx of all kinds of American-made items – not only airplanes, trucks, and tanks but also food and clothing ("American surplus") – into Europe. The American system, which had been a matter for ideological debate and polite conversation in the 1920s, now became a physical presence, an overwhelming force, for millions of people.

Fascination with the American model, particularly among the bourgeoisie, emerges quite clearly from a 1953 IFOP study of French attitudes toward the United States. The study was in two parts. The same questionnaire was presented to a "representative" sample of 1,835 Frenchmen and to a "group of 264 leading personalities selected at random from government and professional directories, including members of the legislative and executive branches, academics, professionals, civil servants, and industrial executives." Only six of these "leading personalities" were Communists; most were Independents or supporters of the Rassemblement des gauches républicaines. Eighty-eight percent of the "leaders" polled approved of the Marshall Plan, 79% approved of the "delivery of war material to France," 77% approved of "American efforts to unify western Europe," and 57% approved of the "presence of Americans in France" (24% had no opinion). Doubts about American policy were expressed in only three areas: the "American attitude toward Indo-China," "American policy with regard to Germany," and "American actions in Morocco," which were disapproved, respectively, by 30%, 37%, and 77% of the leaders polled.

The opinions expressed in the broader, nationwide poll were less favorable to the United States. The differences between the two polls can be traced essentially to the influence of the Communist Party, particularly in the working class. When responses are correlated with "political preferences," there is a marked difference between Communists and non-Communists on all issues.

Communists, for example, were very hostile to the United States (75% stated that the Marshall Plan had been "bad for France"). Looking at responses by occupational group reveals a sharp contrast between blue-collar workers on the one hand and clerical workers, farmers, and cadres on the other. For example, only 42% of blue-collar workers believed that the Marshall Plan had been "good or very good for France," compared with 63% of clerical workers, 65% of cadres, and 53% of farmers. Finally, of those who declared that they had become "cooler" toward the United States after the war, workers were most numerous (33%), while among those who declared that their feelings for America had become "warmer," cadres outnumbered all others (13%). This probably represents the conversion of a part of the old pro-Vichy right to the new "ideals" symbolized by "American democracy."[97]

Statements of fascination with America may seem rather similar superficially, and yet convey very different meanings, depending on the social position and political aims of the person or group making the statement. Further analysis might enable one to distinguish between those for whom the justification for adopting American models lay in the desire to increase France's power and hence national independence (from the United States in particular) as well as to encourage the redistribution of wealth generated by "growth" (as was often the case in the entourage of Pierre Mendès France) and those who saw American democracy as the key to a new, enlightened conservatism. Conservatives resigned to the need for concessions in order to perpetuate the established order hoped that by going along with American plans private industry might prosper and thus remain independent of government control.

A good way to identify conservatives is to examine attitudes toward economic planning. The public/private distinction had been of fundamental importance in France since the nineteenth century, dividing groups and classes in favor of a strong state from proponents of free enterprise. As long as the political climate demanded continuing *de facto* censure of pro-Vichy big business interests and, perhaps to an even greater extent, as long as economic planning was seen by both sides as essential to the success of pro-growth policies (on which private-sector profits depended), the public/private dichotomy was played down.[98] By the mid-1960s, however, things had changed. Industrial and financial conglomerates had gained strength and nearly all big businessmen had been converted to the ideology of management. To them, "the planning commission seemed a survival of outmoded left-wing thinking."[99]

The rationalization of careers

Psychological tools by themselves probably would not have sufficed to bring about the almost miraculous economic and social changes desired by top government officials and progressive businessmen if other institutional changes had not simultaneously affected the "economic ethos" (i.e., attitudes toward time and money, inherited wealth, savings, consumption, and credit, and not unrelated attitudes toward education) of large segments of the bourgeoisie and petite bourgeoisie. This led to important changes in cadres' notions of their careers.

One of the primary goals of management consultants in the 1960s was to rationalize career decisions. The career development movement, an offshoot of the human relations movement, was developed in large firms,[100] specifically, large nationalized firms that adopted methods of personnel management (for cadres only) first tried out in government offices. The purpose of career development was to develop human resources in a scientific and systematic way, taking account of the "needs of each cadre and relying on cooperation between each individual and his superiors. Employees should be able to speak frankly to their superiors about career plans and desires. Cadres should be convinced that job assignments are planned with their career interests in mind. They should also be persuaded that their capacities will be used to the full and that ability is the only limit to advancement." The career rationalization program responded "to needs often expressed by cadres": "to be told early of prospects for advancement," to "be informed of evaluations by superiors," and to "be promoted quickly to positions of real responsibility."[101] As private firms became more and more bureaucratized, career rationalization programs became increasingly common. The purpose of these programs was basically to reduce tensions due to industrial modernization and restructuring. To that end, segments of the bourgeoisie and petite bourgeoisie that came under the sway of large corporations were offered social and economic compensation for the loss of security they suffered as the old system of family capitalism faded away. Under that system higher-level employees had been subject to minimal explicit social controls; many had inherited wealth of their own and/or family and social ties to plant-owners. Discipline was imposed through a complex network of economic, social, professional, and family relations; this system of implicit controls came to seem quite natural to those who worked under it. But modernization required a new system of explicit and acknowledged rules to standardize rewards and punishments, distribute power and profits, and above all to legitimate bureaucratic decisions by involving employees themselves in the system that governed their economic and social destinies. For managers the primary need was to develop not an economically efficient system but a system that seemed *necessary*[102] to those whose futures it controlled. Formalized, hierarchical systems were felt to be rational because they reduced arbitrary decisions to a minimum and concealed aspects of the process that could not be rationalized (in the psychoanalytic sense) in terms of official rules. By this I do not mean to imply that the formal rules actually determined what decisions were made. Objective standards for promotion depended on the growing importance of formal educational credentials and, more generally, of competence, as opposed to wealth or ownership. Objective standards were needed in order to maintain the morale of cadres and to prevent employees who felt that their jobs were beneath their abilities from developing resentment of the employer's arbitrary power.[103] Finally, manipulation of career opportunities proved to be an effective management tool, a way of controlling career choices and encouraging cadres to emulate selected role models.[104]

The basic ploy was to "distinguish between the man and the job": "the job remains ... the same even when the worker changes." In other words, a distinction was drawn between the position, "the place in the organization where a specific kind of work is done, and the occupant of that position, the man who is there at any given time to perform the work."[105] In large, bureaucratized firms the distribution of power and profits cannot be based explicitly on wealth or on family or social connections. Instead, each job has certain formal prerequisites, and candidates are matched up with jobs using various systems of evaluation ranging from the simple to the sophisticated (ranking systems, factor comparisons, hierarchy studies, etc.[106]) – mostly imported from the United States in the 1950s. Once the organizational hierarchy has been established on objective, scientific grounds, each job is assigned its fair salary and its relative value in a classification scheme that reflects the hierarchy of both salaries and responsibilities, and each applicant is evaluated, also scientifically and objectively, by means of interviews, tests, performance reports, questionnaires, etc. Organizations set up in this way can adhere to meritocratic standards and yet remain remarkably flexible: employees can be shifted about at will simply by redefining the job hierarchy (and large firms were subject to constant reorganization) or by adopting new psychological criteria for personnel selection and evaluation. Psychological standards probably proved useful because, even though they were ostensibly designed to reveal a man's character, they were in fact able to pinpoint his social background (this also explains why the scientific judgments of the psychologists so often coincided with the judgments that employers made instinctively or intuitively).[107]

The new moral economy

The rationale behind formalized evaluation procedures was not simply to legitimate hierarchy by introducing meritocratic standards such as education, skill, and efficiency to replace older criteria such as wealth and family connections. Like the retirement system discussed earlier, formalization diminished the influence of inherited wealth and fostered a "need for security" (a phrase that organizational consultants sometimes use with a trace of disdain). The desire to lead a respectable, bourgeois life, free from need, encouraged people to look for jobs that offered certain assurances, certain prospects of regular raises and promotions. One effect of career rationalization was to increase the slope of the income curve. In the past *rentiers* had been content to live on a fixed income, and businessmen had to live with the ups and downs of the market. But now income was supposed to grow steadily, in a predictable manner. Individuals were thus able to reduce their savings and purchase consumer durables, homes, and college educations for their children with money that previously would have been put aside for a rainy day.

All available indicators suggest that a new bourgeois life cycle and new bourgeois household economy based primarily on salaries (as the legitimate mode of appropriation of the profits of capitalism[108]) and secondarily on education (which determined who had access to the higher-paying jobs) finally took hold in the 1950s. CGC polemics denouncing "the squeezing of the salary hierarchy"[109] and the coming "proletarization of cadres"[110] distracted attention from the fact that the actual trend was in the opposite direction: from 1945 to 1951 the salary differential between cadres and ordinary workers increased fourfold.[111] The range of incomes was greater in 1951 than it had been either in 1945[112] or between the two world wars. And it widened still further after salary controls were lifted in 1952.[113] Members of the bourgeoisie who worked for a living found that their purchasing power increased. For example, the purchasing power of cadres in the electrical construction industry was 80% higher in the early 1950s than it had been in 1938. For cadres in the metals industry the figure was 50%. In the same period the purchasing power of manual laborers increased only 7%.[114]

Furthermore, it appears that bourgeois employees of large firms were the primary beneficiaries of institutional changes which, though intended in the minds of their proponents to redistribute income, actually helped to establish a new mode of economic regulation in the years after World War II. To begin with, the "new conception of income" as a "reward intended to allow specific types of workers to meet their legitimate needs" and "the tendency for income to vary with the productivity of the firm or of the economy as a whole"[115] favored bourgeois employees who, because they occupied relatively powerful positions, were able to raise their own pay (union demands were not the only force tending to drive up wages). Bourgeois employees were also able to monopolize for their own benefit social services administered by the works' councils and intended primarily to "improve the condition of workers." These included social clubs, cooperatives, vacation villages, and sports. When it came to benefits, cadres were perfectly willing to consider themselves "workers like the rest." It appears, moreover, that bourgeois employees in the 1950s were quicker than blue-collar and clerical workers to realize the advantages of indirect compensation in the form of social benefits; they championed a system of income redistribution that their administrative and financial skills enabled them to use to their own maximum advantage.[116] They benefited more than other groups from the increase in government revenues and expenditures,[117] particularly expenditures on schools, cultural institutions, hospitals, highways, etc., because they already possessed the physical resources, such as automobiles, and symbolic resources, such as a college education[118] or an appreciation of the advantages of modern medicine,[119] necessary to take full advantage of these collective goods.[120] These changes tended to bring to bourgeois employees in private industry the benefits and guarantees[121] that had previously been enjoyed only by members of the civil service, while continuing to reward them with very high salaries, near the top of the salary range.

As the income of the industrial bourgeoisie increased, as careers became more secure, as public and private insurance plans were established that made cadres feel even more comfortable, and as the economic climate improved (owing to renewed domestic consumption and to postwar reconstruction financed in part by the Marshall Plan), guaranteeing full employment and increased likelihood of promotion, especially for the college-educated, large segments of the bourgeoisie and petite bourgeoisie changed their economic habits and outlook. Money not spent on immediate needs was increasingly used to purchase consumer durables such as automobiles and household appliances, stimulating branches of industry that were destined to play a leading role in the economic growth of the 1960s.[122]

Investments in durable goods and real estate were also aided by the development of new sources of credit, especially the Union de crédit pour le bâtiment, or UCB, established by Jacques de Fouchier in 1951, and the Compagnie bancaire, founded in 1959. These were unusual in that they granted loans not against physical collateral but rather on the basis of personal guarantees, notably the applicant's job stability, career profile, and likelihood of promotion. Such a system of credit can only function in a society in which the future is predictable and calculable, that is, in a bureaucratic society.[123] The value of the personal guarantee actually derived from the lender's calculations of the applicant's chance of success in his career. The same statistical methods that were employed in the first retirement programs for cadres were now extended to the realm of consumption. As Jacques de Fouchier explained with remarkable clarity, bankers could now profit from the new bourgeois life cycle by channeling the flow of funds between generations, lending, on the basis of career prospects, to young couples whose needs were high the funds deposited by older households headed by men whose careers had peaked.[124] Bankers also counted on the fact that many younger members of the bourgeoisie and petite bourgeoisie now worked for large bureaucratic organizations and could anticipate fairly stable pay and regular salary increases. Credit was like an advance against salary, and the banker was merely a temporary substitute for the employer, on whom the young cadre with a promising future counted for eventual raises. Whereas a man was free to use his salary for any and all purposes, when he borrowed he essentially made a choice to use his money for some particular purpose: bankers were fond of describing this as "forced savings," to emphasize the high moral purpose of their endeavors. Credit institutions channeled consumption toward heavy investments in real estate, automobiles, appliances, etc., and thus contributed to the prosperity of the most capitalistic sectors of industry.

Thus the development of consumer credit compensated for the

deflationary effects of what Marx called the "selling of labor power on credit" by those who committed themselves to a career.[125]

As statistics concerning the distribution of durable goods clearly show, bourgeois employees, particularly those who called themselves "cadres," became privileged consumers in the 1950s and especially in the 1960s. The nature and volume of their consumption tended to attract other groups occupying the same professional and social space, and this probably heightened the struggle between groups and classes for the appropriation of various signs of distinction. These status struggles (*luttes de classement*)[126] led to the rapid devaluation of many status symbols (as other classes gained access to goods whose distinctive value depended on their relative scarcity, bourgeois consumption shifted to new products[127]). Commodities became obsolete (symbolically) at an increased rate, thus stimulating production. The distribution of goods among groups and classes shifted upward (without altering relative differences). Although those who would henceforth be called "cadres" set the pace of consumption for other social groups (and thus played a leading role in the daily class struggle), the effects of competition for distinctive goods first made themselves felt among cadres themselves. For cadres differed greatly as to wealth and income and hence as to the volume and nature of their consumption. Yet just as the political representation of the group was monopolized by a leading subgroup (namely, engineers who had studied at the Grandes Ecoles, who served as spokesmen for a diverse assortment of followers), so, too, did the symbols of being a cadre – the life style and forms of consumption promoted by advertising in magazines such as *Paris-Match*, *L'Express*, and *Entreprise* – pertain primarily to this same group of pacesetters (indeed, the advertising often reflected the tastes and values of advertising executives themselves[128]). For it was this upper echelon of cadres that possessed not just the wealth, or economic capital, necessary for this kind of consumption but also, in the case of such highly symbolic goods as books, records, art objects, and so forth, the cultural capital without which appropriation of these kinds of scarce commodities would have been impossible.

Others, recently promoted to cadre level (and especially autodidacts who had come up through the ranks of industry and who had no bourgeois family background), could not fully enjoy their new identity without acquiring the material and cultural symbols of their status group. Indeed, when the cadre's promotion resulted in no noticeable improvement in his working conditions, these status symbols were sometimes the only tangible signs of advancement. But since many cadres were not paid enough to adopt the life style associated with the manager who had made it, they had to make do with ersatz items while awaiting the hoped-for promotion that would make them "real cadres" – as though social identity itself could be bought on credit.

The increased purchasing power of bourgeois employees coupled with changes in their economic behavior accounts for the new type of advertising that one begins to find in magazines such as *L'Express* in the 1960s. Advertisements displayed the kinds of things presumably bought mainly be cadres, such as homes, automobiles, appliances, leather-bound books, radios, televisions, and so forth, along with standard images of "the cadre" (in dark suit and tie, carrying an attaché case, etc.), images that validated the items with which they were associated as genuine articles of cadre consumption. Thus advertising made its own unique contribution to the popularization of the term "cadre" and its associated imagery. It extended to the realm of domestic consumption the representational process which, since the 1930s, had been concentrated mainly in the workplace and the realm of professional relations. But for progressive Catholics, heirs of the anticapitalism of the 1930s and believers in the social doctrine of the Catholic Church (found mainly in the CFTC rather than the CGC after 1950[129]), the two representations of the cadre failed to cohere. Catholics condemned the "factitious pleasures"[130] held out to engineers and cadres and the "use of the term 'cadre' in advertising," which they called "an error that must be corrected" because it "tends to give a false image of the cadre": "Advertising copy is aimed at creating a certain social image. It generally says nothing about [the cadre's] working life, as if advertisers were afraid of diverting their readers' attention from what, to them, is the essential thing, leisure."[131] This is the language of Christian asceticism, which Jean Dubois here uses to describe the life style that advertisers have ascribed to the cadre and the rhetoric of *L'Express* that casts the cadre in the role of the prototypical consumer in mass society. "True cadres," "productive cadres," need to be defended against "the false image of the cadre as consumer" and taught "to avoid becoming fascinated" with the objects that their labor creates; instead of learning to love *things*, the cadre must preserve his "concern for the person" and rediscover "the revolutionary force of Christianity."[132]

A successful group

The introduction of management rhetoric into France and the proliferation of institutions whose purpose was to help the petite bourgeoisie of industry adapt to its new social role by training, managing, and disciplining new cadres certainly helped to objectify cadres as a group, much as the formation of associations of cadres and cadres' unions had done earlier. Cadres, who after the war still formed a vague, ill-defined group[133] whose existence and "representativity" were challenged and who still had to fight for recognition, fifteen years later occupied a central position in the dominant representation of society. The group was *successful* in the sense that it managed to establish objective proofs of its existence. It did not splinter and disintegrate like the middle class (with which cadres had originally been associated). For the middle class proved to be an unstable amalgam, constantly in need of being patched up; its representatives never managed to establish the kind of solid, durable institutions and systems of representation necessary if a social group is to be recognized as an objective reality. To understand how the cadres were able to convince even their original opponents (most notably the Communist Party and the CGT) of their objective existence *qua* group, one must look more closely at the process of objectification.

The first order of business was to acquire legal representation. The collective individual exists, through the mystery of incarnation, in the physical persons to whom it delegates authority. Thus does a "multitude of men" become "a single person" and a group a "personified being" (in Hobbes' phrase).[134] After the Liberation, official negotiating bodies were established to help resolve social conflicts. Without legal recognition and an official place in these negotiating bodies, a group lacked social visibility and could not defend its political and economic interests effectively. The government, which saw itself as the arbiter of social struggles, recognized groups only in the persons of representatives. Those who spoke on behalf of that abstraction, the state, required flesh-and-blood partners, or, as top civil servants often put it, interlocutors. Administrative bodies officially recognized only legally constituted and represented groups. In bureaucratic parlance there are only two kinds of beings: the abstract moral person and the physical person who serves as its representative. This accounts for the alternation (characteristic also of political history) between the abstract and the concrete, between geopolitics and the psychology of leaders, between the legal subject and the human person, between summit meetings involving heads of state and backroom anecdotes about personalities.[135] Legal representation speeds up the process of institutionalization and roots the group's existence in the material order. Objectification of the group in a legally recognized collective person (and of that collective person in an institutional apparatus) helps to make the group more solid and durable than the aggregate of individuals who claim membership and thus sustain the group's existence. For one thing, institutionalization makes it possible for the group to take positions relatively independent of the views of its members.[136] The group elects officers, counselors, etc., who can build on the work of their predecessors. It acquires an existence in law, in buildings, in budgets, in routines and methods, in familiar objects that emphasize its presence in society (much as official reports sometimes speak of the "presence of the Church" or the "presence of France"). Then, too, the group establishes rules and regulations, divides up the work of representation, institutionalizes mechanisms of reproduction, sets up bureaucratic decision-making procedures, and, more generally, establishes a set of routines that come to be taken for granted. Thus its existence becomes less dependent on individual actions (and on its own spokesmen) and hence less vulnerable. It is somewhat reminiscent of the way in which Taylorian methods of scientific management transfer the skills of workers to the organization of the assembly line and thus make the production process relatively independent of the aptitudes of the producers, who have been rendered interchangeable (it is in this sense, and this sense only, that an institution can be compared to a machine or apparatus).

The compleat "cadre" as depicted by official spokesmen for cadres' organizations became a magnetic pole, an image that attracted individuals from other parts of society. With what Goffman might call "dramatic emphasis" these spokesmen simplified the group's definition, thereby helping the group to achieve structural stability, keeping it from being swallowed up by other, larger groups and preventing internal dissension from getting out of hand. The group's outlines seemed to come into focus and stabilize once the proper viewing distance was found. But it first had to be found: too far away and the group merged with its environment, too close and one saw nothing but minute details.

Between 1930 and 1969 cadres developed a quasi-institutionalized system of representation that established the group's existence beyond doubt. What could be more objective than a cadres' training center, a seminar for cadres, an association for the employment of cadres, a national purchasing cooperative, the Fédération national d'achat des cadres (or FNAC), and a cadres' retirement fund? The image of the cadre had struck deep roots and no longer depended on the personal prestige of group spokesmen. The individual who aspired to become a cadre found waiting for him a ready-made group with its own paradigms and stereotypes. He might join the group, but no longer did he have to create it out of whole cloth. It might define him; he no longer had to define it. The group shaped the individual, not the other way around. And no longer did any cadre have to ponder the mystery of the cadre's substance or the group's origins: henceforth these subjects were taboo. It was as though cadres had existed for all eternity.

PART 2
A finished group

3 *The field of representations*

As cadres developed an organizational structure that made the group's existence seem more and more self-evident, what I shall call a "field of representations" was established. The one-dimensional discourse of the founders of the group (spokesmen for a still nascent institution which they closely controlled, whose various statements were to a remarkable degree ideologically consistent) gave way in the 1960s to a range of somewhat divergent representations. These proliferating representations were manipulated by a number of different agencies, chiefly unions but also political groups of various kinds.

The development, in the 1960s, of new organizations representing cadres was both a sign and a consequence of social success. Now that the group possessed an undeniable presence, it could no longer be ignored by unions and political parties battling for control of society. This led to the development of strategies of cooptation and reinterpretation, or rather, of cooptation through reinterpretation. For example, it was not until the 1960s that the CGT attempted (particularly after its 1965 convention) to establish a beachhead among the "new strata" by allocating a substantial budget to a subsidiary organization that had existed in theory since 1948 but had remained dormant since its inception: the Union générale des ingénieurs et cadres (or UGIC, which in 1969 became the Union générale des ingénieurs cadres et techniciens, or UGICT). The

CGT developed organizing campaigns around issues designed to appeal to cadres and publicized "new theoretical analyses" of the "class position of engineers and cadres," analyses elaborated by intellectuals and sociologists associated with the Communist Party. To appeal to cadres, the CGT had to drop its opposition to craft unions as permanent affiliates (especially unions that imposed membership restrictions based on hierarchical position). Efforts by reformers to persuade the CGT to open its ranks to individuals "exercising a portion of the employer's or the government's authority, either directly or by delegation" were thwarted by "structural" problems in the postwar period (as they had been earlier, in 1936–7, when the Federation of Technicians had made a brief appearance on the scene). The reformers had hoped to make room in the union for those engineers and cadres – a small minority – whose work in the Resistance (or at any rate hostility to Vichy) and desire to work with the unions toward "national recovery" had made them sympathetic to the trade-union movement. In the final report of a national conference of cadres and engineers belonging to the Fédération des métaux, dated 10–11 February 1945, we read that

> the very possibility of holding a national conference of cadres and engineers affiliated with one of the leading trade unions proves not only that trade-unionism has demonstrated its value to all classes of workers but also that the need for a total organic unity that will cast aside old prejudices, stale quarrels, sterile fears, and vain mistrust is now evident to all, even those who long disdained or even combatted such unity, as the only way to put across our common concerns.... Clearly we working masses have shaken off the inferiority complex that came from spreading ourselves too thin and kept us on the defensive; we now realize that an alliance between numbers and competence can invigorate us and generate constructive new energy. (Archives of the CGT's Metal Workers' Union)

In the same year the CGT established a "Cartel confédéral des cadres," led by Albert Gazier and Pierre Lebrun. But this organization, whose purpose, according to Gazier, was to create a place where cadres could be "neither isolated nor drowned out," had no legal foundation or standing, which weakened its position and only called attention to the opposition of most union federations to accepting cadres as members. In the great schism of 1947 the majority of cadres in the CGT (who were employed mainly in the public sector or in nationalized firms) therefore joined Force ouvrière or one of the autonomous unions that served employees of the Paris Métro and the SNCF.[1]

The CFTC had attempted to mobilize cadres even before the CGT. It sought to sign up engineers and other cadres who had been influenced by the Social Catholicism of the 1930s and who had joined the CGC after the war. As early as 1944 the CFTC set up the Fédération française des sydnicats d'ingénieurs et de cadres, but up to the 1960s this organization had great difficulty mobilizing its presumed supporters (including its own members, some of whom also belonged to industrial unions). It was not until after the founding of the CFDT in 1964 and the development of a rather original class analysis by the PSU (see below) that the Union confédérale des cadres was created (in 1967).

Success also diversified representations of cadres in another way: as more and more people were attracted from other social groups, they became increasingly heterogeneous. Organizations that claimed to represent all cadres in the 1960s actually represented various subgroups. Since these subgroups had no autonomous social existence, they fought within the group to define the term "cadres" in a way most favorable to themselves. Paradoxically, however, the development of a "field of representations" probably helped to maintain the group's symbolic unity, by allowing subgroups to express their particular interests without undermining the legitimacy of the group as such. Because various organizations were competing for the right to represent *all* cadres, they couched demands that in fact reflected the particular interests of some in universal terms that neutralized their potentially destructive effects. For the different representations of cadres had at least one thing in common: all were based on a shared belief in the objective existence of a category whose definition was the only bone of contention.

The structure and size of "mobilization units" (and their position on a continuum ranging from unified entity to dependent subgroup) are in large part determined by the relationship between the "general interest" and "particular interests."[2] The collective persons who embody what Max Weber called "representation by interested representatives"[3] must somehow cope with a contradiction inherent in their very structure. On the one hand, the power of negotiators depends on the number of people they represent, on the number of people who share the "general interest." (This explains, for example, why unions generally favor standardized pay scales and job classifications rather than "individualized" systems.[4]) On the other hand, it is more difficult to mobilize the members of a large union, for the larger the group, the more heterogeneous its membership and the more local interests need to be suppressed.

Local conflicts, often caused by direct competition for jobs, are especially common and particularly bitter between unions representing similar types of worker. Often there is no officially sanctioned means of alleviating such conflicts. Hence they are particularly threatening to trade-union unity. For when diversity is ignored or suppressed, "local issues" (*particularismes*) can be raised explicitly only through strategies aimed at de-objectifying and hence destroying mobilization units that are the reified product of a prior objectification process. Heterogeneous groups are more likely to endure if provision is made for giving vent to (rather than merely censuring or suppressing) local interests, but without defining them as such and without allowing those who express them to claim a distinct identity that would set them apart from the larger group.

The mobilization of sociologists

Like the middle class in the 1930s, cadres became the focus of a debate in the 1960s over the nature, social position, role, and future of what was considered a new group. At stake in this controversy was nothing less than which of several competing representations of society would prevail. Which would determine the structure of society and its constituent groups and classes? There were, however, clear differences between the way in which cadres were discussed in the 1960s and the way in which the middle class was discussed in the 1930s, differences in form as well as content. Different kinds of arguments were used, and those arguments were justified in different ways. Indeed, in the postwar years conditions affecting the production of social representations changed profoundly. In large part these changes stemmed from the leading role that was accorded to the social sciences, and especially to sociology, from 1950 on, and above all to a new relationship between the government and the universities (where much of the discourse on society was produced). This new relationship was itself a consequence of the development of new, quasi-governmental, quasi-academic institutions.[5] Here again the Commissariat au Plan played a major role. The work of economic planning required the development of a series of monitoring and forecasting agencies and planning commissions, staffed by academics, researchers, top civil servants, union representatives, businessmen, etc. These individuals pooled their skills, exchanged issues and jargons, and through negotiation overcame their distinct, even divergent, professional interests to arrive at something they called the "collective interest." The view of society developed by these "natural research groups" (often led by reform-minded individuals, many of them influenced by Social Catholicism) was intended to be both scientific and statistical, prospective and prescriptive.

In periods of growth individuals or groups who believe that the tide of history is with them generally combine voluntarist attitudes toward social change with a deterministic philosophy of history. To describe the future as the "ineluctable" consequence of a chain of events whose origin lies in the present is, first of all, a performative discourse, intended to act upon the present: the predicted future defines the present, which in turn determines what the future will be. In other words, prospective discourse is a type of performative discourse whose purpose is to bring about a state of affairs that is alleged to exist already. By describing what the social order and class structure of the 1980s would "inevitably" be, planners put themselves in the position of choosing which postwar changes were pertinent, or as they themselves phrased it, "pregnant with the future." In this way they helped to shut off alternative possibilities and to reinforce those existing tendencies that best fit their expectations (and were in part the result of prior, objectively orchestrated, partially coherent actions and reactions).

Based on the theme of growth, expansion, and progress, this ideology bore all the earmarks of what I shall call "scientistic evolutionism," first, because the planners believed and explicitly stated that they possessed a theory of social evolution,[6] and second, because they maintained that science is the motor of all social evolution. Like the Marxists, though in a different way, they believed that history tends in a certain direction. Historical evolution can be controlled, they asserted, by means of science and especially the human sciences. Such a view implies the death of history: if it is correct, the future is inevitable, a mere unfolding in time governed by a logic implicit in the present. On this view, knowledge (especially statistical knowledge) of the present state of society is the key to controlling the future. At the same time, forecasting the future helps to orient action in the present by identifying what changes will prove to be durable and which individuals, groups, and classes deserve to survive and to reproduce. The 1960s saw an abundance of speculation as to the future of French society – covering such topics as the "end of the peasants," the effects of the Common Market, and the "bourgeoisification" of the working class – whose purpose was to impose as scientifically valid and self-evident a specific representation of the social structure and thus through a process of objectification to bring about what was predicted as inevitable: the goal, in effect, was to proclaim a self-fulfilling prophecy.[7]

In this attempt to symbolically reorder society, the definition of cadres played a crucial role, because this new group occupied a position in the social structure where it proved possible to introduce some play into the taxonomies. Thus the success of efforts to change the social definition of such groups and classes as employers or the working class (whose existence seemed undeniable and which had long possessed their own representative organizations and symbols) depended in part at least on the properties ascribed to the new group, which had acquired objective status much more recently and to a much smaller degree. In particular, it was of great importance to define the boundaries of the new group.

Academic sociologists (whose numbers had increased greatly with the proliferation of teaching and research positions) served the planning commissions as "experts," lectured to seminars, colloquia, clubs, and study groups, and published in such journals as *Esprit*, *Preuves*, and *Prospective*, answering questions from enlightened civil servants and modern employers in the name of social science. Sociologists also participated in efforts by the Marxist parties and unions to refurbish their ideologies and reclaim old symbols (the Communist Party and the CGT had all but ignored cadres as long as they maintained their belief in the theory of the "two fundamental classes"). Finally, sociologists directly inspired attempts by the new left to transcend the status quo. Hence one cannot understand the "cadre issue" as it was posed in the 1960s without analyzing the major role that sociologists played in framing the key questions. Conversely, this also means that one cannot analyze sociological discourse concerning cadres without looking at how it was shaped by social and historical circumstances.

Our first finding is this: cadres became a legitimate object of sociological inquiry only after the social objectification of the group was complete. The group first had to complete its own process of formation, unification, and representation, develop its own collective institutions, and win official recognition; in short, it had to enter the arena of political combat before it could become an object of scientific research, a "topic" whose necessity was initially external. When politicians began to talk about cadres as a group and people began to say that cadres had done this or that, qualified experts were called in to explain just *who* these cadres were in terms of some consistent, theoretically justified representation of society (based on one of the rival theories of social evolution current at the time). At this point the rise of the cadres acquired the status of a scientifically important question.

The relation between the growth of the group and sociological interest in it was not one of simple cause and effect. As we shall see in greater detail in chapters 4 and 5 of part 2, the group did not simply grow in size and automatically attract the attention of the sociologists and other specialists in social representation who from 1960 onward took it upon themselves to say what it was and what place it occupied or should occupy in the social structure. In fact, the growth in the number of cadres cannot be explained solely by an increase in the number of supervisory positions in industry as a result of technological change. Nor does the growth in the group's size account for the form that scholarly interest in it took. Some sociologists held that the existence of a cadre group was self-evident, others that it was problematic. For example, Jean-Paul Bachy maintained that cadres were "a rising group but impossible to situate" in the social structure.[8] This proposition, logically absurd on the face of it, actually expresses belief in a prophecy that plays on the ambiguity of the verb "to rise." Are we being told that cadres are actually on the rise or merely that they will rise some day? And does "rise" mean to increase in size or to ascend to a position of dominance (the two are in some sense contradictory, since the number of dominant positions is by definition limited). In any event, the relationship between the growth of the group and the amount of scholarly attention devoted to it was a dialectical one. As the size of the group increased, it naturally attracted more attention. Conversely, however, before everyone could agree that this growth was an obvious and undeniable fact, a notion of what the group was had to exist and methods of recording its size had to be in place (along with systems of classification, nomenclature, etc.). Otherwise there would have been no way of grasping the physical reality of the group as an autonomous entity, distinct from other groups in the social taxonomy with which cadres had always been confused – until a noun was invented to set them apart.

Double dependency

Work on cadres in the 1960s focused on the question of the group's boundaries and membership criteria. In order to understand why this was so, it will be necessary to review briefly how social conditions influenced scholarly views of society in this period. Academic discourse on society is of course always shaped by a complex web of constraints, but the development of institutional links between government and the universities in the 1950s and 1960s revealed these constraints with particular clarity. Scholarly representations of the social world are shaped by both intellectual and political factors. Social theories are symbols, weapons in intellectual combat; together with their associated systems of social classification they are also weapons in social and political struggles.[9] Hence theoretical production in the social sciences enjoys relatively little autonomy *vis-à-vis* outside influences. Social theories are in effect the results of an interaction among conflicting demands, principles of legitimation, and grounds for action. From the realm of politics come demands for rationalization (in the psychoanalytic sense) and legitimation. Sometimes the need is to convert political power into intellectual authority (as, for example, when a politician becomes a professor of political science). At other times it is to convert symbolic authority into political power. And so on. Because the rewards are so many and so varied, so, too, are the individuals who seek to develop "representations" of society and to make their views on social questions known to a broad public. This field of production is therefore not well integrated. Many individuals, representing many different kinds of institution (universities, think-tanks, newspapers, political parties, etc.), are linked in and through competition. All occupy what I have called elsewhere "extended positional space":[10] over the course of their careers they have diversified their investments in many different fields (some more than others).

In order to reconstruct the field in which the debates over cadres developed in the 1960s, one must first understand the objective relationships among individuals occupying a wide range of institutional positions. To begin with, there were academics invested with the most august and traditional symbols of higher learning: the Ecole Normale, the *agrégation*, etc. (e.g. Alain Touraine). There were sociologists associated with the new schools of management that opened their doors in this period (e.g., Michel Crozier). There were trade unionists (e.g., Pierre Belleville). There were also essayists who came to sociology and political economy by way of politics and journalism (e.g., Serge Mallet and André Gorz, who followed very different trajectories). And so on. One must also analyze the complex relationships that existed between these intellectuals and various groups and organizations in the field of politics: the CGC and "third-party" tendencies, the Communist Party and the CGT, the CFDT and the PSU, etc. If one viewed scholarly books and papers as representing nothing other than "disputes among specialists," as scholars tend to do, and gauged the relation of one theorist to another solely by obligatory footnote references and explicit polemics (such as Nicos Poulantzas's critique of Serge Mallet)[11], one would miss many important allusions. The more euphemistically these allusions are phrased (as they generally are in papers intended for consumption solely by other social scientists), the more telling they are, for they refer, beyond individuals and their works, to the organizations that those individuals supposedly represent, at least in the minds of rival scholars: e.g., Serge Mallet stands for the PSU and the CFDT, Michel Crozier stands for "advanced liberalism," etc. If one ignores these external influences, one is in effect admitting that intellectuals do in fact enjoy the kind of independence that they claim for themselves.[12] But if one wishes to recover the historical and social significance of seemingly abstract controversies, one must deliberately suspend the rules of academic propriety, which forbid treating the theoretical discourse of scholars on the same plane as the political rhetoric employed by spokesmen for a party apparatus.

Apparatus: I am well aware that the word, devalued by partisan polemic, is used more as an insult than as a concept. Yet despite its mechanistic connotations it has the virtue of reminding us that all political organizations, from the most informal to the most highly institutionalized, are not mere abstract entities, points in space whose coordinates are "positions" on the issues and similar symbolic distinctions, but real entities in the "world of things" (as Maurice Halbwachs might say). These entities are defined by their power to mobilize people and gain control over things – in other words, by their possession of capital, in the form of men and institutions, including institutions in the field of intellectual endeavor and/or useful to intellectuals, such as magazines, publishing houses, institutional forums, etc. Think of all the advantages that an intellectual derives from being a Communist (or, for similar reasons, from being a Catholic): the means to publish and express his ideas, an audience, and perhaps more than anything else an obligatory set of issues on which to focus his attention. Think, too, of what intellectuals without party affiliations owe to their membership in various groups, clubs, lobbies, and informal networks which are all the more exclusive because their boundaries are not clearly defined. Besides the recognized and explicitly identified party apparatuses, there is in effect a whole series of ambiguous and nameless external agencies that exert effective practical control over institutions within the intellectual sphere and thus play a part in the reinterpretation of practical interests in intellectual terms.

These invisible apparatuses (if I may call them that) accomplish a miracle: they pave the way for the production of a series of homogeneous products (differentiated in minor ways that conceal their agreement on the major issues) that satisfy all external demands without enforcing the kinds of rigid rules that true party apparatuses must enforce in order to obtain strict adherence to the party line. Thus there is a continuum that ranges from the classical party apparatus, which forces intellectuals to toe the line and speak directly in the name of the party, to the loose network of friendships and alliances in which each individual member speaks only in his own name. The less explicit the link to external institutions, the greater the appearance of independence (and hence the more legitimate the discourse ostensibly is).

Scholarly output must therefore meet two kinds of requirements, defined by value systems that are to some degree distinct and appealing to two partially distinct audiences.[13] Specifically, scholarly work must meet certain intellectual standards, which today means that it must pass for social science (concretely, it must qualify for publication in a refereed journal or by a reputable publisher or be acceptable as a thesis by a recognized institution, etc.). At the same time it must also meet the needs of certain external agencies which, in order to legitimate their own practice, require certain instruments, certain tools for gaining symbolic ascendancy over the social world.

These two types of dependency hide each other and thus give intellectual discourse its appearance of autonomy. The "scientificity" of social theoretical discourse and the symbols of academic prestige that surround it conceal its practical functions and give it the appearance of universal validity. Then, too, the fact that social theory alludes to major political debates and fundamental social issues (as distinct from sociologically pertinent questions), coupled with the recognition that practical exigencies take priority over cognitive interests, conceals (in the name of a service ethic that the expert can invoke as readily as the organic intellectual) the way in which social theoretical discourse depends on the theorist's location in the intellectual field, where the value of rival symbolic goods (theories, conceptual systems, empirical data, etc.) depends in part on the degree to which differences among those goods are manifest.

One reason for thinking that there is a homology between the political arena, with its rivals for power, and the intellectual arena, with its rivals for legitimacy as interpreters, is precisely this need for each participant to differentiate himself or itself from the rest.[14] To newcomers, whether individuals or institutions, intellectuals or organizations, society always appears to be the symbolic or pragmatic property of various actors, agencies, and groups, each with its own place in the social structure. Any symbolic restructuring of society (a precondition of any political realignment) must take account of the constraints that rival systems of interpretation impose on the process of ideological production. New interpretations can enter the debate only if they recognize the validity of the questions regarded as fundamental at a particular historical juncture. This is tantamount to accepting as valid the common ground of the various competing theories. Of course, at the same time the new interpretation must differentiate itself from existing ones, whose acceptance by a segment of the public is in itself a kind of verification. Now, at any given moment, the number of different positions compatible with the dominant view of any topic and yet sufficiently differentiated from one another to win the adherence of a broad segment of the public is necessarily limited. This heightens competition among rival interpreters, who, in order to gain visibility within the realm of symbolic production (as well as in the political realm), are forced to do battle with one another for possession of those features and subtleties that distinguish one theory from another. If they fail to do this, the public may fail to recognize their particular product as distinctive and unique.

The truth of these propositions is particularly clear in the case of the cadres: since the number of possible definitions of the group is not unlimited, and since each new interpretation is obliged to distinguish itself from previously appropriated interpretations, the whole range of discussion (*problématique collective*) within which specific distinctions between actors and groups are made can be described as a transformational matrix, in which each version of the typology is based on a specific combination of distinctions defining the position of the cadres in relation to the positions of the two other previously defined and represented groups, the proletariat and the employers (*patronat*). It can be shown that, on the whole, the competing definitions proposed in the 1960s and 1970s were associated with one of the following positions: (1) cadres are a specific, autonomous group occupying an intermediate position between the proletariat and the employers and destined either to coexist with these two groups or, in extreme versions, to replace them (middle-class society as "classless society"); (2) cadres are the natural allies of employers (against the proletariat); (3) cadres are the natural allies of the proletariat (against the employers); and finally, two more complex versions, which involve either (4) consigning the employers to the past and identifying cadres as the new dominant class (technocracy), or (5) consigning the proletariat to the past and identifying cadres as the new working class.[15]

For example, it is difficult to understand the logic behind the invention of the new working class (associated, at least initially, with the CFDT and even more with the PSU) unless one sees that it was intended to solve the following problem: How to assign cadres a place in the social structure (*espace taxinomique*) that recognized the group's specificity and uniqueness (in contrast to what was then the Communist Party position on the question) while at the same time differentiating one's own position from those who held that the cadres were simply an autonomous group, a view associated with third-party ideology and hence branded as right wing? The solution was to produce a left-wing version of the third way distinct from the right-wing version with which this new vision of the future would ordinarily have been connected. Similarly, in order to understand how the Communist Party came to promote cadres from the status of "social parasites" in the 1950s to that of "intermediate working stratum" or "varied strata of employed intellectuals"[16] in the 1960s and to declare that cadres were "historically destined" to join forces with the working class, one must understand how the spread of new representations of society affected competition in the political arena.

Legalism and the obsession with boundaries

There is another reason why it proved possible to reconcile the social and political need for new representations with the constraints of academic discourse: there was an affinity between positivist sociology, with its penchant for abstract classification and construction of taxonomies (or, what comes to the same thing, typologies) composed of discrete, rationally defined, ordered (and usually hierarchically arranged) entities, and positivist legal thinking, which plays an important part in the process of institutionalization and objectification of new collective entities. Positivist sociology has laid down certain standards, or demarcation criteria, for distinguishing between work that is scientific and work that is not. Similarly, various apparatuses established administrative criteria intended to define the audience to which they addressed their appeals. These criteria were intended to transform practical groups into human capital by winning their permanent allegiance. They were also intended to establish a line beyond which retreat was impossible and to set goals for the future.

Legalistic thinking tends to fix and harden objective differences by embodying them in a form of discourse in which factual findings reproduce distinctions of which the facts are signs and in which examples are chosen for their normative value as precedents. This accounts for the existence of a homology between social scientific nomenclature and the language of politics (and especially of politicians). Consider, for example, the statement "Cadres are afraid of the future." As it happens, this comes from a scholarly journal. But it might equally well have been spoken by a representative of the CGC or any other cadre organization. The reason is that political rhetoric is in many ways functionally similar to sociological classification.[17] Group spokesmen, who enunciate the desires of a group's members, who personify the group and give it a voice, behave, implicitly at least, as if all members of the group they claim to *represent* were equivalent, as if all shared the same interests and the same values, and as if the groups were homogeneous and defined by clear boundaries. The use of collective nouns in politics (and polemic) is therefore similar to the use of typologies in sociology. Political rhetoric pretends that social groups or classes are, like classes in logic, homogeneous, finite, and unambiguously defined. It strives for symbolic unity. It provides individuals with an identity, with explicit principles and official membership criteria. It tells them explicitly whom they resemble, in what respect they have something in common with other people that is more essential, more decisive than the issues that divide them. And it enforces belief in the objective, scientifically established, almost natural character of the standards thus established. Technologies of social mobilization or (to use Goffman's term) "alignment" thus simplify the confusing texture of the social fabric; they provide an orderly, stylized representation of society[18] and reduce complexity to manageable proportions by identifying the property or properties that are really or objectively crucial, by constructing, as it were, a set of meridians and parallels that can be projected onto social space in such a way as to make it visible.

Finally, mobilization rhetoric can, if necessary to cement a working alliance, invoke the language of necessity and determination; in other words, it can invoke the external authority that is nowadays invested in science. For to be "determined" means two things. An outcome is determined if it is fixed in advance, stable and immutable; a person is determined if he is decided and resolute, bold and intrepid. Ideological struggles, in which the fundamental issue is to decide which set of mobilization criteria will win out in a given population,[19] are thus struggles to impose both a hierarchy of principles of determination and a hierarchy of sciences. For example, nationalism is generally associated with biological naturalism, while Marxism, in its dogmatic or statist versions, is associated with economic reification.[20]

As we have seen, the struggle to control and mobilize different social groups and classes representing a real or potential social capital (similar in many respects to the struggle between nations for control of territory) is played out not only on the battlefield of practice (in the form of competition for, say, seats on a works' council) but also in the realm of symbolism (over social taxonomies and representations). For symbolism orients and justifies practices, most notably by staking out the legitimate sphere of influence of each of the competing forces, that is, in practical terms, by defining which classes rival organizations or parties may legitimately claim to represent and what means of mobilization are available to them. Establishing the boundaries of a group, definining membership criteria, is one form of political action. Institutionalizing the boundaries between groups is always a political issue. The boundaries between groups (like the boundaries between nations[21]) are not natural, and a group that grows up around a magnetic pole in practice extends only as far as the magnetic pull of that central pole, i.e., until the pull of other attractors is felt with equal force. But when boundaries are objectified and institutionalized by quasi-legal action, they help to create objective differences that tend to justify their location. This is true not only of international boundaries (geographers speak of the "dynamic effects of borders"[22] but also of boundaries between groups and classes, whose distinctive features tend to be reinforced as institutionalization of boundaries makes member agents aware of how they differ from nonmember agents (as is shown, for instance, by H. Tajfel's experiments on social categorization[23]). Here again, legal objectification is something that mobilization technologies have in common with sociological methods of classification (construction of typologies, nomenclatures, codes, etc.). On what basis can one choose a representative sample of cadres? How can one distinguish between small merchants and big merchants? Where does the working class end? All these problems of sociology and statistics are similar, at least in the form in which they are usually framed, to the problems faced by jurists called upon to define what constitutes membership in some institutionalized, i.e., defined and delimited, group: Who is a citizen? Who belongs to a professional group protected by a *numerus clausus*, legal qualifications, etc. As is well known, one of the functions of the law is to fix for all time an existing state of the class struggle, by explicitly locating the boundaries between groups and by inventing criteria for assigning individuals to one group or another. In this sense, jurisprudence is the ultimate social theory, in which an objectification is reified once and for all, giving jurists the power to cause to exist in practice that which they state to be the case, even when the distinctions they introduce are relatively arbitrary ones.

To clarify the connection between substantialist sociology, with its reified representation of the class structure, and jurisprudence and to demonstrate that a common pattern of thought underlies both, let us examine the work of a jurist, Alain Le Bayon, as he sets out to define the "legal status of the cadre."[24] Le Bayon deplores the ambiguity and vagueness of the term "cadre": "The term 'cadre' is difficult to pin down with a precise definition." This, according to our author, is a state of affairs that no jurist can accept. He must make the notion of cadre "more precise." This "preliminary" task is "essential": "The existence of cadres cannot remain *purely de facto*,[25] of no consequence for law. On the contrary, the appearance of this particular category of employees must sooner or later be taken into consideration by the law." In effect, the "status" (*qualité*) of cadre "confers upon the beneficiary definite advantages, both in the realm of labor law and as regards supplementary retirement benefits. In order for an employee to enjoy these advantages his cadre status must be recognized" (p. 79). But, in order "to *define this notion with great precision* ... we must have at hand certain specific criteria." And so on.

Comparable to this jurist's attempt to move from a *de facto* state of affairs to a definition of legal status is the attempt by Marxist sociologists to determine group boundaries and membership criteria in an implicitly legalistic manner. They attempt to define criteria for determining who exploits and who is exploited, who rules and who is oppressed – as one might imagine, the answers to these questions are not immediately obvious. To appreciate the difficulty, consider, for example, the line of the Communist Party and the CGT, which in the 1960s held that cadres could be defined both as "producers of surplus value" and, in another light, as agents responsible for "extracting and collecting surplus value" (though it is not specified whether these are the same or different individuals).[26] This solution to the problem is comparable to the theory of the "average peasant's" dual nature, formulated by Lenin in 1919 as the "basis of current tactics, coercion plus persuasion": "The average peasant cultivates the earth with his hands. He is therefore a worker.... But in time of famine his product – grain – becomes a treasure that gives him the means to speculate and thus to become an exploiter."[27] Today's "cadre problem" forces workers' parties to confront many of the same questions raised by the "peasant problem" in years past. Consider, for example, the problem of distinguishing between "average peasants" and "kulaks." This was put to Lenin in 1920 by members of the Communist section of the Eighth Congress of Soviets, and Lenin answered thus: "The peasants know better than we do.... In the countryside they know perfectly well how to tell the difference."[28] Of course, a few years later manipulation of the definition of kulak was used as a weapon against the small and middle peasantry.[29] Thanks to the "dual nature" theory, it was possible to admit cadres to worker-dominated organizations while maintaining the distinction between "cadre" and "worker" and denying cadre members positions of authority that they might have claimed given the nature of their socially produced skills. It is impossible to understand debates on the cadre issue in the Communist Party and the CGT, especially before 1968 (debates characterized by vacillation between the hope of bringing cadres into the Party and fear of seeing them confounded with other "workers," especially industrial workers) without appreciating the almost obsessional need to protect the working class from bourgeois pollution of any kind, to protect both the "theoretical" purity of the Marxist definition and the "practical" purity of a Party in which the working class played a "leading role." Surely the problem of the internal and external boundaries of the cadre category would have proved less thorny had it not raised an issue of fundamental importance for any worker-dominated party or union: that of the "boundaries" of the "proletariat" and of the relations between it and its external "allies."

Hard-liners

Consider, next, another example of theoreticism in which the relationship between positivism and legalism is particularly clear: the section on cadres in M. Bouvier-Ajam and G. Mury's *Les classes sociales en France*.[30] Based on a 1959 report by Maurice Thorez to the Communist Party's Central Committee and bolstered by numerous excerpts from *Das Kapital*, this text, typical of the work of Communist Party sociologists on the cadres in this period, is entirely taken up with questions of boundaries, which are treated in legalistic fashion. Caught, like technocratic discourse, between the "informative" and the "performative," between "scientific" legitimacy and political legitimacy, between the need to eradicate "theoretical confusions" (p. 66) and the need to correct "dangerous pragmatic orientations" (p. 67), the text in question attempts to draw a line, in two senses: a dividing line between the "working class" and "intermediate strata," and a guiding line, an answer to the question "What should be the relationship between the 'working class' and its 'allies?'"

Recalling Lenin's view that "only a specific class, namely, the urban workers or, more generally, the factory or industrial workers, is capable of leading the masses of the exploited," the authors note that "Lenin, when he wrote *The Great Initiative*, was grappling with Russian reality. In other words, his thinking was shaped by a society in which the classes were sharply divided from one another and industry was concentrated in large firms. *Hence his efforts to enunciate principles were not frustrated by the existence of 'fringe groups' or composite milieux.*"[31] According to Bouvier-Ajam and Mury, this makes "his definition all the more interesting." In other words, Lenin was able to develop a "pure theory" because the social reality he had before his eyes objectively embodied the distinctions on which his theory relied. Hence he could enunciate his "principles" of classification with the utmost clarity, whereas observers in other, more "composite" societies had to face the more complicated question of how to deal with "fringe groups."

Next comes a discussion of the "principles" just mentioned: "According to Lenin, office workers (*employés*) and industrial workers (*ouvriers*) constitute distinct strata or classes, since only the latter actually take part in the production process" (p. 65). One must be careful, however, not to confuse the office workers envisioned here, figments of pure theory, with what is normally meant by the term "office workers," namely, empirical individuals who happen to work in offices: "Again, we must stress that it is the 'office worker' (*employé*) in the Marxist sense that we are trying to define. Needless to say, this characterization does not apply to the wage-earners (*salariés*) who are commonly called 'office workers' (*employés*) but who are part of the collective laborer, the producer of value" (p. 64).

As this example shows, the dilemma faced by this particular version of positivist theorizing is that it cannot completely abandon the usual taxonomies (and eschew the use of words such as *cadres, employés* and *patrons* – borrowed from common parlance – for this would be to cut the party off from ordinary social experience), nor can it abandon itself to them, precisely because it sees the scientific enterprise as a process of rationalist reification of common systems of denotation and classification (together with associated modes of perception). The result is that sociologists adhering to this line are condemned to produce theories whose status is ambiguous, theories that borrow their terminology and taxonomies from common parlance, but, rather than describe how these things are used socially and explore the symbolic interactions to which they give rise, attempt to define them rationally, independent of the practice and experience of social agents. This explains why they are inclined to rely on a technology-based description of the division of labor to provide universal, abstract criteria for distinguishing between social groups and for developing "typologies" based on a version of "obective reality" that owes nothing to either experience or practice. Such divine understanding assumes that the universe consists of substances having nothing whatsoever to do with the ordinary world of appearances, much as one constructs a formal taxonomy by applying rules of inclusion and exclusion derived from a transcendental principle of some sort.[32]

The invention of the "new working class"

One cannot understand the controversy that erupted in the 1960s over the "new working class" without knowing something about the social interests that lay behind the contending theoretical interests and influenced attempts to account theoretically for recent social changes. Once again, struggles over "turf" [power, position etc.] between parties, unions, etc. (*instances de mobilisation*) raged in the background, tending to obscure the issues in the scientific debate. The notion that postwar social and economic changes had produced a new working class was really an argument about "new social strata," and about cadres in particular. The novelty of the new working class thesis lay in the way in which it rearranged the terms of social taxonomy. To what positions in the social structure should the word "worker" be applied? Was today's "worker" the same as yesterday's "proletarian?" Did "cadres" belong to the working class? In the 1950s the idea of a "new middle class" had made it possible to redefine the political implications of the "third way" after the collapse of corporatism. Similarly, in the 1960s, the idea of the new working class aroused considerable enthusiasm in Marxist circles, which can be best understood in light of the history of the relationship between the academic left and the Communist Party. The prophetic claim that the traditional working class would soon give way to a new working class enabled intellectuals who had resigned or been expelled from the Party in the late 1950s to transfer to a new group, still undefined politically, hopes that had been invested after the Liberation in the proletariat and in the Communist Party as its legitimate representative.

Questions that had stirred Marxist parties since the turn of the century were again at the center of the debate: Pauperization or enrichment? Two classes or three? Is the proletariat growing or shrinking? But this time the answers were relatively new. They incorporated ideas about bureaucracy and technocracy that had been developed since the 1930s (often by ex-Trotskyites like Burnham and Rizzi[33]). The new synthesis emphasized the shift from ownership to control, denied the pauperization thesis, noted the growth of the tertiary sector, and defined the proletariat in terms not of poverty but of loss of collective power and individual autonomy, i.e., in terms of liberty. This invalidated existing taxonomies and cast doubt on existing party and union organizations. At the same time it justified efforts to form new kinds of political organizations. More generally, it legitimated the social and political ideas of the political–intellectual avant-garde consisting of individuals expelled from the Communist Party and disenchanted veterans of the reformist left of the 1950s (both Socialists and Catholics). Many were involved with the PSU, at least initially.[34] But those who sought to develop a new picture of society and at the same time to alter the political power structure found that they had to differentiate themselves not only from the Communist Party and the Marxist vulgate but also from the kind of thinking about the middle classes that had developed around the CGC after World War II. The 1960s were not the 1930s: it was no longer enough to allude to a third way to justify one's desire to bring about a revolution while at the same time criticizing the organizations that claimed both to represent the working class and to hold a monopoly on revolutionary ideals, namely, the CGT and the PCF. The new ploy was to engage in a kind of taxonomic manipulation: to create new groups or to alter the boundaries between existing groups, to change the relationship between the objective social structure and the words used to characterize it, and to modify the connotations of words in the social lexicon. This was essentially a political maneuver, since it was aimed at redefining class boundaries, class relations, and class representations and hence at dividing up the political turf in a new way. Nowhere is this maneuver better described than in Pierre Belleville's *Une nouvelle classe ouvrière*, which reformulated Serge Mallet's analyses in terms useful for political and union organizing.[35]

To counter the notion that the proletariat (as traditionally defined) was shrinking relative to other groups and would ultimately be replaced by a broad middle class, and to enhance the influence and political power of the working class, it was necessary to shift the boundary between the middle class and the working class. The working class, in Belleville's words, had to "conquer new frontiers": "*Workers cannot stand by idly and wait for their ranks to swell. They can set out in search of new frontiers. Their boundaries are in dispute.*[36] When workers say that the number of non-self-employed persons is larger than ever before, others respond that income leveling is bringing the vast majority of workers into the middle class."[37] Now, one way for workers to swell their ranks was to claim that "engineers and cadres," who differed from other workers only "in the level of their skills," actually belonged to the working class.[38] For example, at Neyrpic, an "advanced" factory near Grenoble, the CGT, "overtaken" by events, had failed to see that "the leading sectors (*secteurs moteurs*) in the plant are the leading sectors in the struggle"[39] and that the "alliance that was forged to defend Neyrpic ... reflects the heightened consciousness of cadres and engineers as well as students and research workers."[40] For Belleville, the new working class was formed by adding and incorporating new categories of workers to the old working class (in keeping with the logic of union organizing).[41]

Serge Mallet seems at first sight to be proposing something more radical. His theory, based on an evolutionary model, is that a new working class is gradually taking the place of the old. First came the worker as craftsmen, then the worker as laborer, now the worker as engineer: "Does the electronics technician represent the synthesis in a dialectical process in which the oppressed, robotized assembly worker is the antithesis and the old-fashioned industrial mechanic the thesis?"[42] For Mallet, the old working class is associated with traditional sectors of industry (such as "mining, traditional metalworking, construction, food processing, cement," etc.) and is on the wane, while the new working class consists of "workers, technicians, and cadres profoundly 'integrated' into the most advanced, most crucial sectors of industrial society, so 'integrated,' in fact, that they are in a position to see the possibilities for human liberation implicit in technological progress and to rebel against any attempt to foreclose those possibilities." In these advanced sectors, "job changes have brought workers and cadres closer together." Now the relation between them is one of "hierarchy within the same social group." Furthermore, "modern industry encourages subtle gradations, and the distance between the worker, the technician, and the cadre is diminishing steadily."[43]

As "technical hierarchies" replace "social hierarchies," as the "bourgeoisified proletariat" gradually joins consumer society,[44] and as the "proletarianized" middle classes (and even bourgeoisie) go to work for "bureaucratized," "Taylorized" firms in which even intellectual labor is "fragmented" (*parcellisé*), a new, historically unprecedented class will arise, one that obviously will have a great deal in common with the new middle class unless, through a kind of definition by denial, it is identified with the working class whose "revolutionary mission" it is destined to accomplish.[45]

The development of this new theoretical position, which maintained the revolutionary/conservative distinction while neutralizing the opposition between workers and supervisors, made it possible to dismiss as conservatives all who argued that the middle classes enjoyed a certain autonomy: on the one hand the CGC, exquisitely sensitive to any threat of social pollution and ready at a moment's notice to rebuild the symbolic barricades separating cadres from other workers, and on the other hand the CGT with its much subtler view, that by proclaiming an alliance between workers and technicians, engineers, and cadres while keeping cadres isolated from other workers within the union organization, one could maintain the working-class monopoly on revolution and yet argue that the working class and the cadre class, though distinct, shared certain interests in common.

Thus Mallet was able to criticize the effort by the CGT and PCF to incorporate cadres into the Marxist taxonomy and the union and party apparatuses and to accuse both organizations of "third-partyism," tarring the CGT and the CGC with the same brush. The CGT's new position (which was to recognize that cadres do indeed enjoy some measure of autonomy, to admit them into the union, and to defend their interests even though these might conflict with workers' interests, particularly in regard to salaries) could thus be characterized by Mallet as reformist, conservative, and outdated.[46]

The models on which the new working class analyses were based, and the social interests they represented, emerge with particular clarity in works published just after the strikes of May–June 1968, which claim to explain the historical significance of the crisis. What was unique about May '68, we are told, was the arrival on the scene of a new revolutionary class in which students were joined by engineers, technicians, cadres, and research workers (precisely those whom Frédéric Bon and Michel-Antoine Burnier dubbed new intellectuals and Serge Mallet and Alain Touraine called new proletarians[47]). The crisis, it is held, not only revealed an economic and technological mutation but also suggested the decline of the traditional working class and of the PCF and CGT, which were destined to be replaced, respectively, by new social strata and the new left. This no doubt accounts for the great interest that the sociologists and journalists who popularized these new clichés showed in the scattered and relatively insignificant strikes by cadres that accompanied strikes by workers, mainly in large, public-sector firms (see chapter 4 below).

The most systematic statement of the view that there was a connection between the emergence of a new working class and the crisis of May–June 1968 can be found in a work published by Alain Touraine in the fall of 1968.[48] Touraine's interpretation of the crisis is based in part on an evolutionary model, summed up in two contrastages of France: "coal mines, vineyards, and bureaucracy" versus "electronics, chemicals, automobiles, and education" (p. 162), i.e., the past versus the future, the declining classes versus the rising classes, etc. The "old working class" (p. 171), "manual workers in large firms," "producers" (p. 156), "miners" (p. 171), "workers, a group in relative eclipse" (p. 117) – this group, according to Touraine, "is no longer the historical agent of revolution in our society" (p. 157). Motivated mainly by the desire for "higher wages" (p. 173), they were waging a "rear-guard action in declining industries" (p. 168) and had "joined in the Poujadist defense of the weak of every ilk" (p. 177). In contrast, the "new technical workers and engineers" (p. 161), "technicians and research workers" (p. 168), "cadres and technicians" (p. 169), "office workers, designers, and planners" (p. 169), "workers in leading industries" (p. 155) – this was the group that had launched a "new form of class struggle, as different from the old as the State Planning Commission is different from the Comité des forges and IBM is different from a family-owned textile factory" (p. 191). These "rising" occupational groups, among which the CFDT has made "inroads" (p. 160), have shown themselves to be "inventively aggressive" (p. 173), calling for "qualitative changes" (p. 169) in the workplace and bandying about the "slogans of self-management" (p. 173). Henceforth it is they who must be seen as "the primary adversary of the ruling class" (p. 177).

The following year the theme of the new working class and of "May as the revolt of the new intellectuals" was taken up by Roger Garaudy,[49] whose version of this familiar refrain is interesting chiefly for demonstrating that there is no end to the possibilities of symbolic distinction. Totally won over by the new orthodoxy – the celebration of the computer and of the "liberating" virtues of automation, "cybernetics," the society of leisure, the vision of the future without a proletariat – Garaudy was still speaking on behalf of the Communist Party when he wrote *Le grand tournant du socialisme*, which is addressed primarily to an audience of Party members. But he must forge a new position for himself, and he does this by denying that the "new class" that he is talking about is the "new working class," even if it shares all the properties of that class (which, as we have seen, is itself the product of a denial: the new working class is not the new middle class, even if, again, both share all the same properties).

"New working class" or "classless society"?

Gradually shedding its revolutionary aura, the "new working class" thesis was itself absorbed into the dominant ideology only a few years after its appearance and refined to meet the needs and expectations of new segments of the bourgeoisie. As the idea of the new working class became increasingly familiar, it lent itself to different social uses. Although developed initially as a critical response to both the Communist Party and the notion that "middle-class society equals classless society," it was now coopted by those who wished to herald the imminent demise of the working class, both new and old. Because the very idea of the new working class referred implicitly to rival theories, it proved to be an unstable notion that lent itself to a variety of reinterpretations. As with an optical illusion, a slight change in the angle of view – or, in this case, of vocabulary or the order of argument – sufficed to produce a new image, closer to one of the more familiar, established positions. This no doubt accounts for the rapid spread of the "new middle class" idea, which could soon be found in a thousand versions and variations reflecting the expectations of different social groups. Though first used to justify a broader definition of the working class, it later came to signify the decline of the working class and the rise of the middle class. One reason why such cooptation proved so easy was that it actually represented a return to the sources of the "new working class" idea, whose proponents had merely reworked the old argument that automation, the decline of manual labor, expanded educational opportunities, and so forth would ultimately lead to the disappearance of the working class. In order to use the idea of the new working class in support of the new mode of economic and social regulation that developed in the 1950s and 1960s, it therefore sufficed to transform the forecast of "revolution" into an optimistic assessment of the future, based on belief in the "inevitable" benefits of technological progress.

An example can be found in the version of the thesis put forward by Julien Cheverny in *Les cadres nouveaux prolétaires*[50], which helped to popularize the new prophecy. A believer in the "bourgeoisification of workers" (p. 22), Cheverny predicted that automation would eradicate the dividing line between workers and cadres:

> There is no longer . . . any distinction between what the worker does and what the cadre does or between the productive and the unproductive worker or between the secondary and tertiary sector. There is no longer any dividing line between the cadre, in the sense of the planner, supervisor, and overseer, and the worker, in the sense of the person who adapts the technology to the job and puts ideas into practice. . . . Now there are only employees (*agents*) who all exert some influence over production, which no one person controls directly. (p. 72)
>
> One wonders if there will come a time when the very notion of cadre will have to go, when it will become necessary to speak not of cadres but of the intelligentsia of the working class, including the new working class that has been ushered in by automation. (p. 73)

It would not be difficult to follow the spread of the "new working class" idea still further, as it made its way into the very heart of industrial ideology in the 1970s (when, in order to restore the symbolic order shaken by the events of 1968, the ruling class invested in "social" measures and revived "optimistic" views of the "future of the working class," elsewhere described as being on its last legs).[51] One milestone was Michel Drancourt's article, "The New Status of the Worker," which declared that "Karl Marx's proletarian worker is on his way out," because "the evolution of the modern world is improving the condition of the worker" (*Entreprise* 810, 19–25 March 1971, pp. 4–15).

As the substitution of the word "condition" for "class" indicates, the move from intellectual journals to trade magazines came at the cost of some selective simplification. The magazines could afford to dispense with the hedges and subtleties found in books and articles destined for scholarly consumption and retained only those aspects of the "new working class" thesis that seemed useful and appropriate to this new audience.

Traces of the new working class can be found in ideological productions of the most diverse and disparate sort. Once the idea spread from the precursors, the professional cultural producers, to the innumerable reproducers, many of them nameless amateurs, it became more or less indistinguishable from the general ideology of the 1960s and 1970s. In order to understand the intellectual background of the idea one would have to reconstruct the spirit of the age, which the more technical discussions both reaffirmed and camouflaged in the euphemistic terms of "sociological theory." And one would have to understand all the peculiarities of the historical moment that defined that spirit.[52] Any such reconstruction would surely give some weight to two independent phenomena: first, many intellectuals renounced the political hopes and aspirations of the immediate postwar years, especially after the Twentieth Congress of the Communist Party and the assumption of power by de Gaulle put an end to thoughts of near-term political change, and second, the economic growth of the postwar period, which seemed to prove that the optimism of innovative segments of the bourgeoisie had been warranted. Economic growth affected the intellectual climate in two ways. Indirectly, the modernization of some sectors of the economy, the increase in the size of the average production unit, automation, and expanded availability of material and symbolic goods (and of educational opportunities) gave some semblance of credibility to the myth that manual labor was obsolete and that the condition of the working class was improving. But the direct effects of economic change were perhaps even more important: the number of high-level jobs (*positions dominantes*) increased, particularly in the institutions responsible for producing symbolic goods and services (universities, radio and television, polling and market research, advertising, etc.), thus expanding the range of opportunities open to the innovating bourgeoisie and in particular to intellectuals. Hence the promise of a "radiant future" gradually moved from the realm of eschatology into the realm of realistic expectations.

Listen to the words of one informant, who abandoned political activism in order to devote himself to his career.[53]

For me, the main factor was the economic growth of the 1960s. . . . Until 1958 nothing much was happening in my career. When de Gaulle came in in '58, I felt that politically we were done for. . . . We said to ourselves, Now's the time to tend to business. And we caught the crest of the wave. Things started to change socially. Before that none of us had any personal plans. And then society took a strange turn. I remember reading stories in *L'Observateur* about left-wing intellectuals that talked about whiskey and beach houses. I was flabbergasted. We didn't understand what was happening. It was the operators who made out, the wheeler-dealers. Things changed. We had been idealists, but we saw that things were about to change. And then there were real new possibilities.

Better than anyone else Michel Crozier captured the new spirit of the 1960s in an article on intellectuals published in 1964. But Crozier extend to the whole of French society an optimism characteristic mainly of the dominant class, and especially of intellectuals associated with rising segments of that class. The affluent society, he says, will finally put an end to the traditional intellectual, with his bohemianism and his crises of conscience, the intellectual who is conservative *because* he is "revolutionary." Prosperity, says Crozier, will break "the vicious circle of impotence and revolutionary verbiage." It will call forth a new kind of intellectual, free of ideological fetters, ready for action, eager to participate along with young businessmen and executives in the activities of progressive political "clubs," and prepared to use his newfound skills to further the cause of economic development.[54]

Scientific representations and union representations

If social philosophy were addressed solely to specialists, its truth would never be tested. If theorists do on occasion develop representations of society that are not entirely without foundation, the reason is that their theories must to some extent reflect the interests of a nonspecialist audience. Behind each of the theories that claim to define the cadre's position we find groups of people whose members claim the title "cadre" on various grounds and ask to be represented not only for what they are but as typical of cadres in general, as models for others to imitate. To be sure, the characters of the collective persons who inhabit social theory are never direct reflections of the objective properties of the membership of, say, a political party or trade union, if only because group characters are after all nothing more than statistical aggregates. In real life many factors affect membership characteristics, whereas in the realm of representation paradigms always have sharp outlines (thanks to objectification and stylization). Still, it is reasonable to suppose that the various theoretical definitions of the cadre are in part designed to meet the expectations of the (actual or potential) memberships of the various organizations competing for the group's support. In other words, it is as though sociologists and other specialists in the production of social representations – who, as we have seen, are related in various ways to the contending forces in the field of politics and who, even if they were as autonomous as they claim, would have to depend on those forces in various ways (for contacts, access to meetings, knowledge of internal problems, etc.) – have a tendency to define the cadre by attributing to anyone who describes himself as such properties that in fact belong specifically to the segment of the population from which the organization or agency with which they are associated normally recruits its members.

One way to test this hypothesis is to consider cadres' unions. The proportion of cadres belonging to unions is much smaller in private industry than in the public sector. Unionization rates are determined in part by the costs and benefits of union membership, not only for each person taken individually but also for each subgroup of cadres.[55]

The rate of union membership among cadres is generally put at 12–15% (though the definition of "cadre" used to arrive at this figure is rarely specified). It is impossible to state the size of the major cadres' unions with precision (and, in any case, without analyzing the way in which membership is defined it may not even make sense to try to determine a precise figure). The Confédération générale des cadres (CGC) claims 300,000 members, mainly in the private sector (the union has made little headway in the public sector, despite its efforts). The Union générale des ingénieurs, cadres, techniciens (UGICT–CGT) claims a membership of some 200,000 "engineers, cadres, supervisory personnel, and technicians." And the Union confédérale des ingénieurs et cadres (UCC–CFDT) has around 40,000 members. A more accurate index of relative size can be deduced from the results of elections of representatives to various cadres' funds and works councils. In the most recent AGIRC elections, the CGC received 57% of the votes, the CGT 10%, the CFDT 7%, independents 14% and other unions 12%. In works' council elections held in 1974 the CGC received 36.6% of the votes in the third college (engineers and cadres) and 17.1% of the votes in the second college, compared with 11% for the

CFDT and 7.8% for the CGT (which, by way of comparison, received 25% in the second college).[56]

Information gleaned from a variety of sources,[57] each yielding fragmentary information (not all of it statistical) about particular cadre subgroups, suggests that cadres are less likely to join unions if (1) they work for small firms (most notably because the smaller the firm, the more likely the cadres are to come from the traditional self-employed classes or to have been at one-time independent employers themselves); (2) they work in the private sector (cadres' unions are better established, better tolerated, and more powerful in nationalized firms, hence the cost of joining a union is lower); (3) they hold high-level jobs; (4) their jobs are less technical and more involved with sales or finance (or direct supervision of workers); (5) they possess prestigious advanced degrees (from the Grandes Ecoles, say) or are autodidacts (union membership involves costs without compensatory benefits for cadres with prestigious degrees, who already enjoy the greatest job security and best career opportunities, while autodidacts, who owe everything to the firm that has trained them and whose experience is valueless on the job market, run a considerable risk if they join a union[58]); (6) they are young (age reduces career opportunities, so that joining a union represents a smaller risk for an older cadre).[59] Conversely, especially in big firms with large, well-financed, active works' councils, union activity (especially in the CGC) can bring prestige, power, and influence to cadres whose careers have proved disappointing. These same factors seem to explain membership in all cadres' unions (CGC, UGICT–CGT, and UCC–CFDT).

The CGC, toward which employers exhibit "benevolent neutrality," has always aimed its actions more at the government than at employers directly (it even supported employers against the government immediately after World War II). Today it is the most powerful cadres' union and the only one that represents cadres exclusively in all its dealings, from the highest levels of government to the shop floor. Joining this union is therefore a cadre's least risky option (although in some firms the risk is still considerable). This accounts for certain characteristics of its membership. The CGC is better represented than either the UGICT–CGT or the UCC–CFDT in small firms, where management control is tightest.[60] Many of its members are especially vulnerable to direct management controls and pressures. It is commonly estimated that only a third of the members of the CGC are "cadres" as defined by collective bargaining agreements (which generally give a broader definition than is implied by the "coefficient 300 or above" criterion, probably the most restrictive way of looking at the group); the rest are technicians, low-level sales personnel (about 20%), and supervisory personnel, especially foremen (around 35%). The latter two groups include many autodidacts and others of working-class or middle-class background, and those who occupy strategic positions (supervising workers or selling products to other companies) are subject to closer ethical and political scrutiny than are engineers or technicians.[61]

The CGC's membership criteria are broad: there are no restrictions on salary coefficient, and any employee exercising some measure of authority in the firm is accepted. This lax standard reflects the interests of the union, which like any pressure group derives its strength in part from sheer numbers. For the elite of CGC members, the engineers (mainly industrial engineers) and others who hold leadership roles in the union, lower-level cadres, foremen, and salesmen serve as shock troops.

According to one CGC official, the union speaks to all cadres, from executives down to shop foremen and supervisors. The CGC's very broad definition of the term "cadre" fits the union's third-party ideology: its purpose is in part to homogenize the social space between employers and the proletariat, thus helping to create a broad middle class. In defining the place of supervisory personnel in the work force, the CGC uses INSEE socioprofessional categories, adds up the figures for workers classified by one-digit codes (which includes primary and secondary schoolteachers, groups having little in common with the private-sector cadres whom the CGC represents), and comes up with 4,254,000 cadres, or 19.5% of the working population. But the end is not yet in sight: "The growth in the number of supervisory personnel will, like any other growth phenomenon, gradually level off and approach an asymptote, which, with all due allowance for the uncertainties inherent in any such prediction, we would put at one-third of the work force."[62]

All indications are that lower-level cadres far outnumber higher-level cadres and executives on CGC membership rolls. While the minimal risk of joining encourages lower-level cadres to sign up, the benefits to individuals of membership are no longer sufficient to attract large numbers of higher-level cadres. Thus, paradoxically, the CGC, which of all the cadres' unions is most acceptable to employers and closest to them in ideology, is also the one with the lowest percentage of members holding college degrees.[63] There is a clear relationship between the CGC's image of the cadre and the characteristics of its members: the majority of CGC members are lower-level cadres, without advanced degrees, and close to the traditional petite bourgeoisie. They owe their success, or so they believe, to stubborn, hard work and often supervise other workers. Hence they are inclined to accept a traditional view of the cadre as a person in authority, a leader.[64] This makes it possible to be fairly generous in awarding the title while still establishing a clear boundary between cadres and other, subordinate workers (the class from which many CGC members come originally). CGC members naturally favor using the term "cadre" to cover the entire hierarchy from foreman to chief executive officer and are willing to open the union (in a formal sense, at any rate) to all cadres. Members find it reassuring to think that they are part of a vast and powerful middle class, destined to become that chimera of chimeras, the dominant class in the classless society. Somehow this belief magically does away with everyday reminders of their subordinate status.

Since the mid-1960s the CGC has been torn by internal conflict born of tensions between low-level and high-level cadres and between cadres in the public and private sectors. The union is not a monolith. Differences between the rear guard and the advance guard erupted in a series of conflicts between a "conservative" faction led first by Malterre and later by Charpentié and a "reform" faction led by Gilbert Nasse from 1963 to 1966 and, after Nasse's expulsion from the union in 1967,[65] by Jean-Louis Mandinaud, who in 1969 quit the CGC to found the Union des cadres et techniciens (UCT).[66] On one side in these conflicts we find private-sector, relatively low-level cadres from local union branches representing mainly salesmen and foremen, and on the other side cadres from nationalized firms and high-technology, capital-intensive industries. The UCT's strength lies primarily in the state-run electricity monopoly EDF, in the petroleum industry, and in banking (especially Crédit lyonnais, which was headed at the time of its founding by François Bloch-Lainé) and to a lesser extent in chemicals, metals, and aeronautics. Its main demand is for cadres to be allowed to participate in the management of the firm and, relatedly, for increased use of a new form of corporate management referred to in France as *conseil de surveillance* or *conseil à directoires*.[67] The UCT (which sees cadres' unions as the "coming thing in trade unionism ... leading to real and positive changes in corporate organization" – *Cahiers de l'UCT*, no. 2) is to the older CGC locals (which it often accuses of Poujadism) what college-educated managers employed by large, bureaucratized corporations are to the traditional petite bourgeoisie.[68] Its leaders are sympathetic to what they call "German-style social democracy." In some respects these conflicts are merely continuations of now-forgotten postwar battles between the CGC and ex-Resistance fighters who worked for reform from within the bureaucracy.

In contrast to the CGC, the UGICT is the union to which employers are most hostile. Hence a cadre runs a considerable risk by joining the UGICT. The union is affiliated with the CGT, the largest trade-union confederation in France, with close ties to the Communist Party (for example, René Le Guen, former secretary-general of the UGICT, is a member of the PCF's central committee). The UGICT's politics account for the peculiarities of its membership. Its association with the Communist Party tends to drive away those supervisory personnel most vulnerable to pressure from their employers, personnel often occupying strategic positions and under direct management control; it also alienates the better-educated cadres and those of bourgeois background who occupy fairly high-level positions.

Accordingly, the UGICT is least powerful in small and medium-sized firms and in the more traditional sectors of industry, where most cadres either have personal connections with their employers or are former workers or children of workers indebted to their employers for the opportunity to move up to a higher status. For similar reasons, the proportion of lower-level cadres, autodidacts, and direct supervisory personnel (foremen, personnel specialists, etc.) is much lower in the UGICT than in the CGC. In other words, of those cadres who are current or potential union members (a fairly small percentage of all cadres, as we have seen) the number of potential UGICT recruits is quite small. The UGICT is most strongly represented in sectors of industry where trade-unionism is fairly well protected, especially in nationalized firms such as EDF and, to a lesser extent, in metals, automobiles, aeronautics, etc.

The UGICT tends, moreover, to attract cadres with formal degrees, who are comparatively safe from dismissal or other disciplinary action and who face better prospects in the job market than do autodidacts. But UGICT members tend to hold low-prestige degrees, from the lesser engineering schools, technical training institutes (IUT's),[69] etc. Many are employed in manufacturing, but in technical jobs, not in positions where they supervise other workers directly. They are typically production engineers with run-of-the-mill credentials, former technicians promoted to the rank of engineer, etc. Finally, many UGICT members come from working-class families and think of their union "militancy" as a mark of class loyalty.[70]

Thus the differences between the UGICT and the CGC correspond to differences in the characteristics and interests of their members: though similar in their relations to capital and the powers that be (even if the modalities and relations of domination differ), members of the two unions differ in several respects: qualifications (CGC members tend to be autodidacts, UGICT members graduates of relatively unprestigious schools), position in the firm (direct supervision or sales for CGC members, technical functions for UGICT members), and types of employer (private sector for CGC members, public sector for UGICT members). As we saw earlier, the position of the UGICT with respect to cadres is rather ambiguous. It recognizes their specificity but refuses to concede that they form a class. Rather, they are said to constitute a stratum of society with a dual character (they both produce surplus value and collect it) and are termed "allies" of the "working class."[71] This ambiguous attitude is well-suited to the character of the UGICT membership. To be sure, the lower-middle-class cadres who make up the bulk of the union's membership hold no monopoly on ambiguity. But the objective situation in which they find themselves makes it easier for them than for, say, the typical member of the CGC to repudiate the mystifications involved in the image of the cadre as a leader and a company man and to capture the ambiguity of their position at work in the ambiguity of their positions on the issues. For one thing, they enjoy enough advantages over most workers to want to maintain the distance between them and the working class. They do not necessarily favor indiscriminately linking supervisory personnel and workers as exploited employees. Such a move would be in contradiction with their overall social and professional strategies (as one UGICT official puts it, "when you talk about the 'deskilling of foremen,' the foremen are the first to disagree"). In another respect, however, UGICT members, most of whom have some sort of degree and enjoy some measure of job security (especially those who work for nationalized firms in relatively prosperous times) are sufficiently independent-minded to recognize that they are exploited. They also have an interest, especially if they are of working-class origin, in declaring their solidarity with the class whose domination by the bourgeoisie they help to ensure.

The ambiguity in the CGT's positions and its cautious behavior in the past make no sense unless one recognizes that they are the result of an objective contradiction. A union dominated by workers, the CGT cannot increase its appeal to engineers and cadres without recognizing the specificity of a professional and social group that formed outside its sphere of influence and in opposition to its membership, and whose unity is based in part on a negative principle: the *difference* between it and the working class, as concretely embodied in a hierarchy of material and symbolic rewards (i.e., in salary differentials and power relations). The CGT (like the PCF) is therefore obliged to mimic the CGC and employers' organizations and to address cadres as though they constituted an undifferentiated group. It cannot afford to mount an open attack on the group's symbolic unity.

The UCC–CFDT, the union about which we have the best information, differs from both the CGC and the UGICT in that its members include the elite of cadres, the higher status levels of the group. Having given up on the idea of becoming a "mass" union and of battling with its rivals by inflating the size of its membership, the UCC is the only cadres' union to have established a clear boundary between cadres and other non-blue-collar personnel (*non-ouvriers–non-cadres*[72]), limiting its recruitment in the private sector to engineers and cadres as defined – narrowly – by collective convention and in the public sector to those designated "cadre A."

Accordingly, the UCC can claim to be more representative of cadres than either the CGC or the UGICT even though it has a much smaller membership. In the contest for representativity (i.e., for legitimacy), the union with the largest membership is not necessarily the most influential, because cadres as a group are defined by their relative scarcity. Vote totals in union elections do not prove that a union is representative of a particular group unless the union can show that its voters are *entitled* to delegate power to it. Therein lies another paradox of cadre unionism: How is it possible to be the "mass organization" of an "elite group?" The cadres' unions face two contradictory sets of requirements. On the one hand they must increase their membership so as to make themselves "representative" in a quantitative sense. The easiest and most common way to do this is to encourage lower-level cadres to join (this strategy is relatively easy to implement as long as the risks of union membership are not too great, since membership may in itself have symbolic value to those who have only recently become cadres or who have been assimilated by the group). On the other hand, however, the unions must try to maintain their social homogeneity, and accepting too many "dubious" members tends to diminish their "representativity" (in the qualitative sense) and hence their power.

The UCC has a strong presence in the public sector (where it represents 20% of all cadres) and especially in nationalized industries (where it represents 31%), as well as in high-technology private firms (in the chemical, petroleum, and metals industries, for example).[73] Members generally hold high-level degrees: according to various studies 60–80% have attended college (much higher than the proportion in the cadre population at large, no matter what definition of "cadre" one chooses), and around half are graduates of one of the Grandes Ecoles. Finally, the UCC has many more engineers than cadres among its members: 21% are production engineers, and a full 32% are engineers working in research and development (R&D). More than half of all UCC members are associated in one way or another with R&D activities. This figure is remarkable when compared with the distribution of cadre employment reported by some of the more broadly based studies.[74]

It appears that the production engineers associated with the UCC come mainly from the old CFTC (surveys of UCC members, whose average age is 41, show that 35–45% of them belonged to the CFTC). Within the CFDT these are the last representatives of traditional Social Catholicism, which as we have seen exalted the virtues of the leader and the human and social role of leadership. Listen, for example, to the words of one UCC militant, an engineer and the son of an industrialist, who was interviewed by A. Andrieux and J. Lignon:

> I joined the union a year after starting work. As a student I had been politically active, and given my background union activity seemed the natural thing to do. . . . We think that cadres should be listened to, that their opinions should be taken seriously. But that can't happen without some kind of organization. . . . I really like the slogan that the CFDT used last May (May '68): "To live as free and responsible individuals." . . . I am a practicing Catholic. That probably counted for something. And then there was the example of my father. He was an exemplary employer. He really liked other people, and his workers adored him. I used to think that cadres and workers should belong to the same union and that the union should stand up for their interests and serve as an intermediary between employees and management.

But as Andrieux and Lignon have shown, the production engineer – humane leader and buffer between proletariat and employers – has been losing ground to the R&D engineer, who, it should be noted, is generally free of hierarchical responsibilities and liberal in his attitudes. In their study of those who joined or quit the engineers' and cadres' section of the CFTC (and later of the CFDT) in large

French firms in the period 1946–59, Andrieux and Lignon found that production cadres and engineers in manufacturing industries were about as likely to join the union as to resign (28 joined, 23 resigned), whereas 69 R&D engineers joined (more than half after the CFDT split off from the CFTC) and only 17 resigned.[75]

R&D engineers are heavily endowed with cultural capital and are closer to intellectuals in terms of education and work than are most other cadres. Many stem from the Catholic bourgeoisie; more than half come from Paris, and many gained political experience in the JEC or UNEF. The research engineers form the core group of the UCC's cadres. Members of the educated, enlightened, liberal segment of the bourgeoisie (around 30% of UCC members are active in the Socialist Party), they are often receptive, in certain respects at least, to the notion of postindustrial society. Thanks to their positions in the hierarchy and probably also to their class background, they are predisposed to accept, to some extent, the "new working class" thesis and to support related demands for better quality of work and self-management. They work in laboratories or R&D facilities where they do not supervise other workers directly (half of all CFDT members say that they supervise either no other workers or fewer than five workers). What technicians and workers they do supervise are a select group. The clear-cut authority relations characteristic of the production floor are unnecessary in the lab, where authority is legitimated by competence. Of all cadres R&D engineers are most receptive to the idea of gradually eliminating the distinctions between engineers, technicians, and skilled workers (for the only differences between them and their "subordinates" are based on competence and hence, in their eyes, are legitimate).

The idea of a workplace without distinctions helps R&D engineers to relieve the tensions they feel as a result of their ambiguous position between the field [*champ*] of the intellect and that of economic power. Their basic interest is to secure autonomy for themselves, to make decisions independent of financial and marketing considerations. This is the equivalent (in the industrial *champ*) of the autonomy claimed by the universities and more generally by intellectuals *vis-à-vis* the dominant class. Hence R&D engineers are inclined to accept the validity of an analysis according to which the crucial boundary is not between classes, i.e., in this case, between themselves and those who occupy objectively dominated positions in industry, but between, on the one hand, all scientifically and technically skilled workers (regardless of the degree of their skills) and, on the other hand, owners, managers, stockholders, and marketing people – in a word, capitalists, motivated only by the desire to maximize profit.

Finally, because R&D engineers feel no need to defend their status as cadres, which no one would think of challenging, and no need to insist that they be classified as such, which everyone admits, just as everyone agrees that they are part of the bourgeoisie, they can afford to tolerate a rhetoric in which cadres are lumped together with workers and can describe as corporatist or even Poujadist, i.e., narrow, blinkered, and petit-bourgeois, the "special interests" of the CGC and UGICT, unions whose behavior is influenced by the need of lower-level cadres to fight to maintain their status and distinction from other workers.

"Social art" and "social science"

"Theoretical" discussions of cadres generalize to the group as a whole the properties of one or another of its subgroups; what truth there is in such theories is partial and partisan and derives from the relationship between a particular theory and one of the organizations that claims to represent the group as a whole. As in a Rorschach test the group changes form without changing its identity. Depending on how the group is interpreted and defined, on which subgroup from the field of action is singled out for emphasis in the realm of theory, cadres can be classified in many ways. Consequently, the first subgroups to be represented in social thought were those already represented in the realm of political practice. Describing what cadres are, which might have clarified how social conflict affected their definition and objective attributes, was deferred; instead, a particular subgroup was taken to be typical of the group as a whole. But these interpretations were themselves symbolic arms in the struggle over who would represent the cadres. Each attempted to impose as scientifically true and hence as politically and socially correct a restricted definition of the group. Hence it became necessary to differentiate one interpretation from another (though all derived from an underlying consensus); this obscured the relations between those interpretations and the objective structures of the group.

Each new theory of cadres had to respond to existing theories. No one theory could be allowed a monopoly of interpretation. But the accumulation of interlocking theories heightened the symbolic efficacy of each one individually, establishing a context of discussion (*problématique*) in which the key themes were the nature and role of cadres and their substance and position in the social structure. As in any dialectic of subjective and objective, there was an effect of circular reinforcement. Even the theories that denied the existence of cadres as an objective reality made the group seem real by taking it seriously. Represented from many angles and in many ways, cadres became a focus of interest for clubs, unions, and political parties. Social science took an active part in the debate. By converting social interests into objective representations of society, social science increased the probability that its predictions would come true. Wielded as a weapon by rival groups in the field of politics, scientific knowledge of society altered the reality it claimed to be recording by bringing it into the realm of scholarly discourse.

It may be that no a priori, scientifically rational definition of cadres is possible. For to give such a definition is in itself a political act (usually of an unconscious, hence uncontrolled and hidden, sort). The paradox is this: Any rational definition that claims, as social science, to stand outside the field of social practice is in fact, objectively, a demand for official recognition (calling for, say, a revision of the statistical categories used by government agencies) and thus necessarily has practical consequences. For example, the new definition can be used to record data whose significance is not solely scientific, data that have practical import (such as determining who is entitled to certain social or retirement benefits, tax abatements, etc.). Hence the definition of any social group becomes an instrument, and an issue, in group conflict and class struggle, because it serves the interests of a particular group or class.

Accordingly, *social science* (the study of the social order produced by practice, i.e., in part, by social art) and *social art*, which takes the findings of social science and applies them in the field of practice (i.e., in this case, in the class struggle[76]) are caught in a vicious circle, which can be broken only if one moves away from a quasi-legalistic definition of social science as the legitimate agency for the production of systems of social classification. Rather then seek to establish, once and for all, a realistic definition of the object, one may seek instead to analyze how different definitions of the object compete with one another in ordinary social use. These definitions may be produced by statisticians, government agencies, trade unions, political parties, etc. (and need not have been "objectified" in statistical form). The sociologist's primary task is then to collect all data pertaining to whatever subject interests him, no matter what the source of those data. He must then show how data from different sources, established on the basis of different definitions of the object, are dialectically related to other data about the same object.

Not until we have analyzed the contrasting ways in which cadres have been defined can we hope to use the quantities of statistical data that have been collected about them over the past twenty years to reconstruct the objective regularities that underlie all the representations: statistical data are of no use until one has determined how the measuring instrument operates and how every database is shaped by certain social interests. In other words, the field (*champ*) of statistical representation is related in complex ways to the field of political representation (of which it is not a mere reflection). Statistics from different sources are hard to reconcile, not simply for technical reasons that a competent statistician could presumably allow for, but because the variety of definitions and nomenclatures employed in different studies generally derive from conflicts in which the surveyed group has been or is involved.[77]

Many sources of information about cadres in industry are currently available, but each uses a different definition of the group. These may be categorized under five broad heads:[78] (1) studies based on the occupational groups defined by INSEE, such as the "Formation Qualification Profession" study, which include either all personnel classified as C.S. 3 or C.S. 4 ("*professions libérales et cadres supérieurs*" and "*cadres moyens*," respectively) or various additional subcategories. (2) Studies based on the official definition set forth in the regulations of the supplementary retirement fund for cadres (articles 4 and 4 *bis* of the 1947 cadres' retirement program charter define cadres as personnel whose salary coefficient is equal to or greater than 300 on the Parodi–Croizat scale). Only private sector and certain nationalized firms are included. Furthermore, the sample is defined by hierarchical position and included agents who do not perform cadres' functions as defined in appendices to collective bargaining agreements (e.g., Agnès Pitrou's 1973 study of "Cadres and Security," commissioned by the Caisse interprofessionnelle de prévoyance de cadres, or CIPC, and the unpublished 1975 APEC study of cadres and job mobility). Those who are "cadres" according to this definition are not necessarily "cadres" according to the INSEE definition, and vice versa.[79] (3) Studies based on some educational criterion, such as the FASFID study of engineering school graduates who joined the federation – a sample that only partially overlaps engineers and cadres as defined by INSEE, since approximately half of the engineering school graduates interviewed by FASFID called themselves "cadres" (and not "engineers"), while, conversely, half the engineers counted by

INSEE did not graduate from engineering schools (mainly engineers trained on the job by their employer). (4) The periodic studies by the UIMM of "cadres and engineers in the metals industry," which, since they are commissioned by an employers' group, use the definition of cadres specified in the industry's collective bargaining agreement. (5) The study carried out periodically by the magazine *Expansion* and SOFRES on the "price of cadres," which used the forms filled out by applicants for cadre positions and filed with the leading Paris employment agencies. This study yields statistics concerning upper-level cadres in large firms.[80]

The rise of the cadres is the modern form of the traditional rhetorical appeal to the rise of the middle class with which the bourgeoisie has attempted to dampen revolutionary fervor ever since the nineteenth century. To complete our critique of the notion that this supposed rise of the cadres will somehow diminish hostilities between the bourgeoisie and the proletariat, between oppressors and oppressed, we must press on with our analysis, so as to reveal the patterns of thought that govern the interpretation of what appear to be well-established statistical facts.

4 *The university and business*

A new dogma: investment in education

To supporters and detractors alike, the idea that cadres were on the rise and that France was on the verge of being transformed into a middle-class society probably never seemed more firmly established than in the early 1960s. It was supported not only by common-sense arguments derived from first-hand experience but also by statistical data regularly produced by various agencies established in the postwar years[1] and backed up by the pronouncements of economists and social scientists. All indicators seemed to point to the same thing: not only nominal wages but also, since at least the mid-1950s, real wages had been increasing; productivity was up, especially in the most capital-intensive sectors, with repercussions on wages;[2] workers' consumption was also up, and durable goods (such as automobiles and household appliances) were more and more common; urban models of consumption had spread to other segments of society; and so on.[3] Two trends were especially noteworthy: the increase in the number of students and the increase in the number of cadres, which many social theorists viewed as obvious signs of the advent of a "new society." In the wake of accelerated economic growth, technological breakthroughs, and growing automation (which proved to be a major theme of industrial sociology in the 1950s and 1960s) came a social mutation characterized by an increase in the social value of technical skills, democratization of education, reduction of social inequalities, and, most important of all, gradual elimination of the distinction between manual workers and intellectual workers.

The number of students in the faculties of letters, sciences, and law and economics tripled during this period, from approximately

160,000 in 1959–60 to 550,000 in 1974–5. According to INSEE figures, the number of engineers and senior cadres rose from 352,975 in 1954 to 515,762 in 1962, 640,721 in 1968, and 910,040 in 1975.[4] The growth rate for top-level administrative personnel was 3.1% annually between 1962 and 1968 and 5.3% between 1968 and 1975 (or 5.8% if one looks only at the private sector, which accounted for two-thirds of all personnel in this category). For engineers, it was 5.1% from 1962 to 1968 and 4.5% from 1968 to 1975. During the same period the proportion of top administrators and engineers in the work force more than doubled, from 1.9% to 4.2%. The connection between the growth of higher education and the increase in the number of cadres seemed obvious: *cadres supérieurs*, according to the quasi-official INSEE definition, form a group composed, "broadly speaking, of persons practicing professions that in principle require higher education."[5] Thus the connection between educational credentials and professional credentials took a quasi-legal form, often guaranteed by collective bargaining agreement. Until recently, in fact, college graduates who went to work in industry were almost always hired with the title of "cadre."

The finding that the number of students and the number of cadres had increased simultaneously was seized upon by a number of writers in the early 1960s as they attempted to frame new ideologies. The new left came up with the "new working class" and "postindustrial society," while neoliberals argued that capitalism would usher in the "affluent society" and the "end of ideology," which was to be replaced by "rational decision-making techniques."[6] Think of the hopes that were invested at the time in "higher education for the masses" (the contemptuous connotations of the term were not apparent before 1968), and of the political and social consensus that lay just beneath the surface of polemics over modernization and development of the educational system. There was widespread agreement that the development of scientific education would hasten unavoidable technological change and lead to gradual replacement of workers by technicians, engineers, and cadres. Growth and democratization of the educational system would enhance social mobility and deprive the working class of its most dynamic and gifted members. Businessmen were particularly quick to grasp the implications of this optimistic prophecy, promoted by several of the "clubs" of intellectuals formed after de Gaulle came to power in 1958. Until 1968 the business community was strongly in favor of increasing the number of students attending universities,[7] a move that businessmen believed would stimulate economic growth and help maintain social order.

There were in fact economic and technological reasons for business interest in the educational system and the future of the university. Estimates and projections produced by the planning commission and by private industry associations (such as the UIMM[8]) bemoaned the lack of skilled personnel and college graduates and the dearth of technicians, engineers, and cadres. Those who foresaw an era of exponential growth complained of a shortage of "gray matter." On the basis of figures for degrees awarded in the 1950s and 1960s, planners predicted that the gap would continue to widen between the number of jobs created by the dynamics of the economy and the number of graduates qualified to fill them. A shortage of skilled personnel was widely perceived as one of the major obstacles to growth, and the economic gospel imported from the United States in the 1950s and broadly accepted by top civil servants and leading industrialists held that development of the educational system through an increase in educational investments was a major factor in economic development.[9] A prominent feature of American society was said to be the number and quality of its universities, and American professionals were generally believed to enjoy a high level of technical competence.

It is against this background that the interest of industrial leaders and prominent economists in the educational system must be viewed. The main reason for Europe's backwardness and inefficiency, it was held, was the poor quality of education. Not until the educational system had been improved could norms and values imported from America be adopted in Europe. This is the gist of remarks made by Edward F. Denison to a seminar organized by the OECD on the "residual factor":[10]

> More advanced education makes the individual more receptive to new ideas and new ways of doing things.... Plant owners, executives, and managers tend to be more familiar with practices used elsewhere.... More than one foreign observer has attributed this characteristic of American executives, which is less noticeable in executives from other countries, to the fact that a high proportion of managers are college graduates. (p. 39)

In his conclusion Denison adds that

> it is quicker, easier, and cheaper to take production methods from another country and adapt them to local conditions than to discover new methods.... But this probably requires, among other things, technical and managerial talents similar to those required for research. It is there-

fore highly likely that scientific workers, engineers, and educated managers can, by helping to adapt known technologies, contribute more to economic growth in Europe than in the United States. (p. 59)

The widespread belief in these ideas was also related to the particular economic situation of France in the 1960s and to industrial conflicts at that time: progressive employers, and especially top executives in high-technology firms, stressed the need to reduce the number of self-taught cadres.[11] Such cadres were particularly numerous in smaller firms in traditional sectors of industry, where they generally occupied management positions. In a more general sense, the exaltation of competence and formal education in the rhetoric of economic modernization was part of the struggle between two segments of the dominant class: one associated with big businesses operating in the international market, the other comprising traditional segments of the bourgeoisie and petite bourgeoisie bent on the protection of small, family owned firms doing business mainly in domestic and colonial markets.

In the first wave of concentration that followed the opening of French borders to the Common Market, many small businesses came under the control of larger firms. One consequence was that local cadres, many of them autodidacts well on in years, longtime employees who had come up through the ranks, were often replaced by young cadres "parachuted" in from corporate headquarters. Many of those who lost their jobs went without work for long periods, unable to find new jobs equivalent to the old ones they had been forced to relinquish. As a result one began to see "frictional" unemployment among cadres in the mid-1960s. Newspapers began criticizing firms for "putting older cadres out to pasture." This trend peaked between 1965 and 1967, during which time all the major dailies published articles on the plight of the so-called older cadre (e.g., *Le Monde* devoted a series of six articles to this problem in October 1966, and *Le Figaro* in the same year inaugurated a column devoted to the subject, with such headlines as "Humiliated Cadres," etc.).

Development of the educational system, it was assumed, would provide industry with large numbers of skilled young cadres familiar with the techniques of scientific management, human relations, and marketing. These "new men" would be chosen from among the "nation's finest," if need be from families of modest background (to encourage "circulation of elites").[12] The universities were also supposed to train the children of managers of small family businesses to assume positions as subordinates (albeit with "great futures") in large companies. Finally, the interest of big businessmen in development of the educational system was not without ulterior motives: increasing the number of college-educated cadres, technicians, and engineers would slow the rapid rise of salaries paid to these employees in the 1960s.[13]

From scarcity to overproduction

Between 1960 and 1975 the tenor of the discussion of higher education gradually changed: worries about the shortage of skilled personnel and hopes that the universities might contribute to the modernization of French industry gave way to denunciations of overproduction of graduates and attacks on the dysfunctional effects and the futility and cost of mass higher education.

That the system of higher education had grown inordinately was the main thesis of an article by Louis Lévy-Garboua on "contradictions in the mass university," an article premised on a market model of higher education. The "decline in students' employment opportunities" was due, according to Lévy-Garboua, to a disproportion between the "influx of students" and the magnitude of "economic growth," between the "supply of degrees" and the "size of the gross national product." The author seems to assume that everyone who had graduated from college over the past fifteen years had applied for work simultaneously, and that competition for jobs within this reserve army of bourgeois labor had driven down job levels and salaries. "During this period [beginning in 1962] ... the influx of students far outpaced economic growth.... This is partly responsible for the degradation of the students' position." In another passage that makes clear that he is referring to the field of industry, Lévy-Garboua writes that "demand for college graduates must have increased less rapidly than the gross national product in the 1960s, because the concentration of industrial, agricultural, and artisanal enterprises and the capital-intensive use of new technology steadily reduced the need for manpower."[14]

The major flaw in this analysis is that it makes no use of the results of the many studies of the structure of the cadre population or of employment of graduates who completed their studies in the late 1960s and early 1970s. The cadre studies show that the proportion of self-taught cadres, which varies from sector to sector and survey to survey but is always high (ranging from 30% to 70% of all cadres, depending on the criteria used to define the group), does not seem to have diminished (e.g., according to the UIMM's surveys it went from 38.8% in 1962 to 39.8% in 1970 to 40% in 1975).[15]

Table 1. *Degrees held by cadres, according to various sources (in percent)*

	SOFRES– Expansion *survey 1976*	*UIMM survey 1977*	*INSEE FQP2 1970*		*APEC survey 1975*		*CIPC survey 1973*	
None or primary school only			26.0		9.1		25.0	
Secondary, no bac.	27.0	45.0	23.0	65.1	31.5		24.0	73.0
Secondary, with bac.			9.0		7.2	51.3	24.0	
Some college			7.1		10.5			
M.A.	5.0	3.5	0.3				12.0	
M.S.	5.5	4.0	0.1			10.7		
Law or Economics	6.7		4.3					
Doctorate	3.0					5.7		
Institute of Political Studies	2.6		0.8					
Small business schools	14.0		3.5					
ESCAE	3.3		2.6			12.5		
HEC	4.9		1.1					
Small engineering schools	17.2		23.0	26.1				15.0
CNAM	3.0		4.2					
Arts et Métiers	2.8		6.4					
Ecole centrale	2.0		3.0			13.0		
Ecole des Mines	0.9		1.5					
Ecole polytechnique	2.1		1.4					

This finding is difficult to reconcile with the hypothesis that the job market gradually became saturated with college graduates, for earlier predictions had been that autodidacts would gradually be replaced by graduates. Employment studies reveal that between 1960 and 1975 business continued to recruit most of its young cadres from the management and business schools and the engineering schools (which are estimated to have produced 30–50% of all new cadres[16]); now, the number of graduates of these schools did increase over this time period (mainly due to the increase in the number of such institutions) but far less rapidly than the number of graduates of the universities. One study carried out by the Université de Paris-Dauphine at the behest of the APEC shows that of 80,000 graduates in 1970, 68,000 came from the universities and 12,000 from the engineering and business schools. But 68% of the young cadres hired by industry graduated from the latter, compared to only 6% from the universities. Similar differences are observed between faculties: only one to five percent of cadres graduated from faculties of letters, which enrolled the largest number of students and in which the increase in enrollment was especially large. Even the science faculties, whose curriculum is formally similar to that offered by the engineering schools, produced far fewer cadres than the faculties of law and economics (which accounted for 4–7% of cadres hired), whose enrollment remained much smaller than that of the faculty of letters despite an equally impressive rise. The large numbers of students who graduated from the universities between 1960 and 1975 took jobs for the most part outside industry. The vast majority of them (80–100% depending on the study[17]) went to work in the public sector (slightly more than half as teachers, the rest as civil servants or in other public jobs). In other words, the major quantitative changes in the system of higher education had only minor effects on the nature and direction of the flow of students from the schools into the work force.

Despite numerous feminist-sounding declarations of intention, traditional hiring and promotional criteria were maintained. These tended to exclude women from positions of authority and power in industry (indeed, women who internalized the objective reality of the situation eliminated themselves). This certainly helped to reduce pressures on the job market by removing a large group of university graduates from the competition for positions. Women with equivalent educational credentials are still less likely than men to become cadres in private firms (according to a study by the Centre d'études de l'emploi, 9% of women with law degrees, 13% with economics degrees, and 20% with degrees in political science became cadres, compared with 24%, 50%, and 52%, respectively, for men). The proportion of women in the student body varies from faculty to faculty, but it is always high; yet, although the proportion of female students increased sharply in this period, the number of women hired as industrial cadres was negligible in the 1960s and increased only very slightly and very slowly over the next decade.

Comparative analysis shows that the percentage of upper-level administrative cadres who were women rose from 11.1% in 1966 to 13.4% in 1968 and to 17.1% in 1975. But most of this increase was due to massive hiring of women in the public sector, where the percentage of female upper-level civil servants (as classified by the INSEE's *code des métiers*) rose from 15% in 1968 to 26% in 1975. According to the CEREQ study, 90% of female graduates in the liberal arts and 60–90% of female graduates in the sciences (depending on the level of degree) went into teaching; most female graduates in law, economics, and political science took jobs in the state bureaucracy, which explains why the percentage of upper-level female civil servants with college degrees increased from 36.9% in

1968 to 59.7% in 1975 – a greater increase than for their male counterparts, for whom the comparable figures were 54.6% in 1968 and 62.4% in 1975 (these statistics have not been published before and are based on analysis of the census data for 1968 and 1975).

Women who do obtain positions of authority or responsibility in industry – a male world governed by masculine values – generally owe their status, power, and even professional identity to the men for whom they work: it is common to speak of a cadre's secretary as his "second wife."[18] Work relations in such situations reproduce family relations. A 1975 APEC study of new members of a cadres' retirement fund showed that female cadres, who accounted for 13% of the sample, were paid considerably less than their male colleagues and generally became cadres fairly late in their careers, usually by internal promotion in a small firm, where they served as executive assistants (i.e., they had no direct power over subordinates). Most seem to have been secretaries, bookkeepers, or private secretaries who had worked for the same firm, and even the same boss, for long periods. For these women, a promotion to cadre does not necessarily imply a change of job or even salary, and its rewards are mainly symbolic, compensation for years of loyal service.

It is probably in the professions with the highest proportion of women that female college graduates are most likely to achieve some measure of autonomy from men. It can be shown that the status of women teachers is less gender-related (and hence less subordinate) than the status of women in industry, because the teaching profession is largely female-oriented,[19] and role models for male teachers require them to exhibit many of the virtues socially defined as feminine.

How did it happen that the number of self-taught cadres remained quite high in a period when the number of college graduates on the job market, particularly graduates in the liberal arts, sciences, law, and economics, increased markedly? To answer this question, it should be noted that the job market is neither homogeneous nor transparent, and that there is no automatic mechanism for adjusting supply to demand.[20] Economic models, whether based on a single market or on a hierarchy of segmented markets, fail to take account of the selection and recruitment norms that officially or (more commonly) unofficially govern the reproduction of specific occupational groups.[21] They also forget that the statistical evidence, namely, the parallel increase in the number of cadres and the number of college graduates, does not support the notion that there is a direct relationship between embodied cultural capital (or, if you

Table 2. *Growth of higher education*

	Business schools		*Engineering schools*					*Institutes of politics*	*Law and Economics*		*Sciences*		*Letters*	
	T	% of F	A	B	C	T	% of F		T	% of F	T	% of F	T	% of F
1957–58	4907		3285	4840	8301	16,762		3087						
1958–59									34,229	25.1	61,725	29.7	55,653	56.5
1959–60	4879		3566	5585	12,348	21,497		3890	34,171	26.6	67,627	30.7	59,265	57.6
1960–61	5210		3655	5773	13,515	22,943		3347	34,231	29.5	70,217	32.0	64,415	62.0
1961–62	5538		3653	6497	15,566	25,716	4.3	4451	38,449	29.3	75,282	32.1	73,376	63.3
1962–63	5538	13.0	3683	6250	16,338	26,251	4.4	4481	45,468	28.4	88,595	31.5	88,734	63.5
1963–64	7125	12.8	3693	5979	17,331	27,003	5.0	5106	53,650	29.4	100,498	30.7	103,484	63.7
1964–65	7069	13.0	3800	6470	17,364	27,634	4.7	5641	74,267	25.3	113,084	30.1	122,972	62.3
1965–66	7026	14.8	4084	6218	17,391	27,693		5240	86,733	25.3	125,552	30.0	137,008	63.1
1966–67			4011	6741	17,784	28,536	4.8		99,664	26.7	129,607	30.9	157,477	63.6
1967–68	9952		4204	6883	18,116	29,205	5.0	7283	114,382	29.8	137,111	31.8	171,168	65.2
1968–69	10,002		4169	6548	18,208	28,925	5.1	9768	126,074	31.1	100,085	31.1	144,746	64.6
1969–70	8266		4103	6020	19,035	29,268	5.2		138,676	31.1	122,825		218,258	
1970–71	8868	15.1			19,529				149,019		118,390		233,390	
1971–72	9110	17.5	4413	6628	21,114	32,155	6.7		153,581	31.9	120,808	30.6	246,735	
1972–73	9542	20.4	4798	7341	23,065	35,204	7.5		165,694		120,142		254,851	
1973–74	9697	21.3	4850	7644	22,400	34,894	8.1		171,104	35.8	123,703	32.9	257,338	66.7
1974–75	9596	25.2	4913	8257	21,692	34,862			181,379	37.2	123,576	32.5	241,809	65.8
1975–76	10,232	27.7	4998	8272	21,779	35,049			186,838	38.9	127,406	32.5	253,508	65.3
1976–77	10,707	30.8	4823	8335	22,685	35,174	11.9		178,501	41.7	122,721	33.7	251,663	65.1
1977–78	10,990	33.0	4893	8165	25,478	36,536		9271	180,695	42.7	126,072	33.4	255,110	64.9

Sources: Ministry of National Education, Statistiques des ensseignements techniques supérieurs, sections concerning students of business and engineering schools. Statistiques des enseignements, tableaux et informations, sections concerning university students from 1958 to 1978. For certain years and certain subjects (such as sales training), Statistiques de la France (1967–1970). Statistics concerning engineering and business schools are scattered and frequently incomplete: numbers of students are not given for all years and all schools, and students in schools of ambiguous status (such as military medical schools) were in some years included in the number of engineering students. In short, the estimates given in this table should be treated with caution (especially for the small business schools, most of which are private and may not have been included in official statistics for all years). The data here are intended mainly to indicate trends.

Engineering school students have been divided into three groups, using the classification introduced by the periodic *Expansion* survey of cadre salaries (the total may exceed the sum of the three categories, because certain schools could not be isolated). There is reason to believe that the *Expansion* classification, intended primarily to help cadres evaluate the salary level they might reasonably expect, actually reflects distinctions important in the labor market, or at any rate that segment of the market in which large firms recruit their cadres, often through employment agencies (this is the base of the *Expansion* survey). The breakdown shows that engineering schools had smaller student bodies than the science faculties, and that the higher a school stood in the hierarchy, the less the size of its student body increased. (Cf. P. Beaudeux and J. F. Rouge, "Le prix des cadres in 1978," *L'Expansion*, June 1978). The classification used in the *Expansion*–SOFRES poll is the following: Engineering Schools, Category A: Polytechnique, Ponts et Chaussées, Mines (Paris, Saint-Etienne, Nancy), Centrale (Paris), Sup Aéro, Sup Elec, Institut national agronomique (INA), Télécom.; Engineering Schools, Category B: Arts et Métiers, Ecole nationale supérieure d'électronique-hydraulique, Mathématiques appliquées et génie physique (Grenoble), Ecole nationale supérieure d'électrotechnique-électronique (Toulouse), Ecole centrale (Lyon), Institut industriel du Nord (IDN), Arts et Métiers catholiques (Lille), Physique et chimie (Paris), Ecole nationale supérieure du pétrole et des moteurs à combustion interne, Ecole nationale de géologie appliquée et de prospective minière (Nancy); Engineering Schools, Category C. other engineering schools.

prefer, skill) and the technical requirements of the job. This is because the statistics are based on forms filled out by individuals and record the language that people ordinarily use: the language of professional titles and educational credentials.[22] Now, in the case of cadres, at any rate, all signs suggest that the award of the professional title is governed by a logic different from that which governs educational achievement, and different, too, from that which governs the division of labor and hence the number and type of jobs available.

Competence and skill

Criticisms of higher education as out of date, practically useless, divorced from real life, and hence unsuited to business needs – commonly voiced by businessmen and also by liberal economists to explain why there is such poor communication between the educational system and the economic system – are not as empty as they may seem. For there is in fact little connection between training received in college and what is actually done on the job. Indeed this is one of the most basic and enduring properties of the industrial field.[23]

It has been shown, for example, that the curriculum of the Grandes Ecoles, particularly those specializing in science, is not necessarily better suited than the curriculum of the universities to the kinds of administrative and managerial positions that graduates of the more prestigious schools are able to obtain, in some cases immediately after graduation.[24] Technical aspects of the curriculum do not determine career success. For example, data from the regular survey carried out by the magazine *Expansion* (which uses a fairly detailed system for coding educational background and job classifications)[25] show that even in jobs that would appear to be highly technical, as in the computer field, a substantial proportion of cadres have no scientific or technical training (46% of the data processing professionals surveyed held degrees in the liberal arts, political science, or law, or had attended business schools or were self-taught). The lack of connection between education and employment emerges even more clearly when one looks at jobs requiring less specific skills, such as positions in administration or sales. Among sales personnel, for example, we find that 24% were graduates of engineering schools, 13% were graduates of the universities or political science institutes, and 44% were autodidacts.

This lack of fit between education and employment is no accident but the result, at least in part, of a deliberate policy. Employers are tireless in their praise of mobility, adaptability, and willingness to be recycled – all qualities highly valued and sought after (as can be seen in career guides for cadres[26]), because employees who possess them will readily accept reassignment to new jobs or new locations as the needs of the economy dictate. These qualities were particularly prized in the period 1960–1975, when buyouts and mergers were common and legislation made it difficult to fire cadres and replace them with new workers having different skills. Shifting employees from job to job and department to department without regard to their educational background and experience and in accordance with apparently arbitrary criteria also serves objectively to remind cadres, especially those who are college graduates, that their value depends entirely on how much their services are worth to the company, hence on what they learn "on the job" that has direct relevance to the company's concerns, and not on general knowledge acquired at school. Thus it is not the man but the company that is the measure of all things. Management techniques that encourage mobility and flexibility among cadres, preparing them for change by means of recycling seminars and group dynamics sessions are instruments of domination (for, as Max Weber says, "in ordinary life domination is above all else *administration*"[27]). Their purpose is to make employees and particularly lower-level and would-be cadres aware that their relatively privileged positions are due not to their personal qualities but to the good will of the organization that employs them.

The recruitment of cadres is not governed by technology alone, and the firms that hire them require not just machines, devices whose operation requires technically competent agents, but also human capital that must be mobilized for production and profit. In contrast to government, which employs relatively few blue-collar workers – more in some areas than in others, however, and more, in any case, than are employed in institutions of cultural production and diffusion – industry employs agents belonging to all social classes in plants that are not only places of organized, coordinated production but are also battlefields. At the lowest level are the workers: concrete individuals in need of supervision, abstract producers whose labor must generate a profit, and members of the working class, an organized collectivity with its own leaders that can be, or is, mobilized for action. It is impossible to understand the systematic differences not only in political attitudes but more generally, perhaps, in values and life style among the various segments of the moyenne and petite bourgeoisie without recognizing that these are related to the structure of the field in which the members of these various class segments work, earn their livings, and perhaps find their respective *raisons d'être*. This is particularly true of the groups that occupy the middle ground in class relations. Structurally ambiguous and unstable, these groups face very different constraints depending on the social context in which they play their intermediary role: jobs that objectively contribute to the discipline of the lower orders vary in nature depending on where they are performed. In the field of cultural production and diffusion, a series of mediations come between daily practice and the contributions that this practice makes to maintaining the social order. Where control and coercion cannot be dissimulated and where the class struggle is a more overt part of everyday experience, however, the relationship between supervisors and supervised is more direct (in industry, for instance, one speaks of "front-line cadres").

In the factory, as in the army (or navy, which served as a model of organization for the earliest factories), the relationship between cadres or officers and their subordinates can always – even today, despite cooperation, human relations, and job enrichment – regress to the level of pure force, and not just in the symbolic sense (as the holding of cadres as hostages by workers has shown). It is because the factory is the primary battlefield on which the class struggle is waged that qualities of leadership and other manly virtues inculcated by schools such as the Ecole des arts et métiers and Ecole centrale, whose graduates have traditionally assumed positions of authority in industry, are so highly praised and sought after. This also explains, at least in part, why there has been such strong opposition to allowing women to assume posts of responsibility and authority in industry, especially in plants where the workers come mainly from the lower classes and subscribe to a masculine system of values. Such workers are less likely to have internalized an alternative principle of legitimation such as educational achievement, which women could then use as grounds for arguing that gender is not an issue.

The proportion of women among upper-level cadres (using the INSEE definition) is therefore lowest in sectors with a high proportion of blue-collar workers, especially when the majority of those workers are men. In the metals industry, with 73.3% blue-collar workers (only 2.9% of whom are women), only 2.3% of upper-level cadres are women. The same is true of the automobile industry, in which the work force is 70.6% blue collar. Even though 15% of the workers are women, only 2.4% of top-level cadres are women. As this example shows, an increase in the proportion of women in the blue-collar work force does not necessarily lead to a corresponding increase in the proportion of female cadres. In the textile industry, for example, with 77% blue-collar workers, 57% of whom are women, less than 6% of the cadres are women. The proportion of female cadres is noticeably higher, however, in sectors employing few blue-collar workers: 8.2% in banking, for instance, and 17.8% in the national and local bureaucracies and the social security administration (INSEE, *Recensement de 1968, sondage au 1/20, population active*, p. 174). This pattern stands out even more clearly when we look not at branches of industry but at individual companies. Fewer than 2% of cadres are female in the following firms: Usinor, Peugeot, Télémécanique, PUK (Ugine Steels), Houillères du Nord, and Renault. By contrast, more than 20% of cadres are female at Oréal, Nouvelles Galeries, Hachette Librairie, Credit Industriel et Commercial, and the Banque Nationale de Paris (see *Cadres C.F.D.T.*, 228, April–May 1979).

Industrial class relations affect employers' attitudes toward the universities as well as academics' attitudes toward the private sector, though usually in implicit ways. These attitudes are partially responsible for businessmen's distrust of students and for students' absence from the cadre job market, where the value ascribed to their degrees and, more generally, to themselves as individuals does not correspond to their investments, that is, to the time they have devoted to their studies and to their image of themselves and their futures. In repudiating hierarchy and hierarchical relations the students are in fact denying the existence of class relations. This serves two purposes. First, it expresses the students' resistance to such aspects of industrial life as fixed hours, short deadlines, expense accounts, and supervision by superiors, associates, and clients, all of which contradict the image fostered by higher education (particularly in the liberal arts) of intellectual excellence as a disinterested vocation, a product of pure research. In other words, the students are repudiating all signs of the subordination of intellectual interests to economic interests and of the young cardre–intellectual to his employers, signs that the cadre belongs not to himself but to the firm that employs him and pays him to work just like anyone else.[28] Students are also expressing their reluctance to assume leadership positions (as one says in the jargon of industry), to define themselves as managers, and thus to claim in an explicit way the privileges available to those who hold the proper educational credentials and job titles. In other words, they want to stand apart, to belong to no class, to escape – symbolically – from the relations of class domination. For in the universities, although there is constant talk of class (generally with a touch of guilty conscience), the concept somehow lacks reality because concrete instances of class domination are lacking. It is interesting, moreover, that the two principles of opposition to hierarchical relations are closely related. Subordinates, for example, are never so clearly aware of their subordinate status as when they must pass on to *their* subordinates orders given to them by their superiors).

Public and private

The mode of class relations that is objectively embedded in the structural properties of a specific field is surely one of the mediations (which agents may choose to express or deny, depending on their positions and specific interests) that determines how the job market (governed by the opposition between the private and public sector) is related to the system of higher education (governed by the opposition between the universities and the Grandes Ecoles). This relationship is the product of many convergent factors, among which social background is of paramount importance. For similar reasons we find a relationship between the political opinions expressed by students and the various factors that determine their educational and professional careers. Broadly speaking, university students comprise the "left," whereas the students of the engineering and especially the business schools comprise the "right." Thus the political taxonomies parallel the opposition between the universities and the Grandes Ecoles, as well as between the segments of the petite and moyenne bourgeoisie associated with the public sector (teachers, civil servants, administrators, etc.), traditionally regarded as left-wing, and the segments associated with the private sector (merchants, industrialists, etc.), traditionally regarded as right-wing (and whose children are present in large numbers in the business schools). In other words, data about the career plans and political preferences of students are in large part redundant. The preference indicated for the private or public sector itself corresponds to the objective likelihood that a student will wind up in one sector or the other.

A poll of 4,475 students carried out in 1977 by the magazine *Etudiant* studied students of engineering and business schools as well as various university faculties; the poll tells us of students' political

Table 3. *Survey of students*

in percent	*Business and management*	*Engineering schools*	*Law schools*	*Science faculties*	*Arts and Letters*
plan to join union after obtaining job	13.8	14.7	22.7	21.0	26.0
want to work in private industry	60.5	55.4	23.6	16.5	9.3
want to work in civil service, nationalized firm, teaching, or research	14.6	29.6	41.7	70.9	64.7
would work at Peugeot	15.2	17.7	9.7	8.4	4.0
would work for post office	2.0	3.9	6.8	14.8	12.6
confident of finding job appropriate to training and desires	53.6	55.9	32.4	30.0	23.5
more than two hours a day extra-academic reading	12.1	4.5	15.4	11.7	24.1
Read the *Figaro* regularly or occasionally	33.8	21.7	28.0	19.4	13.2
Will vote Communist or extreme left in next elections	9.9	7.4	14.6	17.6	21.5
Will vote for Giscard or Chirac in next elections (i.e., center or center-right)	35.0	30.6	27.4	17.3	13.1

Sources: Survey of 4,475 students in 23 academic cities carried out in 1977 by the magazine *L'Etudiant*

opinions and career plans. Their expressed preferences in fact reflect internalized values that can be correlated with specific segments of the educational and job markets. For example, the proportion of students who plan to go into private industry drops sharply when one moves from the business schools (65%) and engineering schools (55.4%) to the law schools (23.6%), faculties of science (16.5%), and faculties of letters (9.3%). The proportion who plan to go into teaching, research, or the civil service varies inversely. Similarly, the proportion who said they would prefer to work for Peugeot (the paradigm of the large, traditional private firm, family owned, paternalistic, and highly disciplined)[29] drops as one moves from business and engineering students to the faculties of sciences and letters; the proportion who said they would prefer to work for the state-owned postal and telecommunications service (PTT) varied inversely, from 2% of business students and 3.9% of engineering students to 14.8% of science majors and 12.6% of liberal arts majors. Attitudes toward politics and trade unions vary in the same sense as career plans. For example, the proportion of readers of *Le Figaro* [considered a right-wing newspaper – Trans.] ranged from 33.8% of business students to 28% of law students to 21.7% of engineering students to 19.4% of the future scientists to 13.2% of the liberal arts majors. Similarly, the percentage of students who said they would vote for either Valéry Giscard d'Estaing or Jacques Chirac [the two right-wing candidates – Trans.] in the 1981 presidential elections ranged from 35% of the business students to 30.6% of the engineering students to 27.4% of the law students to 17.3% of the science students and 13.1% of the liberal arts majors. Finally, the proportion of students who planned to join a union as soon as they found a job was lowest in the business schools (13.8%) and engineering schools (14.7%) and highest in the universities (21.1% in the science faculties, 22.7% in the law faculties, and 26% in the faculties of letters). Thus the political attitudes of students prior to entry into working life are generally in accord with the political attitudes tolerated in the professional environments where they are most likely to find employment. Whether a student declares himself or herself to be on the left or on the right is in part determined by the same factors that determine where he or she will find work, social background in particular. Thus, the intention to join a union becomes much more common as we move from students whose fathers are industrialists (12.5%) or self-employed professionals (16%) to students whose fathers are white-collar (28.8%) or blue-collar (35.7%) workers. Political choices are determined by job expectations and various objective factors that incline students of lower-class background to think of working for the PTT (which has a reputation for rapid promotion and is chosen by 19% of blue-collar workers' children compared with 4.6% of industrialists' children) and young people whose parents are industrialists, executives, or self-employed professionals to set their sights on the dominant positions in the industrial field.

When a firm hires new cadres, it is not content merely to buy embodied cultural capital at the going market price. As one executive put it, "we want men," playing on the ambiguity between the military and humanistic connotations of the word "men." Deciphered, what he means to say is that the firm wants solid individuals with all their social and characterological attributes, all the vices and virtues of their class and educational background. "Beginning cadres," who play a strategic role in industrial class relations, must be counted on not to defect in case of strike or labor conflict. Their loyalty to the firm and its top executives and values (and to the business community in general) is of fundamental importance to management, especially since legislation has made it increasingly difficult to get rid of unsatisfactory personnel. This is especially true for cadres who are college graduates, for their degrees, sanctioned by authorities external to the firm, give them a measure of authority of their own, of independence from the company, and protect them from the sort of direct coercion that can be brought to bear on autodidacts. The industrial literature makes this point in its own way when it criticizes college graduates as pretentious, lacking in ability (which is not too serious, since the company can always train its own men), and, worst of all, insubordinate, inflexible, and inclined to challenge company norms and values and the internal hierarchy (especially in small- and medium-sized firms, where beginning cadres are often better educated than their superiors).

Engineering and business schools, many of them private institutions and generally closely connected with business and industry, offer the greatest guarantees to corporate recruiters, because they select students on the basis of the same values that prevail in industry, values that they seek to reinforce in their students, many of whom come from the families of cadres and businessmen. One of the functions of modern employment agencies and the like, with their psychological tests and whatnot, is to confirm the preselection accomplished by the educational system. Such confirmation was unnecessary when cadres were hired mainly through family and social connections, ensuring that candidates had connections to industry (often as the sons of plant owners) and had profoundly and precociously internalized prevailing industrial values (this is still often the case in smaller firms, which rarely rely on employment agencies). As firms grew in size and became increasingly bureaucratic, however, employment agencies proliferated. A job market for cadres developed, which, though not quite as perfect a market as the technocrats sometimes claim, nevertheless did acquire some measure of autonomy, as is shown by the tendency for salaries in different sectors of industry to equalize over time. Testing has several functions. To begin with, the tests remind college graduates that their degree is not everything and that the ultimate verdict lies with the company, not with the university. Thus testing demonstrates the independence and autonomy of the industrial field by cutting across, if only symbolically, the educational hierarchies. The tests also compensate for uncertainties in the educational section procedure. For even schools most subject to the influence of industry always maintain some degree of autonomy, relying on such selection criteria as examination scores and mathematical prowess that allow some social undesirables to slip through.

Employment agencies expanded steadily in the late 1960s and early 1970s (showing a 50% increase in gross revenues between 1973 and 1975). Agencies recruited 5,500 cadres in 1970 and 7,000 in 1974. Given the selection procedures, this means that 20,000 to 30,000 cadres filed applications and took various tests. In other words, the agencies may have recruited as many as 5% of the cadres hired in 1965, 15% of those hired in 1971, and 25% of those hired in 1975, serving mainly large firms, 25% of them multinationals and 35% French-owned. Another indicator of the growth of employment agencies is that they accounted for 45–50% of the classified advertisements in *Le Monde* and *Le Figaro* in 1970, triple the percentage for 1965.[30] Rationalization of the mechanisms of social control governing the hiring of supervisory personnel explains why, according to a 1971 SOFRES poll, 50% of upper-level cadres had been subjected to psychological testing of some sort, compared with an average 24% for the working population as a whole. Twenty-two percent of the upper-level cadres (as defined by the one-digit INSEE codes, including teachers who are not, for the moment at any rate, subject to psychological testing in hiring and promotion) had been tested at some point in their careers. The percentage of those tested increased with level of education (ranging from 12% of those with only a primary education to 49% of those with college degrees) and decreased with age (from 21% of those between 25 and 34 to 7% of those over 50).[31] Confirmation of the hypothesis that the primary purpose of testing is to ensure conformity of the agent's "habitus" with prevailing industrial values can be found in the fact that "headhunters" (who, unlike employment agencies, maintain computer files on currently employed cadres and try to entice people away from their jobs) never make use of tests, which they regarded as pointless and inappropriate, and rely exclusively on interviews.[32] In any case, the use of outside employment agencies and licensed psychological consultants to do what an experienced personnel manager could no doubt accomplish on his own, using his usual skills and knowledge of the terrain, may perhaps owe some of its popularity to the fact that it lends a certain legitimacy to hiring procedures. Delegating hiring to outside agents, or specialists, who remain officially neutral with respect to internal conflicts, makes the selection of employees seem the result of a rational and objective, indeed scientific, procedure. This can be important, especially when there is internal division over which candidate to hire or when management prefers to hire someone from outside rather than promote internally.

Given the facts that most of the influx of new students from the lower and middle classes went not to the business schools but to the universities, where they majored mainly in science and the liberal arts, and that, for a person with a given degree, the lower his or her class background, the less likely he or she was to become a cadre, it seems reasonable to assume that democratization of the university did not appreciably alter the mechanisms of social reproduction in industry: children of workers who went to college were more likely to turn to other kinds of work than to return to industry.

Students in business and engineering schools come from higher class backgrounds than students in the faculties of letters and sciences; the more prestigious the school, the greater the disparity. Since the late 1960s student recruitment has been for the most part socially stable; the most prestigious business schools are even more elitist than they were, and the universities are accepting an ever increasing proportion of children of industrial and office workers (this apparent democratization has been counterbalanced by a decline in the social value of a college degree). Indeed, there are greater contrasts between the social backgrounds of students in different types of higher educational institutions than one would think from statistics published by the Ministry of National Education, in which the method of aggregation is such as to conceal these social effects. Other indices, such as the high proportion of children of self-employed individuals (artisans, merchants, and industrialists) attending the smaller business schools, or, again, the high proportion of children of white-collar workers and middle-level cadres (probably mainly technicians in the private sector) attending the smaller engineering schools, suggest that the schools that lead to employment in the private sector are attended mainly by students whose fathers are already employed there.

The social selection that takes place upon entry into the system of higher education is reinforced upon entry into working life: given two students with the same educational background, the one with the higher social background is more likely to obtain a job as a cadre. The CEREQ study of universities and the job market showed, for example, that 40% of graduates holding Masters' degrees in economics were employed in the government bureaucracy if their fathers were blue-collar workers and 50% if their father were white-collar office workers, compared with only 32% of those whose fathers were upper-level cadres or self-employed professionals and 24% of those whose fathers were moderate to large-scale merchants.

Similarly, a study by the Centre d'études de l'emploi showed that 63% of 1970 graduates who obtained managerial or executive-level positions in industry, commerce, and finance had fathers who were either self-employed professionals, upper-level cadres, industrialists, or large-scale merchants (with children of the latter two groups alone accounting for 21% of the total). Graduates of lower- or middle-class background were more numerous in the public sector: 30% of upper-level cadre positions in the government bureaucracy were held by graduates whose fathers were "blue-collar workers, white-collar workers, artisans, small merchants, farmers, or service personnel."[33]

These patterns suggest that, for those of lower social origins, upward mobility into cadre positions is mainly a matter of working one's way up through the ranks. As the continuing high proportion of autodidacts indicates, for those of humble origin on-the-job training is more likely than formal education to lead to cadre positions, even if the job titles associated with those positions often imply a high level of educational achievement.

The value of a diploma

These mechanisms of student orientation suggest that the increase in the number of college graduates affected the public sector (especially education and social services) very differently from the private sector. Broadly speaking, the absorption of most of the new graduates by the public sector heightened an already noticeable difference between the public and private sectors with respect to the rate of concentration of certified cultural capital (*taux de concentration de capital culturel certifié*).

In 1972 some 2,944,083 men and women, or 14.4% of the work force, were employed by national and local government agencies, compared with 12,164,662 in the private sector, or 59.7% of the work force. Yet the public sector employed 28.7% of those people in the work force with a degree beyond the baccalaureate. Another study shows 16.9% of public sector employees with a degree beyond the baccalaureate, compared with 4.4% of private sector employees (INSEE 1972 employment study, D 33–34, table FORM 14). Among senior administrative cadres, only 30% of the men and 20% of the women hold college degrees overall, but if we restrict our attention to those employed by the government, half have college degrees. The state employs only one-fifth of senior administrative cadres but "consumes" more than a third of the college graduates in this group.[34] The same 1972 study shows that the percentage of college graduates entering public service in the year before the study (33.2%) is much higher than the percentage of college graduates in the public sector as a whole (16.9%), as is the percentage of public sector employees under age thirty-five with college degrees. Similar changes occurred in the private sector, but to a lesser degree: 6.3% of those who entered the private sector in the year before the study had college degrees compared with 4.6% of employees under thirty-five and 4.4% of all private sector employees.

Thus it was mainly public sector expansion in the 1960s that enabled recent graduates to enter the bourgeois job market (*marché du travail bourgeois*) and earn a relatively good return on their degrees, whose value increased sharply. This was particularly true of the teaching profession, in which the vast majority of science and especially liberal arts majors found employment. The increase in the number of primary and secondary school students due to demographic growth and increased rates of school attendance, coupled with the scarcity of teachers (which was frequently deplored in the 1960s[35]), tended to lower hiring standards for teachers in secondary and higher education.[36] The number of jobs in the government bureaucracy also increased sharply in the 1960s. Early in the decade there was a crisis in civil service recruitment, reflected in a dearth of candidates taking civil service examinations. For example, only two-fifths of the jobs on offer with the tax inspection service were filled, because too few candidates signed up for the examination (of 400 posts available, 125 were filled from a pool of 162 candidates). In another examination for the position of assistant secretary in 1965, only 259 of 586 available positions were filled.[37] But when public sector jobs dried up in the late 1960s and early 1970s, it appears that new university graduates did not then set their sights on the private sector (as they would have done had demand in that market been highly elastic). On the contrary, most continued to seek jobs in the public sector and were willing to accept lower pay, especially for entry level positions, and greater uncertainty about the future, coupled with extended periods of preparation for internal examinations. The result was an increase in the number of people holding unstable jobs of ambiguous status: minor posts, "holding positions," assistantships, and temporary appointments of one kind or another. The shortage of jobs in the public sector meant that many people held positions of lower rank than they might have been entitled to expect in view of their educational credentials (thus devaluing the college degree); it also meant that internal civil service promotion examinations took on a new importance. Previously, most college graduates had attempted to enter the civil service at a high level by scoring well on the so-called external examinations. Now, with increased competition for jobs, this was increasingly difficult to do. But if many students believed that the "royal gate" had closed, they also felt that it might just be possible to enter via the back door, that is, to join the civil service at a relatively low level and then score well on the internal promotion examinations. This led to profound changes in the way in which internal promotion was used within the service and, more generally, to changes in the implicit rules governing the behavior of civil service personnel. Many began civil service careers in low-level jobs. But the system of internal examinations (which made it possible to skip one or more echelons instead of climbing the ladder one step at a time, as with normal promotions) offered a good chance of making up for lost time, even if a low starting grade generally meant slower promotion and a lower rank at the end of one's career (unless one started very young). These new promotion mechanisms considerably reduced the chances of autodidacts without college degrees (which had been fairly good under the old system, especially in such agencies as the PTT); they also increased the importance of social capital and social background as factors in obtaining civil service promotions.

The shortage of candidates taking external civil service examinations in the period 1960–5 encouraged promotion of autodidacts, since the internal examinations provided more "category A" civil servants than the external examinations.[38] This trend was reversed in the late 1960s, as the number of candidates in the external examinations increased. For example, in the external examination for entry into the Centre d'études supérieures of the social security administration, the ratio of the number of candidates to the number of posts on offer went from 1:2 in 1962 to 2:4 in 1968, 4:2 in 1970, 10:6 in 1972 and 15:5 in 1973.[39] Correspondingly, the level of educational achievement of civil service candidates increased sharply in the 1970s. One external examination (for *attaché d'administration* and *intendance universitaire*, where the ratio of female to male candidates was 2 to 1) was officially open to candidates who had completed two years of college. But while no candidates in the 1972–3 examination held degrees higher than *licence*, 16.4% of the 1974–5 candidates and 15.3% of the 1976–7 candidates held a *maîtrise*.[40]

The rate of internal recruitment remained high in the late 1960s and early 1970s, due mainly to the unions' concerns that internal promotion not be neglected. This concealed important changes, as the system of internal promotion was put to uses other than those originally intended for it. At the same time the characteristics of the candidates, especially the successful ones, changed. Although the maximum age for filing an application was raised thanks to union pressure, the actual age of candidates, and especially of those who passed the internal examinations, fell. For example, 46% of the candidates taking the internal examination for *attaché d'administration* and *intendance universitaire* were over 35 in 1964, compared with only 31% in 1974. In many cases it appears that college graduates declined to take external examinations for which their degrees made them eligible, but in which competition became intense after 1968, preferring instead either to take lower-level examinations where their chances were better (thus reducing the chances of those who held the minimum-level degree required to take the same examinations) or to accept contract employment that would enable them to build up the necessary time in grade. They then entered the bureaucracy at a level that theoretically did not require a degree as high as the one they held, and later joined the "A group" by passing an internal examination, where their chance of success was greater than that of candidates without degrees, whose promotion was thus blocked or slowed: in the ENS–PTT, for example (access to which was formerly limited to category A civil servants), 32% of the students entered the civil service at level A, 58% at level B, and 10% at level C in 1970, compared with 68%, 23%, and 2%, respectively, in 1974.

This trend was further encouraged by changes in the internal examinations (which had previously emphasized practical knowledge). The tests were revised to be more like the external examinations and, in general, more like the kinds of examination given in universities. For example, in the internal examination for assistant secretaryships in 1974 (in which 31.5% of the candidates held a degree beyond the baccalaureate), the percentages of applicants who received passing grades were as follows: 18% of candidates with diplomas lower than the baccalaureate, 34% of candidates with baccalaureates, 22% of candidates with degrees above the baccalaureate but below the *licence*, and 57% of candidates with a *licence* or higher. This overqualification phenomenon, once limited to examinations for the ENA,[41] spread to all civil service examinations.

The private sector, which as we have seen was largely closed to graduates of the universities, evolved in a different direction. In the early 1960s, the value of those diplomas that were negotiable on the cadre job market (chiefly degrees from engineering and business schools) tended to increase; the supply of graduates fell far short of demand, which had increased rapidly as a result of several independent factors: increased production, industrial reorganization, and introduction of American-style management ideology and practices (affecting both organization and production). Another development, related in complex ways to the increase in demand for graduates, was a growing belief that in order to hold a position of power in a large firm one needed the proper educational credentials. Increasingly, when a firm-owner hired a child or relative to work in the firm, he did so only after the educational system had given proof of competence.[42] But in contrast to the public sector, the tightness of the job market in the private sector proved favorable to graduates of the "right" schools, which remained highly selective, at least until the full effects of the economic crisis made themselves felt toward the end of the 1970s.

In an area where studies are few and far between and results are often hard to come by,[43] the available data suggest that the income of cadres in France, and especially of executives (*cadres dirigeants*), are higher than the income of their counterparts in other European countries and have remained at a high level since the early 1960s (see, for example, the annual studies published by the Management Centre Europe, or MCE[44]). The ratio of the average income of a senior cadre in the private sector to the average worker's income remained almost unchanged from 1963 to 1973 (4:2 in 1963, 4:0 in 1973), reaching a peak of 4:6 in 1967 when the tight market was especially favorable to college graduates in the private sector.[45] The relative value of degrees from various institutions of higher learning also remained stable. Take the entry level income of a graduate of the Ecole Polytechnique as our standard of reference (Polytechnicians being always in demand). Compare this with the average starting salary of graduates of, say, the Institut supérieur d'électronique du Nord (though any other institution would do just as well). This remained fixed at 87% of the Polytechnician's starting salary over the period 1970–7, even though the average nominal salary of the Polytechnician doubled in the meantime.[46] These quantitative indices are confirmed by the experience of informants. Economic journalists, personnel managers, and employment agency heads agree that the value of these kinds of diplomas held steady until the late 1970s. Those who attended the "right" schools, especially if they came from the "right" families (i.e., if they were children of owners or senior cadres), remained relatively scarce in an environment where autodidacts were common; this legitimated the high value placed on them, the high salaries they were paid, and the brilliant career prospects that lay open to them.

Right-wing cadres and left-wing cadres

Despite major changes in industry in this period (such as concentration, internationalization, bureaucratization, increased government intervention, etc.), the agencies that dominated the industrial field maintained control of the mechanisms of reproduction (namely, private or dependent educational institutions that legitimated the power of the dominant agents, coupled with internal mechanisms of promotion that kept dominated agents in line) and thus preserved the crucial independence of *private* enterprise. But the defensive reactions that preserved the internal order of private industry shifted the burden of most of the socially "undesirable" consequences of the expansion of higher education to the public sector (or at any rate shifted the burden of those consequences that were felt to be undesirable by those who wielded economic power). The first and most obvious of these consequences was resentment on the part of college graduates who saw their diplomas diminished in value and the profits of their education, both monetary and symbolic, eaten away, frustrating ambitions fostered by educational success. Such resentment manifested itself far more often and with far greater force in the public sector than in the private sector, where young cadres who had attended the Grandes Ecoles declared themselves to be much more satisfied with their lot and hence far more willing to accept and respect the values prevailing in the organizations for which they worked.

A poll conducted by the magazine *Etudiant* showed, for example, that the proportion of students who "believe they will easily find a job matching their qualifications and desires" was highest among students in the engineering schools (55.9%) and business schools (53.6%) and lowest among students in the faculties of letters (23.5%), law (32.4%), and sciences (30%). This contrast persists after students leave school and enter the work force. A 1973 APEC-sponsored study of "occupational integration of recent graduates" showed that dissatisfaction related to a gap between career plans and actual employment was much more common among teachers, civil servants, and other public sector employees than among cadres in industry. To the question "Do you feel that the job you hold is above, below, or equal to your training?" 35% of the teachers, 33% of the civil servants, and 35% of other public sector employees answered "below," compared with only 18% of cadres. Similarly, 44% of the cadres feel that their careers have "gotten off to a good start," compared with 24% of public sector employees, 26% of teachers, and 30% of civil servants.

Relations between the educational and job markets may also have helped in a more subtle and covert fashion to keep things calm in industry by diverting those students most likely to challenge the prevailing social and economic order into sectors of the economy where their antiauthoritarian and antihierarchical sentiments could find expression at less cost to themselves and at less risk to the dominant segment of the dominant class. New forms of social protest and subversion, born in the universities before and after 1968, were carried by students into the places that employed them, but these were mainly in sectors in which, as we saw earlier, there were no blue-collar workers. Hence declarations and demonstrations of solidarity with the working class remained essentially symbolic and did not disrupt regular institutional functions. Such declarations and demonstrations would have been less well tolerated in industry, where maintaining discipline was a constant concern of employers from the early 1960s on. Hierarchical relations between top management and senior supervisory and production personnel evolved differently in the public and private sectors. In the private sector, the usual control mechanisms continued to ensure that cadres would subscribe to the values and policies of company owners (usually boards of directors representing assorted financial interests). Thus the reassuring image of a harmonious community of views could be maintained, at least to outsiders. In the public sector, however, basic policy was set by politicized top management, who often clashed with civil-servant managers; conflict was sharpest in institutions responsible for cultural production and diffusion, over which the politicians were constantly trying to reassert their authority.

For example, it is well known that a majority of teachers vote left, chiefly for the Socialist Party (one poll showed 46% of teachers intending to vote for the PS, compared with only 27% of the voting population as a whole, and 15% voting Communist).[47] Conversely, cadres in private firms, among whom "contrary to a widespread notion the PS has enjoyed little success,"[48] more often support parties of the right (the declared preference of 50% of engineers, 51% of senior cadres, and 54% of executives) than parties of the left (preferred by 23%, 21%, and 14% respectively).[49] The political differences between non-self-employed bourgeois in the private and public sectors emerge particularly clearly from an analysis of the vote in the March 1978 legislative elections based on a poll of 4,500 persons by the Centre d'étude de la vie politique française: 79% of senior cadres in the private sector voted for right-wing parties (UDF, PR, CDS, radicals, and extreme right); 58% of senior cadres in the public sector (including civil servants) and 75% of teachers voted for left-wing parties (PCF, PSU, PS, MRG, and extreme left).[50]

This correlation between political attitudes and employment in either the public or private sector is, of course, most striking when one contrasts extremes, cadres in private industry, say, with teachers; but it remains marked even in more homogeneous samples. Gérard Grunberg and René Mouriaux, in their study of cadres' attitudes toward politics and unions (based on a sample that excludes not only teachers but other public sector cadres), show clear differences between the political attitudes of cadres in private firms and non-civil-service cadres in the public and nationalized sector: the latter are much more likely to belong to a union (40% versus 22%), much more supportive of unions that accept both cadres and non-cadres (41% versus 26%), and less likely to declare themselves right-wing (44% versus 53%) than their private sector counterparts.[51]

These divisions reflect the dualist logic of politics. They can be related to the private/public sector distinction and to the class segments associated with each sector. The reasons for these intersectoral differences are historical and involve what I shall call the "mode of reproduction" prevalent in each case (inherited wealth in the private sector versus reproduction through education in the public sector, etc.). These differences form part of the "habitus" of each agent and become "objectified" in political, moral, institutional, and family traditions. It appears that the expansion of higher education in the 1960s and 1970s and the channeling of most graduates into the public sector revived and heightened this old opposition while infusing it with new content. Hence, in order to understand values that were described in the early 1970s as "new,"[52] values that were systematized and stylized in a process of collective invention (in which young, college-educated workers in the public sector played a leading role), we must understand what these values (and the epithet "marginal" often used to describe them) owed to the fact that so many recent graduates were working in institutions located on the margins of the productive apparatus, which offered advantages (such as job security, free time, relative affluence, etc.) that tended to encourage these marginal employees to transform partly negative conditions into a new *art de vivre*. The new values may have been conceived originally in opposition to the values prevailing in private industry, to which students had no access. Behind this lay two essential principles: first, a rejection of the work ethic (in Weber's sense), of the spirit of capitalism, of the quest for profit, and of rational work organization as tirelessly preached by the missionaries of productivity and American-style management; and second (in an objective choice not independent of the foregoing), a recognition of intellectual values and, more precisely, a taste for free and gratuitous learning. Combining these two principles led to placing a very high estimate on the value of free time as opposed to work time, of nonworking life as opposed to working life, and, in general, of the private – private life and family life and family and cultural recreations. Paradoxically, the "heroic" virtues of the public man wholly identified with his work are today most commonly associated with private industry.

This can be seen through an analysis of the results of a 1978 private poll of a sample of 300 young cadres ranging in age from 28 to 32, 96 of whom were employed in the public sector and 207 in the private sector. Half lived in Paris and half in the provinces, and all had annual incomes greater than 70,000 francs per year.[53] Given that the cadres in this sample belonged to the upper levels of the group (80% were college graduates, for example) and, further, that the differences between private and public sector agents tend to decrease as one moves from the petite and moyenne bourgeoisie to higher levels of the social hierarchy (as is suggested by the phenomenon known in French as *pantouflage*, in which senior civil servants quit the civil service to take jobs in private industry), we may assume that the systematic differences that the poll reveals between public and private sector cadres would emerge with even greater clarity from a poll based on a broader sample of cadres.

The poll reveals that public sector cadres are concerned about working conditions, desire flexible hours (for greater free time and a better quality of life), want enough time to live, prefer to devote themselves to their families even if work must suffer a little, and enjoy reading, going to the movies and theater, and participating in

Table 4. *Young cadres in the public and private sectors*

in percent	*public*	*private*
Would like:		
—flexible hours	23	12
—good working conditions	14	8
—rapid promotion	5	10
What is most lacking:		
—free time	61	55
—quick success	14	24
Family:		
—when a person has responsibilities, the family inevitably suffers	51	62
—one must devote sufficient time to family life even if work suffers	46	36
Economy:		
—one must accept the workings of the market	42	62
—the government should intervene more	47	37
Political Parties:		
—Socialist or Communist Party (left)	38	26
—Independent Republicans or RPR (right)	24	39
Expect to have a better career:		
—in a large firm	57	38
—in a small-to-medium sized firm	39	60
—working for someone else	75	63
—heading one's own company	17	34
Derive most pleasure from:		
—group activities	22	17
—reading	24	16
—going to movies	23	16
—sports	28	35
Favorite politician:		
—Mitterrand	21	14
—Giscard	36	45
—Rocard	43	38
Unions:		
—a cadres' union should be entirely independent of the workers' unions	34	53

Source: Survey conducted by COFREMCA in 1978, based on a sample of 300 senior cadres, aged 28 to 32, 68% of whom worked in the private sector and 32% in the public sector. Forty-three percent were Parisians, 46% held engineering-school or business-school degrees, and 31% university degrees.

group activities. By way of contrast, private sector cadres are interested mainly in rapid advancement and quick success; they agree with the statement that "when one has responsibilities, the family inevitably suffers"; and for recreation they prefer sports to cultural activities.

These different life styles and values are associated with conflicting opinions about economics (private sector cadres believe in "letting the market function," while young public sector cadres believe in "greater government intervention")[54] and politics. Young private sector cadres prefer the UDF and RPR [right-wing parties – Trans.], and young public sector cadres prefer the Socialists. The latter are more favorable towards self-management and to joint action between workers' unions and cadres' unions. The life styles most common in the public sector are also most common among cadres who declare themselves to be "on the left." Thus to be left-wing means to devote oneself to one's family even if work must suffer a bit, to take the time to live, to cultivate ease of communication, to participate in group activities, etc. Conversely, to be right-wing means to seek a high salary, to desire quick success, to have more money, and to believe that "when one has responsibilities, one's family inevitably suffers somewhat." More generally, right-wingers subscribe to the values of the "man of action" or, as today's management specialists like to say, the achiever; their dynamism contrasts with the more laid back, drop-in style of the public sector marginals.

Recognition of the sharp and therefore visible differences between cadres in private industry and cadres in the public sector should not lead to reification of the contrast between two models of excellence, a contrast that happens to be objectified in what is today's strongest institutional division but could easily be transferred to various other domains. These differences are the result of an internalized social taxonomy that determines how members of the bourgeoisie and petite bourgeoisie explain their own behavior and thereby not only control but to a certain extent engender the social order. A few examples may help to clarify what I mean. In large private firms, for instance, research and development engineers are to sales cadres what public sector cadres are to private sector cadres when we consider the bourgeoisie as a whole. Similarly, in the government's cultural bureaucracies, the relationship of administrators and sales representatives to creative personnel is just the reverse (e.g., television producers complain of the obstacles put in their way by "those damned cadres"). And so on. These differences are based in part on the attributes of the agents (R&D engineers in large, high-technology firms have much in common with, say, CNRS researchers), in part on the nature of the jobs they fill (especially with respect to the distinction between those jobs that bear directly on investment yields and returns to capital and those that are more closely associated with cultural investments; as in any case where economic and cultural values clash, this distinction brings in a whole series of other distinctions, between interest and disinterest, the material and the spiritual, and so on).

In private industry, research cadres and (to a lesser degree) development cadres differ in a number of ways from administrative and especially sales cadres. This opposition parallels the opposition between public sector and private sector cadres. Thus, for example, R & D cadres are more likely to be college graduates than sales and administrative cadres. Engineers are most common, followed by graduates of the science faculties of the universities (especially in research departments). For the most part they are employed in large firms in advanced sectors of industry, which are, generally speaking, the only private companies that maintain their own research departments. Conversely, one finds the highest proportion of autodidacts among sales and administrative cadres (especially in small- and medium-sized firms, where they often occupy management positions). Similarly, cadres working in research and quality control are more likely to describe themselves as left-wing (44% and 40% respectively, compared with 28% of administrative cadres and 24% of sales cadres).[55] Research cadres (who are especially numerous in the CFDT) generally do not have direct supervisory responsibilities. Around half are children of upper- or middle-level cadres.[56] Compare this with manufacturing cadres, many of whom have a working-class background and only a third of whom are children of senior cadres. Around half are themselves former workers or foremen who have risen through the ranks and whose primary responsibility is to supervise and inspect the work of blue-collar workers. In the 1974 presidential elections 44% of the research engineers claim to have voted for François Mitterrand [the candidate of the left – Trans.], compared with 24% of the manufacturing cadres, 44% of whom supported Valéry Giscard d'Estaing (compared with only 21% of the research engineers).[57]

The same logic very likely dictated the polarization of cadres that took place during the crisis of May–June 1968, as is suggested by data from a 1969 study of the Marseilles region conducted by the

Laboratoire d'économie et de sociologie du travail:[58] cadres who took part in the strike came mainly from large public sector firms, especially those using advanced technologies such as the Commissariat à l'énergie atomique, and from R & D firms employing mainly engineers and research workers (these accounted for 41% of the sample but 61% of the strikers). Conversely, striking cadres were underrepresented in private industry and in traditional sectors such as construction, metals, foodstuffs, etc.

Similarly, analysis of striking cadres by type of job shows that the percentage of strikers was highest among research engineers with no supervisory responsibilities and lowest among cadres in administration and sales. Finally, 61% of CFDT members (many of whom work in technical or research departments) declared that the demands of cadres stood at the "intersection of workers' and students' demands," compared with only 24% of CGT members, and 44% declared that cadres were mainly "influenced by the student movement," compared with only 16% of CGT members.[59]

More detailed analysis would no doubt reveal similar splits within units smaller and apparently more homogeneous than sectors or even firms, and one could show that the same patterns of opposition operate in smaller and smaller domains, one contained within another. Within each frame of reference, it is as if agents with contrasting attributes tend to gravitate toward opposite extremes.

The same system of oppositions also seems to have operated within the universities, where cadres served as a model for some and a countermodel for others. The subject of cadres became a matter of considerable debate and controversy in the years leading up to the crisis of May 1968.

The modernization of the university

The new standard of excellence that took shape even as cadres were institutionalizing themselves *qua* group took hold outside as well as inside the domain of private industry. The new standard or social representation attracted attention, diffuse and surreptitious though it may have been, among intellectuals and in the universities, especially in the "modern" disciplines that were called upon to play a role in industrial development, such as applied physics and, in a rather different way, psychology. In groups such as the Association d'études pour l'expansion de la recherche scientifique and the Club Jean-Moulin and meetings such as the Caen Colloquium of November 1966, modernist industrialists, progressive civil servants, and large numbers of academics (many of them scientists, mostly young and inclined to challenge, as spokesmen for their disciplines, the traditional hierarchical values of the universities) met to discuss reforming the system of higher education. The conceptual model for educational reform was the same as the model for the modernization of industry. The overriding theme in both cases was one of opening borders and ending "protectionism" in order to enjoy the salutary effects of competition stemming from "integration into international economic life."[60]

Nothing is more instructive in this regard than to read the 1964 special issue of *Esprit* on higher education, in which the principal themes of reform are discussed.[61] Bernard Cagnac, a lecturer in science at Orsay, declared that in order to achieve "mass higher education that will prepare youths over the age of 18 for careers" it would be necessary to destroy what was sometimes called the "university ghetto" (*Esprit*, p. 59). Roger Grégoire, a member of the Conseil d'Etat, had this to say: "Like all of France, the universities have lived under a protectionist regime. They will come back to life only if they are willing to open their borders" (*Esprit*, p. 823). To begin with, the boundary between the universities and industry would have to be eliminated. This meant treating the universities as businesses whose productivity had to be increased in order to make them competitive with other enterprises of the same type (a leitmotif in this line of criticism is the comparison of French universities with their American and Soviet counterparts). The goals, or, as Catholic civil servants and industrialists are fond of putting it, the "finalities" of the universities must be adjusted to the needs of the economic system: "The techniques of long-range economic and social forecasting should make it possible to formulate goals for the universities," wrote Claude Gruson (*Esprit*, p. 709). Much technocratic thinking about higher education was based on an analogy, not always explicitly stated, between the Malthusian forces in the economic sphere (i.e., segments of the bourgeoisie and petite bourgeoisie whose interests were bound up with small business and local and colonial markets and which were nostalgic for the "age of petit-bourgeois radicalism"[62]) and the conservative forces in higher education (tenured professors in traditional disciplines, etc.). The struggle against the mandarins was thus one reason for the tacit accord in the years leading up to the crisis of May 1968 between representatives of outside economic interests – senior civil servants and industrialists – and young, innovative instructor-researchers in the universities who at the time still occupied subordinate positions in the academic hierarchy. These young teachers worked mainly in the natural and social sciences. They campaigned in favor of research and authority based on scientific value rather than on the possession of a chair, which, it was charged, many old-fashioned professors viewed as their inalienable property. At the Caen Colloquium, for example, criticism was leveled at the system of "chairs, which constitute minor, isolated fiefdoms."[63]

For instance, one Parisian banker, R. Schlumberger, attacked the fundamental conservatism of the teaching profession, which he likened to the conservatism of artisans, and called for radical changes in the protected environment of higher education:

> The universities today are one of the last national institutions that have not been shaken to the foundations by the twentieth-century revolution.... One of the major difficulties seems to lie in the universities themselves, and particularly in the teaching corps. Assuming, as is certainly the case, that the universities cannot command sufficient resources to deal with the growth in the number of students while at the same time maintaining their current protected environment and antiquated artisanal methods, will they be willing to accept radical changes? ... Many are the friends of higher education who fear its fundamental conservatism in this regard. (*Esprit*, p. 712)

Various groups campaigned for what one might call an "internationalization of the cultural capital" transferred by the universities; among the targets of criticism in this campaign were what was termed "old-fashioned humanist culture," which the critics argued should be replaced by the "new" scientific culture. More generally, native French intellectual traditions were denounced as provincial and archaic, and praise was reserved for disciplines and schools that had developed most fully in the United States. Finally, changes in working conditions, chiefly in the exact sciences but also to some extent in the human sciences, tended to familiarize academics and researchers with a model less remote from the industrial model than had been the case in previous generations: increases in the budget for higher education and research, not only for operating expenditures and capital improvements but also for salaries, increased the number of positions of power (so that important professors and heads of research laboratories spent much of their time at the ministry of education or dealing with various budgetary committees) and accelerated academic promotions, which, much as in industry, could be managed rationally so as to maximize the return (and not solely the intellectual return) on "intellectual investment." In response to the *Esprit* survey, one professor drew a jesting portrait of the professor of the future, which may be the objectification of a collective fantasy: "His standard of living is that of a successful physician or top manager in industry. He is an important member of the community and promotes intellectual activity in his province. He is simultaneously active in teaching, publishing, and missions abroad. Students respect him, yet his door is often wide open" (*Esprit*, p. 824).

It was at least in part in opposition to forecasts of the modernization, rationalization, and profit orientation of higher education and to attempts to bring the universities closer to industry that the student movement was organized in the period 1964–6. The technocrats, statistics in hand, saw a vision of utopia in which students would become cadres, even though all the objective mechanisms of selection and orientation tended to channel most university students away from industry. Against this view was raised the virtuous indignation of the "revolutionary" prophecy, which predicted that students would rise in rebellion against a fate that others sought to impose on them, namely, the fate of the cadre.[64] Given the very absence of organized protest, it is unlikely that this destiny would ever have been realized.

The Sorbonne in the 1960s

Between the end of the war in Algeria and May 1968, the ideological rhetoric that accompanied factional struggles within the UNEF for control of what people had begun to call the "student movement" was, like all mobilization rhetoric, primarily intended to define the term "student" and to impose some firm identity on what was a particularly unstable and heterogeneous group. To do this it was necessary to identify something that all students shared in common, something more fundamental than the differences that divided them (among other things, sex, discipline, and above all social background).[65] For all factions involved in this struggle, the image of the cadre prevalent in the 1960s became the antimodel. During the planning and implementation of the Fouchet reform and especially in the period 1964–6, a critique of the "technocratic university" was developed by students in the faculties of letters, especially at the Sorbonne (the leaders of the student movement, Antoine Griset, Marc Kravetz, and Jean-Louis Peninou, were from 1962 to 1965 representatives of the Fédération des groupes d'étude de lettres, or FGEL).[66] The central theme of this critique was that neocapitalist powers wished to technocratize the universities and through specialization, orientation, and selection transform the mass of students into a mass of future cadres, of specialized and blinkered automata; neocapitalism sought to fashion an army of obedient little cadres, to supply industry's need for human robots.[67] Academic life subjected the student to a form of alienation that foreshadowed and familiarized him with the alienation that he would experience on the job. In other words, the student movement subscribed to the predictions of the reformists but attached a negative value to the outcome.[68]

Cadres were particularly well suited to play the role of antimodel in these new ideologies because of the ambiguity surrounding their identity and the heterogeneity of the group. Thus statements about cadres could convey multiple messages. In speaking of cadres one could refer both to those who wielded technocratic power and to those who controlled the major capitalist firms; to petty bosses who tyrannized workers and to so-called intellectual workers, new proletarians compelled to perform fragmented tasks. So protests against the transformation of the university into a "cadre-making machine" could also claim to be urging students to refuse to participate in capitalist exploitation and supervision of the working class and at the same time pose as an elitist rebellion against a system that held out the promise not of intellectual, creative work but of petty, undignified labor (the "fragmentation of knowledge," which was said to be an instrument for the "social conditioning of the future cadre," was obviously conceived as something similar to the fragmentation of work in industry).

Thus the rhetoric of the student movement wavered between an ostentatious refusal of privilege and anxiety at not being able to gain access to privilege. But it was obsessed not so much by the notion of the "top manager" (who perhaps comes closest to the students' definition of the cadre as the "watchdog of capital") as by the "*petty* cadre" (the term recurs constantly), the "subaltern," the modern incarnation of the eternal "petit bourgeois." We also find the same obsessional images that have always filled the elitist fantasies of intellectual segments of the bourgeoisie, such as the "anonymous masses" (of "intellectual apprentices"[69]), the "horde," the "common run," the "machine" (the "academic machine"), the "robot," and the "automaton" (with its related imagery of "programming," "programmed instruction," and the "programmed society"). This accounts for the exaltation, which today seems somewhat surprising, of *culture* (this was before the cultural revolution), of "true, general culture" as opposed to "specialized knowledge" ("ersatz pre-sliced culture"), which "reduces all culture to the lowest common denominator." It also accounts for another leitmotif of student rhetoric, the prediction of imminent "unemployment," especially in the faculties of letters. Now, unemployment was not only non-existent at the time, it was also hard to see where it would come from, at least on the basis of objective indicators and projections, and the planners tirelessly repeated that all college graduates would find jobs commensurate with their qualifications. The fear of unemployment and the fear of being relegated to low-level cadre posts are frequently mentioned together,[70] perhaps reflecting the same anxiety and the same nostalgia for a time when college students were relatively few in number and more or less free of institutional (i.e. academic) constraints and could be certain of finding work that would bring them at least the symbolic rewards of the bourgeois intellectual (in teaching, law, medicine, etc.); these included "respect," autonomy, control over one's time and work schedule, and above all a monopoly on philosophical reflection and thought, that is, a form of spiritual power.

In order to interpret the rhetoric of student mobilization, one must recall the prevailing intellectual climate in the faculties of letters, especially at the Sorbonne where the movement was born. This will also make clear what the movement owed to professors who relayed theories and topics of current scholarly interest to their students.[71] For liberal arts students, especially the philosophy and sociology majors who formed the university's political cadres, political commitment was, as Yvette Delsaut has shown,[72] a way of indicating one's acceptance of the intellectual role, characterized by absence of obligation (a free schedule, an undemanding program, etc.) and opposition to scholarly discipline and professional constraints. It is clear that "proclaimed indifference to political commitment was inversely proportional to the degree of integration into the academic environment." For example, the highest proportion of students declaring themselves indifferent to politics is found among women, provincials, and students of middle- or lower-class background. It appears, then, that political debate was "one way among others of learning the intellectual trade" through manipulation of subtle shades of difference, the basis of all symbolic distinctions. These attitudes were particularly evident among sociology students. Still new in the university curriculum, sociology in the 1960s occupied a privileged position in the intellectual sphere; sociology departments were prepared to accept students with a particularly highly developed theoretical bent and a taste for political analysis (among whom the percentage of males and of children of the intellectual bourgeoisie was higher than in most other academic disciplines).[73]

We can now understand why the question of "number" was so important in the system of contradictions characteristic of student mobilization rhetoric. The increase in the number of students, made visible and almost palpable in this case by the crowding of lecture halls, suggested a danger of unemployment, disqualification, etc.[74] But the logic of mobilization at work here, patterned after the workers' movement and aimed at unifying the student masses and turning a heterogeneous collection into a unified and powerful group, made it impossible to fight against this "danger." Explicit opposition to the increase in the number of students was out of the question, for it would have contradicted the universalizing intention behind this new form of "revolutionary" discourse. Hence selection (and any other form of "flow control"), which might have seemed a rational response to the catastrophic predictions made by the student unions (and which was perhaps implicitly, or, rather, unconsciously, demanded by the students) was of all the reform proposals the one that aroused the greatest hostility and thus helped to mobilize large numbers of students. The idea of basing selection on academic achievement aroused individual fears of exclusion (especially, no doubt, in disciplines like philosophy and sociology, in which students were most attached to the exemptions and freedoms of student life and – not unrelatedly – most politicized), so that in order to defend the interests of each individual (which would have required reducing the number of students or limiting access to certain courses) it was necessary to demand that everyone be granted equal access to scarce privileges.

The working bourgeoisie

This is probably the best place to discuss the historical context surrounding the development in the late 1960s of modes of existence and principles of identity whose most prominent attributes were at least originally a simple inversion of standards of excellence associated with the cadre archetype: these include the repudiation of productivism, of the profit motive, of the spirit of competition, and of careerism and the celebration of the local, the regional, etc. These new attitudes were associated mainly with the public sector, especially in its more intellectual zones (such as cultural production and diffusion), that is, in the zones that rapidly absorbed most of the students produced by an educational system in which there had never before existed so great a contradiction between expressed intentions (to manufacture cadres) and objective mechanisms of selection and orientation.

After May 1968 the dominant segments of the dominant class – major industrialists and top civil servants – abandoned many of the hopes they had placed in the universities, intellectuals, and social sciences and renounced the utopian notion that consensus could be achieved by "rational" means, namely, the maximization of efficiency and profit. From this point on, "the general diagnosis is quite clear. Between the university and the economy there is an abyss, an abyss between two worlds that know nothing of each other and that seem to take pleasure in erecting obstacles to mutual understanding."[75] No doubt one could show, moreover, that conflicts between, on the one hand, the petite and moyenne bourgeoisie associated with the public sector and, on the other hand, big business and its representatives in the civil service and in politics (and private sector cadres) played a major role in the political struggles of the late 1960s and 1970s.[76] It seems that cadres, who had previously been defined mainly by contrast with traditional segments of the bourgeoisie and petite bourgeoisie, were now incorporated into relatively new systems of classification, which overlapped older systems without replacing them altogether. As "bureaucratization" (to use an old Trotskyite expression) continued apace, and as strife between those with inherited wealth and others associated with the centers of capital accumulation and concentration (or, to put it another way, conflict between what Robert Boyer calls the "mode of competitive regulation" and the "mode of monopolistic regulation"[77]) became less sharp and less bitter, another division developed within the bourgeoisie and petite bourgeoise: on one side stood agents destined to occupy privileged positions in major business organizations, and on the other side those who benefited primarily from their association with institutions of redistribution, planning, statistical monitoring, control, and cultural production and diffusion. This contradiction, though not new, became particularly severe during the past decade. It is characterized by a series of related but not identical oppositions: between a "protected" sector imbued with the spirit of public service and cultural detachment (*spiritualisme culturel*) whose members refuse to recognize the constraints of the market, and an "exposed" sector, exposed in the sense that it must increasingly face international competition and to an ever greater degree must operate in the Third World;[78] between regionalism (or nationalism) and multinationalism; between the spiritual and the material; between utopianism and realism; and so on.

It is easy enough to find instances of the new social images associated with the term "cadre" as used not in the dominant sense (i.e., of modernist cadres contrasted with the old-fashioned bourgeoisie) but in the new sense (i.e., efficient, hard-headed managers contrasted with cultivated, utopian marginals). The value of each term in the opposition depends, of course, on where in "social space" a given utterance is produced. Take, for example, the following excerpt from Maurice Clavel's column in *Le Nouvel Observateur*, published in 1972:

Hexagone broadcast an important program on cadres.... Many cadres were there – young cadres, would-be cadres.... There was a lot of talk about standards of living, retirement, salary range, taxes, promotions, hierarchy, and careers.... This world is absolutely frightful, though the people in it are not to blame.... Humor is out of the question. Things are too bleak.... How can one help hating these young elites? ... These days, you see, I prefer the generals, who by dint of having cooled their heels for so long in the barren wastes of the fatherland may one fine day populate the countryside by returning home themselves. And similarly – I only seem to be changing the subject – I prefer the traditional Christians, with their dogma intact, worried about divine transcendence and convinced that they have nothing whatsoever to do with society as it is now constituted.... Cadres ... will be tomorrow's enemy – for alas, an enemy is a necessary thing! And there will be a fight.[79]

The same opposition is invoked, however, by spokesmen for what is today the dominant faction in the industrial field as an argument in favor of the internationalization of capital. Alain Cotta, for instance, speaks of two "economic strategies": a strategy of adaptation to the "expanding world market," and a strategy "of retreat into fortress France." According to Cotta, the contrast between these two strategies defines a new division in society:

It is quite likely, even, that our country, faithful to its radical history, will succeed in not choosing; that under the influence of various domestic economic, social, and political factors there will arise two complementary spheres of activity, each as different from the other as both are necessary. The first comprises a world of far-flung export industries subject to international competition, peopled by men who spend much of their lives in the airports and chain-operated hotels without which life would be impossible on a planet where industrialization will one day be less uneven than it is now. The second is presumably the incarnation of our historical tendencies to regulate the economy, to convert others to speak our language, and, more democratically, to assert our cultural identity – essential for any nation and especially for a Mediterranean nation. It will consist of men who are less mobile, of organizations whose vocation is purely domestic, and of redistributive institutions. The split between these two worlds should not be confused with present-day political oppositions or with the overworked distinctions between public and private, mercantile and non-mercantile. It will be *sui generis* and will develop slowly, along with social tensions whose exact intensity it is difficult to predict; and once again it will take the monotonous forecasters by surprise.[80]

Both right-wing and left-wing rhetoric about the frustrations of the middle classes (which would be less interesting if it were less "interested," i.e., if the middle class were not always a sought-after prize of political, and more precisely electoral, conflict), with its endless denunciations of the "malaise of cadres", or the "freezing of teachers' promotions," at times expresses nothing more than the economic and ethical conflicts that arise between left- and right-wing segments of the bourgeoisie and petite bourgeoisie. Even radical oppositions may conceal common interests that can be defended more easily if they remain tacit. Hostile segments of the bourgeoisie and petite bourgeoisie share at least one common interest, namely, that the various factors that contributed to the swelling of their ranks continue to operate (and these factors may owe less to technological determinism than the prophets of growth believe). In order to interpret the considerable growth of the bourgeoisie and petite bourgeoisie over the past twenty years (assuming, for statistical purposes, that the relevant taxonomies have remained unchanged over this period), it is surely not enough to point to the increase in industrial productivity, however undeniable its effects. This is particularly true when we look at agents classified as senior cadres in the private sector, as well as senior cadres and teachers in the public sector (the parallel growth curves for these groups is a problem in itself, given the fact that growth in each case was due to relatively independent factors). Among the other factors to be considered, particular attention probably ought to be paid to the social effects of the new international division of labor. Take Germany, for example, a country in many ways comparable to France: the number of workers employed in subsidiaries of West German firms in the Third World (at least 25% German-owned) is 20% of the number of workers employed in German territory (and this proportion would certainly be higher if firms subcontracting to German firms were included in the total).[81] Thus there is good reason to wonder about the relation of various phenomena affecting the in-

Table 5. *Middle-class employees in public and private sectors, according to census data for 1954, 1962, 1968, and 1975*

	1954						*1962*					
	public sector	% of F	*private sector*	% of F	*total*	% of F	*public sector*	% of F	*private sector*	% of F	*total*	% of F
Teachers, professionals	63,560	38.6	17,600	42.6	81,160	39.5	93,400	43.1	25,340	44.3	118,740	43.1
Engineers	116,000	9.2	81,140	2.1	353,160	6.9	35,100	4.4	102,880	3.6	137,980	3.1
Top administrative cadres			156,020	7.7			159,340	12.6	210,580	11.8	369,920	12.1

	1968						*1975*					
	public sector	% of F	*private sector*	% of F	*total*	% of F	*public sector*	% of F	*private sector*	% of F	*total*	% of F
Teachers, professionals	153,020	43.7	47,740	43.5	200,760	45.2	279,860	46.9	74,700	45.9	354,560	46.7
Engineers	49,940	4.2	136,800	3.0	186,740	3.4	61,240	4.9	185,580	3.7	246,820	4.0
Top administrative cadres	172,180	15.2	275,220	11.2	447,400	12.7	238,440	23.5	405,940	13.7	644,280	17.3

Note: F = females

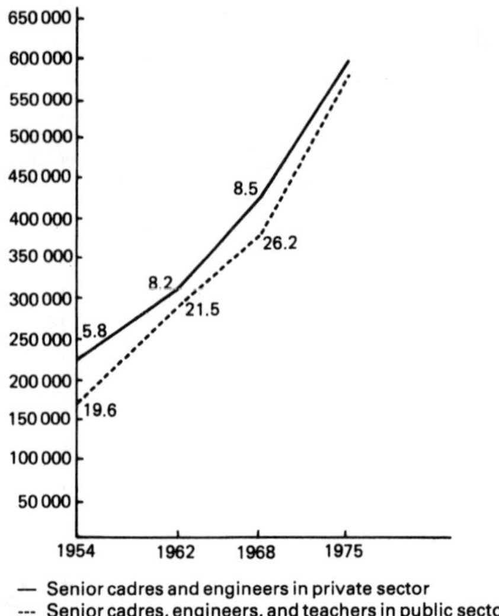

dustrialized nations of Western Europe, such as the growth of the tertiary sector, the middle classes, the number of cadres, etc. (the basis of so much optimism in the 1960s), to the increasing exploitation of an all but inexhaustible reserve of workers living in what has come to be called the "periphery" of the industrialized world, workers who are in competition with one another and largely powerless in the struggle with their exploiters.[82]

Yet it is not enough simply to recall the macroeconomic conditions that made possible the increase in the number of bourgeois employees if our goal is to understand how the term "cadre" gradually won general acceptance and attracted the interest of scattered segments of the bourgeoisie and petite bourgeoisie. In gathering statistics one generally assigns names to artificially defined social aggregates, names that make these aggregates seem more homogeneous than they really are. In order to break down this apparent homogeneity, we must next analyze the way in which cadres exerted a force of attraction on the members of other social groups, individuals who lacked many of the attributes associated with the cadre archetype. Indeed, this lack becomes increasingly apparent as one moves farther and farther away from the original archetype. People occupying many different positions in industry all claimed the title "cadre." Once we have identified what these positions were, we can then speculate about the structural properties of the field and attempt to follow the careers of different kinds of cadres over the course of their working lives.

5 *Careers*

A heterogeneous space

"Careers" are a subject of inexhaustible interest for cadres, as is shown by the proliferation of guides, studies, and other sources of information about career opportunities and prospects, and yet this is one of the most difficult aspects of professional life to investigate using statistical methods. Suppose one wanted to determine the probability that an individual with a given set of attributes will occupy a given series of positions. To do so one would have to assume the existence of a homogeneous social space, in which positions labeled by a given name would exhibit identical characteristics *at all points in the space*. In particular, there would have to exist a stable relationship between educational capital and job definition, between the academic degree and the job title – a relationship that would remain stable across all institutions, firms, agencies, and so on, as well as over. These conditions are not met in industry, a complex array of entities of varying size and legal status (the company, the subsidiary, the plant, the department, etc.). Nor is the position of each of these entities relative to the production process or the power structure determined by its official legal status.[1] Within this heterogeneous and complex structure, those in control of each unit (possibly not the officially designated owner or CEO – yet another impediment to unraveling the true power structure) have the power to assign job titles. But nominally identical titles may conceal actual diversity. The titles in common use in industry today, such as director of marketing, sales manager, internal auditor, and so on, constitute a shared vocabulary, in the sense that a limited number (around one hundred) job titles are used throughout industry to characterize both the job specialty and hierarchical rank of cadres. Yet a given title in one firm may not correspond to the same title in another firm. Unlike the government bureaucracy, industry has not been subjected to an institutional process of unification. Hence the same title, say, "sales manager," can refer to something quite different depending on whether we are looking at a large firm or a small one (in which supervisory responsibilities are unevenly shared). Thus the value of a given position depends both on its place within the structure of the firm and on the place of the firm within the field of industry.

A fundamental property of any "field" is the degree to which its system of titles and positions is unified, standardized, and institutionalized. Accordingly, it is impossible to compare the government bureaucratic field with the industrial field without taking into account the standardization process to which the former has been subjected over the past century, largely under pressure from the unions and especially through campaigns for salary parity for civil servants of equivalent rank employed in different departments of the bureaucracy.[2] No doubt one could show more generally that statistical measurement depends on "institutionalized spaces" (and hence on social spheres subject to state administration), because no meaningful statistics can be gathered unless there exists a universally recognized, standard nomenclature whose terms have almost legal force.[3]

In other words, it is impossible to study individual careers unless one has previously analyzed the specific properties of the field (and not simply the "market"[4]) within which those careers unfold. Is the field homogeneous, and has the parity between different job titles been fixed through a process of organization and unification? These points are all too often neglected in studies of social mobility, many of which rely on rigid distinctions between individuals and jobs, agents and positions. I am thinking, in particular, of so-called structural methods developed in recent years in the United States.[5] The underlying assumption in such approaches is that careers are a natural phenomenon, that it is somehow foreordained that individuals will move from job to job and from echelon to echelon within some kind of hierarchy. But this way of organizing professional life is only one of several possibilities, a product of social technologies operating in definite historical circumstances. The implicit assumption that there is a rigid distinction between agents and positions is best satisfied by the kinds of "homogeneous spaces" that one finds in bureaucratic organizations, especially when regulated by explicit legislation. Under these conditions the value of a position does not depend on the individual who fills it, and the reified organizational structure can be perpetuated. Even in this case, however, "positional analysis" is artificial in that it reflects the formal rather than the informal organization, unless care is taken to allow for the way in which the informal organization is manipulated in practice.

Any attempt to analyze career patterns (as in the positivist, British and American tradition of "professionalization" and "organizational mobility" studies) will face certain problems. Grappling with these problems does at least have the virtue of calling attention to certain basic properties of the industrial field that must be grasped if we are to understand how cadres' careers develop. Specifically, there is a contradiction between, on the one hand, the need for "rationalization," transparency, and long-term planning (as reflected in formal organization charts, career planning, etc.) – a need which since the 1950s has been associated with meritocratic principles of legitimation – and, on the other hand, the underlying structure of the industrial field, a complex network of power relations revolving around vaguely defined entities, jobs, titles, etc. The nominal homogenization effected by the introduction of "management" methods probably made the field even more opaque, for a common vocabulary is now used by agents occupying positions quite unequal in power (e.g., a department supervisor in a large department store and the vice-president for sales of a major auto manufacturer) to describe their respective activities (promotion, advertising, networking, marketing, administrative control, etc.) and positions (leader, manager, man in charge, chief salesman, etc.). The language of management, the official jargon of business, tends to dissimulate or to find euphemisms for objective differences that were once expressed rather openly.

The official nomenclature of titles facilitates some semblance of communication only if the agents involved take account of a fairly large number of explicit or, more often, implicit signs of status. Titles would have almost no practical predictive value if agents did not make use of other available information, such as the age, social background, and education of the person holding the title, the size and importance of the firm employing him, etc. Since each indicator taken by itself is ambiguous, the only way to make any sense of an individual case is to consider many different indicators at once. For example, having a large number of subordinates may be a sign of high status if the subordinates themselves occupy fairly high positions in the hierarchy, or it may be a sign of low status if the subordinates are blue-collar or clerical workers: a shop manager or foreman may have more people working under him than a corporate comptroller. The cadres interviewed recognized this when they said of each indicator presented to them, "That doesn't mean anything." Each indicator makes sense only in relation to all the others. Apparently "native speakers" of this industrial language have the ability to assemble seemingly insignificant clues into meaningful patterns.

The fact that the industrial field is relatively opaque no doubt plays an important part in the reproduction of social hierarchies, for it places lower-level cadres, autodidacts and/or individuals of middle- or lower-class background under an even greater handicap than they would be otherwise. Capital in the form of information, on which rational career planning in a bureaucratic world largely depends, is very unevenly distributed via the power structure and perhaps even more via informal relational networks (family, friends, family connections, and so forth). By calling upon these networks one can obtain information needed for making (or unmaking) profitable investments (as in the stock market, one's profit depends chiefly on the quality of one's predictions).[6] Agents occupying strategic positions in various power structures can arrange for information to be funneled to them. More than that, they can cause events to happen (say, by reorganizing a department), advance knowledge of which is precisely the kind of scarce information that cadres prize. Here again, rather oddly, the introduction of management methods probably made the professional world of cadres more intractable and less predictable than it was by adducing simplification and rationalization as grounds for frequent reorganization. Informational inequalities are exacerbated when mergers lead to major restructuring and people in subordinate positions find that painfully acquired knowledge is no longer worth anything.

During periods of restructuring, the very identity of those company officials on whom the fate of cadres depends is in doubt. Who is "in charge"? Are one's direct superiors really in control? They themselves hide behind orders from the top and complain of limitations on their freedom to maneuver ("I got you that bonus – it wasn't easy, but it was the best I could do"). Perhaps the strings are really being pulled by higher-ups. But these higher-ups are in many cases inaccessible, or they may insist that everything be handled through channels (and lower-ranking officials may severely punish any attempt to "go over their heads"). In any case, a person may believe someone to be in charge who is really in the dark, so that his statements and promises are in fact worthless ("When he said that something or other was going to happen because one of the top executives had told him so, it didn't take two weeks before everyone knew it wasn't true"). These same mechanisms protect people in positions of power by directing resentment toward underlings, who are where they are precisely in order to divert criticism from the top, or else toward officials of high enough rank that nothing can be done about their alleged misdeeds. The opacity of the overall structure, the secrecy that shrouds the decision-making process, and the gap between official information and "rumors" passed on through informal networks all serve to channel collective resentment toward certain designated scapegoats. In the case of a merger, these are often officials of the larger company. These scapegoats become the focal point of the anxieties and fantasies of those who "feel threatened," which in many cases means nearly everyone in the firm. What cadres say about their companies in such cases is filled with unspoken insinuations and allusions to shadowy figures: "It seems that so-and-so . . ."; "A certain unsavory character arrived and the shit really hit the fan"; "A gentleman I won't name . . ."; and so on.

Lower-level cadres, autodidacts who have risen through the ranks and who, having reached their current position relatively late, are not included in informal informational networks, tend to stick quite closely to the formal image of the organization as depicted in the official organization chart and to abide strictly by the formal rules governing promotion. Hence they are more likely than other cadres to overestimate their likelihood of success, believing that they can in fact obtain positions that are formally open to them even though their real chance of succeeding is nil. In other words, the obstacles and pitfalls confronting the sociologist are the same as those confronting the agents themselves, particularly those at the bottom of the heap, who share with the outside investigator a lack of the kind of tacit knowledge that defines native competence

Characteristics of firms and social attributes of cadres

As the foregoing remarks suggest, all but insurmountable problems of method confront any attempt to uncover the way in which agents' attributes relate to company characteristics. For example, the size of a firm (as measured by the number of employees), useful as it is as an index, must be viewed with caution. The significance of the number depends on whether the unit considered is a single plant or an entire firm, an independent or a subsidiary of another firm, a production plant or a corporate headquarters, etc. It also depends on the informant's position in the circuits of production and power. This is particularly true in large conglomerates. In theory, at least, all cadres serve under one corporate management. Yet in interviews with cadres the answers they give depend on where they sit in the corporate structure. The higher their position, the more they tend to answer questions about the size of the company by referring to the corporation as a whole. The lower they sit, the farther they are from corporate headquarters and top management, the more they tend to refer to their own subsidiary or plant. These differences in perception correspond to objective differences in field of activity, range of opportunity, and power.[7] In large corporations, for example, high-level cadres are recruited directly at the corporate level, intermediate-level cadres at the division level, and low-level cadres at the plant level. Inequalities of power and range of opportunity within a given corporation or division emerge with particular clarity in cases of merger: cadres employed by the parent company gain access to top slots in the subsidiary, whereas cadres employed by the new subsidiary find that their range of opportunities has been reduced, since they can no longer aspire to top positions in their own company. Company size is far from the most ambiguous of industrial indices, moreover. Similar remarks could be made about such indices as "sector" (a large corporation may have subsidiaries working in high-technology sectors and other subsidiaries operating in more traditional sectors). Other indices, such as "gross revenues" (more or less independent of number of employees) and "growth rate," are also fraught with ambiguities.[8]

I have no miraculous remedy for these problems, which are inherent in the structure of the field itself. Yet there are, I think, two indices that do help to clarify the relation between cadres' social attributes and the firms that employ them. Given the nature of currently available statistics, however, these indices must be inferred indirectly. The first relates to what I shall call the degree of dispersion or concentration in a given branch of industry. For example, J.-P. Gorgé and A. Tandré[9] have contrasted what they call "concentrated sectors" with what they call "dispersed sectors." Dispersed sectors are those in which a large number of relatively small firms operate. Concentrated sectors are those dominated by a few relatively large firms. Concentrated sectors tend to become more concentrated under the combined effects of government intervention and corporate mergers. In them we find both privately owned companies and publicly owned corporations (though the distinction is not always easy to make) and almost equal numbers of nationalized firms, French-owned private firms, and multinationals, chiefly under American control (a quarter of the personnel involved in mergers in the past fifteen years have worked for foreign-controlled firms, which have played a major role in the trend toward increased concentration).[10]

The second index mentioned above is especially relevant to the study of cadres. It has to do with a firm's capital structure (and is not independent of the degree of concentration or dispersion discussed above, of which size is a rough indicator).[11] This capital-structure index is a composite of capital intensity (i.e., the ratio of physical or constant capital to labor or embodied capital) and another index that measures the degree to which firms invest in cultural capital. Capital-intensive industries tend to be relatively concentrated and labor-intensive industries tend to be relatively dispersed. Similarly, we can also classify firms according to the amount of cultural capital concentrated in them and the degree to which they make use of that cultural capital, either directly as a factor of production or indirectly in the form of nonproductive services.[12]

Using these two indices, we can now classify the various sectors of industry. Some industries are highly dispersed, that is, characterized by large numbers of relatively small production units. Their capital intensity is low, because the employment of a large, relatively unskilled, and low-paid work force encourages continued use of older, technologically backward machinery. This description characterizes traditional consumer goods sectors such as textiles, wood and leather products, clothing, and so on. It is also true of construction and public works and to a lesser extent of the food processing industry.[13] Other industries are highly concentrated (and their concentration has tended to increase over the past fifteen years). They are highly capital intensive but at the same time rely heavily on cultural capital.[14] They use modern high-technology equipment and maintain research and development departments. This description applies to such capital goods producers as the aircraft industry, electrical machinery manufacturing, electronics, precision instruments, machine tools, etc. Between these two extremes one finds a wide variety of intermediate cases. Some sectors are highly concentrated and capital intensive but use relatively little cultural capital (such as the steel industry and, more generally, other materials processing industries). Here, the employment of a relatively unskilled and low-paid work force encourages, as in the consumer goods industries, the use of older, technologically backward machinery. Still other sectors exhibit low capital intensity but rely heavily on cultural capital. These may be concentrated (banking and insurance) or relatively dispersed (e.g., the service sector, with its management consultants, employment agencies, etc.).

These distinctions are relevant when it comes to analyzing the distribution of cadres across the industrial field. For example, all studies exhibit certain patterns dependent on firm size: the smaller the firm, the higher the percentage of autodidacts and the lower the percentage of younger cadres.[15] These findings are not independent, moreover, since autodidacts generally become cadres only by rising through the ranks over the course of a long career. More precisely, it is in large firms in concentrated sectors with high capital intensity and above all where cultural capital is of great importance that one finds the highest proportion of senior cadres and engineers possessing all the attributes generally associated with the title "cadre" in its widely accepted social interpretation. Cadres employed by large firms in industries that rely heavily on cultural capital are most likely to be well educated: for example, 71% of cadres in the aircraft, electrical machinery, and electronics industries continued their studies after age 20, and 72% did not enter the work force until they were 20 or older. The corresponding figures for the chemical industry are 92% and 92%, and for the petroleum industry, 72% and 83%. Most were hired with the title "cadre" (the initial job classification was engineer or senior cadre for 51% in the first group of industries, 56% in the petroleum industry, and 73% in the chemical industry). It is also in large firms in these sectors that cadres are most likely to work in research and development (35% in the automobiles, aviation, electrical machinery, etc., and 46% in chemicals, compared with 10% in small consumer goods plants and 2% in retail sales).[16] Cadres in high-technology sectors (employed mainly by large firms) are also younger (24% were under 35 in the metals industry, 35% in the chemical industry, 28% in the petroleum industry) and more likely to reside in the Paris region, along with cadres employed by major service firms such as banks and insurance companies (41% of the cadres in metals lived in the Paris area, 46% of those in chemicals, and 36% of those in petroleum).

By way of contrast, it is in the smaller production units (employing fewer than 100 employees) in the consumer goods sector[17] (characterized by low capital intensity and reduced importance of cultural capital), as well as in retail sales, transportation (and probably in parts of the service sector) that we find the highest proportion of senior cadres and engineers who completed their studies and entered working life before age 20 (60% and 52% respectively in the consumer goods sector and 65% and 57% in retail sales[18]), who did not attend college (65% and 80%), and who live in rural villages and towns with fewer than 5,000 inhabitants (10% and 18%). Cadres in these small, traditional firms (along with cadres in retail sales and services with similar attributes) are also most likely to hold jobs in administration or management and most likely to have fathers who are self-employed or employers (45% in the consumer goods sector, 47% in retail sales).[19]

Cadre or boss?

These patterns suggest the existence of a dual job market for cadres. Despite some tendency toward standardized hiring criteria and salaries since the development of independent employment agencies and the proliferation of published information about salary levels (in *Expansion, Express, Point*, etc.), together with the increasing influence of large corporations using formally rationalized hiring procedures, there continues to exist, and perhaps even to prosper, a more traditional and less "transparent" job market.[20] In this market, in which the "buyers" are large numbers of small firms, access to supervisory and managerial positions comes mainly through family and social connections, and salary level is established through direct (and usually secret) negotiations between the cadre and his employer.[21] An APEC study of cadres who changed jobs[22] showed that self-taught cadres, most commonly employed by small firms, found their jobs through "connections" more frequently than other cadres (40%, compared with 29% of the cadres who had graduated from engineering schools, for example).[23]

The fact that one finds personal ties and traditional relationships between cadres and employers in small firms may obscure a more profound similarity. The social attributes of cadres in the dispersed sectors are in fact quite similar to the social attributes of their

Table 6. *Social characteristics of cadres by sector and size of firm*

Sectors	*No. of employees*	*No higher education*	*Business or engineering degree*	*Finished school before age 20*	*Entered workforce before age 20*	*Administrative or management functions*	*Sales function*	*Methods, quality control or design functions*	*Research functions*	*Live in towns with pupulation under 5,000*	*Under 35 yrs of age*	*Entry position engineer of senior cadre*	*Entry position blue collar or clerk*	*Father in management, commerce, or trade*	*Father blue-collar worker*
1. Commercial	less than 100	80	9	65	58	51	42	—	2	10	19	13	52	47	14
	100 and more	57	9	57	46	45	45	—	3	5	12	18	45	34	21
2. Consumer goods	less than 100	65	14	60	52	42	33	8	2	18	18	26	49	45	18
	100 and more	53	22	29	31	38	22	17	3	15	14	36	44	35	24
3. Transport	less than 100	61	19	57	52	44	28	9	2	15	22	34	50	21	17
	100 and more	64	15	46	35	30	22	7	—	2	22	48	41	4	30
4. Banking	less than 100	63	8	59	56	52	31	6	—	8	18	12	54	29	14
	100 and more	52	11	45	41	45	24	11	5	2	16	21	45	20	21
5. Metals & Mining	less than 100	47	24	40	36	39	37	13	4	2	11	32	37	33	23
	100 and more	50	31	33	32	22	24	18	7	7	22	45	36	11	37
6. Automobile	less than 100	57	24	46	42	27	37	17	3	9	22	26	44	26	25
	100 and more	28	46	29	28	22	23	29	6	3	24	51	25	15	26
7. Petroleum	less than 100	25	35	19	19	43	22	17	8	13	9	56	17	29	18
	100 and more	18	50	28	17	22	22	22	17	6	28	56	28	14	21
8. Chemicals	less than 100	42	33	17	14	42	25	11	19	5	14	64	22	15	12
	100 and more	10	49	8	5	16	11	5	40	2	35	73	13	28	9

employers. Apparently the increase in the number of employees classified as "senior administrative cadres" over the period 1950–79 reflects, at least in part, a simple change in terminology: a fairly large number of what used to be called "owners of industrial or commercial businesses" now refer to themselves as company employees, even though they may directly or indirectly hold a controlling interest in its stock. This is a common and long-used practice in large corporations and holding companies, whose top officials (whether "heirs" or "managers") often grace themselves with the title "cadre," just like the most obscure of their department heads (which helps to conceal the concentration of capital). Increasingly, it seems, the outward signs of ownership and inherited wealth, which used to be the pride of what the PME charter refers to as the *patronat réel*, have been abandoned by the heads of small companies, particularly since the mid-1960s. Hence statistics that seem to show a decline in the relative and absolute numbers of company owners and a simultaneous increase in the number of cadres actually obscure a complex process of relabeling, redefinition, and reorientation.

Corporation law in France makes it quite easy to blur the distinction between employer and cadre or employer and employee and allows employers to enjoy the advantage of a dual status. In the usual type of corporation "directors of quite different status and function can coexist": the chief executive officer (*président-directeur général*) cannot claim the status of "worker" (*salarié*), but his executive vice-president (*directeur général adjoint*) is considered a "technical manager" and hence a worker, even though his actual power over day-to-day operations may be more extensive than the CEO's. The distinction is harder to draw for corporations governed by the law of 1966, headed by a "directorate" that combines functions formerly shared by the board of directors and the chief executive officer. In many cases it appears that the 1966 law, which permitted technical managers to be named CEOs and CEOs to be named technical managers, encouraged owners to redefine themselves as "managers" so as to gain the legal and tax advantages enjoyed by those classified as "workers."[24]

This change in terminology partially accounts for the relatively high proportion of autodidacts among managers of small firms. For example, a UIMM study shows that "management cadres" (*cadres de direction*) account for 16.7% of all cadres in firms with 100–250 workers but for only 3.7% of cadres in firms with more than 10,000 workers. Thus the decrease in the percentage of cadres classed as "management" in firms of all sizes in the metals industry, from 10.7% in 1966 to 5.9% in 1975, is certainly the result of increasing concentration in the industry during this period. The proportionate number of high-level positions (including management positions) in an organization increases as the size of the organization decreases. In small firms the cadres who work alongside the owner (often a member of his family or a close friend[25]) frequently boast of prestigious titles having little or nothing to do with their actual roles in the firm. Consider, for example, the case of a 27-year-old sales manager in a company employing fifty-five workers and specializing in the manufacture of materials handling equipment. This man was interviewed by a reporter for the newsletter published by the Centre national des jeunes cadres. This typical "young cadre" was a relative of the company's owner and, as the headline introducing the interview noted, both "a worker and a stockholder," "employee and employer." The man described himself as "judge and witness," since he "helps in setting his own salary" and in selecting his job title. The variation in the proportion of cadres who are college graduates with the size of the firm therefore cannot be explained solely in economic terms, although it is often argued that small firms cannot afford to pay the going rate for college graduates. As the *Expansion*–SOFRES polls show, cadres in traditional and comparatively unprosperous industries such as textiles claim to be paid far more than the going rate paid to other cadres occupying similar positions and with similar educational backgrounds. The mystery disappears when one realizes that cadres in this and other, similar, industries are often members of their employers' families and claim their share of the profits on the family capital in the legally sanctioned form of salary.

In traditional firms, then, cadres negotiate their salaries and perquisites directly with the "owner," whereas in large corporations job descriptions and salaries are more standardized (nationalized firms offering the most extreme example). These differences reflect two distinct "modes of domination and extraction." The distinction here is not simply between those who directly claim a share of profits (the "owners") and those who merely sell their labor power ("workers"). One mode of profit extraction is direct: the appropriation of company profits depends on the power of domination exerted directly over a given firm. It is distinguished chiefly in this, that the identity, value, and fate of those who profit from the company's activities are directly linked to the fate of the company: they prosper if the company prospers and suffer if the company suffers. The other mode of domination and extraction[26] is structural: profits are shared indirectly among individuals who occupy institutionalized positions in a power structure. In this case, the relationship between the agent and the firm from which he extracts his share of profit is mediated through the bourgeois job market, which determines the value of cadres, that is, the rate of extraction that cadres can expect to obtain, usually in the form of salary. Each mode shapes the relationship between individual interests and company interests in a different way and thus determines the nature of the solidarity that binds agents to employers. In traditional firms individuals are closely bound to the firms whose profits they share. They generally cannot quit their jobs without losing their share of the profits. By contrast, in large firms, both the cadres and the bureaucracies that employ their services are comparatively free to end their relationship if the market so dictates. Thus the careers of cadres in large firms are dependent not so much on the firm's success (though success does have some effect, since it influences the availability of jobs within the firm) as on external market conditions, including market size (which is largely determined by educational achievement). It appears, in fact, that one of the chief advantages of an officially sanctioned (i.e., universally recognized) degree, and especially of a degree from one of the Grandes Ecoles, is to certify the value of the holder to buyers in a vast job market, and thus to ensure the individual's independence by separating his fate from that of his employer.[27] In other words, cadres in large firms move from one position to another within the firm until they encounter some obstacle to further promotion, whereupon they move to another, similar firm. In small firms, on the other hand, where the number of cadre positions is small, the hierarchy narrow, and opportunities for promotion limited, a cadre's career depends on the firm's growth. As the number of subordinates increases, the division of labor among supervisors tends to raise the status of existing positions in the hierarchy, enabling cadres to increase their power and remuneration without necessarily changing their title or functions.[28]

One must be careful, however, to avoid the danger inherent in the construction of typologies, that of creating a hard-and-fast distinction where in fact there is a subtle gradation of intermediate cases. Within a single large corporation, in fact, very different types of units can coexist, largely ignorant of one another (especially where the various divisions of a corporation are linked mainly at the financial level).[29] A firm can have fancy corporate marketing departments, high-tech laboratories, and the glass-and-steel office buildings that are the hallmark of modern capitalism, and still maintain a far-flung network of small, traditionally managed manufacturing plants, usually located in small provincial towns far from the Paris headquarters and staffed by ex-farmers (or, nowadays, located even as far away as the Third World's "industrial zones").

A geographical region – a "country," say – achieves unity only when interpersonal relations, values, and symbolic systems have been unified to a considerable degree. By contrast, an industrial corporation can function in an integrated manner while remaining organizationally diverse, so long as overall cohesion is ensured through financial management and control of cash flows between corporate divisions. "Corporate spirit" (the industrial equivalent of "national consciousness") cannot develop in the absence of a history, a shared "culture," and a collection of common symbols. Creating these requires delicate and costly collective effort (including ceremonies, commemorations, trips to corporate headquarters, and so on). But such corporate spirit is really necessary only where a large number of employees must be motivated to do work requiring a considerable degree of emotional and cultural investment (in a large research laboratory, say, or in the R & D facilities of a company like IBM, whose profits depend primarily on returns to investments in cultural capital). In most other cases, however, simple auditing controls provide a cheap, impersonal, rather abstract way to oversee the operations of a large corporation.[30] A good example is a small electronics component manufacturer in Hong Kong, managed in a traditional way by a plant manager who supervises a work force of adolescents or even children. The profits of this firm may eventually show up in the bottom line of a financial statement prepared in Paris or New York by young financial managers whose work is competent, even impeccable, but who may have no idea how the profits they are paid to tot up are earned. Such "managers" have little or nothing in common with the agents who produce the profits in which they share.[31]

There is, however, no need to go so far afield to see the effects of the separation between cultural control and budgetary control. Take, for example, a company that employs 300 people in the manufacture of industrial instruments (with a 5–10% share of the French market). The company was founded twenty years ago by an engineer, a graduate of the Ecole Centrale and scion of an old but declining industrial family, who, after many years of working for other people, decided to "take the plunge" and purchase manufacturing licenses from an American firm; ten years later his company was taken over by the American concern that had supplied the technology. But the original founder remains as president of the new division. To judge by the management manuals, this company is in many ways contradictory. Depending on which characteristics one chooses to focus on, one could describe it as "typically French and traditional" or as "totally Americanized." For instance, much emphasis is placed on modern methods of organization and selection (including handwriting analysis, use of outside consultants, etc.). The number of cadres is high, and according to the formal organization chart department heads retain a large measure of autonomy, in accordance with the wishes of the Americans who bought the company. But interviews with a number of informants (from the sales manager to the CEO's executive secretary) revealed a widely shared belief that "nothing is delegated" and that the CEO, a "paranoid sadist," runs the show himself and "takes daily pleasure in humiliating his subordinates." Every morning he assembles his management team for the "mail ceremony" and heaps sarcasm upon insult ("We let him do as he likes and think about other things, because we're paid well"). American control over the firm is limited to budgetary matters; monthly figures are sent to the parent company, which conducts three audits annually. The CEO has limited latitude to make investments, purchase licenses, and so on, but he is free to deal with his subordinates as he pleases as long as profits continue to flow to the parent firm.

Thus the number of ambiguous positions in industry has increased dramatically in recent years. In the chambers of commerce one finds heads of small firms affiliated with major corporations rubbing elbows with one-time independents now employed as cadres in small, legally autonomous firms that are in fact subcontractors to large corporations and totally at their mercy. An explanation of how this came to pass would require a detailed description of recent industrial changes. Very briefly, complex investment networks, centralized and yet diversified, have grown up to link dispersed production units in a "seamless web" composed of "many diverse strands."[32] One of the tools of employee management is manipulation of the official "boundaries" and limits of different production units (shops, departments, subsidiaries, plants, companies, corporations, etc.). A current trend is to shorten chains of command in large corporations and to move away from "centralization" and toward new forms of organization in which smaller units operate independently under the aegis of larger corporations ("entrepreneurship within the corporation," as one slogan has it). A fairly new way of "integrating cadres into the firm," this method relies on both market and bureaucratic constraints. The performance of these smaller units can be monitored by way of data on costs, prices, delivery delays, and output, leaving managers free to decide how best to achieve corporate goals. In some companies adherence to explicit orders from corporate management and even more to implicit and ambiguous norms (pertaining even to intimate personal matters such as appearance and politics) count just as much as performance.

Consider, for example, the case of V, who heads a production unit of 155 employees in a small town in Normandy. This plant is owned by a company that is the subsidiary of two other companies belonging to a huge electrical and electronics conglomerate. The factory in Normandy was purchased by the giant corporation some years ago, but the old plant manager (age 58) was kept on, along with an engineer who assisted him (a former technician and the son of a blue-collar worker, age 42). Both men are autodidacts. They are the only cadres in the plant. Working under them are a dozen technicians, an office staff, and 125 female workers, mostly unskilled, who do wiring and assembly of small lots of electrical equipment. V's position is ambiguous. Depending on one's point of view, he is either an insignificant local *patron* or a low-level cadre employed by a giant corporation. The son of local merchants, he rose through the ranks and is "quite well-known in the area," where he has spent his entire career. He is a "local luminary," a close associate of the mayor (who also serves as UDR deputy from the region), and plays an active role in CNPF activities at the local level. He can often be seen at the "receptions that the prefect holds for industrialists of the region" and belongs to a regional trade association composed of some fifty local "executives" (i.e., owners of small businesses or plant managers employed by large corporations), who meet periodically to "discuss over a bottle of whiskey questions of wages, workers, and regional problems." With this strong community base, V is able to exercise the traditional authority role expected of him in a plant where most of the employees live in the town or its environs. His role is tailored to the workers he supervises: women, many of them very young, largely unskilled, often daughters of blue-collar workers or farmers. By his own admission V's technical knowledge is no longer up to the requirements of production. His job is more that of a personnel manager ("What one needs to know to run a factory these days is social law"). He is also something of a father-figure, someone who has known his workers since they were born and who is able to keep close tabs on their activities ("if a worker is five minutes late, I know it at once"). His major responsibility is to maintain good relations with the labor inspectors ("It's like with judges: there are the Reds and then there are the others"), whom he takes to lunch at company expense in a restaurant near the plant favored by managers.

V saw the strikes of May–June 1968 from the standpoint of a local *patron* ("My wife was insulted in the street because she was the boss's wife, you understand. I had to send her to live with her parents"). In general, he supports the forces of law and order in this small working-class town, where "everybody knows everybody else," "class struggle" is an everyday affair, and "labor disputes" often involve people who have other scores to settle ("May '68 was worse in the provinces than in Paris, because there were no unions, no union leadership. The workers weren't used to that, weren't used to striking, and they ran amok"). Receiving guests and attending receptions, taking people out to lunch, participating in local groups, holding a semi-official position in the town, and earning the workers' "respect" and fear are V's basic symbolic rewards. Lacking any real power to influence plant operations, he sees the signs of respect that are shown him as marks of his belonging to a group that he admires: "industrialists" as they have traditionally been known – genuine *patrons*.

But to the corporation that employs him, V is a relatively low-level cadre, who according to one informant "doesn't earn as much as a senior manager" and is "less important than the messenger boys at corporate headquarters." He has no financial autonomy, is not allowed to hire or fire, must seek approval for promotions and wage increases, and has to furnish detailed monthly reports of plant activities to corporate headquarters. V's relations with his superiors are based on bureaucratic procedures (monthly statements, etc.) and proceed strictly "through channels." He almost never goes to Paris and knows only one person at corporate headquarters, his immediate superior. Yet he lives in constant fear of the parent company and especially of "early retirement." Although he has no chance of promotion, he can be sacked and replaced if production should falter ("As long as you're making a profit, nobody bothers you"). When he speaks of the corporation that employs him, for which he works "just like any other worker," V is no longer a "boss." He defines himself in relation to another pole of attraction: he is a "cadre" who must deal with remote and haughty "executives." He is quick to express his resentment in the clichéd language of middle-class organizations, which from 1936 to the present have tirelessly reminded us of the "silent and modest anguish" of the "misunderstood, humiliated, unpopular cadre," caught "in a pincers between *patronat* and *prolétariat*." V says that he is "punished when things go badly but never rewarded when things go well." He would like to receive some sort of "performance bonus" ("so I can buy my wife a present when the plant is rolling along smoothly"). He complains most of all about lack of support in his daily struggle to obtain the best performance from his workers: "The big-shots are willing to sacrifice us. Punishments nowadays are handed out to cadres." When his "cup runneth over" he talks about "joining the CGC" yet nevertheless refrains from taking a step that for him constitutes the ultimate rebellion. As one might suspect, V finds that his two positions, "boss" on the local level and "cadre" on the corporate (or multinational) level, sometimes conflict. The mayor, for example, often presses him to hire the mayor's political flunkies: "I don't dare tell him I'm not allowed to hire anybody without corporate approval. I'd look like a kid in short pants if I said that."

More generally, the establishment of scattered, autonomous production units has, according to one executive of a small company that is part of a larger corporation, enabled firms to "diversify their risks," "avoid problems associated with having large numbers of workers concentrated in one place," and "fight the unions."[33] This development is no doubt one aspect of a large-scale transformation of the industrial structure.[34] Many firms have dispersed their operations widely. In some cases fictitious companies have been created to conceal maneuvers of this kind.[35] Other aspects of this transformation of industry include increased reliance on temporary labor[36] and subcontracting,[37] job-market segmentation, and diversification of methods of discipline and social control. Small plants, managed by traditional managers but actually operating as part of large corporations, have survived in part because this type of organization is optimal for dealing with the most vulnerable segments of the working class (especially in newly urbanized areas[38]), particularly when the plant manager is himself of working-class background, as often seems to be the case. Taken together, these structural changes have tended to reduce the tension between cadres employed by "bureaucratic" firms and "independent" plant managers. Agents are distinguished by their place in the power structure and by their salaries rather than by their legal status.

The vulgarization of the "cadre" title

Still, the transformation of once independent owners into cadres is not enough to account for either the increase in the number of cadres or the development of systematic differences among cadres occupying different positions in the industrial field. Another important factor has been the vulgarization of the cadre title, which has been handed out indiscriminately to agents lacking educational credentials and wielding little or no power. This phenomenon is presumably responsible in large part for the increase in the number (and diversity) of cadres in the 1960s. In order to understand the "rise of the cadres" we must recognize that it has come about as a result of two essentially independent processes. On the one hand the increase in the cadre population is certainly related to the growth of the "tertiary sector,"[39] especially in the areas of sales, service, and administration. This phenomenon is itself a consequence not so much of the "technology explosion" as of the growth in the size of capital and commodity markets[40] coupled with the development of new relationships among legally independent firms (e.g., conglomerates). The net result has been increased bureaucratization in industry.[41] But this still does not explain why so many people want to become, or to be recognized as, cadres (including managers, engineers,[42] industrialists, merchants, wholesalers, salesmen, etc.). Satisfying this demand served the interests of those who control the economy. By fostering individual career hopes firms kept pressure on their employees and increased competition for "promotions." This pressure was felt not just on the fringes of the cadre group (among technicians, secretaries, and the like) but also in the upper echelons of the working class.

Of 100 self-taught cadres who took courses to upgrade their skills at the Centre d'études supérieures industrielles in Nantes in 1974–5, 46% had first entered the work force as blue-collar workers (usually skilled), 29.5% as clerical workers, 21.5% as technicians, and 3% as cadres.[43] Similarly, a study conducted by Agnès Pitrou at the behest of the CIPC (of a sample of members of a cadres' retirement fund) shows that only 44% of cadres entered the work force as cadres (14% as senior cadres and 30% as middle-level cadres); 22% started as blue-collar workers and 29% as clerical workers.

There are obvious social and political advantages to promoting autodidacts, technicians, clerical workers, and skilled laborers (whose loyalty and conformity to company norms have been ensured by a lengthy process of socialization and selection) rather than hiring recent graduates straight out of school.[44] The very existence of the cadre title sets up a barrier, a boundary that can be crossed only at some cost and that therefore represents a definite value.[45] Two sets of rewards and punishments are involved: one material, the other symbolic. The prospect of promotion enforces obedience and encourages employees to contribute in ways that are not always compensated by commensurate rewards (especially salaries). This is particularly true of individuals who become cadres relatively late in life, especially those whose job it is to supervise other workers directly (foremen, personnel managers, etc.). Many of these are autodidacts, often of working-class origin, whose prospects of promotion depend mainly on a "good attitude" and loyalty to the firm.[46]

A 1975 APEC study of new members of a cadres' retirement fund showed that, of those who had not previously been members of such a fund and who had been promoted without changing employer (12% of the total sample), 68% were earning only slightly more than they had before promotion and 12% had received no raise at all. Relatively old (25% were over 40), not well educated (77% had no degrees beyond the baccalaureate), and high in seniority (62% had worked for their present employers for at least ten years), these "old retainers" had for the most part been promoted in name only as a reward for "loyal and faithful service." Nevertheless, "promotions to cadre" are still prized, and this creates certain divisions between workers: for example, technicians with credentials from technical schools or junior colleges claim a priority over autodidacts that management does not always recognize.[47]

The magnetic attraction of cadre positions has been particularly strong when the economy is in good shape, especially in periods of full employment. It was impossible to prevent "symbolic inflation" of the title, which, since it is granted to private individuals by innumerable private organizations, cannot easily be monitored or standardized. Like the dubbing of knights long ago, award of the title "cadre" depends solely on the pleasure of the parties involved, practically as well as legally.[48] Companies may make anyone a cadre, and they use this freedom quite lavishly. As long as top management retains control over (if not ownership of) the corporate capital, the basis of their power, there is little for them to fear from the consequences normally associated with "inflation of honors" (the value of any title usually declines as the number of people who hold it increases).[49] Indeed, employing large numbers of cadres may well bring prestige to a company in the eyes of clients, competitors, and other subsidiaries of the same firm (which explains why salesmen are so often renamed "sales engineers"). This is particularly true of smaller firms, which, as they gain familiarity with American-inspired management models, demonstrate their "modernity" and "efficiency" by filling their organization charts with new and often superfluous positions such as "marketing director" or "public relations manager."

Clearly, the number of so-called cadres would not have increased as sharply as it did if many different groups and agencies had not found such an increase to their advantage. In fact, all the inflation process needed to get going, especially in a period of full employment, was for the various forces at work to be allowed to run their course (since each employer was ostensibly free to promote or decline to promote any employee who asked to be made a cadre, and since each employee was free to quit if his or her request went unsatisfied). The vulgarization of the title did not affect the selection mechanisms that ensured a close correspondence between the social attributes of agents and the positions open to them, not only upon entry into the work force but throughout their careers. This limited the social risks of "honorific inflation" without eliminating the symbolic profits, which remained high as long as economic growth helped to blur the disparity between the subjective and objective career prospects of individual agents

Career uncertainties

The increase in the number of agents who claimed the cadre title certainly helped to make the cadre group more heterogeneous. Cadres were quite different from one another socially. They held very different kinds of positions at work. And their compensation varied widely, depending mainly on their educational achievement and social background. To cite just one example from an abundant literature, Michel Cézard's work at INSEE, based on the results of the Formation–Qualification–Profession survey of 1970, showed that the higher an engineer's social background, the more likely he was to hold a degree from an engineering school (56.5% of the engineers who were sons of senior cadres held such degrees, compared with only 33.3% of engineers whose fathers were blue-collar workers). Furthermore, about one-half of the engineers whose fathers were workers or farmers usually held jobs directly related to production (e.g., in manufacturing or tooling[50]), compared with only one-third of those whose fathers were senior cadres. Similarly, only 4.3% of senior cadres whose fathers were workers or farmers held degrees equivalent to an engineering school degree, compared with 24.7% of those whose fathers were senior cadres; the former were also less likely to hold administrative or management positions than the latter.[51]

The relation between educational achievement and salary is also quite clear, no matter what statistical sources we use. For example, a 1975 APEC study showed that 57% of cadres holding the baccalaureate or a lower degree earned less than 50,000 francs per year, compared with 20% of engineering and business school graduates, 22% of whom earned more than 80,000 francs per year. Similar remarks apply to the relation between social background and salary: 60% of cadres whose fathers were workers earned less than 36,000 francs per year, compared with 34% of cadres whose fathers were self-employed professionals or senior cadres. What is more, 40% of the latter group earned more than 52,000 francs per year, compared with 14% of the former. The salary range looks even wider when one combines both educational achievement and social background: 46% of cadres with good degrees and of relatively upper-class background earned more than 52,000 francs annually in 1973, compared with 10% of cadres without good degrees and of working-class background (source: CIPC survey).

There is, moreover, a tendency to underestimate the effects of education and social background as a result of sampling the distribution of cadres at one particular time and then lumping together individuals of different ages and at different stages in their careers. Aggregate statistics obscure the link between an agent's educational and social capital and his position, which emerges much more clearly when we correct for age and allow for objective differences between nominally similar positions. Cadres with different types of degrees, different social backgrounds, and unequal promotion prospects may hold fairly similar positions (so that they appear to be in competition) and earn roughly comparable salaries when still young. But when we look at the slope of the salary curve as a function of type of degree and age, the differences increase noticeably after age 35 or 40. It is as if the educational factor produces a delayed reaction, whose effects do not become visible before the second half of a man's career.

The FASFID studies deal with a relatively homogeneous population, namely, the graduates of engineering schools (both Grandes Ecoles and less prestigious institutions). These show that salary range broadens considerably with age. The ratio between the first and ninth decile is 1 to 2 at age 30 and 1 to 4 at age 55. More precisely, the salary gap between engineers and middle-level cadres on the one hand and chief engineers and senior cadres on the other hand is smallest at age 33 (400 francs in 1968) and largest at age 57 (2,300 francs). In effect, the salaries of the former hold more or less steady after age 35, whereas the compensations received by the latter increase sharply from that age on.[52] These results are confirmed by analysis of the raw data for the 1977 study, which showed that salary differences as a function of age are related to promotions from "lower-level" functions (in manufacturing, research, and so on, involving the exploitation of technical skills) to "higher-level" functions (in finance, administration, management, etc.).[53]

In order to gauge the full effect of social determinations we must therefore examine the relationship between objective career prospects and social attributes at various career stages. This is quite difficult, because in real life people are not only promoted and demoted but also change jobs, moving from one firm to another (perhaps from a major corporation to a smaller subcontractor) or from one department to another within the same firm (from manufacturing, say, to sales). In large firms cadres on an optimal career path move from stage to stage through a hierarchy of functions, from manufacturing (or, for Grandes Ecoles graduates, research) to finance and top-level staff positions.[54]

It is as if the value of a cadre position were determined not only by its social distance from blue-collar work but also by its spatial or even physical distance. The highest positions are those in which one need not be aware of labor, laborers, or production but only of such abstractions as commodity and cash flows, high-technology processes, and investments. Such positions are found at corporate headquarters, which differ from the factory in every respect – from décor to interpersonal relations – and which are inhabited largely by cadres. In order to understand how bourgeois sensitivity to the proximity of the working class and even to the sight of workers has changed since the nineteenth century, and to gauge the extent to which the idea of production has been repressed and the relations of production have been glossed over, one has only to compare a leading nineteenth-century firm like Le Creusot, whose works manager had his château right in the middle of the industrial zone, with a modern corporation like Renault, whose corporate offices were moved in the 1970s from the company's Boulogne plant into luxurious modern quarters.

Of the entry level engineers included in the 1977 FASFID survey, 40% worked in research and development. This percentage decreases steadily with age, from 35% of engineers under 30 to 28% of those between 30 and 34 to less than 20% of those over 45. The percentage of engineers in sales positions peaks at age 35 (at 18%). And the percentage working in administration, finance, or personnel management climbs steadily up to age 50. The APEC study (more broadly based than the FASFID survey) yields similar results: entry level cadres (17% of the sample), most with college degrees (90%), go into research and development (30% of the total sample, and 43% of those who graduated from engineering schools) and production (26%), for the most part in large firms (53% work for companies employing more than 1,000 workers) in highly concentrated sectors (like metals, 22% and electricity–electronics, 12%).

Cadres with diplomas, particularly in science or engineering, obtain the highest salaries in firms that rely heavily on cultural capital, many of them fairly large-scale operations. Educational capital yields its best returns early in a person's career, when little or no capital of other sorts is available. Companies buy the up-to-date knowledge of young graduates and thus add to their stocks of cultural capital at low cost (the "cost of production" having been borne by the educational system). Large companies also hire young autodidacts (though entry level autodidacts are older on the average than entry level college graduates), generally to work in their production and even more often in their sales departments in jobs that are physically or psychologically demanding, requiring "authority" in the case of shop managers or "flair," "glibness," and "street smarts" in the case of salesmen.

For example, the APEC study showed that cadres promoted after moving from one company to another (particularly common among salesmen and technicians) were relatively young (half under 30) and not especially well educated (59% had the baccalaureate or less and 30% had attended two-year colleges). They started work early

(73% before age 22), so that half of them had ten years' seniority before becoming cadres and being included in the study. The vast majority (91%) said that they had quit their previous job because they were not paid enough or their chances of promotion were minimal. Poorly paid in their old jobs (66% earned less than 40,000 francs per year), these "new cadres" received the greatest salary increases of any group in the study (48% were earning "slightly more" than they had before and 31% "a great deal more"); they were also most satisfied with their new jobs (77% preferred the new job to the old).

Like lower-level cadres, college graduates of bourgeois background must often begin their careers in jobs defined by others, not infrequently reporting to superiors who are not as well educated as themselves. They must make do with salaries below those paid to older employees of similar social background and hence accept a "standard of living" below that of their parents. They are not able to enjoy immediately all the privileges implicit in their educational credentials and social origin. On the job they must work alongside petit-bourgeois autodidacts, who, since they hold positions of equivalent rank, must be treated formally as equals and colleagues. These adversities are temporary, but they sometimes make well-educated, upper-class cadres feel that they are "workers like the rest," in "solidarity with other workers" and equally "exploited." It is in the second part of a person's professional life that the post-graduation mechanisms of social selection produce their full effects, as some individuals move from line jobs into positions of power that no longer demand much in the way of technical knowledge, know-how, and energy, or, rather, demand something else besides, including such qualities as distinguished appearance, good manners, tact, and good taste, which are socially acquired in the family and hence associated with an upper-class background.

It seems, then, that in the cadre job market the value of technical competence relative to that of social competence varies with age. Direct investment of technical competence in production tends to diminish, or at any rate to decline in value, as an individual grows older (this has been called the "obsolescence of knowledge"[55]). Conversely, the (socially acquired) skills needed not to produce *per se* but to administer the production process (such as the ability to delegate tasks to others, to manipulate interemployee conflicts, and to motivate and use other people) increase as a cadre begins to grasp more and more of what is going on both inside and outside the company. Cadres of middle- or lower-class background must generally rely on technical knowledge, energy, and ambition alone. Hence their value on the (internal and external) job market declines as they grow older. The less well educated a person is, the more rapidly his value decreases. Educational credentials tend to limit the effects of knowledge obsolescence by perpetuating the social value attached to knowledge acquired in a person's youth (this is clear in the case of graduates of the Grandes Ecoles). Cadres of upper-class background, on the other hand, generally see their value increase over the course of their careers, because they can call upon an extensive network of contacts from their first day on the job and can take advantage of still other contacts made through work.

Whether or not social capital maintains its value depends in part on the positions that a person occupies. In a well-planned career the social capital invested in each new position grows in magnitude. Social capital is useful for more than just obtaining a job (by "pulling strings"). It is really an investment (comparable in every way to an economic investment). Without an investment of social capital an institutionally defined position such as "financial manager" has no value, or perhaps it would be better to say that the potential value of the position cannot be *realized*.[56]

This is particularly true of executive positions, for the power of an executive depends on his ability to use his extensive contacts (especially with senior government officials) for the benefit of the company.[57] But it is also true of lower-level positions, whose occupants cannot do their jobs without calling on contacts within the company itself. In fact, what defines the "real manager" is his intimate knowledge of how the company works and his ability to manipulate men without violating any of the company's formal bureaucratic rules.[58] Consider, for example, a chief of marketing: his work largely involves contacts with people in many different positions, from manufacturing department heads to sales managers to data processing managers. The formal authority associated with his position is never sufficient by itself to mobilize all the people he needs to do his job; he must possess some legitimacy of his own (this is one function of educational credentials),[59] and he must maintain, beyond merely professional relations with his colleagues, relations of a more personal sort extending over a long period of time and sustained by mutual services, by a series of gifts and countergifts (and in fact, many marketing heads have done lengthy stints in research, manufacturing, training, and sales departments). In the psychological systems invented by the "career development specialists," the socially acquired aptitude to motivate and use other people is considered a personality trait. It is supposed to be the expression of an "extroverted, open, dynamic personality, with a feeling for human contact, tact, and intuition, psychologically perceptive, and capable of establishing good communication with fellow employees."[60] Career planning techniques, personality inventories, and the like use psychological terms to characterize what are in fact socially defined aptitudes for executive responsibility. By such means the elimination from consideration of self-taught cadres (and others of lower- and middle-class background) can be justified on "rational grounds." In important ways this helps to maintain the mechanisms that reproduce the industrial power structure. For example, what organization consultants call the "span of control that a man is capable of assuming" is said to vary from individual to individual and, for a given individual, over the course of working life. According to Octave Gélinier, this trait exhibits "the characteristics of a biological phenomenon, of maturation followed by decline."[61] In fact, it appears to reflect the kinds of competence – predominantly technical or predominantly social – required of cadres at different levels of the hierarchy and hence at different stages of life.

These mechanisms help to explain the ways in which education and social background influence the careers of cadres. Self-taught cadres of lower-class origin, unable to gain promotion in larger firms, must look to smaller, less prestigious, more traditionally managed firms (many of which serve as subcontractors to larger companies). These small firms may find it advantageous to hire people with experience of the way things are done in the major corporations.[62] Thanks to this mechanism, the percentage of self-taught and older cadres tends to be higher in less concentrated sectors of industry.

One way to understand the declining career patterns of many cadres who receive an early promotion, only to find that in order to hold onto a valued title they must abandon early hopes and make concession after concession, is to look at cadres in the APEC study who found jobs after being laid off from a previous job (18% of the total sample). Forty-four percent were over 40 years old and 49% had not attended college. Fifty-seven percent started work before they were 22, yet 38% said that they did not become cadres until after age 30. They found it far more difficult to find work than cadres who had resigned from their previous jobs (though in many cases resignation, encouraged by the employer, is nothing less than a covert form of dismissal; see below). On the average they went without work for 22 weeks, compared with 18 weeks for those cadres who had resigned before signing a contract for a new job. In general they were forced to take jobs at a lower level than the ones they had been forced to leave. This was also the group least satisfied with its new employment. In order to remain in the job market they had been forced, apparently, to accept work with smaller firms (39% had worked for firms employing fewer than 50 people in their first jobs, compared with 58% in their second jobs, while 30% had worked for firms employing more than 500 workers in their first jobs, compared with only 17% in their second jobs). They frequently said that they had been forced to make concessions concerning the size of the firm (27%), location (35%), and salary (45%). It is also in this group that we find the highest percentage of cadres who earned the same (29%) or less (31%) than on their previous job. For autodidacts, the higher the previous salary, the greater the salary cut: 18% of those who had earned more than 90,000 francs had higher salaries in their new jobs, compared with 79% of those who earned less than 30,000 francs.[63] Salary changes were correlated with changes in company size: 57% of those who went to work for smaller firms earned higher salaries, compared with 66% of those who took jobs with larger firms. The higher the old salary, the greater the disparity: 50% of those who earned 90,000 francs before changing jobs and who went to work for larger firms earned more than they had before, compared with only 23% of those who went to work for smaller firms. Note, finally, that those who say that they were forced "to make concessions" regarding the size of the firm were found most commonly in the traditional sectors, such as textiles, wood products, paper, construction, and so forth, and among self-taught cadres: 68% of the autodidacts found work in firms with fewer than 500 employees and 32% in firms with more than 500 employees, compared with 56% and 43%, respectively, of cadres who had earned university degrees and 37% and 55%, respectively, of cadres who held degrees from engineering and business schools.

Thus cadres may either gain value with age or lose it, just as some objects like paintings and other "collectibles" become rarer and more valued and prized as they grow old, while others, worn out and useless, lose their value until they become ready for the scrap heap. But cadres do not stand still as they grow old. Just like art objects, they pass from one segment of the market to another. A painting may go from a rural antique dealer to an auction to a dealer in rare paintings, while a used car may be passed on from a doctor or an executive to a small merchant and from there to a peasant. The same is true of cadres. Autodidacts are like automobiles, moving from major markets when "new" to increasingly peripheral markets as they become "used" and lose their symbolic value. This kind of downward mobility (accompanied by a stagnant or even declining salary) may not show up in statistical analyses, which reflect only job titles and may give the illusion of upward mobility (e.g., in the case of a man who goes from sales engineer with a large firm to sales manager of a small one).

Analysis of the professional and social trajectories of cadres shows, finally, that the career mishaps (and periods of unemployment after the age of 40) that are so common among cadres without solid position, degrees, or contacts are not simply the result of hard times or economic change or the expansion of higher education, as was commonly believed in the late 1960s and early 1970s, or of the economic crisis, as is commonly believed today. Rather, such mishaps are in fact produced by the structural mechanisms responsible for the reproduction of the industrial field. Over time, the number of autodidacts gaining promotion to cadre positions has remained fairly constant. This suggests that unemployment among self-taught cadres over age 40, for which there is evidence as early as the mid-1960s, in a period of full employment, is not caused ultimately by "competition between college graduates and internally promoted cadres," which allegedly developed in the wake of expanding higher education.[64] Similarly, the restructuring of the economy in the 1970s surely contributed to unemployment among older cadres, but it was not the decisive cause.[65] Many older cadres were autodidacts, bound to a single firm, often a smaller firm, or even to a single plant or person, and in many cases their jobs were eliminated when their company was bought out by a larger corporation. It is from this group, apparently, that most of the cadres came who were unemployed in the period of full employment before the recent economic crisis. This phenomenon should be seen in relation to the objective mechanisms that developed in the 1960s to regulate cadre promotions. These mechanisms led to the promotion of many autodidacts to cadre rank at about age 30, only to relegate them to marginal positions or to eliminate their jobs entirely a few years later. One effect of this rapid turnover of cadres was to heighten competition between older cadres and aggressive, newly promoted younger cadres, even when the age difference involved was quite insignificant.

For example, a 1971 UNEDIC study of 1,029 cadres showed that 87% of the fund's subscribers at that time were over 40; only 22%

held degrees from a university or Grande Ecole, 35% had either no degree at all or a degree below the baccalaureate, 15% had the baccalaureate, and 28% held some sort of technical degree. Seventy-nine percent did not begin work as cadres: 45% had previously been clerical workers, 21% blue-collar workers, and 13% technicians. Forty-seven percent said that they had completed their training on the job, and many had spent their entire career in the same firm (especially the older and less well educated), where they often held fairly high positions: 65% were department heads or higher, and 37% were executives of one sort or another; 34% worked in sales. Half of the cadres who were laid off had no warning that they were about to lose their jobs and first learned of the decision by registered letter. Many worked for small- and medium-sized firms and appear to have lost their jobs in the wake of reorganizations, consolidations, or mergers,[66] which led to large-scale layoffs. Some 20% lost their jobs because the company they worked for shut down;[67] this accounts for the relatively small number of resignations (11% overall, and 17% of cadres between 40 and 50 years of age). Interview data suggest that in 40% of these cases resignations were obtained by coercion. The same study shows that self-taught cadres who lost their jobs in the second half of their careers had great difficulty finding work in 1971, and the older they were, the more difficult it was. The percentage of those who were out of work for more than six months ranges from 26% of the under-40 age group to 36% of the 40–50 age group, to 55% of the 50–60 age group. After one year of unemployment 50% of the dismissed cadres gave up looking for cadre-level jobs. At the time the questionnaire was sent out, 155 of the cadres who responded had succeeded in obtaining new jobs; 50% of these were earning less than they had earned before, and 38% had reduced responsibilities. Forty-one percent had found a job through contacts. Yet even those who could not find a job and faced the prospect of a reduced standard of living or, for older men, early retirement, continued to dream of independence, a "small shop of one's own," perhaps, "somewhere in the provinces," or even a "store." One former electrical worker who had received a degree from CNAM at age 32 and who had been out of work for several months had this to say:

> I really wanted to work for myself, and my big dream would be to make it, just so that I could have that independence. . . . When you work for somebody else, especially as a senior cadre, you've got to pretend that you always agree with the boss. . . . I don't want my son to work in industry. He can be a doctor, an artist, a lawyer, a real-estate agent, a notary. . . .

But I don't want him to work in that system, and if he doesn't take to school, well, then I'd rather see him a plumber or an auto mechanic, as long as he's independent.[68]

Processes of exclusion

As we have seen, relatively uneducated cadres of relatively low social background tend to falter in the second halves of their careers. The downward slide often begins with a move from one plant to another within the same company (e.g., from Paris to the provinces, from a technical or sales job to a production job, etc.). In large firms one of the functions of geographical mobility, and more generally of changes of position, department, plant, or what have you, is to make exclusion less visible and less predictable.[69] A shift from one department to another or one city to another may mean many things. It can just as easily signal a promotion as a first step toward dismissal. The meaning of a shift emerges only later, as when a cadre is left with no choice but to resign. It would take too long to describe the many mechanisms by which self-taught cadres are forced toward the periphery of the industrial field. Since the beginning of the economic crisis in the mid-1970s, when "large-scale layoffs for economic reasons" helped to "get the fat out" of many companies (at least in the eyes of management consultants), there has been a tendency to ease people out of their jobs rather than to fire them outright: this gradual process, which demoralizes people and destroys their self-esteem, has proved to be the most economical means – in both material and symbolic senses – of achieving "personnel reduction."[70] What has happened is that there is now a lower tolerance than in the past for the more direct and visible forms of exploitation (especially in the upper echelons). In addition, companies want to keep their images, and the image of business generally, untarnished if possible. Labor legislation and union power have made it costly to fire employees (companies have to pay severance pay, unemployment benefits, and so on).[71] All these things have played a part in the paradoxical "humanization" of the process of exclusion (to borrow a term often applied to reforms in the operation of so-called total institutions). This humanization is also linked to a more general trend in evidence in a number of different fields: direct acts of authority or, if you will, of violence, committed by a physical person acting in the name of a moral person yet still responsible for his or her own actions (such as disinheritance, excommunication, expulsion, exclusion, dismissal, etc.), are increasingly being replaced by seemingly impersonal processes, which appear to be inexorable because they act over long periods of time and affect many different individuals.

While it is wrong to interpret these exclusionary processes as the result of some sort of "conspiracy," as the victims often do, it is no doubt equally wrong to describe them as "perverse" effects of neutral economic and social mechanism, as many "liberal" economists and, more recently, sociologists have done.[72] Exclusion is a management tool for coping with the contradictions inherent in certain types of career patterns.

As usual, it is Octave Gélinier who, with the bluff frankness of the puritanical entrepreneur certain that he knows the way to salvation, has most clearly explained the tried and true techniques for getting rid of unwanted subordinates. Similar techniques have long been used in what Erving Goffman calls "total institutions": for example, religious orders and political parties that demand unequivocal support from their members can use the emotional energy invested in them to manipulate individual members and lead them to destruction. But Gélinier was probably among the first to state these techniques explicitly as principles of action in the context of a quasi-technical discussion that would not have been possible if the human sciences and organization theory had not bestowed upon such *social technologies* a sort of neutrality, an aura of necessity and dignity that silenced the expressions of moral outrage they would otherwise have provoked. Listen to Gélinier:

> We come now to the most common case, the cadre without much seniority who has not violated any particular rule. Take as an example a man 45 years of age. He has worked for the company for five years and was promoted two years ago to sales manager, and after a "trial period" during which he received normal support, it is found that he is clearly not up to the job. To keep him in his present position is impossible. This would jeopardize the company's success for the twenty years remaining until the man reaches age 65, and it would mean forgetting about the company's primary purpose, which is to create wealth. It would be to lapse into feudal attitudes, to let the course of events be determined by a mixture of chance and entrenched positions rather than by assessment of actual performance. Finally, it would be to show little regard for other employees (and especially cadres), for to keep an inefficient man in a position of authority is demoralizing to others. Whenever a man's position is at stake, the matter must be examined gravely and with full awareness of the company's economic and human responsibilities. What is more, to dismiss a man with no warning invariably upsets other cadres, who identify with their colleague and feel threatened themselves. If the decision to get rid of the man must

stand, the groundwork should be laid carefully, keeping the following suggestions in mind: (a) *State the problem objectively*: The first requirement is to lay on the table the facts and circumstances surrounding the man's failure and the reasons for his dismissal. Stating the problem objectively is necessary for the sake of the individual involved and even more for the sake of his colleagues. What must be avoided at all costs is any suggestion that the decision to dismiss is merely a "whim of the prince" regarding a subject who has "ceased to please." To make the man's failure objectively obvious, one should assess his performance in the standard way: point out the various policies, goals, programs, and budgets whose requirements the employee has failed to meet and detail specific instances of errors he has committed. (b) *Judge the man's performance, not his character*: Objective evaluation should deal with job performance, not with the man's value or character, which must not be impugned.... (c) *Exert psychological pressure on the individual*: This may be necessary in the case of a cadre who refuses to admit his failure. Psychological pressure is legitimate and effective only when backed up by objective facts and only when confined to judgments of professional performance. It should be designed to help the individual set aside his alibis and excuses and recognize the facts that signify his failure. Normally he will feel the discomfort that we all feel whenever our actions are subjected to deep scrutiny, the most common symptom being a period of insomnia. With most men these signs of stress will generally lead to a sudden perception of their inadequacy. When this happens the individual himself will often take the initiative in negotiating the terms of his departure. If he does not do so, it is appropriate to help him reorient his thinking. This is one possible purpose of the final interview.[73]

It would be easy to multiply examples of the use of such manipulative techniques and of their often disastrous consequences. Consider, for example, the case of Joseph, a student in an adult education course given at a university in the Paris area where, though he described himself as "having no hope of getting back into industry," he had enrolled in a job retraining program:

I am 49 years old. I worked for the same company for ten years, first in Toulouse, then in Paris. I began as a worker and ended as head of a laboratory. We manufactured electrical equipment. At a certain point my position in the company became very difficult, and they made my life absolutely impossible. A competitor offered me a job, and I stayed there for a year, but in the end they fell flat on their face and I went down with the company.... Now it's getting to be impossible for me to work in the industry, because I was completely devastated by those two experiences and I just can't find my footing any more.... I had become a troublemaker.... I had worked for the company for a long time, and I had a lot of friends. I sniped at people and they didn't forgive me.... For example ... I ... I did just as I pleased, see. I didn't realize that ... I thought that what they wanted me to do was idiotic, so I didn't do it. They gave me so much grief that I reacted violently. Not toward top management, they thought I was OK, but the technical managers and especially the research engineers, the ones in the research lab, I didn't get along with them at all, and then one fine day I put out a memo explaining how the outfit operated. That caused a terrible uproar and I was exiled to Paris with a warning that at the next opportunity I would be out the door. They made my life impossible.

The power of these exclusionary processes can be seen with particular clarity in the case of cadres without college degrees working in sales, who, like the boxers with whom they sometimes like to compare themselves, have no capital other than youth, vitality, and energy. The sales manager of one large service firm, a very "distinguished, efficient, clear-sighted" man, had this to say:

What do you want me to do with my super-salesmen afterward? With all the good will in the world I could never turn them into sales advisers in the provincial branches. They don't have what it takes. I have one guy who started out as a butcher. That fellow would sell anything, and in saying that I don't mean to be dismissive. He sells, he sticks his foot in the door, he laughs, he blathers. . . . But later on? He won't be of any use. He doesn't have what it takes. If they're young, if they've got drive, they make a lot of money very quickly. My butcher drives a Mercedes, when all I've got is an R5. He really takes himself for a cadre. You've got to see him. But later on? The best thing that could happen to him would be to become sales manager of some small outfit. Really.

As this interview suggests, a crisis is quite likely to occur in the career of a salesman of modest social background when he reaches the age of 40. Yet this crisis cannot generally be foreseen, at least not by those who are potential victims. For them there is only one avenue of promotion. Yet it is risky to rise too fast; success itself can cause a man's downfall. The very diversity of career patterns in industry makes it hard to predict whether or not a particular individual with particular social attributes will succeed in any given job. That the importance of educational credentials varies with age and stage of career only aggravates the problem.

Let me indicate briefly the stages in this process of rise and decline. To begin with, the percentage of blue-collar workers, clerical employees, and technicians who rise to cadre status by taking jobs in sales is quite small, so that the few who are selected tend to overinvest in their jobs and to place all their hopes in the firm that "gave them their chance." They tend to be older upon entering the sales force, and to remain in sales longer, than college graduates, who often start out as salesmen. There comes a point when they are no longer considered sufficiently young, dynamic, or successful to hold positions the company needs to try out promising young graduates – positions described by insiders as the "company nursery."[74] Successful salesmen quickly earn fairly high salaries, moreover. If they do not rise in the hierarchy, it becomes too expensive to maintain them in their jobs. Company executives therefore tend to expect more of salesmen as they grow older and to think of replacing them with younger or less well-educated men willing to work for less. But by this point the cadre trained on the job is too old to quit, because his chances of finding an equally well-paid job elsewhere are not good. Self-taught cadres, especially those of middle- or lower-class background, have almost no hope of obtaining positions of power, which are monopolized by graduates of the Grandes Ecoles and/or cadres of upper-class background with inside contacts. Thus a point of no return is reached when the self-taught cadre can no longer either hope for promotion, quit, or feel secure in his present position. The company, for its part, cannot suddenly dismiss him for no reason without running the risk of tarnishing its image and demoralizing other employees. Nor can it demote him to a lesser position (which may still rank above skilled workers and technicians, who also have to contend with loss of status in the second stage of their careers). Unless a way is found to allow sidelined employees to "cool out"[75] within the company, dismissal must inevitably conclude this subtly orchestrated technique of persuasion and punishment.

One sales engineer tells the following story about a situation that he himself is unlikely to face since he is a Grande Ecole graduate:

> I knew a guy in the outfit I used to work for, they wanted him to resign. But he stayed on. In the end, though, he handed in his resignation. It was a pretty sordid affair, really. He was in his forties by then, so you see the problem. He wasn't a bad fellow, a good worker, but he had a way of shooting off his mouth and finally somebody said to him, "When the hell are you leaving? We can't stand having you around any more." That kind of thing. They were always giving him trouble. But he dug in his heels. He must have said to himself, It's not possible, I shouldn't give in to those kinds of threats, I shouldn't do it. Finally, a new guy joined personnel and took charge of the matter. A retired army officer and a first-class bastard, incidentally. He won out in the end in the following way. I heard the story directly from the person involved. "I went to see him," this guy told me, "and he offered me a cigarette, talked things over, and then he said, You know, things can't go on like this. Everybody's suffering. You've got to do something. You've got to make the effort." And so on. So this fellow, after all he'd been through, along comes a guy who offers him a cigarette and sweet-talks him and he signs his resignation on the dotted line.

These techniques are seldom used on engineers who have graduated from one of the Grandes Ecoles, unless they engage in political activity embarrassing to the firm. Consider the case of a graduate of the Ecole Centrale, of bourgeois background but an active Communist and member of the CGT:

At first they promised me a lot if I gave up the union. When that didn't work they stripped me of all responsibility. First the manager came to see me: "With a prestigious degree like yours, and plenty of connections" – because my father had been an executive with a big company – "you really should quit the CGT. I'm telling you this man-to-man, one engineer to another." I don't know why, but I kept on.... Since I refused to quit the union, after a year the management took away all my powers. And to try to break me, to force me to resign, they assigned me to the job of monitoring all the thermometers in the plant. For three months I walked around checking thermometers. Every morning when I came in I said, Look, I'd like another job, and they said to me, Are you sure that such-and-such a gauge is working properly? Go check it out. I'd come back the next day: Yes, it's working. Really? But are you sure you checked the gauges in the shop? And so on.... Often your colleagues just stand around and watch. There's a kind of pressure in a plant that encourages them to think that management has the right to expect cadres to be loyal servants. They say, he's in the union so he's done for, all he had to do was keep a low profile. And then, there's fear, just plain fear: everybody feels threatened.... After a while some guys refuse to shake your hand.

As these examples show, time plays a crucial role. The exclusionary process is necessarily long and costly, because its function is one of dissimulation and hence its outcome must be made to appear inevitable. A man's investments must be impounded or destroyed and belief in his worth must be undermined. This belief rests on two foundations: the subjective judgments of coworkers and the objective performance of the employee. The degradation of a cadre's status becomes a kind of self-fulfilling prophecy, a product of the dialectical relation between actions taken by superiors and rivals and reactions by the threatened individual. At the first signs of dismissal (which may involve nothing more than withdrawal of previously granted privileges), the threatened person may take defensive measures; these can be self-destructive, especially if he overestimates his value on the internal job market. The dynamic of the exclusionary process itself causes him to make mistakes and fail to achieve his goals, which in turn justifies the attempt to get rid of him. Time is also the price the company must pay to secure the oft-noted neutrality of the man's peer group: cadres who might contest the sudden, arbitrary dismissal of one of their own as a threat to their survival and dignity are obliged to admit that the dismissed employee has misbehaved and that his punishment was inevitable and "necessary." Those who remain behind then reestablish order by censuring their dismissed colleague: "He was good for nothing, he was starting to slack off," etc. To go against this collective judgment is too costly for any single individual, and to go along can prove advantageous.

Thus stripping a cadre gradually of the symbols of his status turns out to be just as effective as coercion, because he derives his identity and pride from his role, which comes to him, along with all its attributes, as a syncretic whole. Under scrutiny a man's whole identity can fall apart. This is particularly true of cadres trained on the job, whose promotion to cadre status is often experienced as a "rebirth" and who, in order to overcome their status anxiety, constantly look to their fellow workers for reassurance. With such men, already uncertain of their identities, allowing them to keep their salaries and titles while denying them work appropriate to their status is the best possible way of reminding them that job titles mean nothing, and hence that they themselves are nothing. In times of crisis the power of those who really run the company is clearest, for that power includes the ability to create and destroy symbolic tokens and hence to influence employees' images of themselves and self-esteem.

Listen to one purchasing agent, age 33, an autodidact, and still rising rapidly in his firm:

What I like is that I have power. It's great, it makes me laugh. I eat regularly with executives in their sixties who hold the door for me, who take care of all sorts of little things, and it gives me a lot of pleasure. I enjoy myself. It's pleasant to be kow-towed to by a guy who's 60 years old and makes four grand a month. . . . I have the power to reprimand people, and I like that, too. To know you can tell somebody off is terrific. You get used to it, and after that you can't accept a lower position. In my company right now, when top management wants to punish one of the managers they demote him to assistant manager with the same salary. It drives them crazy. Money doesn't count. Would you sweep the sidewalk if they paid you the same salary you're getting now? Not for long. . . . Once the wind goes out of your sails, you're done for. The boss starts giving you a hard time, or somebody else does. It doesn't matter, it's all worked out, it's part of a plan: you make the guy so unhappy that he leaves. For instance, they'll transfer you from one department to another. Or they'll assign you work below your level. You're supposed to be an executive and they treat you like an errand boy. If the man's got a weak character, he'll resign. To hold out you've got to be tough. They don't invite you to meetings and conferences, they don't tell you what's going on, so you look like a jerk.... That hasn't happened to me yet. But I'm still young. The chickens will come home to roost when I'm 40 or 45, that's when it happens, when it's too late to get out. Because of your age and your salary you can't find anything equivalent on the outside. In my case, I was trained on the job, and that training is worthless to another outfit. So I'm stuck here. Right now there's still time to leave. But I tell myself I should stick around, because I've still got a shot at a better job. And so in ten years, when I no longer have a shot, it will be too late to think of leaving. When that happens they'll stick me on the sidelines somewhere and I'll fight to keep my job.

In other words, it is by depriving cadres of the power conferred upon them as employees of a firm that those who wield real power best demonstrate how powerful they are. The uncertainty of the cadre's position is nowhere more evident than in the field of power relations. Indeed, a subordinate position inside the company often gives access to outward signs of power that can be used in dealings outside the firm. In order to stay afloat, a sales executive, say, must know how to change his attitudes, his "character," and even his physical bearing as he moves from exercising authority outside the firm to submitting to authority inside the firm. If he works for a major company he personally benefits from his company's position in the market and may forget, like any bureaucrat, that his power can be taken away at any moment and that it gives him no real authority, especially not inside the company. If a top executive begins to take himself too seriously, to get "drunk on power" and carry on as though his was the starring role, he can be bypassed by major stockholders who meet socially and agree between themselves on some course of action,[76] or, as a final warning, his authority to represent the firm in outside dealings may be withdrawn.

Integration rituals

In order to analyze these exclusionary processes completely and understand how purely symbolic pressures and irritations – pressures that might not even bother employees less identified with the company and hence less implicated in their own domination – can be so powerful that "no one can withstand them for long," we must first notice that manipulation on the way down is merely a necessary counterpart of manipulation on the way up: it is because cadres invest so heavily in their work that forced divestiture – or, as the military so eloquently puts it, degradation – hits them so hard. The social technologies of exclusion are in fact identical with the technologies of inclusion or integration, whose purpose is to consolidate corporate unity.

As companies grow larger and larger, integration of new employees is increasingly accomplished by means of explicit techniques. In most large firms new cadres must take courses whose chief purpose is to integrate them into the firm: sales training courses, management training programs, orientation seminars, and so on. It is especially important to instill the "company spirit" in new cadres who will be assigned to key jobs (i.e., jobs on which the company's reputation may depend), especially when these are not subject to direct supervision, including such personnel as purchasing agents, salesmen, industrial engineers, and even production engineers assigned to remote job sites or to branch plants in the Third World. In large companies the integration ritual typically lasts from a few days to a few weeks, preferably in a place isolated from the outside world.

Consider, for example, the orientation program attended by seven engineers newly hired by a large industrial service firm (two-thirds of whose operations are outside France). One of the tasks assigned to the new recruits was to prepare a 500-page report on the orientation program itself, and it is from this document that the following excerpts have been taken. The training course was held in a Renaissance château described as "a rural residential setting." Its purpose, according to the welcoming brochure, "is to facilitate your integration into our company by providing you with all the information you will need and introducing you to many of your fellow ORIF employees." During this training period the novice is expected "to acquire certain traits, certain attitudes typical of ORIF engineers." He is also expected to understand the "ethical outlook" and "conception of man peculiar to this company." The purpose of the training is not so much to convey knowledge as to instill a certain "spirit." The point is "to make you aware of belonging to a group," to create something like a "family": when participants are introduced, for instance, such private matters as hobbies are emphasized as much as educational and professional background. The techniques used are typical of psychosocial engineering, including "brainstorming sessions" designed to "break down taboos" by allowing each man to "say whatever is on his mind," "role-playing sessions" during which each participant views the others with a critical eye, and instruction in "how to give a briefing so as to create a dynamic impression." Each technique teaches a way of doing things, a "style" supposedly characteristic of engineers working for this particular "outfit." But it is above all the simple fact of being "together all the time" that shapes the new recruits. From the "morning constitutional" to "discussions over dinner or drinks" everyone is together, and "in the development of the group the moments of relaxation were probably just as important as the training exercises," for they "did much to encourage trainees to relinquish their more or less individualistic habits and commit themselves to a collective endeavor."

One of the strengths of this method of indoctrination derives, paradoxically enough, from the fact that participants are advised to keep training, instructors, and methods in perspective and not to let enthusiasm carry them away. In France in the 1980s most young cadres know something about the human sciences, and many shared as adolescents in the "spirit of May '68." With such men, using techniques designed for retraining blue-collar foremen in the 1950s are useless. Recruits are free to describe the manipulations to which they have been subjected in the language of the human sciences (sociology, psychoanalysis, etc.): "Some will say that we have been subjected to a process of decomposition and reconstruction." This helps to exorcise the "symbolic violence" inflicted on them and thus to ensure the success of the process. The "journal" kept by the trainees serves a similar purpose; its rather brittle "in jokes" (e.g., "the transfer of amorous technologies") are reminiscent of the ritual humor often associated with *esprit de corps*. The training is successful only if all the trainees leave "satisfied," with all their doubts and criticisms put to rest. "We SAO men [SAO stands for *stage d'accueil ORIF*, or ORIF orientation training] learned to live and work together as a group." They "improved communication and developed a group spirit" initially by learning to "distrust" themselves, the first step toward dependency.

In large firms whose owners cannot be physically present to lead their "men" or even their cadres (and especially in American-based multinationals), techniques of integration and control, or of control through integration, are particularly prominent during the initiation period following promotion to cadre rank. These techniques color all aspects of company life, subtly blending anxiety with comfort, and liberalism, not to say permissiveness, with coercion and even violence. Everything possible is done to show cadres that the company is "attentive to their problems," to make them feel secure and to encourage them to confide in their superiors.[77] Yet everyone knows that at every business meeting and seminar, on every business trip, at every "informal" gathering at a colleague's home or at the company health club, each employee is scrutinized by his colleagues, especially his rivals and superiors, who make discreet judgments about his manners, bearing, and attitudes: "Things don't seem to be going well for him at home, it's no wonder his sales are down."

Here is an account of social control methods used by one high-technology multinational, as described by a disgruntled cadre, age 40 and an engineering school graduate:

You might start with a caricature: the clothes we wear... White shirt, three-piece suit – people call us "penguins."... Shave off the beard, of course, but I was about to say other things come first. More serious things. In sales training and in the cadre orientation program they teach you to be aggressive, particularly in selling.... They tell you about the climate, the right tone to take.... But the most important thing is that the company goes all out to make sure that its employees are beholden to it: an engineer will be given highly specialized training, he'll be state-of-the-art in some narrow area of technology, but he's not really qualified for anything.... The more he becomes specialized in some particular product, the more beholden he is to the company.... The worst off are the salesmen who haven't been to college. They're completely beholden. How can those poor guys possibly sell anything outside the company?... Here, you know, the atmosphere is reformed: they listen to you. Suppose you have a complaint.... You go and tell some people about it, they're all nice guys, they listen politely, they'd really like to help. It throws you for a loop.... You always feel that at any moment they're going to break out the cookies. They add their own complaints to yours. Three months later they've still done nothing.... Very few people are fired outright. They're much more flexible, they keep a file on you and they use it when necessary. I wrote a memo a few years ago about recruitment in the personnel department. They tell you they want a file on political opinions, union membership, habits, debts, the wife, what she spends, and so on.... They know everything, there's always some guy willing to talk.... I was surprised in my department until I found out who the informer was.... Guys are watched by guys who are watched by other guys and so on.... The personnel managers talk to one another, they hang out in the cafeteria, they keep their ears open.... And meetings galore.... I saw one manager use an opinion poll that was guaranteed to be secret against people. He got hold of it somehow.... The middle managers all take management courses. They teach them that they should take you out to lunch whenever there's a problem. I know one case, a group that had problems, they invited all the guys to lunch.... I even know one secretary who took it into her head to invite the four guys who worked under her to lunch. And she picked up the tab! Its wonderful to reach that point, that degree of integration.

One of the fundamental ideas implicit in the modern approach to "human resource management" is not new. It is to make people constantly aware of the *presence* of the institution. For it is a general rule of total institutions – whether armies, boarding schools, convents, or businesses – that a person left to his own devices, left alone to harbor fantasies and resentments, is a person lost to the institution and potentially dangerous. One need look no further to understand why business is always interested in "enlisting the support" of cadres, particularly in time of crisis. In the years after the 1968 crisis a favorite theme among personnel managers in large, "socially progressive" firms was the need to "talk things over" with cadres, to "keep cadres informed," something one would have thought too obvious to mention. Business drew at least three lessons from the crisis. First, cadres must be made to feel that the company relies on them constantly. Otherwise there is a danger that, like "students," they will become "turned off" or, worse, that they will turn to active protest to vent their resentment at being shunted aside. Second, businessmen learned that "authority" and hierarchy no longer went unquestioned. Hence they sought to establish informal channels of communication that worked outside the formal hierarchy; even if these played no technical role in the operations of the firm, they at least introduced a sort of formal democracy and some semblance of "self-management." Finally, business leaders learned how important it was to keep themselves informed about what is going on at lower echelons, using traditional methods (volunteer or paid informers) and/or formal procedures guaranteeing anonymity.

Listen to the owner of a large electrical machinery manufacturer, writing in 1968:[78]

> In one of my first annual letters to the Company's cadres, I cited this sentence from Péguy: "A man who breaks rocks with a pick-axe must know why he is breaking rocks." And I added: "We all need to know the reason for what we are doing." This, in my view, is essential for effective and confident collaboration in any collective endeavor. The events of May and June have thrown new light on the desire and need of employees to participate in all aspects of company operations. The participation of cadres is crucial to this company. Without it, our goals cannot be met.

Management therefore set up "working groups" outside the normal hierarchical channels, whose members were "chosen by engineers and cadres who in 1968 gave some thought to the company's human relations problems and suggested to management solutions to those problems." In another large electrical machinery firm, four new "groups" were set up: a "senior cadres' group," a "council of shop foremen," a "council of technical and administrative supervisors," and a "committee of junior engineers" – as if, facing new dangers, socially minded employers were reinventing tried-and-true corporatist techniques. In another company (a machine-tool manufacturer), meetings were organized for cadres in each department to "reach consensus about the firm's purpose and set common goals for cadres of many different backgrounds who have joined this relatively new company." It was also arranged that "six cadres will have lunch with the President every month and speak to him directly and personally." Finally, "ombudsmen" were selected in each major division of the company. Their job was to pass on to top management information of the sort that generally got lost somewhere "in channels." It would be easy to multiply examples of this sort. For instance, in one large corporation with many regional subsidiaries and therefore quite difficult to manage, top management administered a very sophisticated opinion poll to all employees in 1970. The questionnaire included 97 questions of the following sort: "Do you like your job? (1) I love it. (2) I like it quite well. (3) I like it. (4) I can take it or leave it. (5) I do not like it." In its final report management claimed to be delighted with the sincerity of the responses and the almost universal satisfaction expressed by employees.

We must be careful, however, not to overestimate the effectiveness of these new methods for maintaining order. They work best on individuals carefully selected and trained to think of work relations as competitive, a view that tends to break down practical solidarities and to replace them with a vague sense of belonging to some abstractly defined group, such as the "company," the "corporation," or the "cadres." Of the many factors that have helped to spread this competitive view of work relations, none has been more important than the growing popularity of adult education. The availability of training courses fosters hopes of promotion, however vague and uncertain. This has encouraged aspirations that have made competition on the job harsher and more bitter, especially among blue-collar and white-collar workers and technicians just below cadre level, who must compete with one another for coveted promotions.

The institutionalization of autodidacticism

The institutionalization of adult education was a logical consequence of steps taken in the 1950s to develop new ways of controlling middle-level employees and regulating their careers (or, to be more precise, new ways of regulating and controlling behavior through the manipulation of career prospects). This certainly encouraged many employees to overestimate their chances of obtaining positions that were in fact reserved for graduates of the Grandes Ecoles. Adult education, today used primarily by technicians and lower-level cadres working for large firms, is related to the normal educational system in complex ways.[79] Promoted in the 1950s and 1960s by those who believed that "cultural backwardness" was the reason for France's "industrial backwardness," the institutionalization of adult education is one more sign of the growing importance of education among the various institutions of social reproduction.

State-sponsored adult education is available to all persons recognized under the law as "workers." It has an assigned place in the formal organization of technical education. For example, an ONISEP brochure on technological education dated April 1973 devotes a paragraph to adult education and informs future holders of technical diplomas (including the CAP, BEP, BT, BTS, and Bac) that after graduation they may choose either to enter the work force directly or to continue their studies in an adult education program. In other words, adult education is intended not only for adults already working in industry but also for young students who have completed their regular training but wish to improve their skills.

Looked at from another angle, however, adult education seems to have been conceived from the outset as a way of introducing some leeway into the relationship between educational credentials and jobs.[80] This is particularly true in the case of middle-level occupational certifications and technical degrees, whose value has declined as their numbers have increased. Adult education provides a way of basing "promotion" on educational achievement and merit, which makes personnel decisions appear legitimate and necessary without depriving companies of control over the careers of their employees. It is usually up to management to decide which workers will receive adult training. Lack of training can be used to justify lack of promotion. Furthermore, training leads to horizontal mobility at least as often as it leads to vertical mobility. To use the language of managers, it is supposed to promote "adaptation of cadres."

Adaptation is the main thing, the necessary and sufficient condition of mobility, and adaptation is first and foremost a question of attitude. If your 45- and 50-year-old cadres have problems on the job, the reason is that they are usually incapable of adapting to new kinds of organization and new work methods. They feel lost, overwhelmed.... How often have I seen, in my company and others, men who after a certain point are useless because they can't change their attitudes toward their colleagues and work methods.... I am convinced that behavioral problems are more important in the end than any other kind of problem.

These arguments, put forward by Jean Chenevier, Vice-President of British Petroleum (*Cahiers du C.R.C.* 13, 1969), to counter the arguments of other industrialists opposed to the institutionalization of adult education,[81] help to make clear the reasons behind the "constructive" and "cooperative" attitude of the CNPF in the negotiations with the unions that led to the signing, in 1970, of a national agreement on occupational training: adult education was designed to be an instrument for managing the careers of cadres. A side-benefit was that it made industry more independent of the normal educational system (a primary objective after May 1968).[82] It did this by accelerating the trend toward "privatization" of the instruments of training, already evident in the system of Grandes Ecoles for engineers and even more in schools of business and management. At the same time it strengthened the hand of management in dealing with those employees (mainly cadres) who held college degrees by introducing some flexibility into the relation between job level, job content, and educational achievement and above all by legitimating the notion that these need not be rigidly linked. One worry of employers was that once adult education was institutionalized and administered by the "state" it might be used by workers as a means of guaranteeing job security and would thus supplant the universities. In the report cited above Jean Chenevier writes that "adult education must not reinforce needs for protection and promotion" and, further, that there should be no "automatic link between training and promotion" of the sort demanded by "certain unions" and others who "dream of organizing – a typically French excess, alas – a vast and compulsory system."

In general, workers who enroll in adult education earn more than other workers with equivalent amounts of normal schooling who do not enroll (although it is impossible to determine whether this is a result of adult education in itself or of other factors, such as age). Still, there is no firm link between adult education and improvement of one's professional situation. The passage of the adult education bill does not seem to have increased the likelihood of promotion as a result of enrollment in further training. The 1970 Formation–Qualification–Profession study showed that no job change ensued for 48% of those who completed an adult education course (and for 59% of those who took such a course on their own, rather than their employer's, initiative).[83] An APEC study carried out in August 1977 showed that adult training was "approved" by employers in slightly less than half the cases examined.[84]

Nevertheless, the official character and even the very existence of adult education did indeed foster hopes of promotion in many individuals. The outcome being uncertain, this made the selection of rational career strategies (i.e., strategies in which the means were appropriate to a predictable set of ends) more difficult, and this in turn heightened competition among employees of equivalent rank. For example, Christian de Montlibert has shown that those who enroll in adult education programs, mainly technicians of middle-class background and better educated than most other technicians, are less supportive of other workers of equivalent rank and markedly less supportive of collective action by workers. They prefer individual competition. Only 24% say that they have been union members at one time or another, compared with 43% of the group as a whole, and only 33% prefer to work as part of a team, compared with 50% of the larger group.[85]

Autodidacts have always experienced tension between their competence and cultural aspirations on the one hand and the level of job they hope to attain on the other hand. Today, however, it seems that this tension is an inevitable byproduct of the mechanisms that govern the relation between the educational market and the job market, between the educational system and the productive apparatus. With these changes competition that was once most intense at the time of entry into the work force has been extended throughout working life. This is especially true of individuals without prestigious degrees but not totally without hope of promotion: a system of deferred gratifications (often deferred forever) keeps them "in the running" and, indeed, keeps them "running" until they are well on in years, whereas in previous generations individuals in similar positions were already preparing for retirement. As long as the link between the adult "catch-up" programs and promotion is sufficiently indeterminate or obscure, there is no danger that employees will reduce their efforts to a level commensurate with their real chance of success. Whether the game is worth the candle is a question that remains up in the air, so everyone has no choice but to get down to work. What technician comes to work without a textbook in his "attaché case," ready to study for that senior technician's license or to compete for promotion to the rank of engineer? The decision to continue one's studies beyond the age normally set aside for them used to be an individual (which is not to say a socially indeterminate) matter. It was the hope of upward mobility that persuaded some people that prolonging the period of uncertainty about the future was worthwhile. Today, however, the need to pursue further study after graduation is increasingly a career necessity, which whole categories of workers cannot avoid.

A pathology of "promotion"

By heightening competition for promotion, adult education increased the burdens of professional life, in some cases to a considerable degree. It became increasingly difficult for autodidacts to obtain needed knowledge, and they had to work very hard for promotion. Self-improvement required an ascetic way of life and careful husbanding of all available resources.

To gauge just how hard individuals have to work to make up for deficiencies in their education and how social factors affect upwardly mobile cadres, it is useful to consider a poll of readers of the magazine *Science et vie*, which is read mainly by upwardly mobile workers (not counting students). This magazine dispenses a type of knowledge valued by industry, the knowledge of the traditional engineer. For upwardly mobile workers it is a way of keeping up, usually in conjunction with adult education and other training. As one young technician put it, "*Science et vie* teaches me a great deal, which helps me not to appear too ignorant even in the presence of upper-class people."

Thus the idea of inserting a questionnaire into *Science et vie* (henceforth abbreviated SV) seemed a good way of sampling a cross-section of people from disparate social groups but who shared certain attributes, and in particular showed similar attitudes toward "social mobility" and "culture."[86] In fact, the magazine's readers did turn out to belong to nominally different categories (including workers, technicians, and engineers), but they differed not so much in attitude and outlook as in age: older readers, mainly "in-house engineers" who liked to read about scientific discoveries, were the embodiment of the dreams and hopes of younger readers seeking to rise to a higher station.

Excluding secondary and technical school pupils and students at the lesser engineering schools, of whom there are quite a few among the SV readership, most of the magazine's readers work in industry or commerce: 11.8% are blue-collar workers, 7.5% are clerical workers, 21.8% are technicians, 12.2% are cadres, and 9% are engineers. Most began reading the magazine when they were adolescents (68% before age 21). The higher their position in life, the older they are: the average age of workers is 33, foremen 39, engineers 45, senior cadres 49; the only exception to this rule is the technicians, whose average age is only 28. Thus the length of time that a person has been reading the magazine is roughly proportional to his position. These patterns suggest that a selection process is at work: readers begin reading SV in adolescence and, if they feel the need to bridge the gap between their actual job and the ambitions they formed during their years in school, continue to read the magazine after they begin work. For young workers forced to leave school and unable to qualify for jobs as engineers or cadres, an interest in science and technology indicates a desire to resist the forces of the job market, a determination not to give in, to seize the opportunity to realize hopes fostered by their families while they were still in school, before their failure to qualify for admission to higher education. This interest tends to evaporate, however, if promotion is delayed too long and career hopes turn out to be unrealistic. Such a mechanism accounts for the characteristic features of this self-selected sample. For example, blue-collar workers, underrepresented in the sample group, are much better educated than the average for their social class: 30% of the semiskilled workers who read SV hold a certificate equivalent to the BEPC, 17% a degree equivalent to the baccalaureate, and 17% a professional certification of some kind. As for skilled workers, who responded to the questionnaire in much greater numbers than their semiskilled colleagues, 27% have a BEPC or equivalent, 5% a baccalaureate or equivalent, and 62% a professional certification. As for the senior cadres and engineers, they, too, are highly upwardly mobile (74% of the cadres and 50% of the engineers), and half have recently taken refresher courses of one kind or another.[87]

The aspiring cadres and future "in-house" engineers examined in this survey for the most part lead sober lives; they must manage things carefully in order to meet the costs of advancement in time as well as money (obliged to attend courses, they cannot work overtime and must spend money on books, records, and other educational materials). The need to husband scarce resources even determines how these men relate to their own bodies: they make rational and economical use of their physical resources and train themselves (almost like athletes preparing for competition) to get as much as they can out of themselves (by learning how to cope with fatigue, for example, or practicing techniques of healing and relaxation).[88] The ability to control one's body is the ability to control one's "self," important if one is to stick to a prescribed course. Similarly, many ambitious young workers and technicians evince a kind of sexual asceticism, stemming from fears that "a woman" might cause them to waste the "free time" they now use to better themselves. One unmarried office worker, age 36, mentioned that he "was trying to study for an exam by correspondence. Completing this course in one year was unusual, but it could be done. I could have done it [*embarrassed silence*], but let's just say I made some foolish choices. I got interested in a girl. I shouldn't have. I had other things to do. That cost me a year." Controlling sexuality makes celibacy bearable, and celibacy is one of the most common costs of extracurricular studies. In order to devote full time to "primitive accumulation" of career capital one must, according to one 35-year-old technician, "not have children or a family.... [You have] to live with your mother, sit up straight, eat, and get back to your books." Of SV readers between ages 25 and 34, 32% were still bachelors, compared with 25% of the population as a whole. Furthermore, among readers over age 30, 26.4% of the bachelors had taken or were taking evening courses to prepare for an examination of some sort, compared with only 19.8% of married readers in the same age group.[89]

Given the high cost of becoming a cadre, it is hardly surprising that those who overcome all the obstacles tend to overinvest psychologically in their new roles and positions. This makes them quite vulnerable to manipulation (e.g., by depriving them of the symbols of cadre status), the purpose of which is to impose a system of values. Hence prolonged unemployment hits cadres, and especially autodidacts, particularly hard, often resulting in "psychological disturbance," "depression" (the UNEDIC study cited above found that 30% of the respondents reported being depressed), and even physical ailments. One could no doubt show that there exists what I might call a "pathology of promotion and demotion," whose symptoms are classified sometimes as psychological disorders, sometimes as somatic disorders.

As Edwin M. Lemert has shown in a well-known study,[90] certain forms of paranoia are directly related to demotion and exclusion in large bureaucratic organizations. These processes can create a paranoid disposition in the absence of positive character structure. Lemert studied ten inpatients with obvious paranoid symptoms who were confined in California hospitals after experiencing difficulties in their bureaucratic jobs. On the basis of detailed investigation of the conditions under which their first "symptoms" appeared, Lemert found that the onset of paranoid delusions could be related to objective processes of exclusion, which the victims inevitably perceived as "conspiracies." Hence the common idea that the paranoid invents the conspiracy against him is incorrect and incomplete. Exclusion of the "paranoid" from communication networks keeps him from finding out what other people think of him and correcting his interpretations of social reality. In these circumstances, occupational anxiety can easily develop into "insanity." The paranoid's investment in his role then enables him to serve the organization in yet another capacity, that of "scapegoat."

Many studies have been made of psychosomatic disorders associated with problems of social mobility and job-related conflict.[91] A particularly difficult position is that of low-level managers, who must cope with both the hostility of underlings, for whom they are company discipline incarnate, and the disapproval and lack of support of higher-ups. Stomach ulcers are commonly found in individuals whose rise in status has been accompanied by sharp conflict.[92]

A. Zaleznik, M. F. Kets de Vries, and J. Howard studied psychosomatic symptoms in 2,000 employees of a large Canadian publisher.[93] The employees interviewed were asked not only about health matters but also about career plans, job satisfaction, family background, and other subjects. The study was carried out during a company reorganization marred by internal conflict, especially between English-speaking and French-speaking employees. Zaleznik and his collaborators show that there was a strong negative correlation between prevalence of psychosomatic symptoms (insomnia, drug abuse, cardiovascular and gastrointestinal problems, allergies, etc.) and position in the hierarchy: these symptoms were least common among managers (about 25% of the sample) and very common among administrative staff (25%) and operational personnel (50% of the sample), even though people in the latter two categories come from very different backgrounds and are dissimilar in many other respects (the former being mainly "salesman types," the latter "intellectuals"). Clearly, then, somatic response to institutional conflict is directly related to personal dissatisfaction and above all, according to the authors of the study, to status uncertainty. It is highest in positions that carry with them a high degree of responsibility but a low level of authority. A similar finding was obtained by P. Castelnuovo-Tedesco in a study of stomach ulcers.[94]

Conversely, these authors refute the widely accepted notion that managers with "heavy responsibilities" are particularly subject to cardiovascular problems. Numerous studies have shown that the prevalence of cardiovascular symptoms increases not only with the objective level of job responsibility but also, perhaps even more, with the frequency and intensity of job-related conflicts.[95] A decrease in job level or even work load can be more deleterious to a man's health than a major increase in "responsibilities" that comes in the normal course of a professional career.

It is not difficult to find many other indices of daily stress in the lives of upwardly mobile cadres. Consider their relation to language, for example: the obsession with the *mot juste*, the attachment to nominal signs of status such as titles, forms of address, and so forth, and the insistence on following "directives" "to the letter" (to the point that one is sometimes reminded of medical definitions of "obsessional neurosis": "a disease of bookkeepers," as one eminent psychiatrist put it with rather haughty contempt). Before reaching their present positions, many upwardly mobile cadres had to overcome numerous obstacles and to deal with the stress of being placed repeatedly in ambiguous situations; obsessive behavior is very likely a result of such experiences. In the most commonplace situations, autodidacts will feel torn between habits acquired early in life and rules, often ambiguous and vague, internalized at a much later stage. In other words, they will feel torn between their original identity and the identity they hope to attain. Like anyone who can no longer take his surroundings for granted, the self-taught cadre therefore falls back upon explicitly stated rules. Rules help to compensate for the loss of an instinctive sense of how to behave. This may be one reason for the "rigidity" that is so often characteristic of the upwardly mobile petit bourgeois. That which has been named, categorized, and labeled is supposed to have a definite, palpable reality; words do not lie. Language is thus invested with great authority; the playful use of words is ruled out, as is any interaction between words and experience. To industrial psychologists rigidity is a "characterological" trait often cited as a reason for not promoting a low-level cadre. But in reality it has to do with the dialectic of the clear and the vague, and hence with language. Rigid behavior reflects an inability to allow for the ambiguities of real life and to maintain the proper distance between oneself and one's use of language. The "rigid personality," which recognizes no gap between words and things and views the world as a false image of the truth contained in words, is caught in the toils of language, as though ignorant of the fact that we usually try to "say what we mean." Practical nominalism of this sort cannot deal with the fact that ordinary behavior is underdetermined or that fleeting gestures and "unimportant" conversations can convey meaning; nor can it cope with ambiguity, with the fact that one person may combine many contradictory attributes. Cadres with this kind of mind are always looking for "solid" individuals, people "you can trust." They require "truth" and tirelessly scrutinize others for the "authenticity" that they themselves are summarily denied.

Conclusion: the cohesion of a fluid group

The most "cadre-like" of "cadres"

Before raising the question of the relationship between individual cadres and the collective personality that cadres have fashioned for themselves and that in turn has fashioned them, or, to put it another way, before examining the relationship between individual cadres and their social identity, I felt obliged to analyze the cadre group's sociological attributes (such as heterogeneity) and to show how these attributes could be explained in terms of the group's origins and history (in keeping with the Durkheimian dictate that social facts be explained in terms of other social facts and not by reference to some external principle, be it biological, economic, or psychological). Knowledge of the history of the group and its structures is the key to understanding those fleeting everyday phenomena that seem at first sight to be consequences of individual psychology and yet prove refractory to individualist methods, including polling and other statistical techniques which have proved incapable of establishing the collective context that gives individual opinions their meaning.

Hence it is impossible to speculate about the origins and properties of the cognitive instruments (classifications, categories, concepts, etc.) in terms of which individual agents conceive of the group and of their membership in it without relating those instruments to the group's structure and history. Of course these cognitive instruments turn out to be internalized, reified products of the group's history and structure, and their use helps to reproduce the group.

Indeed, the mental categories in terms of which the group is conceptualized seem to have a structure that reflects the structure of the group itself. Here, of course, I am assuming that it makes sense to speak of a "structure" of mental categories. It is common in sociology to think of social categories as homogeneous, discrete sets. What I am proposing here, however, is a different kind of logic, which I shall call "practical logic,"[1] the key tenet of which is that social categories are organized around a central kernel but have no precise boundaries, so that one can never say definitively of any particular person that he or she is or is not a member.

Interdisciplinary work in anthropology and cognitive and social psychology, particularly that of Eleonor Rosch,[2] has shown that, unlike the nomenclatures normally used in academic disciplines, "popular" or practical taxonomies (i.e., taxonomies not objectified in totalizing representations such as schemata, trees, graphs, tables, etc.[3] and not legitimated by a body of specialists) do not consist of homogeneous "classes" or categories separated by sharp boundaries or clear defining criteria (as was assumed in earlier work in what is usually called "componential analysis"[4]).

Using experimental technique Rosch shows that, unlike constructed concepts, which are definable in terms of bundles of pertinent traits, the semantic categories of natural languages are not sharply differentiated. Their role in the cognitive process is governed by a different kind of logic. Each mental category is organized around a core meaning based on those objects that best exemplify the properties of the category, that is, on paradigmatic examples. Around these clear-cut cases we find a halo of other member objects, grouped in order of decreasing resemblance to the paradigm. It follows, first of all, that the category possesses an internal structure, that it is not composed of undifferentiated and equivalent elements (and Rosch further states that it is merely an artifact of the usual experimental procedures that all members of a category seem to be equivalent and that this leads to the erroneous assumption that natural categories can be modeled after artificial concepts). It also follows that natural categories have no definite boundaries.

First tested in the realm of color perception[5] and shape perception (where the paradigms are the "good shapes" of Gestalt psychology), Rosch's hypotheses have since been confirmed in other areas, where the existence of paradigmatic central meanings cannot be explained as a consequence of the visual system's structure and function. For example, Rosch has studied the category "dogs." Her results appear to show that, for individuals in North America at least, some dogs are "more doggy" than others. For example, retrievers, with their long ears and upright tails, are "good examples" of dogs. They occupy a central position in the category. Pekinese, by contrast, are "bad examples." But individual speakers are trained, mainly in school, to use categories in an academic way, and they have internalized the scientifically legitimated zoological taxonomies; hence they clearly know that Pekinese are formally – or, as it were, *legally* – dogs, equivalent to any other member of the dog class. But if one asks them to think of "dogs in general," they will think spontaneously of retrievers, as if in ordinary usage speakers avoid consideration of borderline cases and concentrate instead of "good examples." Vagueness is therefore a property inherent in concept formation.[6]

Just as some reds are "redder" and some dogs "doggier" than others, it is easy to show that not all members of the category "cadre" are "good examples." Various individuals were asked to give three examples of "very cadre-like cadres" (*cadres très cadres*), indicating such characteristics as the nature of their work, their age, sex, education, income, name and size of firm, place of residence, and even the make of automobile they drove (these examples could be made up in whole or in part, as was the case with about half of the respondents sampled, or they could be based on actual friends or associates). This questionnaire was given not only to cadres of various sorts but also to individuals from quite different parts of the social spectrum (such as schoolteachers). This method made it possible to obtain a range of opinions about the nature of the "exemplary" cadre, or perhaps one should say the "imaginary" cadre, without simply accepting an a priori definition and then designing a statistical survey around it. In fact, the results show that the broader definitions are quite at variance with the commoner "ideal" representations of the cadre.[7] For example, the average "ideal" cadre is better educated than the average cadre in any of the statistical samples (with graduates of the Ecole des Hautes Etudes Commerciales particularly overrepresented). The "ideal" cadre is also much more likely to live in Paris and is generally in his 40s, in the "prime of life." An exceptionally high percentage of respondents indicated that their ideal cadre worked in sales, marketing, or advertising rather than production. Few were civil servants (although nothing in the instructions suggested restricting attention to the private sector). Smaller plants and firms are underrepresented, and larger companies, especially such major, high-profile firms as BSN, Péchiney, and especially IBM, were often cited. When small firms were mentioned, they were usually

Table 7. *Specimen sample and statistical sample*

in percent	*Specimen sample*					*Statistical sample*
	Group A *graduates* *large firm* (n = 48)	*Group B* *autodidact* *unemployed* (n = 49)	*Group C* *sales* *large firms* (n = 43)	*Group D* *teacher* *pri. and* (n = 52)	*Total* (n = 192)	*Reference sample* (*INSEE FQP2*)
No degree above bac.	5	39	20	11	19	56
Engineering or business school	67	31	40	38	44	26
Sales, marketing, finance	66	24	45	16	35	28
Production, methods, maintenance	9	13	18	11	11	31
Aged 35–49	71	57	69	58	59	35
Live in Paris area	87	90	75	78	80	41
Work in firm of fewer than 500 employees	23	28	36	27	26	75

Percentages are based on total number within each group.

advertising agencies or industrial service firms. What emerges from these results, then, in a stylized image of the "high-level cadre," whose attributes have a very strong emblematic value: business school, IBM, marketing, advertising, computers, Mercedes or BMW, and so forth, recur frequently. These are the *salient points* of the representation. Such exemplary cases come spontaneously to mind when the name of the category is mentioned, defining, in stylized, schematic terms, a core group, proximity to which in a sense determines membership in the cadre category. In other words, when asked to give a substantive (as opposed to an abstract) definition of the word "cadre," the persons questioned automatically gave paradigmatic examples rather than try to think about marginal cases, about individuals on the boundaries of this fluid category. In this respect the mental representation is a faithful image of the structure of the category itself. The "good examples" fit the stylized images established by the group's process of self-representation. Here we see a conflict between two implicit definitions of "representativity": a statistical definition, based on the notion that there exists a clearly defined parent population of which the statistical "sample" is a perfect small-scale model, a sort of *trompe-l'oeil* representation, and a political definition, a product of political strife, from which the socially dominant image of the group is derived. This situation is not the same as in the case of categories of shapes and colors (for which cognitive psychology has an apparent predilection, probably because these categories seem ideally "abstract," i.e., independent of social and historical determinations). Here the structure of the mental category cannot be explained or justified in terms of "natural" – that is, physiological – properties of the instruments of perception.[8] In the case of cadres, the focal point of the category is occupied by exemplars that reflect, in a stylized way, the attributes associated with those physical persons who have monopolized the instruments of social and political representation of the group as a whole. These "salient" examples are a product of the conflicts and struggles associated with the group's formation, with its history, which thus survives as a faint trace, a pattern impressed upon mental structures.

To make clear what distinguishes mental categories associated with social groups from mental categories associated with "natural" objects (shapes, colors, zoological or botanical species, etc.) it is not enough, however, simply to say that the former are a product of history. There is a more fundamental reason for the difference: social categories are instruments used by individuals to classify members of the society to which they themselves belong. Individuals who apply these instruments to other individuals also determine their own position in society. Thus interests are at stake, and the use of such instruments is never neutral or passive. For example, one can recognize that the dominant representation is dominant without acknowledging that it is "true" (i.e., representative, this time in a quasi-statistical sense). Or one can challenge it and accept it at the same time as part of a complex strategy of some sort. Notice, for example, that the official image of the cadre group most closely resembles the ideal images described by individuals in group A (those in a dominant position) and group D (those who stand outside the group themselves and hence feel less personally threatened by what they have been asked to do). By way of contrast, those in group B (mainly self-taught, unemployed cadres whose position in the group is subordinate and threatened) show both that they know what the dominant representation is and that they challenge it; they do this by choosing both examples that resemble the core group and others that occupy more marginal positions, while describing the latter as more "typical" or more "representative" than the former. In this they perform a fundamental political act, which is to challenge political representativity in the name of statistical representativity; they refuse to allow those who occupy the positions of power in the group to speak and act in the group's behalf, to incarnate the group in their person.

The existence of dominant representations, one of whose functions here is no doubt to reinforce group cohesion by providing agents with prominent points of reference and enabling them to communicate indirectly, by means of what Thomas Schelling has called "tacit bargaining,"[9] therefore seems to be in constant jeopardy. How, then, does the group reproduce its internal differences and yet maintain its unity (which is not entirely a false front)? In order to answer this question it may be necessary to abandon the oversimplified notion that group cohesion results either from similarity of its members or from the imposition, on a heterogeneous collection, of a dominant, official representation, and to examine instead the way in which the mechanisms that govern agents' views of their relative positions and trajectories help to prevent implicit internal divisions from developing into open splits.

Differences and divisions

A case in point: the existence of dominant representations of the cadre group cannot by itself explain why the group does not fragment into a number of smaller groups with names and specific identities of their own. What, then, accounts for the endurance of the collective personality despite the diversity of the actual physical persons who see themselves as sharing in it, even though their attributes and interests may differ from those of the group as a whole? No answer to this question is possible until we have analyzed why many cadres, particularly autodidacts in lower-echelon positions and/or cadres of working-class background, tended to overestimate their chances for promotion and success, especially during the period when the size of the cadre group was growing rapidly (1950–1974). It was this overestimation that led them to enter into hopeless competition with cadres holding advanced degrees and of relatively upper-class background.

These two series of questions have a common set of answers. If the *objective differences* revealed by statistical analysis were to take the form of *explicit differences*, identified and institutionalized as such; if, for example, the distinction between "management" and "staff" were the same at all times and in all places and reflected, say, differences in educational background (rather like the distinction between "high-school teachers" and "college professors"); and if the structures of both the category and the industrial field were reasonably transparent; then agents with the smallest objective probability of obtaining high-level positions would be dissuaded from entering into competition with those more likely to succeed. It would then be easier for them to define themselves in opposition to those who occupy the dominant positions in industry and hence to develop their own standards of excellence and their own organizations. But this is not the case. It is because cadres constitute such a fluid group, with no universally accepted, explicit criteria for membership and no clearly defined boundaries, and, further, because the institutional system (firms) underlying the category is itself a hodgepodge of interdependent and overlapping entities, that agents are willing to enter into competition, overestimate their power and their chances for promotion, and deceive themselves about their prospects, about what they are and what they may become. This self-deception is greatest among lower-level cadres around 30 years of age, that is, at the time of life when career investments are being made: it is as if the all-out effort required of those who would compete despite innumerable handicaps requires them to repress whatever tacit knowledge they may possess of their objective chances. Often it is not until ten or fifteen years later that the "sense of reality" returns with a vengeance, but too late, for the die has already been cast. At this point individuals who had invested all their hopes in their careers may choose to "take their distance" from norms that they can now see to be arbitrary and incoherent; they begin to think of their past lives and of society in general as a puppet show in which some evil genius pulls all the strings.

These mechanisms, whose effect is to distort the social perceptions, the internalized social image, of lower-level cadres at a crucial stage in their careers, operate with maximal efficiency in the period of expansion preceding the crisis of 1974. This was true for several reasons. First, industrial firms were undergoing constant reorganization. As we have seen, older frames of reference, shaped by socialization in the family and school and at the workplace, were disrupted by these changes. Economic growth increased the number of positions of relative power in industry, and hence the probability of promotion to such positions seemed to increase. But this was true for everyone, and everyone's subjective estimate of the likelihood of promotion also increased. Thus the number of people who competed for promotion to the available positions rose, as much as and probably even more than the number of positions available, because the forecasting instruments were in such disarray that subjective hopes increased out of all proportion to objective chances. It was enough that "chances" should exist, but in indeterminate and unascertainable numbers, for large numbers of individuals to be encouraged to compete. Initial and subsequent mechanisms of social selection continued to operate throughout this period much as they had before; expansion increased the general likelihood of promotion without reducing the *relative* handicaps of those least well equipped to compete, either because they lacked sufficient education or because their lower- or middle-class background precluded access to high positions.

The interaction of reciprocal images

Whatever interfered with the perception of social space helped to make the cadre group more cohesive, countering the centrifugal tendencies that would have existed had explicit internal divisions or stable, transparent systems of evaluation and prediction been in place. The group endured precisely because its boundaries were fluid. Marcel Mauss speaks of "cohesion achieved through similarity and difference, as in the weaving of fabric or wicker baskets, cohesion through friction, if you will, which allows diverse social structures to mesh with one another, to intertwine," in such a way as to form a complex whole in which "each group is intertwined with all the others and organized through reciprocal exchange, through interaction."[10] The implicit definition of the term "cadre" varied from one subgroup to another. This allowed individuals belonging to different factions to use the same word to describe themselves and to maintain what Goffman calls a "working consensus" that could never have been achieved had all ambiguity been eliminated. In such an environment unity is indeed a product of division, because the sensitivity to individual differences makes doubtful the outcome of any attempt to mobilize a faction in opposition. No principle of differentiation or identification seems powerful enough to permit subgroups to develop within the larger group whose members might feel sufficiently united to overlook secondary differences.

Any individual may compare himself to other individuals in many different ways. At the individual level these comparisons need not be consistent or "coherent" (in the sense in which Lenski speaks of "status coherence"). Consistency holds only at the aggregate level, which by definition is inaccessible to individual knowledge. People do not ordinarily know the statistical relations among various status indicators (they may possess such knowledge intuitively, but repress it). Hence they can claim, in perfect good faith, that status indicators do not by themselves reveal a person's social position. Each person may feel that he or she is in competition with everyone else (tacitly assuming that there is just one market and some minimum degree of interindividual comparability) and yet maintain that every individual is unique. In this world of difference, uncertainty, and hence suspicion (toward others) as well as refuge (for oneself, when scrutinized by others), "one never knows" and "nothing means anything." For people lacking scientific and/or political organizing principles to help decide which properties are "fundamental" and which are "secondary" (i.e., irrelevant or purely "individual"), the exception always appears to be the rule. This is particularly true of individuals who have found the energy needed to pursue their careers by repressing perception of social patterns and emphasizing real or apparent exceptions to those patterns (people will often justify industrial selection methods, for example, by pointing to a few top executives who never went to college and "started with nothing"). Such examples are "heartening," provided no hard questions are asked about the likelihood of following in their footsteps. If one's notion of causality is not statistical but purely deterministic, then everything seems to be indeterminate. There are exceptions to every rule: salary is not always commensurate with education (mainly because it also depends on age, sex, size of firm, etc.); power is not always commensurate with title; some corporate executives never went to college; some graduates of prestigious schools fail to make it to the top; the "salary is low" but the "benefits are great"; the title is "not prestigious" but the "job involves responsibilities." There is no end to the terms and symbols that cadres use to gauge and measure one another, and no end to the ways in which these terms and symbols can be used to obscure true hierarchy and cloud prognostication. The effect of this is to liberate cadres, but their freedom is essentially symbolic, not to say fantastic: they are free to plan and maneuver in ways whose relation to reality is sometimes so tenuous that one hesitates to call them "strategies."

The group remains intact despite internal differences because it satisfies, at least in a symbolic way, the interests of all its members. A cycle of internal exchanges runs through it, in which the circulating commodity is precisely the name of the group, its emblem: regardless of a person's objective position, it is in his interest to call himself a cadre, to define himself as such, provided others do the same. In other words, subgroups benefit from association with other subgroups of the larger group. Lower-level cadres are attached to a title for which many of them had to fight hard and which is valuable because it is also claimed by their superiors. Thus cadres in the lower echelons share a set of symbols with those who dominate them, directly or indirectly. Such sharing does not, of course, preclude criticism or resentment. The shared symbolism is useful to those who occupy positions of power in industry and yet claim to be "cadres like the rest." It helps them to conceal their identity: in surveys, for instance, those who wield real power are confounded with their subordinates in a single category. It also legitimates their authority. This legitimation is possible only because the fluidity of the cadre group's boundaries keeps internal divisions from taking an explicit, institutionalized form. Access to the "elite" is today said to be "meritocratic" because desirable positions are obtained through competition (subtly biased as it is); there can be no legitimate victor without disappointed rivals.

Belief in the group is maintained by the material and symbolic benefits that cadres derive from membership. Even the most disillusioned and disabused informants, who when "fed up" willingly lay their resentments at the feet of the sympathetic, outside observer and "critic" that they imagine the sociologist to be, never go so far as to question the existence of the category, which they regard an unquestionable even when doubtful or confused about its content. For anyone can call himself a "cadre" and insist that the group exists while at the same time arguing that others who also claim membership are not really cadres. Or he may say that he is not a "real cadre" even though he calls himself one, but that others are "real" and that one day he will be too. Or, again, he may argue that since he is a "real cadre" he has no need to define himself as such (role-distancing) and that those who call themselves "cadres" are attached to the title precisely because they do not "really" deserve it. And so on.

Senior cadres, "distinguished," aloof, upper-class executives who serve as role models for the group as a whole, are sometimes condescending in their descriptions of the behaviour by which their juniors try to assert that they, too, are cadres. Such men can readily provide the sociological investigator with quite convincing "analyses" (convincing precisely because they are expressed in language that conforms to the rules of learned discourse) of the way in which upwardly mobile autodidacts surround themselves with symbols of their status (luxury cars, attaché cases, tailor-made suits). But this apparently objective and disabused manner is in fact a way of marking the distance that separates them from the "common run" of cadres as well as asserting their own identity by demonstrating the symbolic power they wield over the self-images of others. "They" (the lower-level cadres) think that they are "cadres" because "we" make them believe; "we" create their "alienated" self-image; "we" look at them from the outside; "we" manipulate" them and watch ourselves doing so; "being a cadre means nothing to me but to them it makes sense"; "they believe that they play a part in decision-making, and we let them believe it"; "they'd rather have expense accounts than good salaries, because the expense account is the sign of a real cadre"; "every morning they thank God that they're cadres"; "to have status that others don't have is what they want, and we pump them up with that image"; "you've always got to be patting them on the back, letting them think they run the plant." Middle managers are not real "executives": "Things are quite different from what most cadres imagine, but we need to have people who think that the company would collapse without them and that they keep the ship on an even keel." By presenting themselves as disabused and cynical, executives who wield (or think they wield) real power demonstrate their unique privilege, the authenticity that puts their cadre status beyond doubt. But this defining authenticity also places them above the group, and everything that they say is intended to deny that belonging to a cadre organization has anything to do with their social identity: they are cadres only for others, for those whose essence is to believe that they are cadres and who by multiplying signs of belonging succeed only in proving that they do not really belong. Top executives define themselves as cadres only so that others who are not "really" cadres can identify with them. Thus the really high-ranking cadre can make it seem doubtful that anyone at all is a cadre without for one moment doubting the existence of the category itself, as though it were a thing, an "objective" fact.

Each agent forms his own peculiar image of other agents in the "field," and there is no position that enables a person to see things as they "really are." Lower-level cadres, for example, are not as blindly attached to their status symbols as many executives think. Many have a fairly comprehensive understanding of their situation (especially older cadres who have worked for a number of different firms and, to an even greater degree, those who have been fired, unemployed, or suffered in other ways). They are not unaware of the group's internal divisions and to varying degrees are conscious of contrasting norms and role models. Outside the workplace lower-level cadres are perfectly willing to express themselves "personally" and individually and often exhibit the same ironic distance from their positions as their superiors (which of course is also a way of distancing their superiors): the people on top, they say, force us to be what we are, or, rather, to appear to be different from what we "really" are. They can speak of themselves in the objective language of social psychology and discuss their "façades," their "play-acting," their "false fronts," their show of "zeal" and "eagerness" as means of pleasing "bosses" whom they describe as fairly stupid and invested in their "cadre roles" to an almost caricatural degree. Indeed, the bosses are especially eager for their subordinates to behave in this way because they themselves are far from fitting the mold of the "ideal" cadre. For low-ranking cadres the "real cadre" is someone more self-confident, more fortunate, better educated, and more powerful than either themselves or their direct supervisors. One cannot escape from this hall of mirrors by saying that for low-level cadres the "real cadre" is the owner of the firm, because they normally agree that the owner is not a cadre and that by his very nature he belongs to some other group. Thus both lower-level cadres and their supervisors may not recognize themselves or any of their coworkers as authentic cadres and yet continue to believe in the objective existence of the category.

The strength of weak aggregates

The relation between a group and its individual members is often complex, characterized by a mixture of belief and incredulity, enthusiasm and disillusionment. One function of militant activity in political parties and labor unions is to cope with this complexity. The existence of competing unions, partially contrasting social images, contradictory group definitions, and spokesmen who may be rivals or accomplices of one another enables individuals both to contest possibly "radical" group values and to believe in the reality of the "cadre phenomenon." The "otherness" that agents experience in their daily interactions is institutionalized at the level of the social representation, where its effect, paradoxically, is to reinforce the collective identity. Competition among rival organizations helps to create a unified field of battle. The cadre who belongs to a worker-dominated union such as the CGT or CFDT believes that by questioning the "trademark" of the cadre he is taking his distance from the group and seeing through the false image that cadres have of themselves. Often he will also question the unions' images of the cadres. But it is always *as a cadre* that he goes about his union activity in association with other cadres and in opposition to other organizations that also define themselves in terms of the cadre group. Behind challenges to a group's self-image one always finds struggles over who will represent the group, struggles that presuppose belief in the group's existence. These political actions and reactions make the group's *presence* more overwhelming and difficult to question but at the same time more opaque. In other words, what appears to weaken the group may also strengthen it. The cadre group's powers of attraction are enhanced by its own weakness and fluidity and by the laxity of its requirements. It is malleable, and depending on how one looks at it it may either stand out or fade into the background, like Henry James' "figure in the carpet." Or, to borrow another Gestalt metaphor, like mud as described by Francis Ponge: "It lies at the edge of the nonplastic. It tempts us with shapes only to discourage us in the end." But even this failing is no defect, and it would be wrong to think that the harshest mobilization strategies are necessarily the most efficient. Because mobilization technologies invariably result in both inclusion and exclusion, aggregation and separation, they always threaten to destroy the collectives that they help to create (as is clear in the case of sectarian groups). Since destructive potential is always proportionate to constructive power, suboptimal strategies may in fact be best if longevity is important.

In short, the cadre group is able to unify its membership and to quell internal hostilities precisely because it remains ill defined and indeterminate.[11] Adopting a common name is tantamount to creating a political alliance that need not be regarded as such. Accords between cadres organizations (such as the CGC) and the middle-class movement or employers' groups (as in the 1950s) and campaigns against the public sector and the government in the postwar years may simply be official and superficial manifestations of a more deepseated conservatism. Cadres have done much to maintain the social order simply by existing as a group and gathering dispersed and in some respects hostile elements together in a single symbolic unit. Low-ranking cadres have paid for their titles with their bodies and their votes. They swelled the ranks of cadre organizations and served as troops ready to be mobilized by the dominant segments of the bourgeoisie. Those who "represented" this captive audience tirelessly repeated that cadres enjoyed a privileged position far above the working class ("privilege" is a word that frequently appears in advertising directed at cadres). At the same time they insisted on the cadre's underlying unhappiness ("cadres are not liked") and, as if to keep the troops on their guard, spoke of a deep "malaise." Of course the word "malaise" is ambiguous, because it can connote disappointed hopes, bitterness at having to take orders, or fear of being confounded with the "masses" (this is frequently what is meant by talk of the "proletarization of cadres").[12] There was no danger in reminding cadres of their malaise, however, because any potential rebellion would have required cadres to turn against other cadres, thus destroying the unity of the group. Rebellion remained impossible as long as the officially formulated discontent was experienced by individuals as a generic but undefinable malady.

This tacit alliance between the industrial bourgeoisie and the cadres resulted in direct economic benefits to the former (in the form of retirement systems, ceilings on social security payments, tax reductions, and so forth). The widespread use of the cadre title helped to suppress latent conflicts between different segments of the bourgeoisie and petite bourgeoisie, as did the creation of a cadres' job market, which to some extent standardized hiring criteria and salaries. Energies that could not be collectively mobilized were channeled into individual competition, where outcomes *seem* to be unpredictable but are in fact determined by ascertainable laws (this helped to bring about the new conservative view of the social order that replaced corporatism after the war). This account applies in particular to the politically crucial conflict between the traditional bourgeoisie, whose interests lay with family firms operating in local markets, and technically trained and socially innovative segments of the grande bourgeoisie, whose interests lay with the development of large-scale industry and the internationalization of production and trade. The increase in the number of cadres also stabilized potentially hostile relations between the grande bourgeoisie, which holds economic power, and the "masses" of petits bourgeois who occupy middle-management positions in large firms: the cadre/non-cadre distinction became the focal point of the latter group's expectations and strategies, after which what Piaget calls the "centering effect" prevented low-level cadres from taking a comprehensive look at their position. The title "cadre" was applied to agents of very different social origin, educational background, and income. A Parisian executive, a Grande Ecole graduate from an old bourgeois family, has little in common with a former blue-collar worker promoted to foreman in a large company or a provincial plant manager in charge of a company doing subcontracting to a large corporation, or with an aerospace researcher employed by the CNRS. Widespread use of the cadre title altered the symbolic order to correspond with the new structure of industry, where formal unification under the aegis of giant corporations often conceals the perpetuation and perhaps even the deepening of existing differences and inequalities. But this symbolic unification also restored an earlier, undifferentiated state, prior to the formation of the cadre group, when there was still no clear distinction between plant owners and their "collaborators," as they were then called. With one difference, however: in the past, cadres identified with plant owners, whereas now owners often identify with cadres. The existence of a sharp distinction between the two groups may be associated historically with the period of transition between two types of industrial organization.

The authentic and the inauthentic

This book began with the question of the existence of the cadre group. Along the way I tried not to lose sight of this group character, which I hope to have shown was neither an artifact nor a fantasy. But it has been difficult to identify the group's precise contours, at least in the sense that one can identify the precise contours of other elementary social units. Except perhaps in the original core group of engineers, we have never found a pragmatic collective or organization tacitly held together by common attributes and shared objective interests. This, of course, brings up the question of membership. No matter what the group, membership criteria are never self-evident. Almost as soon as a group forms it begins to include some and exclude others; it incorporates and rejects, assimilates and expels, opens and closes its ranks. Through constant effort, only a small part of which is preserved in the written record, the group is *constructed* (much as the objects of social science are constructed, and by not dissimilar techniques). It acquires a structure of its own with a center and a periphery, "authentic" representatives and borderline cases, building or underlying structures (distribution structures of scarce goods), which limit the number, variety, and freedom to maneuver of potential members and the powers of attraction of the titles and representations associated with the group (not to the point of wholly determining the outcome, however). At any point, the set of possible operations (unions, intersections, partitions, etc.) is not determined solely by economic or morphological mechanisms but depends also on historical and political circumstances, that is, on the degree to which antagonistic or competing groups are mobilized and on the strategies that they adopt.

Another thing that our investigations failed to turn up was a moment of "historical fusion," that is, a moment in which objective diversity is suddenly transformed, in the urgency of battle, into organic unity. The group deceives those whom it attracts; not all members benefit from membership to the same degree. Even "membership" does not have the same meaning for all, except in a formal sense; the boundaries of the group are fluid, and some members "belong" more than others. The dominant representation of cadres, formulated and popularized when the group was first organized, is not based on generic properties of the group as a whole: tailored to fit the engineers who shaped the collectivity (and who long monopolized its social power), the dominant image becomes less and less appropriate as one moves farther and farther from the core group. It is the more marginal members who are most misled by accepting the group image. In this connection, incidentally, "marginal" does not imply that the individuals so described mean deliberately to be atypical or asocial but merely that, because of their ambiguous attributes and equidistance from several different poles of attraction, they must either define themselves in negative terms ("neither cadre nor owner nor artisan nor worker") or else borrow their image from one of several different poles – which ever one happens, at a given moment in history or in the life cycle of the group, to exert the strongest attraction.

Hence it is incorrect to describe the relation between individual agents and the group to which they belong (as Lukačs does) in terms of "class consciousness," based on the assumption that society is composed of "a number of clearly distinguished basic types whose characteristics are determined by the types of positions available in the process of production."[13] Class consciousness, Lukačs writes, "consists in fact of the appropriate and rational reactions imputed to a particular typical position in the process of production."[14] But in order to determine what these appropriate, rational reactions are, one must assume that social groups can be characterized in terms of their interests and other objective criteria around which awareness of a shared situation can crystallize, thereby enabling individuals to join with others to form groups conceived as organic entities. Only on this condition can organized collective practice, assisted by political "explanation," enable individuals to see clearly how their underlying situation relates to their "consciousness," thus transforming "objective" membership into "subjective" knowledge. Such a mechanistic definition of "class consciousness" has always been in favor with party officials, for whom it serves as a sort of professional ideology (since their job is precisely to mobilize party members by demonstrating that they share "objective" grounds for action in common). It does not hold true for groups like the cadre group, which formed in successive stages around an original core, much as a crystal forms around a "seed." In the case of cadres, it makes no sense to contrast "a small number of determinate typical situations" with the variety of individual consciousness. In order to understand the formation of the group and the relationship between individual members and the collectivity, we must in fact stand the stated formula on its head and contrast the diversity of objective situations with the relatively small number of "position names" incorporated into various stylized social models. An individual cannot acquire a coherent and meaningful identity unless he or she identifies with some legitimate, that is, collectively recognized, representation. A priori, however, there is no reason to describe identification with some institutionalized pole of attraction as emancipating rather than "alienating" or authentic rather than inauthentic. Proximity to the pole of attraction determines which description is correct in each individual case. An "authentic" social existence is possible only for those whose objective position in relation to the underlying structures coincides with an institutionalized and represented point of social space. "Authenticity," which in social terms signifies nothing more than conformity to some socially recognized standard of excellence (and which is therefore best expressed in tautology: "he is what he is"), is accorded only to those individuals whose attributes correspond to their socially defined identities – in other words, to individuals for whom there exists a collectively recognized social identity corresponding to the position that they occupy in the realm of objective distributions. Only collective action can dispel inauthenticity. Only when explicitly and collectively defined as "typical," that is, specific *and* universal, can individuality move beyond the realm of the ineffable, the private, and the insignificant – beyond local singularity. But what is thereby gained is irrevocably lost to others, because when a new group enters the order of representation other possible forms of organization are invariably repressed.

Epilogue: the car in the garage

It was in May 1977 that I recorded the interview with which the present work begins. Almost exactly four years later, M, the man who had told me his life story, let me know through common friends at whose home we had first met that he wished to see me again, to speak to me, because he had "other things" to tell me, things that "would interest a sociologist." He wanted, that is, to fill me in on the rest of his adventures and misadventures with his new employer, a company which, after the initial years of euphoria, he now saw as an "outfit like any other."

I also learned that he had left Paris. He was now living in a village between a forest and an industrial park about 70 kilometers south of the city in a small house, a "family property," which he had once used as a weekend house but had since made his primary residence. He commuted to Paris every day to work: four hours of travel daily. Having been ill for three weeks, he was able to spend some time with me – "all afternoon if you like" – which in normal circumstances would have been impossible. He met me at the train station. Since we hadn't met for four years and might not recognize each other he told me that he would be driving a green Citroën 6CV, a Visa model with four doors and a hatchback. Our conversation took place around a picnic table in M's back yard. Despite the heat he wore a wool jacket over his sport coat. He had untied his tie but left his shirt collar buttoned.

His story, excerpts from which will follow in due course, reflects his efforts to prepare for the new ordeals he would soon be facing (he expected to be forced to resign from his position in the near future). But this time, unlike the last, he found it difficult to tell a coherent story, probably because he had now explored the whole spectrum of industry, from the smallest of traditional firms to the largest of multinational corporations. Everywhere he had met with backstabbing and failure. Hence it was no longer so easy for him to define himself as a salesman, a cadre, or a sales engineer and to maintain his ambitions while continuing to believe that somewhere, in some other firm, he would find a reality that corresponded to his idealistic image of business and of the social role in which he had invested his hopes, that there did indeed exist a place in the world where a man could truly accomplish something. As he himself admitted, he had lost his faith. He mentioned Japan again, but perfunctorily this time. In any case Japan was too remote, too inaccessible, to be anything other than a mythical beacon of hope (though he did mention, without real enthusiasm, the possibility of offering his services to a Japanese subsidiary of some French firm). His years of experimentation were over, he now knew the world of industry and perhaps society as well, and the metaphor that occurred to him spontaneously (he advised me to bear it in mind, unaware that it was already central to social psychology) was that of the contrast between the dining-room of a restaurant and the kitchen: the difference between the sham and the reality, the official and the hidden, the fraudulent and the authentic. I was reminded of Erving Goffman and the Shetland Islands where Goffman went on the advice of W. L. Warner to do community research and ended up forging the basic concepts of his social theories while dining in a hotel and watching waitresses pass through a swinging door from the "stage" where he was dining to the "wings" where his dinner was being prepared.[1]

M was not completely alone or empty-handed, however, in his effort, apparently far-reaching and final, to de-invest from his job. For the ideology of the post-1968 period – with its pottery and its sheep, its exaltation of nature and its love of culture, its critique of production and consumption and its comforting celebration of the "simple life" – had by now spread its influence to cadres. This ideology, of course, has much in common with Catholic notions of resignation and sanctity and may fulfill the same psychological and social functions. Inevitably, the changes in M's thinking had led him to anticipate a move from one extreme to the other of the petite bourgeoisie: he spoke now of looking for a job with one of the "nationalized firms" that he had so harshly criticized in the past, and this for him meant entering into a period tantamount to "pre-retirement." His friends tell me that he voted left for the first time in his life in the most recent elections. But youthful difficulties in internalizing cadre culture and disciplining or repressing instincts fostered by his family upbringing had cropped up again now that his adopted world had rejected him. His new rhetoric, no less borrowed than the old though from different sources, again suggests a fairly incoherent ideology, which no doubt reflects the incoherence of his objective situation. He combines two themes, for example, which though not contradictory *per se* derive from hostile ideological camps (a fact of which M seems to be unaware): on the one hand he is critical of consumer society and favors a movement "back to the roots," while on the other hand he is misogynist in a way that many lovers of nature and the earth would no doubt characterize as macho if not fascist.

This apparent paradox would be incomprehensible if we knew nothing about the mishaps that landed M in his new predicament. After the retirement of a superior whom he had hoped to succeed, M's attitude went from consternation to rebellion as he was first passed over in favor of an "ambitious young cadre" from corporate headquarters and then shunted off to a subsidiary and forced to work under a man to whom he referred as a "boy scout" or "Good Samaritan" in a plant where the atmosphere was "relaxed" to a point that M judged to be incompatible with the company's "image" and "position." What is more, important staff positions were held by women, which gave the whole department what M saw as a "feminine" look (in M's mind this was not unrelated to the relaxed atmosphere). As for himself, he had this to say: "Me? I'm not a woman, at least until somebody proves the contrary." Just as in his previous jobs, M's troubles began when he started to take his role and his title too seriously and insisted upon recognition and consideration that the firm refused to give him. But what was unprecedented in this case, making his situation particularly intolerable and outrageous, was the fact that the humiliations he was now forced to endure came at the hands of women. From his first day in the department M was cast into what he regarded as a female hell: gossip, idle chatter, close supervision, irritations, excessive "mothering," and snide remarks. He began complaining to his superiors, who dismissed his complaints out of hand. He then attempted to retreat, but since his sales fell at about the same time he was shut out of his peer group and eventually brought to the brink of resignation.

In this case, career control and "cooling out" mechanisms did not work; M was made to feel that he had no choice but to resign.

His problems are surely connected with his personality: M is at once the victim and the instrument of his misfortunes, both persecutor and persecuted. But his repeated failures raise certain questions, and to reformulate these in psychological terms is really to miss the point. The reason for the repetition is that the system indefatigably renews individual hopes and expectations whose fulfillment social conditions do not permit. But these expectations are collective and historical, and the character structure of the individual reflects (in this case to a remarkable degree) the properties of the group, whose structural instability is perpetuated by the insecurity, anxiety, and aggression of its members. Collective biography, moreover, enables us to identify the stage at which socially regressive investments became established: when the "rise of the cadres" happened to coincide with economic growth; when the bourgeoisie, recently redefined, seemed open and accessible; and when there were opportunities to be seized and places to be had, open to anyone who felt capable, who wanted success badly enough, and who "had what it takes." An earlier period comes irresistibly to mind. One thinks of the desperation of the petite bourgeoisie in the 1930s. And of Raymond Queneau's character Toto in *Les enfants du limon*, the model worker who works hard to raise himself up and become an engineer and who, after the Depression hits, escapes unemployment by joining a fascist league: "Injustice for him lay not in the various inequalities that distinguish one man from another. He did not ask why beauty and ugliness were unevenly distributed, or why wealth was unequally divided. For him it was no injustice that some are strong and others weak. Rather, it was injustice that the strong, which to him meant the sharp ones, the movers, among whom he numbered himself, should be allowed to succumb."

There are plenty of other things in life, you know. There's nature, listen, you hear the birds? It's great. . . . I decided to leave Paris for a number of reasons. Monetary reasons in part: rents in Paris are high, at least if you want to live in an old section. It's expensive. We were paying on the order of 3,600 francs a month. And since we needed to breathe, we had to leave town every weekend. Three hours on the road, the traffic, the aggravation. . . . The choice was between continuing to pay our rent and paying to fix up this place out here. So we decided to settle here for good. I'm in sales, I'm not in the office twenty-four hours a day. I have clients all over France, not just in this area, so I often end up coming home late at night. . . . The corporation is in the throes of a complete reorganization. We were told that the average age in our department is 37 compared with 28 in the other departments. That gives you some idea what's really going on, because in the meantime they've hired a lot of young people. They've started pushing us out. They hassle us all the time.... At first things were all right. My boss was an intelligent fellow. But he left and they sent us this conceited young jackass who walks in step and clicks his heels every morning, talks to three people at once, and juggles five phone calls at the same time. But the guy turns out to be pretty much of a nothing. He got the job through pull. He's a great pal of Mr So-and-so, so you can't say anything. I couldn't believe it. I didn't catch on. It didn't fit with my philosophy.... After my transfer I was sent to this really sweet department, you know, with a boy scout for a boss. Everybody's on a first-name basis and they all go around clapping each other on the back. I was kind of surprised, because in business you don't see people clapping each other on the back very often and calling each other by their first names, at least not for very long. But then our sales dropped, and whenever that happens the higher-ups crack down. They watch what we're doing. I have six or seven people looking over my shoulder, directly or indirectly. It's intolerable, unbearable.... To keep up sales you've got to have contacts in the laboratories, the design departments, and the purchasing offices. This kind of selling keeps you really busy, and as I was saying I've got twenty-five or thirty companies to visit all over France – that's companies, not individuals. Nobody can do a job like that by himself, it's impossible. As long as times are good and the market is humming, orders come in more or less by themselves. But when they stop you've got to be visiting twenty plants at once.... Every sales engineer is backed up by an accounts manager. Now, these are women, and unfortunately they lack technical training. But they don't report to the sales engineer. You see what a mess that creates. You work with these people but you have no authority over them.... These women want to know where you are at all times, who you're going to see, in what company, at what time you're going to be with So-and-so, whether you had lunch with him, and so on, so they can report to one of the higher-ups, one of the sales managers. Who repeats it to the department head, who repeats it to the division manager, who repeats it to the VP for sales. And suddenly at the end of the year this VP for sales decides to freeze your salary. That happened to me. The department head is the boy scout, the choir boy. A great pal, couldn't be nicer, terrific, until one day you're sandbagged. That's hypocrisy for you.... One day my boss noticed that my sales were off. He asked me for an explanation, and I gave him one. It was quite simple, really: the government had stopped buying, so demand had collapsed. When I couldn't come up with any predictions I got a dressing-down, and then at the end of the year when the boy scout went to see the division manager, somebody asked what he thought of So-and-so. Oh, So-and-so's not on top of things. What's that you say? So-and-so not on top of things? We can't have that. So he goes and repeats this story to the VP, and the VP freezes my salary. Then my boss calls me in and he looks really broken up, like he's at a funeral or some-

thing, tears in his eyes. I know it's not your fault, he says. You're right on top of things. The market's soft right now. . . . I didn't go along, see, I even got into a shouting match with the big brass, you understand, blah blah blah. But look, if you get your orders up to two million as I was saying a moment ago, I can straighten things out. OK. In January, when my status came up for review, this guy, the Jesuit, puts on a new attitude. He bawls me out for a whole list of things. Now he's figured out that the top brass won't let the matter drop and he's got troubles of his own, they've greased the floor under him, so he's got to find scapegoats. They tried reorganizing the department while he was away on vacation. A lousy thing to do. The guy was away on vacation. He's 48 years old and there are two other guys in the department handling similar product lines. Product engineers. Now these product engineers saw that something was amiss. They're not jerks, and they tried to get the division manager to reshuffle the deck. So the boss called me in April, just before my heart thing, and he said to me, You know, it's a sad business. Your salary's still frozen. I think it might be in your best interest to look for a job somewhere else. And then he added, There's a shakeup going on. I'm in the same boat. Oh, really? I said. Have you been fired or what? So he says to me, Yes, you can say that in a manner of speaking I've been fired. So for your own good, in your own interest, I advise you to find another job. Well, that really got to me. At first I was happy in that outfit. I hadn't seen the whole operation, you understand. It's a bit like going to a restaurant. Remember that image. You go in, you see a nice table, a beautiful waitress, well dressed and all, impeccable, and then you go back to the kitchen and you're horrified, cockroaches all over the place, filthy people running around, cigar butts on the floor, you name it. . . . Take the training courses, for example. They started out telling us, We're the best, Such-and-such Corporation, a multinational, great career opportunities, just wait and see. I believed them. . . . Periodically there are training courses, retraining courses. You've got to leave on a Sunday, on your own time. You get down there at seven or eight in the morning. You eat cafeteria-style. Then you get a briefing by some company big-shot who felt like taking a trip or who happens to have a country house nearby. Then you work until ten at night. You go to bed and the next morning you start over at 7 a.m. and work the whole day. They tell you about the company, how to approach clients, how you're supposed to sell, how you're supposed to do your job. I got nothing out of it. . . . And then they have these ridiculous communications sessions. Once a year. This year we spent three days with the VP for sales. Everybody taps everybody else on the chest and eats at the same table and dances and swims together, everybody does everything and then each person is supposed to say what he thinks. But if you ever really said what was on your mind, your goose would be cooked. . . .

Practically every time I traveled out to the provinces the sales manager and department head came with me. Those trips cost the company five or six thou-

sand francs. These guys come in at ten o'clock and at noon they take everybody out to lunch. At three o'clock it's back to the office: duty calls. What did they do? They spent some money and they went out to lunch. . . . Quite recently a terrible thing happened. . . . But they certainly didn't tell the brass that they had made a mistake and sent the client the figures for our production costs. I've got the photocopy. They destroyed the original, but I was quicker than they were, I had time to make a copy. I can go up to the head office and say, There are your experts for you. There's the letter they sent out while they were telling you I don't have what it takes to make the grade. Sure, I know you've got to back them up, but I just thought you ought to know, in the interests of the company. But if I did that I'd be out the door in three minutes, for sure. In a Japanese company if a cadre goes to see management they give him a medal. . . . I have a secret file that I can show you if you like. Take this example that comes to mind. I give my secretary the draft of a letter. She's 18, this secretary. I was the one who kept her from getting fired. You know how it is. She was the new girl in the department, and you know women, they're a little like dogs, if one of them is wounded all the rest will gang up on her. So I stuck up for her. She's young, I said, I've got a daughter her age, you ought to keep her on. It was a dumb thing to do, but it's my nature to be tolerant and kind and it gets me in trouble. So anyway, I gave this kid the draft of a letter. She's supposed to be a stenographer and typist, and anyway even a typist should be able to take the general ideas and turn out a decent letter if she wants to get ahead. So then I leave on a trip. I'm gone three days. When I come back I find my draft in my mailbox with a red scrawl all over it, like in grade school, in my boss's handwriting: To give a draft like this to a secretary is unacceptable. It shows you have no regard for her or for anyone else and that you're willing to waste other people's time. Moral: I can't ask this 18-year-old secretary to do anything any more. That's finished. Another example: I leave on a trip with my office in perfect order, because it's my principle never to leave anything lying around. The typist, who spends the whole day gabbing with her girlfriend and even drove a couple of the bosses crazy with her incessant chatter, comes in and throws the mail on my desk, just like that. When I come back I find a wad of paper taped to my door with a note on it: Mr So-and-so, would you kindly see to it that your office is in order when you are absent. From the sales manager. Please see Mr So-and-so. Treats me like a doormat: I've got to go speak to the sales coordinator. So who's in charge? Her or me? . . .

Women, at work, it's always difficult. It's a bordello. So I complained, several times. I might as well have been talking to a stone wall. . . . So what if the clients don't like it. The women are always right. They give the sales manager cigars. I'm no woman, at least until somebody proves the contrary. . . . In the old days it used to be, Good morning, Mr Engineer, how are you? Nowadays I come to the office and they, How're ya' doin', kid? No, I mean, they don't talk that way to me, but they do to some of my younger colleagues. So the kid answers, Fine, honey, what's up? To a married woman of thirty. And then when the kid has to ask this woman to do something serious, he's surprised when she tells him to get lost, or vice versa. You lose all your authority. Since I'm 40 and the girl's 18, I don't say, Hi, honey. She doesn't like it so she doesn't type my letters and tells me to go to hell. And I can't do a thing about it. She doesn't work for me.... Always the same jokes. And what's even nastier, with the women in particular, is that they make clothes for some of the men free of charge. One day I took one of the girls aside and said to her, Look, Mrs Brown, it's gone on long enough with Mr Smith, one of the engineers, he's a jerk and so forth but you don't see how serious it is. So she goes and complains to the boy scout who tells me I'm in the wrong. Sure. I'm no misogynist, not at all. But I've never worked with women around me. It's nothing but trouble. It's OK if you have a couple of old biddies, or better still just one, because as soon as you get two or three women in the office you've got a mess on your hands, it's unbearable. Or else you've got to have full authority to crack down when necessary. But if your people don't report to you, you might as well hang it up.... I never want to work as hard as I've worked in the past. I've had some tough times. If I'm fired and if I have the courage I'll go and throw pots or raise sheep. That's what everybody wants to do. And be done with those jerks for good.... In any case I'll try to find a job with a big corporation so I can have some job security and keep bread on the table for my family. But it's not what I'd call a vocation any more. I don't say I'd like to do export sales, go to Saudi Arabia or Mexico because my job this, my job that. Just look at the classifieds. There are plenty of jobs like that. To hell with them. I'm not the kind of guy who lists all the countries he's been to on his business card. That's over. I had those crazy ideas for a time. When I was 30 or 35. But it's over now. The need to run after God knows what, a top job so you can buy yourself the latest car or a vacation in California. To hell with it. I've lost my faith.... I'm going to look for a job with a nationalized company. Not because I don't want to work, but I want to work at something simple. Where I come from, Auvergne, the peasants are simple. You've got to stay simple. Maybe that's the way we were meant to go, just to follow our herd instincts. Don't worry, I'll have my pleasures. As Victor Hugo used to say, just give me my pipe and my walking-stick and I'm off for a walk in the fields. Or I'll take an old refrigerator motor and make a compressor out of it. But I won't work night and day any more. I'll work to earn a living and that's it.... I've finally understood that you've got to work in order to make money and not the other way around. You've got to put in your hours in order to keep in step with yourself. But the rest is for your family, for reading. "Leisure" is a word I don't like to use, because whenever people talk about leisure there's a word they don't mention but that hovers there in the background, and that's money. I have leisure but no money. We'll go for a walk in the forest and you'll see, it's terrific, it's wonderful, and it doesn't cost a red cent. Whereas those idiots work like mad all year to pay for a month's vacation. . . . Some friends of mine, cadres, just bought a house. If they don't buy the Mercedes that goes with it, they'll be beside themselves. That's their problem. It's not mine any longer. I live in the country. Look, there's lettuce, there are potatoes, there's a farm across the road with chickens, rabbits, eggs. I'm a happy guy. . . . Every once in a while one of my colleagues will startle me by saying something intelligent or realistic. But they're afraid. People are afraid. One of them came to see me the other night. You know, he said, the same thing's happening to me that happened to you. I told him it couldn't happen to a nicer guy, because for a year I'd been asking him for help to avoid this kind of unpleasantness and now he finally gets off his duff. But he was in a total panic, this guy, whereas I've kept my cool. Although I did have what they called a nervous depression, some skin reactions. But I had those reactions because I couldn't pick up the chair and throw it in their faces. I'll tell you though, if I could have picked up that chair or an attaché-case or something and thrown it at them, preferably in the middle of a meeting to cause a stir, that would have done me more good than the three bottles of pick-me-ups the doc gave me. Only you know, the blacklist works pretty well. Hello, you have a Mr So-and-so working there? What's he like? Oh my God, that bastard, he threw a chair at one of the executives, put the guy in the hospital, what a scene. So I held it all in until one night it exploded inside, you understand. So the wife called the doc, and you wouldn't believe what I went through after that!

There was still an hour until the next train. We took the walk that M had mentioned, after which he showed me his house and told me about his plans for fixing it up and still more about his worries ("If I quit, how am I going to pay back the hundred thousand francs I've borrowed?"). We came to a huge building that served as woodshed, garage, and workshop and that M had built with his own hands. There, on a drawing board, were the plans for his house as it would look after the renovations. He had drawn them himself – a "professional job," since he had long ago studied drafting in technical school. Now that he is on sick leave, M spends most of his days in this shed. He draws, does odd jobs, repairs the lawnmower or his son's electronic toys that lie strewn amid a hundred other objects: garden tools, a broken refrigerator, old furniture, wood saved from demolished houses, and what have you. At the far end, polished, gleaming, chrome-plated, "like new," is a metallic-gray convertible sports car with leather seats, purchased used ten years ago and now up on blocks, its cylinders filled with oil, but still "ready to run like a Swiss watch." Yet the car remains, immobile, unused. "I really should make up my mind to sell it."

Notes

Introduction 1: one man's story

1. Some sales representatives with engineering degrees call themselves *ingénieurs d'affaires* in order to distinguish themselves from mere *agents technico-commerciaux* who with the connivance of their companies "usurp" the title of engineer. There seem to be many similar conflicts (some of them reported in the professional magazines) in fuzzy border areas, where the *cadre technico-commercial* clashes with the VRP (*voyageur, représentant, placier*), an older and less prestigious title.
2. The term "self-taught cadre" is used in industry to refer to employees classed as cadres but who hold no advanced degrees. It suggests a certain relationship between a man's position in the hierarchy of educational achievement and his position in the hierarchy of jobs and ranks within industry. Because having an advanced degree is part of the social definition of the cadre, cadres without such degrees (who may be in the majority, since they account for one-third to two-thirds of all cadres, depending on how one defines the term "cadre") are characterized in terms of a negative attribute.

Introduction 2: A question of sociology

1. See Pierre Bourdieu and Luc Boltanski, "Le titre et le poste," *Actes de la recherche en sciences sociales* 2, 1975, pp. 95–107.
2. Ludwing Wittgenstein, *The Blue and the Brown Notebooks.*
3. See Luc Boltanski, "Taxinomies populaires, taxinomies savantes: les objets de consommation et leur classement," *Revue française de sociologie* vol. 11, no. 1, 1970, pp. 34–44.
4. Pierre Bourdieu, *La distinction* (Paris: Editions de Minuit, 1979), pp. 147–52.
5. Political science commonly treats social groups as objects exterior and prior to political practices. Hence it takes as its special object of study political behavior (i.e., in most cases, electoral behavior) and

seeks to correlate a typology of behavior with a typology of groups or (in terms of an economic model) to relate consumer choices to political supply. In this type of political science the group typology (whether defined in terms of social classes or occupational groups) is taken as given prior to political practice, which the political scientist treats as an instrument but not as an object of analysis.

6. Raymond Boudon is right to criticize, in his preface to the French edition of Mancur Olson's *Logic of Collective Action*, the naïve realism of "certain sociological works" that "treat groups as though they were persons," as though "endowed with will and consciousness" (p. 7). To rectify the error of treating groups as collective subjects, he proposes another brand of sociology, based on marginalist economics, in which the only actors are real individuals whose behavior is said to be determined entirely by the desire to maximize their self-interest. The criticism falls short of its goal, however, because it neglects the fact that sociologists who speak of collective subjects are merely mimicking (admittedly without analysis) one of the most common forms of social practice and especially of political practice. The questions that these common forms of practice raise for sociology (and secondarily the question of the relationship between political behavior and the way in which sociology defines its objects) are evaded, however, by the recourse to "interactionist" sociology, a regressive solution to a real problem. What must be analyzed first, even before we can understand the actions of individuals, are the processes through which individuals form groups, adopt collective representations, create institutions and appoint spokesmen to *personify* them, and thus create social forms that have all the appearances of collective persons – not only in the eyes of sociologists (who simply take them as they present themselves) but also in the eyes of the actors themselves, whose own actions give the impression that these collective subjects are real.
7. P. Ansart, *Naissance de l'anarchisme* (Paris: Presses Universitaires de France, 1970).
8. Paper delivered to the CREDOC seminar, January 1981.
9. Edmond Maire, *Reconstruire l'espoir* (Paris: Editions du Seuil, 1980), pp. 117–21: 'The composition and representativity of organized labor have remained largely unchanged for the past thirty years, while the work force was rapidly expanding and diversifying in response to economic, technological, and social evolution.... In fact, skilled (male) workers in heavy industry have dominated the labor movement for more than a century, identifying themselves with the entire working class and speaking in its name. The only other major group to join forces with organized labor has been the government employees. This composition of the labor movement explains, I think, the traditional imagery, which tends to overemphasize the skilled worker and to favor a series of programs for the emancipation of workers that would tend to make all of them government

employees and to shift the burden of every problem onto the welfare state.... This situation cannot be remedied merely by tacking new social and occupational groups onto the group that is supposed to represent the hard core of the working class. Instead, we must learn to diversify our understanding of workers' aspirations.'

10. Cf. Erving Goffman, *The Presentation of Self in Everyday Life.*
11. Cf. e.g. Marc Ferro, "La naissance du système bureaucratique en U.R.S.S.," *Annales E.S.C.* 2, 1976, pp. 243–67.
12. On history as a means of unveiling the collective unconscious, see Emile Durkheim, *Education et sociologie* (Paris: Presses Universitaires de France, 1966), p. 119.

1 The crisis of the 1930s and the mobilization of the "middle class"

1. Cf. A Desrosières "Eléments pour l'histoire des nomenclatures socio-professionnelles," in *Pour une histoire de la statistique* (Paris: INSEE, 1977), pp. 155–232.
2. On the ideology of the third way, see Pierre Bourdieu and Luc Boltanski, "La production de l'idéologie dominante," *Actes de la recherche en sciences sociales* 5–6, 1976, pp. 3–73. The division of society into three classes – bourgeoisie, middle class, and proletariat – was a commonplace of French economic and political thought in the nineteenth century. The "appeal to the middle classes" (cf. J. Weiller, "Les appels aux classes moyennes," *Annales du droit et des sciences sociales*, vol. 2, no. 2, 1934, pp. 353–92) and bourgeois discourse concerning the "defense of the middle classes" constituted a defensive strategy (especially after the crisis of 1837–40) against the "socialist peril" and early attempts to organize the working class. The defense of small production enabled liberal economists to justify aspects of their teaching seemingly called into question by the rise of industrial and financial aristocracies. For example, Blanqui condemned, essentially for political reasons, a society composed solely of "capitalists" and "proletarians": "the rich will eat the poor and society will totter" (A. Blanqui, *Cours d'économie industrielle* (Paris: Guillaumin, 1840), p. 189, cited in F. Demier, "Le rôle des classes moyennes dans la formation du libéralisme," paper delivered to the round table of the Association française de science politique on the "middle classes," 27 Nov. 1980).

   No doubt one could show, more generally, that the question of social classes in its various historical guises (particularly that of corporatism) arose in an effort to evade and overcome, in symbolic terms at any rate, the inevitable and insuperable facts of the socialist movement and the organization of the proletariat. This no doubt accounts for the spiraling of ideological themes, as in myth, where narrative is created out of a series of variations around a central opposition. The synchronic and diachronic interplay of differences among various ideological producers yields a series of different and opposing ideologies, even though all derive from the same fund of basic raw materials.

3. Cf. P. Droulers, *Politique sociale et christianisme. Le Père Desbuquois et l'action populaire* (Paris: Editions ouvrières, 1969), p. 11.
4. The Social Catholic movement, which was recognized by the church hierarchy in the period between the wars, originally developed in legitimist circles in the nineteenth century. Legitimist Social Catholics did not aim to adapt the church to the "modern world" or to the "liberal society" created by the revolution of 1789. Rather, in the spirit of counterrevolution, they hoped to hit upon a means of "overcoming" liberalism. From the beginning, then, Social Catholicism was opposed to "two fundamental errors," "collectivist socialism" and "liberalism" (both politico–social liberalism and economic liberalism). Cf. J. M. Mayeur, "Le catholicisme social en France," *Mouvement social* 77, 1971, pp. 113–21, and E. Poulat, *Eglise contre bourgeoisie* (Paris: Casterman, 1977), esp. pp. 135–61. Thus by the second half of the nineteenth century Social Catholics were producing programs that had to await the 1930s for political and social conditions favorable to their diffusion.
5. The USIC still occupies the same headquarters in the rue de Varenne, though it is now called the Mouvement des cadres, ingénieurs, et dirigeants chrétiens (MCC).
6. On the relationship between the prestigious scientific institutions of higher learning and the Jesuit preparatory schools, see M. de Saint Martin, *Les fonctions sociales de l'enseignement scientifique* (Paris: Mouton, 1971), esp. pp. 88–9.
7. Cf. H. Clerc, *Pour sauver les classes moyennes* (Paris: Tallandier, 1939), p. 20.
8. G. Lamirand, *Le rôle social de l'ingénieur* (Paris: Plon, 1954), pp. 263–4.
9. See, for example, P. Alamigeon, *Les cadres de l'industrie française* (Paris: Presses Universitaires de France, 1945), p. 112.
10. See H. Michel, *Les courants de pensée de la résistance* (Paris: Presses Universitaires de France, 1962), p. 378, and A. Calmette, *L'O.C.M., histoire d'un mouvement de résistance de 1940 à 1946* (Paris: PUF, 1961), p. 214.
11. H. Mougin, 'Un projet d'enquête sur les classes moyennes en France,' *Inventaire III, les classes moyennes* (Paris: Centre de documentation sociale de l'Ecole normale supérieure, 1939, pp. 287–343.
12. In many respects the middle-class movements were similar in structure to the veterans' movements in the interwar period, which have been studied by Antoine Prost (though to be sure their ability to mobilize was far less developed). The veterans' groups had a dual structure: at the grass roots one finds a mass movement composed of local mutual aid groups not unlike traditional confraternities. But the movement was controlled by the "*petite et moyenne bourgeoisie*," and the higher one goes in the hierarchy of the veterans' groups, the higher the social level of the men holding office. The veterans' organizations

operated as lobbying groups with the legislature and executive. See Antoine Prost, *Les anciens combattants et la société française 1914–1939* (Paris: Presses de la Fondation nationale des sciences politiques, 1977), 3 vols., esp. vol. 2, pp. 159–79. Other movements, such as the Associations de parents d'élèves, were similarly structured.

13. One exception is surely Pierre Poujade's UDCA, a movement composed exclusively of petit-bourgeois members and totally rejected by the bourgeoisie. This social isolation was probably a factor in the movement's rapid decline. See D. Borne, *Petits bourgeois en révolte, le mouvement Poujade* (Paris: Flammarion, 1977). The Poujadist movement was kept at a distance by the middle-class movements that reconstituted themselves after the war under the leadership of Roger Millot – see below, as well as J. Meynaud, *Les groupes de pression en France* (Paris: Armand Colin, 1960), p. 93. There was a violent clash between Pierre Poujade and Léon Gingembre, founder and president of the Confédération générale des petites et moyennes enterprises. See H. W. Ehrmann, *La politique du patronat français, 1936–1955* (Paris: Armand Colin, 1959), pp. 163–4.
14. Is it therefore, like the peasantry, an "object class?" See P. Bourdieu, "La paysannerie, une classe objet," *Actes de la recherche en sciences sociales* 17–18, 1977, pp. 2–5.
15. For example, between January and May of 1937 studies of the middle classes were published in *Les Journées industrielles* ("L'obscur martyrologue des classes moyennes"); *Le Journal* ("Pour le rassemblement des classes moyennes"); *Europe nouvelle; Marianne* (an article by Jules Romains); *L'Humanité* (Marcel Cachin); *Vu; Le temps; Cahiers français* (Pierre Frédérix), etc. On political struggles involving the middle classes, see J. Lhomme, *Le problème des classes* (Paris: Sirey, 1938), pp. 288–9.
16. Cf. J. Touchard, *La gauche en France depuis 1900* (Paris: Editions du Seuil, 1977), esp. pp. 188–206.
17. Communists in the Popular Front government showed great solicitude for the middle classes and especially for small employers, who had to be reassured and won over: between 10 June 1936 and 27 March 1937 the Communist group in the Chamber of Deputies filed 115 bills: 63 of these directly or indirectly affected the middle classes. See A. Havez, "La défense des classes moyennes et l'action du groupe parlementaire communiste," *Cahier du bolchevisme*, 1 July 1937.
18. Cf. e.g. G. Politzer, "La composition sociale de la population en France," *Cahiers du bolchevisme*, 12–13 July 1936.
19. On the Socialist Party and the question of the middle classes, cf. A. Gergounioux, "Le néo-socialisme. Marcel Déat: réformisme traditionnel ou esprit des années 30," *Revue historique* 528, Oct.–Dec. 1978, pp. 389–412, and A. Gergounioux, "La S.F.I.O. et les classes moyennes (1905–1939)," paper delivered to the round table of the Association française de science politique on the "middle classes", 27 Nov. 1980.

20. In German social-democratic tradition the debate over the middle classes was based on the opposition between "catastrophe" and "evolution." The Kautsky–Bernstein polemic turned on the question whether or not the "law" of concentration of capital and pauperization of the proletariat was valid. But the issues were ambiguous, as Louis Pinto has shown. For "if the rise of the new middle class could be used to indicate the limits of validity of this law, it could also be used to illustrate its universal validity by extending it to groups other than those involved in the relations of production, thus suggesting yet another 'contradiction.'" In fact, the middle-class issue was closely related to the "intellectual question": one way to characterize the "rising" middle class was in terms of its own specific mode of pauperization, via "overproduction of intellectuals" and creation of an "intellectual proletariat." Thus the Marxist approach to the middle classes could be linked to another version of the "catastrophist" view: the right-wing elitism of writers associated with the Action française, who viewed the proliferation of "intellectuals" (a term which for them had pejorative connotations, suggesting "plodding" academics of lower-class origins as opposed to "artists" and "men of culture") as a sign of the "rise of the masses." See L. Pinto, "Les intellectuels et les classes moyennes. Quelques hypothèses sur la constitution d'une catégorie," paper delivered to the round table of the Association française de science politique on the "middle classes," 27 Nov. 1980.
21. The goal of rallying all people exploited by the plutocracy, owners and nonowners alike, and of establishing national unity on that basis also influenced the movement in favor of economic planning that developed in the same political circles. For example, Robert Lacoste, in a lecture on planism delivered in 1937 at the Centre polytechnicien d'études économiques (X-crise) stated that "the Plan ... is an offer of alliance from the working class to the middle strata and technicians" (cited in J. Amoyal, "Les origines socialistes et syndicalistes de la planification en France," *Mouvement social* 87, April–June 1974, pp. 137–70). See also M. Margairaz, "Les socialistes face à l'économie et à la société en juin 36," *Mouvement social* 93, Oct.–Dec. 1975, pp. 98–108.
22. See G. Dupeux, *Le Front populaire et les élections de 1936* (Paris: Armand Colin, 1959), esp. pp. 175–7. Serge Berstein, "La vie du parti radical, la fédération de Saône-et-Loire de 1919 à 1939," *Revue Française de science politique* vol. 20, no. 1, 1970, pp. 1136–80, shows that radicals in the Saône-et-Loire federations, led mainly by farmers, merchants, and civil servants, were "crushed between moderates and socialists" in the 1936 elections and were gradually "abandoned by the notables," who moved to the right. In the 1930s the economic crisis drove to the right the small businessmen and artisans who had previously supported the radical party. It was in order to put a halt to these defections that the party leadership moved rightward. Cf. S. Berstein, *Histoire du parti radical*, vol. 1: *A la recherche de l'âge d'or* (Paris:

Fondation nationale des sciences politiques, 1980), pp. 259–317.

23. See J. D. Reynaud, *Les syndicats en France* (Paris: Editions du Seuil, 1975), p. 118. This federation resulted from the merger of the Federation of Draftsmen with the Union of Industrial Technicians and Office Workers. The success of the movement was apparently short-lived, and the number of affiliates dropped sharply after 1938. Internal political struggles and above all the hostility of union leaders, who saw the Federation of Technicians as a "potential second confederation with a hierarchical structure," were important factors in its decline. See R. Mouriaux, "C.G.T., structures syndicales et attitudes à l'égard des cadres, 1936–1948," paper read to the colloquium of Le Creusot "Engineers and Society," 23 Oct. 1980.
24. In keeping with the official position of the Jesuits of Action populaire: cf. René Remond, *Les catholiques, le communisme et les crises, 1929–1939* (Paris: Armand Colin, 1960), p. 162.
25. In this organization "provincial cells" were supposed to "revive and set in motion the Association des classes moyennes, a simple and effective way of forming an open, nonpolitical association of anti-Marxist groups hesitant to fall under the domination of any party." See P. Fridenson, *Histoires des usines Renault*, vol. 1: *Naissance de la grande entreprise* (Paris: Editions du Seuil, 1972), p. 258.
26. F. Jacquin, *Les cadres de l'industrie et du commerce en France* (Paris: Armand Colin, 1955), p. 176.
27. Cf. G. Izard, *Les classes moyennes* (Paris: Editions Rieder, 1938), pp. 49–50. Another example: on 10 October 1936 "the whole press, some three hundred newspapers throughout the country," published "a document drawn up by major employers" stating, among other things, that "the legislation stemming from the Matignon Accords will ultimately destroy the middle classes." Cited by H. Guillemin, *Nationalistes et natinaux 1870–1940* (Paris: Gallimard, 1974), p. 257.
28. Collective bargaining procedures had existed since 1919 but were little used before 1936. Contracts numbering 112 were signed in 1929, compared with only 29 in 1935. The law of 24 June 1936 was intended, according to the account of motives it contains, to make "collective bargaining the law for employer–employee relations in the various branches of economic activity": 2336 contracts were signed in 1936; 2259 in the first few months of 1937. In all, between June 1936 and August 1939, 5620 contracts were signed. See A. Sauvy, *Histoire économique de la France entre les deux guerres* (Paris: Fayard, 1967), vol. 2, p. 401. Obtaining specific contracts for engineers was described as a major victory by engineers' organizations. Three contracts were signed in the Paris area in 1937 with engineers in the chemical, metals, and construction industries, and seven contracts were signed in the provinces, nearly all in metals. These contracts dealt with salaries and working conditions (duration of work, calculation of seniority, rules on holding more than one job, absences, patents, etc.). They also provided for "engineers' delegates" (anal-

ogous to workers' delegates). The contracts further defined the position of engineer and the attributes that an individual must have in order to hold such a position: for example, the contract in the chemicals industry in the Paris area recognized the existence of "self-taught engineers," defined as "technicians who, through scientific and professional study, have acquired technical knowhow based on general knowledge that places them, in professional terms, on a par with graduate engineers in regard to manufacturing, research and testing, etc." Contracts with engineers proliferated in subsequent years, although their number remained far below that of labor contracts with workers.

29. S. Weil, "Remarques sur les enseignements à tirer des conflits du Nord," in *La condition ouvrière* (Paris: Gallimard, 1951), pp. 268–78 (I wish to thank Antoine Prost, who drew my attention to the 1937 disturbances and to the reporting of Simone Weil).
30. H. de Man, *Au-delà du marxisme* (Brussels: Editions L'églantine, 1927).
31. A. Desqueyrat, *Classes moyennes françaises, crise, programme, organisation* (Paris: Spes, 1939), p. 109.
32. *Esprit* is mentioned in the *Echo de l'USIC* in the late thirties as an "avant-garde Catholic review" that took "ardent" but dangerous positions. The influence of *Ordre nouveau* began earlier and seems to have been more profound. In 1935, for example, Daniel-Rops delivered a lecture to USIC engineers on the subject of "French youth." In it he preached on behalf of Ordre nouveau in favor of a rapprochement between young people of "the extreme left and the extreme right," who have "deep in their hearts the same hopes and the same certainties." He also called for a third way opposed to both "Russian communism" and "American Fordism," both of which were said to result in "the negation of man."
33. Cf. J. L. Loubet del Bayle, *Les non-conformistes des années 30* (Paris: Editions du Seuil, 1969), p. 355.
34. Created in 1904 and at first kept confidential, the Semaines sociales de France became the centerpiece of Catholic action in the interwar years. At these annual meetings a topical theme was discussed by ecclesiastics, militants from Catholic action movements and Christian unions, industrial leaders, and academics (mainly professors of law and economics). Each lecture was attended by several thousand people. The Semaines sociales were thus a factory for the production of ideology and an opportunity (through confrontation and dialogue) for Social Catholicism to adjust its doctrine to the demands of modernity (the crisis, corporatism, classes, etc.). At the same time they provided a means of diffusing this ideology and a "political club" in which future actions were planned (e.g., the Popular Democratic Party was created during one Semaine sociale). Cf. A. Coutrot and F. Dreyfus, *Les forces religieuses dans la société française* (Paris: Armand Colin, 1965), pp. 79–80. The USIC was represented at the Semaines

sociales by its delegate general, Delacommune. A graduate of the Ecole Centrale and one-time industrialist, Delacommune joined the permanent staff of the USIC in 1934. In 1936 he played a leading role in organizing the Syndicat des ingénieurs salariés (SIS).

35. *Cahiers de l'action religieuse et sociale*, Sept. 1939.
36. *Le problème des classes dans la communauté nationale et dans l'ordre humain, Semaines sociales de France: Bordeaux 1939* (Lyon: Chroniques Sociales de France, 1939), p. 537.
37. Catholic social action and Christian democracy developed earlier and faster in Belgium than anywhere else. See R. Rezsohazy, *Origines et formation du catholicisme social en Belgique, 1842–1909* (Louvain: Publications universitaires, 1958), esp. pp. 79–98. For example, Christian syndicalism developed around the turn of the century and by 1935 claimed more than 300,000 adherents. See abbé R. Kothen, *La pensée sociale des catholiques* (Louvain: E. M. Warny, 1945), pp. 329–88. The Christian Democrats were also behind the broad-based middle-class movement. In the late nineteenth century the Catholics who came to power in 1884 assumed responsibility for the petit bourgeois question in an effort to stem the tide of socialism. The Catholics, for whom maintaining the middle class, the buffer class between the capitalist bourgeoisie and the working class, was a factor of social peace, gave official legal recognition to the middle class. See G. Kurgan Van Hentenryk, "La petite entreprise depuis la fin de l'ancien régime jusqu'à nos jours," paper delivered to the Nanterre colloquium on the middle classes, Oct. 1978. In 1899 the Ministry of Labor created a Bureau for the Middle Classes. Between the two World Wars a middle-class policy was elaborated, chiefly under the impetus of the Christian Democrat Hector Lambrechts. See his *La représentation des classes moyennes* (Ghent: Editions de l'Association belge pour le développement des classes moyennes, 1931). In 1928 a Conseil supérieur des classes moyennes was established, along with an Institut des classes moyennes. An "administrative definition" of the middle class was also adopted (see Lambrechts, pp. 24–5). This process of political institutionalization was accompanied by great mountains of ideological literature.
38. Abbé O. Mélon, *L'ordre social et les classes moyennes* (Ghent: Association belge pour le développement des classes moyennes, 1933).
39. Desqueyrat, *Classes moyennes françaises*, p. 37.
40. For example, Pierre Frédérix, *Etat des forces en France* (Paris: Gallimard, 1935) distinguishes rural forces, workers' forces, middle-class forces, oligarchic forces, and moral and intellectual forces. According to Frédérix, *the old bourgeoisie had disintegrated*: "The upper crust has joined the oligarchy. Lower down we meet the 'middle classes,' a confused mixture that extends beyond the boundaries of the bourgeoisie on all sides" (p. 66).
41. *Le problème des classes dans la communauté nationale et dans l'ordre humain, Semaine sociale de Bordeaux, op. cit.*, pp. 2–3.

42. Cf. e.g. Frédérix, *Etat des forces*, p. 70.
43. See Zeev Sternhell, *La droite révolutionnaire* (Paris: Editions du Seuil, 1978).
44. De Man, *Au-delà du marxisme.*
45. Bertrand de Jouvenel, *L'économie dirigée* (Paris: Librairie Valois, 1928).
46. Marcel Déat, *Perspectives socialistes* (Paris: Librairie Valois, 1930).
47. Cited by A. Philip, *Henri de Man et la crise doctrinale du socialisme* (Paris: J. Gamber, 1928).
48. "To overcome the crisis by grouping together the immense mass of producers against the aberrations of a disorderly economy: that is the essence of 'planism.'" From Marcel Déat, "Vers une politique cartésienne," in Centre de documentation sociale de l'Ecole normale supérieure, *Inventaire II: L'économique et le politique* (Paris: Félix Alcan, 1937), pp. 205–27. Marcel Déat was at one point secretary of the Centre de documentation sociale of the Ecole normale.
49. "The Marxist accentuation of class claims has come at the expense of the broader notion of social community as well as the narrower notion of the individual." de Man, *Au-delà du marxisme*, p. 107.
50. Frédérix, *Etat des forces*, pp. 36–7.
51. W. Oualid, "Les classes moyennes," in *Mélanges dédiés à M. le professeur Henry Truchy* (Paris: Libraire Sirey, 1938), pp. 419–31, shows similarly that "the middle class" represents "half of the active population."
52. On the use of statistical weapons in the 1936 conflicts between middle-class groups and the CGT, see e.g., T. Petringenar, *Le rôle des classes moyennes da la société contemporaine* (M. Lavergne, 1940), p. 13: "In 1936 . . . in the statistics compiled to demonstrate the strength of either the working class or the middle class, the same individuals were sometimes counted as part of the proletariat, sometimes as part of the middle classes. Supervisors, technicians, and office workers were considered proletarians by some because they were paid employees, even if they enjoyed some measure of independence, and as 'middle-level professionals' by others because their attitudes resembled those of groups that in no way felt themselves to be proletarian."
53. Confédération générale des syndicats de classes moyennes, *Déclaration confédérale sur le syndicalisme des classes moyennes* (Paris, 1938), p. 24.
54. With classes as with nations, the more heterogeneous the entity that one wishes to bind together, the more the language of unification tends to take on spiritualist and voluntarist overtones. Where differences abound there remains only the will to be united and to share common ideals and values, which need not be practiced to be recognized and celebrated. See my *Le bonheur suisse* (Paris: Editions de Minuit, 1966).
55. *Le problème des classes dans la communauté nationale et dans l'ordre humain, op. cit.*, p. 180. See also P. Frédérix, "Les classes moyennes," *Cahiers*

français, June 1937: "The metal worker who saves his earnings in order to buy a small shop and go into business for himself is already a part of the middle class." Conversely, "the skilled worker who, rather than go into business for himself, prefers to earn a high salary in a large factory where it would be difficult to replace him if he went on vacation is not part of the middle class."

56. On the distinction made, in "Ordre nouveau-style" personalism, between the individual and the person, see Loubet del Bayle, *Les non-conformistes*, pp. 342–3. "Individual man is material, corporeal, and social man.... Personal man is reasonable, spiritual, superior man." Man "*qua* individual is totally submerged in the collectivity but *qua* person cannot be reduced to collective terms." The individual was of course associated with materialism and capitalism, where the satisfaction of material needs reigned supreme (and represented by the United States), as well as with collectivism (embodied in the USSR).
57. Desqueyrat, *Classes moyennes françaises*, p. 211.
58. See J. P. Flavin, "Le radical-socialisme dans le départment du Nord, 1914–1936," *Revue française de science politique* vol. 24, no. 2, 1974, pp. 236–77.
59. Prost, *Les anciens combattants*, clearly illustrates the conflict between these two segments of the petite bourgeoisie. There were two principal veterans' organizations. One, the union nationale des combattants (UNC), was more or less right wing (with ties to the leagues and especially to La Roque's Croix de feu). Its political program is somewhat reminiscent of the program of the middle-class movement. The other, the Union fédérale (UF), was close to the Radical Party and to the Socialists and "defended the republican, secular tradition." Socially speaking, the UNC represented the *petite* and *moyenne* bourgeoisie of the private sector, determined to defend small business, and the UF represented the *petite* and *moyenne* bourgeoisie of the public sector. UNC sections were led by small industrialists, businessmen, wholesale dealers, engineers, physicians, etc. By contrast, in the UF, 22% of whose leadership positions were filled by elementary and secondary school teachers, "middle-class civil servants dominated."
60. Abbé G. Lecordier, *Les classes moyennes en marche* (Paris: Bloud et Gay, 1950), p. 382.
61. See M. Didier and E. Malinvaud, "La concentration de l'industrie s'est-elle accentuée depuis 1900?" *Economie et statistiques*, vol. 1, no. 2, 1969, pp. 3–10.
62. See L. Cahen, "Evolution de la population active en France depuis cent ans d'après les dénombrements quinquennaux," *Etudes et conjoncture* 3, May–June 1953, pp. 230–88.
63. See J. C. Toutain, "La population de la France de 1700 à 1959," *Cahiers de l'I.S.E.A.*, series AF, 3, suppl. 133, Jan. 1963, p. 148. Cahen (see n. 62) shows similarly that the banking and insurance sector

grew at a particularly rapid rate in this period.

64. See Desrosières, *Pour une histoire de la statistique.*
65. Toutain, "La population." See also P. Depoid, "Structure professionnelle de la France," *Revue d'economie politique*, vol. 53, no. 1, 1939, pp. 47–87.
66. Toutain, "La population."
67. F. Simiand, *Le salaire* (Paris: Félix Alcan, 1932), vol. 1, pp. 150–1.
68. J. R. Bonneau, "La fragilité du contrat de cadre," *Revue des affaires sociales*, July–Sept. 1977, pp. 77–93.
69. See P. Cam, "Juges rouges et droit du travail," *Actes de la recherche en sciences sociales* 19, 1978, pp. 2–28.
70. See C.-A. Michalet, *Les placements des épargnants français de 1915 à nos jours* (Paris: Presses Universitaires de France, 1968), esp. pp. 277–86. "Concern for security" led "investors" to react slowly to the decline in the value of money. "The money illusion was important throughout the interwar period" (*ibid.*, p. 298). Hence "the number of declarations including debentures increased steadily until 1934." See P. Cornut, *Répartition de la fortune privée en France par département et nature des biens au cours de la première moitié du XXe siècle* (Paris: Armand Colin, 1963), p. 90.
71. A commentary on bourgeois reactions to inflation may be found in J. Arthuys, *Comment éviter la banqueroute* (Paris: Nouvelle librairie nationale, 1922).
72. From 1919 to 1928 inflation reduced the real income of bondholders by one-half. See Sauvy, *Le salaire*, vol. 1, p. 156.
73. Besides bourgeois employees and professionals whose unearned income accounted for only part of their total income (sometimes the most important part), in 1926 there were 400,000 people who lived entirely on unearned income (rents, dividends, interest, etc.) and practiced no profession.
74. Sauvy, *Le salaire*, vol. 1, p. 423.
75. The fact that increasing numbers of bourgeois were drawn into the work force as their unearned income dwindled bears some resemblance to changes affecting much of the working class in the same period, as many workers, absorbed "by large urban industrial concentrations" and forced to meet new productivity norms, gradually found the "domestic conditions for reconstitution of their labor power" undermined: in other words, they were no longer able to keep fruit and vegetable gardens, small animals, small farms, etc. Cf. B. Coriat, *L'atelier et le chronomètre* (Paris: Christian Bourgeois, 1979), pp. 103–6.
76. See Toutain, "La population," pp. 230–42.
77. M. Perrot, *Le mode de vie des familles bourgeoises* (Paris: Armand Colin, 1961), pp. 105–6.
78. See B. Théret, "Les grandes tendances de développement des dépenses publiques en France de 1815 à 1971," *Critiques de l'économie politique*, new series, 3, 1978, pp. 57–87.

79. "So little is known about the salaries paid to cadres and office workers in the private sector that I prefer to offer no judgment on the matter." Sauvy, *Le salaire*, vol. 2, p. 411.
80. BIT, *Les conditions de vie des ingénieurs et chimistes* (Geneva, 1924), p. 71.
81. Economic concentration increased greatly during the period. For example, the percentage of industrial workers employed in firms of more than 500 workers rose from 12% in 1906 to 22% in 1931. See J. J. Carré, P. Dubois, and E. Malinvaud, *La croissance française* (Paris: Editions du Seuil, 1972), p. 24. Even more important, the 1930s saw an increase in the number of financial interlocks among firms, leading to concentration at the holding-company level. See Jules Denuc, "Structure des entreprises," *Revue d'économie politique*, vol. 53, no. 1, 1939, pp. 220–70. Denuc sees the growing number of financial interlocks, the creation of conglomerates, and even personal relations between directors of different corporations as one of the fundamental economic phenomena of the 1930s.
82. K. J. Müller, "French fascism and modernization," *Journal of Contemporary History* vol. 2, no. 4, 1976, pp. 75–108. Müller shows that it was the major employers in the modern and dynamic sectors that maintained the closest contacts (through subsidies, etc.) with the most traditionalist fascist groups.
83. See Touchard, *La gauche en France*, p. 223. The crisis had very different effects on firms in what was then called the "sheltered sector" (large firms protected by understandings with other firms) and firms in the "unsheltered sector" (small firms buffeted by competition). For example, the distribution of dividends by sector in 1935, taking the year 1919 as a base (= 100), was 118 for very large firms (like the electricity utility) and 33 for firms in the "unsheltered sector." See J. Dessirier, "L'économie française devant la dévaluation monétaire: Secteurs 'abrité' et 'non-abrités.' Retour vers l'équilibre," *Revue d'economie politique*, 1936, pp. 1527–84.
84. Sauvy, *Le salaire*, vol. 2, p. 137. Another index: changes in flows of funds into and out of savings accounts, the bulk of which were held by people in the middle class. From 1929 to 1932 deposits consistently exceeded withdrawls. But from 1933 on the opposite was true, and the pace of withdrawls increased early in 1936. See Dupeux, *op. cit.*, p. 40.
85. H. Hatzfeld, *Du paupérisme à la sécurité sociale, 1850–1940* (Paris: Armand Colin, 1971), esp. pp. 295ff.
86. The CGPF was closely associated with the Comité des forges, particularly through the UIMM. After 1936, some small and medium industrialists denied that the group represented them. For example, the Union des industries textiles, whose membership included many small mill-owners, quit the CGPF after the Matignon Accords. See B. Brizay, *Le patronat: histoire, structure, stratégie du CNPF* (Paris: Editions du Seuil, 1975), pp. 46–8, 49. Within the CGPF a committee of small and medium industrialists and businessmen was formed, one of the

leaders of which was Léon Gingembre, a graduate of the Ecole libre des sciences politiques, former lawyer, and manager of his family's needle-making business in L'Aigle.

87. On *dirigiste* tendencies in the Esprit group, see Michel Winock, *Histoire politique de la revue Esprit, 1930–1950* (Paris: Editions du Seuil, 1975), pp. 95–103.
88. For a full description of *dirigiste* currents in the 1930s, see R. F. Kuisel, "Technocrats and Public Economic Policy: From the Third to the Fourth Republic," *The Journal of Economic History*, vol. 2, no. 1, 1973, pp. 53–100. By 1934 "planism" was a commonplace among intellectuals and politicians who eventually found themselves, after the rise of fascism, the war, and the Occupation, at opposite extremes of the political spectrum. Planism was also a favorite theme of the revisionist and technician factions of the Socialist Party. For example, from 1934 to 1940 Marcel Déat chaired a committee for economic planning on which sat Henri Cler, Robert Lacoste, and Jean Coutrot, the founder of the group X-crise. See A. Bergounioux, "Le néo-socialisme." Also in 1934, Henri de Man organized, at Paul Desjardin's home in the abbey of Pontigny (where Jean Coutrot also held meetings), a gathering devoted to popularizing the idea of economic planning. This idea was greeted with enthusiasm by the group "Révolution constructive" (whose members included Robert Marjolin and Claude Lévi-Strauss), which also took great interest in what it called "the Roosevelt experiments." See G. Lefranc, "La diffusion des idées planistes en France," *Revue européenne des sciences sociales. Cahiers Vilfredo Pareto*, vol. 12, no. 31, 1974, pp. 151–67, an issue devoted to Henri de Man. In the early 1930s de Man's ambiguous position enabled him to span the gap between the "neosocialists" and the young right of Ordre nouveau (on which see, in the same issue of the *Revue européenne des sciences sociales*, A. G. Slama, "Henri de Man et les néo-traditionalistes français," pp. 169–88). De Man's influence helps to explain certain similarities between *dirigiste* tendencies that developed in the Resistance and the thinking of the "Vichy technocrats." On this point, see G. de Margerie, "Sur l'enseignement économique à la faculté de droit de Paris à l'époque de Vichy," *Recherches et travaux de l'Institute d'histoire économique et sociale de l'université de Paris I* 9, Oct. 1980, pp. 55–103.
89. M. Bouvier-Ajam, *La doctrine corporative* (Paris: Librairie Sirey, 1937), p. 11.
90. "The maximum degree of violence that a methodical revolutionary, a Sorel familiar with recent progress in science, would allow himself, would surely be the concentration camp, but without privation or torture: the concentration camp designed as a sanatorium, a temporary rest home, with teachers and nurses, which would be used to temporarily isolate until they were cured people whom one had not been able to convince, in order to prevent them from harming themselves or others. Another problem to be dealt with in a similar way, perhaps, is

the problem of psychological equilibrium in industry. Since the use of these methods for such purposes exceeds the current state of our knowledge, I have included below an account of a purely empirical experiment successfully carried out with shop delegates." Jean Coutrot, *Les leçons de juin 1936, l'humanisme économique* (Paris: Centre polytechnicien d'études économiques, 1936), p. 32.

91. The rate of growth of French industrial output declined from an average 2.6% per year in 1913–29 to an average 1.1% in 1929–38. See Carré, Dubois, Malinvaud, *op. cit.*
92. Between 1900 and 1940 more engineering schools were founded than in the eighteenth and nineteenth centuries combined (45 compared with 41), 23 in the period 1900–18 and 22 in the period 1919–40. Most of these schools were founded in the years of expansion immediately following World War I. These figures are based on the list of government-accredited engineering schools published in La Documentation Française, "Les écoles d'ingénieurs," *Notes et études documentaires* (4045–4047), Dec. 1973. This led to a considerable increase in the number of engineering graduates annually, which rose from around 1000 in 1900 to 4000 in 1920. During the Depression the number of new graduates declined steady and had fallen to about 2000 annually in 1940. But the increase in the number of engineers had been so great in previous years that the number of graduate engineers on the job continued to grow, from 55,089 in 1920 to 83,000 in 1930 to 99,000 in 1940 (figures based on "Les formation d'ingénieurs en France," Paris, CEFI, 1979). It is virtually impossible to guess at the number of engineers who were either self-taught or equipped with a diploma not recognized by the government's Accreditation Commission.
93. The devaluation of the title "engineer' was in a sense made official by collective bargaining agreements. For example, the contract signed by chemical engineers in the Paris region on 30 January 1937 stipulated that 'engineers, as defined in the present contract, shall in principle be subject to the salary schedule below, regardless of the duties they perform. On an exceptional basis, however, in view of current placement difficulties, engineers who expressly consent may be employed in positions in which they will not be obliged to use all the capacities recognized by their diplomas, in which case they shall be paid according to the position they actually fill.
94. The devaluation of diplomas and the collapse of cultural capital in a time of economic crisis were factors that contributed to the spread of "*völkisch* attitudes" among intellectuals and academics in the Weimar Republic, an ominous sign of the coming of Nazism. See Pierre Bourdieu, "L'ontologie politique de Martin Heidegger," *Actes de la recherche en sciences sociales*, vol. 1, no. 5–6, 1975, pp. 109–56.
95. Terry Shinn, "La profession d'ingénieur, 1750–1920," *Revue française de sociologie*, vol. 19, no. 1, 1978, pp. 39–72.
96. See Robert O. Paxton, *La France de Vichy, 1940–1944* (Paris: Editions

du Seuil, 1973), pp. 204–14.

97. Concerning traditional images of the officer, see Louis Pinto, "L'armée, le contingent et les classes sociales," *Actes de la recherche en sciences sociales*, vol. 1, no. 3, 1975, pp. 18–40. These civilian "officers" are also officers in the army reserve. Consider, for example, the advice given to *gadzarts* (even though they occupy a relatively low position in the hierarchy of graduate engineers): "Prepare for military service with the intention of becoming reserve officers. The military and the nation are increasingly indistinguishable, and military ranks will have their equivalence in the civilian hierarchy. Whatever your opinions may be, there is no valid reason not to try to excel in the army as elsewhere, and the experience of your elders suggests that you must take your proper place in the military hierarchy" (Société des anciens élèves des Ecoles nationales d'arts et métiers, *Le choix d'une profession pour les ingénieurs A et M*, Paris, 1938, p. 20). Factories developed at least as much out of a desire to control and discipline the work force as out of technological needs associated with new machinery. Military analogies have been common since the earliest days of the factory system. As Stephen Marglin points out, "military comparisons abound in the remarks of observers contemporary with the first factories. Boswell described Matthew Boulton, Watt's partner in the manufacture of steam engines, as a 'captain brandishing his sword amidst his troops'" (Marglin, "Origines et fonctions de la parcellisation des tâches," in André Gorz (ed.), *Critique de la division du travail*, Paris, Editions du Seuil, 1973, pp. 84–92).
98. "[The CGC] accepts all supervisory personnel, regardless of their rank in the hierarchy. Any employee who wields a 'modicum of authority' may join the CGC. Thus a substantial proportion of its members come from the *middle* (supervisor) and *lower* (foreman) ranks." See P. Meunier, "Le syndicalisme des cadres," *Droit social* 11 Nov. 1970, pp. 506–16.
99. *Cadres de France*, August 1945: 'If it is left up to the bureaucracy and the government to determine the nature of the representative bodies, then virtually no freedom remains to the unions (*applause*). Union freedom remains intact, on the other hand, if the standards of representativity are fixed either by convention, by law, or by decision of the courts. For then the bureaucracy no longer has the right to deny that a union is representative, as long as it fulfills the legal requirements in this regard.... Consider for a moment how the most representative unions are currently determined. Who has the right to make this decision in each case? As soon as one allows a comparative standard such as 'the most representative,' it is obvious that a judgment has to be made, a judgment that cannot be pinned down in clear, precise terms and formulated in a law. The whole question has to be submitted to someone's judgment. This is where the bureaucracy steps in, to determine in each case which organization is most representative. Now, it is extremely important that the bureaucrats not be allowed

free rein in this realm. These judgments must be made under the control of the courts in accordance with clear rules fixed in advance.

100. *Patron mais* . . . is the title of a book by Claude Neuschwander (Paris: Editions du Seuil, 1975): the implication is that the author is a "boss" (*patron*), yes, "but" (*mais*) on the left, a veteran of the Lip struggle and the PSU.
101. Like Emmanuel Berl. See Patrick Modiano, *Interrogatoire* (Paris: Gallimard, 1976).
102. Like Bertrand de Jouvenel. See his *Un voyageur dans le siècle* (Paris: Robert Laffont, 1979).
103. Similar remarks apply to any crisis. As Léon Blum said of Dreyfus, "Had he not been Dreyfus would he even have been a *dreyfusard*?" See Blum, *Souvenirs sur l'Affaire* (Paris: Gallimard, 1936), p. 12.
104. For example, the 1 January 1947 issue of *Le Creuset* contains the following: "It is with the greatest pleasure that we learn that by decree of 29 November 1946 our friend Roger Millot, vice-president of the CGC, has been awarded the Medal of the French Resistance. We rejoice in this award for two reasons: not only is it just compensation for our friend's years of brilliant service, but for us it is also a splendid reply to those who dare to cast doubt on the patriotism of the CGC's founders." See also *La voix des cadres*, 18 Feb. 1946: "Some people maintain that the leaders of the CGC represent the spirit of Vichy." In the immediate postwar period the CGC constantly denounced the "excesses of the purge" and the "injustices" of which certain of its members were the "victims": 'We must speak out forcefully against the sanctions that have been imposed on those comrades who, having taken advantage of the Charter to defend the interests of the corporation, simultaneously joined Resistance organizations and proved their loyalty to the present government to such a degree that no suspicion can possibly attach to them. All too often we find that the purge committees that are punishing our comrades are guided by the desire not to carry out a true purge but rather to unseat the leaders of our union, to strip them of their most dynamic members, and to issue a warning that in some cases drives them into other camps. . . I ask all of you to join with us in protesting such abuses' (*Cadres de France*, August 1945). See also "Lettre ouverte à M. Croizat," *Cadres de France* (March 1946), editorial by Jean Ducros in *Le Creuset*, April 1947, etc.
105. On the class struggle in the period 1945–47, see Grégoire Madjarian, *Conflits, pouvoirs et société à la Libération* (Paris: Union générale d'édition, 1980).
106. *Le Creuset*, March 1947. See also *Cadres de France*, June 1946: "The *Journal officiel* of 29 May 1946 published two decrees, one nominating the members of the board of Charbonnages de France, the other nominating the members of the Superior Council for Electricity and Gas. A sad similarity: the representatives of the employees were chosen from M. Marcel Paul's staff. Why not say that nationalization

means state-ization? And that only the representatives of the government are authorized to serve as directors, albeit camouflaged as representatives of a union that becomes more state-ized with each passing day."

107. In this the CGC followed big business, on the whole quite hostile to the nationalizations. The heads of nationalized firms (like Pierre Lefaucheux and Louis Armand) took part in the resistance, either in organizations connected with the CGT or, more commonly, in the Organisation civile et militaire, the group joined by the few employers who took a stand against Vichy. In the postwar period they opposed the traditional, "family-centered," Vichy-leaning segments of the business community. These conflicts faded with the shifts in allegiance that occurred in late 1947 and disappeared entirely in subsequent years. According to Ehrmann, the reconciliation took place at a dinner organized by the ACADI, in the fall of 1951. See Ehrmann, *op. cit.*, pp. 292–9.
108. See Alfred Sauvy, *De Paul Reynaud à Charles de Gaulle* (Paris: Casterman, 1972), pp. 60–1. In the late 1950s Pierre Dreyfus was the embodiment of the modern "manager" as opposed to the traditional "*patron.*" Roger Priouret, a writer for *L'Express* and one of the first to prophesy the "coming of the managers," describes him thus: "[Dreyfus] is no nineteenth-century-style *patron.* Nor is he a functionary who follows the orders of the government: he truly belongs to a social category that is *sui generis.*" See Priouret, *La République des députés* (Paris: Grasset, 1959), p. 240. In the 1950s and 1960s Renault was considered a prime example of a "managerial" firm managed in a meritocratic manner: "Access to top-level positions appears to be relatively open, and promotion can carry a man right to the very top: there are former workers and foremen in top management posts." N. Delefortrie-Soubeyroux, *Les dirigeants de l'industrie française* (Paris: Armand Colin, 1961), p. 135.
109. Pierre Dreyfus, *La liberté de réussir* (Paris: J. C. Simoën, 1977), pp. 50–2.
110. The circumstance that was used to justify the formation of the Comité national de liaison et d'action des classes moyennes was the opposition of the "independent professions" to the broadening of Social Security as provided in the 1946 law. See H. Roson, "Les classes moyennes," in P. Laroque (ed.), *Succès et faiblesses de l'effort social français* (Paris: Armand Colin, 1961), p. 224.
111. A plant manager, Catholic, and graduate of the business school HEC, Malterre "discovered" cadre unionism in 1936. He joined the CGC in 1945. See *André Malterre ou l'honneur des cadres* (Paris: Editions France-Empire, 1976).
112. Lecordier, *op. cit.*
113. See the special issue of *France-Documents* devoted to the "middle classes," April 1950.
114. L. Purtschet, *Le Rassemblement du peuple français* (Paris: Editions Cujas,

1965), p. 119.

115. P. Guiol, "L'action ouvrière du R.P.F. et le thème de l'association capital-travail, 1947–1955," thesis, Paris, Ecole des Hautes Etudes en Sciences Sociales, 1978, p. 90.
116. *Ibid.*, pp. 85–9.
117. Bourdieu, *La distinction.*
118. Desrosières, *art. cit.*
119. On the establishment of retirement programs after the war and the effect of changing social definitions of old age on retirement institutions, see R. Lenoir, "L'invention du 'troisième âge,' et la constitution du champ des agents de gestion de la vieillesse," *Actes de la recherche en sciences sociales* 26–27, 1979, pp. 57–82.
120. In a CGC publication on retirement for cadres we read: "The CGC for its part regards the cadres' retirement program as an irreversible achievement. It takes the position that any attempt to undo the program is an attack on cadres themselves that challenges their existence as a *group*" (my italics). See CGC, *La retraite des cadres* (Paris: Chotard, 1976), p. 12.
121. R. Mathieu, "Les cadres," in CERS, *Sécurité sociale et conflits de classes* (Paris: Editions ouvrières, 1962), pp. 75–100.
122. A. Le Bayon, *Notion et statut juridique des cadres de l'entreprise privée* (Paris: Librairie générale de droit et de jurisprudence, 1971), esp. pp. 75–6.
123. See *Cadres de France*, August 1945: "It was essential to adopt a policy that would enable cadres to receive automatically any increases granted to workers and other employees" (owing to inflation).
124. Robert Boyer, "Les salaires en longue période," *Economie et statistique* 103, 1978, pp. 27–57. Boyer shows that these changes are effects of the evolution of the system in the period 1936–50 and that they suggest that "monopolistic regulation" of the economy supplanted the "competition-regulated" system that still prevailed between the wars.
125. The distinction between "real employers" and "mere managers" set forth by Léon Gingembre remains central to the doctrine of the CGPME, which, like corporatists of the 1930s, defines "small business" not in terms of legal status or even size in the strict sense but rather by the presence at the head of the firm of an owner who "personally and directly shoulders the financial, technical, social, and moral responsibilities of the firm." Cf. the *Statut général des petites et moyennes entreprises*, first filed 5 January 1945, amended in 1976.
126. Robert Boyer, "La crise actuelle: une mise au point en perspective historique. Quelques réflexions à partir d'une analyse du capitalisme français en longue période," *Critique de l'économie politique* 7–8, Apr.–Sept. 1979, pp. 5–113.
127. See for example the series of articles published in *Le Figaro* starting 12 November 1964 on "young cadres," entitled "L'autre jeunesse, celle qui travaille."

2 The fascination with the United States and the importation of management

1. The Marshall Plan, the productivity missions to the United States, and the role of American "experts" in France receive little attention, for example, in the books of Claude Gruson, *Origine et espoirs de la planification française* (Paris: Dunod, 1968), several chapters of which are devoted to the period 1945–55, and Jean-Jacques Carré, Paul Dubois, and Edmond Malinvaud, *La croissance française*, which devotes only a few lines to "missions abroad" (a fine euphemism!) between 1949 and 1952 (p. 605). A brief survey, surely incomplete, of the literature in social and economic history failed to turn up a single article on either the "productivity missions" or the "productivity campaign."
2. See Fernand Braudel and Ernest Labrousse, *Histoire économique et sociale de la Frances* (Paris: Presses Universitaires de France, 1980), 2:785–6. Industrial restructuring accelerated after 1952: of the 50 largest corporations in 1952, only 26 remained on the list under the same name in 1962. See P. Bourdieu and M. de Saint Martin, "Le patronat,' *Actes de la recherche en sciences sociales* 20–21(1978):3–82.
3. In 1953 American technical assistance provided 30 million dollars in loans and guarantees to private companies that would commit themselves to "improving their productivity" and to establishing "appropriate arrangements for equitably sharing the profits resulting from enhanced output and productivity between consumers, workers, and owners." This aid, which went along with "defense support" and resulted from the Blair–Moody amendment to the mutual security bill, was supposed to facilitate "financing of projects likely to stimulate a free-enterprise economy." See M. Elgozy, *L'aide économique des Etats-Unis à la France, plan Marshall et 'Defense support'"* (Paris: Documentation française, 1953), p. 37.
4. See J. Gimbel, *The Origins of the Marshall Plan* (Stanford: Stanford University Press, 1976), esp. pp. 228ff.
5. See *Actions et problèmes de productivité*, first report of the Comité national de la productivité 1950–53, Paris, 1953.
6. P. L. Mathieu, *La politique française de productivité depuis la guerre*. Memoir of the IEP under the direction of Jean Fourastié, Paris, 1961.
7. Report of the Commissariat au Plan, 14 April 1949, submitted by the "electrical construction group" upon its return from a visit to the United States: *Notes et études documentaires* (1296), 15 Mar. 1950, p. 15.
8. OECE, *Les problèmes de gestion des entreprises. Opinions américaines, opinions européennes*, Paris, Oct. 1954, p. 13.
9. By way of example, here is the list of documents that accompanied the 1951 report of the productivity mission on "cadres and supervisors": "Principal responsibilities of supervisors; Authors' note on training in the USA; program for the visit to the Johnson and John-

son Corporation; Human relations program of the Maynard Institute; Ways to establish a training program; How to conduct a discussion meeting; How to improve work methods; How to deal with personnel problems." The program of the Maynard Institute, which was translated in the body of the report, included the following topic headings: "Introduction to individual differences; Identification of components of temperament; Controlling your behavior; Self-interest versus society; On the tendency to make plans; Principles of the salesman's art; The art of stimulating the desire to buy."

10. "L'agence européenne de productivité," *Notes et études documentaires* (2604), Dec. 1959, p. 10.
11. *Recueil de documents, op. cit.*, p. 16.
12. This did not preclude hope of one day seeing the unions wither away: "We believe that this community of views is possible only in companies from which the dual leadership of unions and employers will have disappeared, not, of course, by banning the union but through the employer's taking upon himself the responsibility to defend the interests of workers in all areas where union action has proved to be necessary." See R. Nordling, "Comment réaliser une communauté de vues et d'intérêts entre la direction et le personnel de l'entreprise," *Rapport du Comité national de l'organisation française au IXe congrès de l'organisation scientifique* (Brussels, 1951).
13. "L'agence européenne de productivité," *op. cit.*
14. *Actions et problèmes de productivité, op. cit.*, p. 412.
15. *Recueil de documents sur la productivité, op. cit.*, p. 16.
16. The critique of French managers and French business is one of the leitmotifs of American management literature, including the most respectable academic works on the subject. It is used as the justification of an evolutionary view of human society: underdeveloped countries → France → United States. A typical example is J. T. Dunlop *et al.*, *Industrialism and Industrial Man* (Cambridge, Mass.: Harvard University Press, 1960), which features a series of portraits of the "elites" of various countries, whose social and ethical characteristics are related to the "stage" of economic development of each country.
17. OECE, *op. cit.*, pp. 14ff.
18. T. A. Wilson, *The Marshall Plan* (New York: Headline Series, 1977), pp. 43–4.
19. The habit of clandestinity – Uri describes his work with Monnet and Hirsch under the First Plan in the following terms: "From my mansard-roofed office in the Commissariat au Plan, I was broadly responsible for French economic policy. As a method ours was very efficient: three clandestine agents who did everything. And the governments did as they were told." Cited in F. Fourquet, *Les comptes de la puissance. Histoire de la comptabilité nationale et du Plan* (Paris: Encres, 1980), p. 87.
20. Jean Monnet, *Mémoires* (Paris: Fayard, 1976), pp. 276–7. Louis

Armand later summed up the endless prattle about productivity in the following terms: "Economically speaking, one American is worth three Frenchmen." See Louis Armand and Michel Drancourt, *Plaidoyer pour l'avenir* (Paris: Calmann-Lévy, 1961), p. 76.

21 Today one has access to numerous and detailed sources of information about Pierre Mendès France and his entourage and even more about the Servan-Schreiber family. In addition to interviews I used mainly the following: P. Mendès France, *Choisir* (Paris: Stock, 1974), and idem., *La vérité guidait leurs pas* (Paris: Gallimard, 1976), especially the chapter on Georges Boris, pp. 231–48; C. Gruson, *Programmer l'espérance* (Paris: Stock, 1976); F. Bloch-Lainé, *Profession: fonctionnaire* (Paris: Editions du Seuil, 1976); P. Dreyfus, *op. cit.*, and above all the indispensable work of François Fourquet, *Les comptes de la puissance*. On the Schreiber family and L'Express, I consulted E. Schreiber, *Raconte encore* (Paris: Presses de la Cité, 1968); J.-C. Servan-Schreiber, *Le huron de la famille* (Paris: Calmann-Lévy, 1979); J.-J. Servan-Schreiber, interview with Roger Priouret in Priouret, *La France et le management* (Paris: Stock, 1972); S. Siritzky and F. Roth, *Le roman de l'Express, 1953–1978* (Paris: M. Jullian, 1979); and M. Jamet, "L'Express de Jean-Jacques Servan-Schreiber" (thesis, 3e cycle, Paris, 1979).

22. 'National accounting was a purely administrative creation, for which Bloch-Lainé and I were responsible. Bloch-Lainé mainly, for he was in charge of the political end.... Some politicians, though, did understand the need for national accounting and planning. Mendès played a major role. From 1952 until 1954, when he became *président du Conseil*, he had an office near ours, and he came not every day but several times a week. He paid close attention to what we were doing and intervened on occasion. His accession to power was in various ways of considerable help to us.'

Furthermore, 'it was during Mendès France's prime ministership that we began to play a real political role.... Several members of my team worked directly with Mendès, such as Simon Nora and Jean Serisé. Above all, in the first weeks of his government Mendès convened, to work out his economic program, a commission that included a number of civil servants: Hirsch, Gabriel Ardant, then commissioner-general for productivity, Bloch-Lainé, Pierre Dreyfus, and Pierre Besse. We kept the minutes of the meetings and were responsible for drafting the reports.' See Gruson, *Programmer*, pp. 79 and 88.

23. It is in relation to this shared past that one must read, for example, the pages in which François Bloch-Lainé proclaims the replacement of the leading elites: 'It is true that the bourgeois castes, whose post-Liberation merits did not obviously make up for their previous demerits (during and prior to the war), reaped the benefits of an economic expansion for which they were not primarily responsible. For them, the "divine surprise" of the 1950s and 1960s followed on

the heels of the earlier surprise of 1940. . . . I admit that the mandarin castes, composed of graduates of the Grandes Ecoles, may have displaced the old high-society families from the "inner sanctum" only to join fortunes with and consecrate the position of those same families rather than sweep them from the stage. Yet I remain convinced that that replacement was like a bomb, and not a dud. The mandarins may have seemed to be absorbed by the old society families, but an upheaval ensued whose first signs went almost unnoticed. Changes came quickly, but they were only the beginning. What the resistance fighters, fresh from the bush, few in number, and concerned (perhaps overly so) with the maneuvers of the Stalinists on the home front, patched together but failed to carry through almost twenty years ago, the new wave of technocrats, fresh from their schools, will finish within ten years. The replacement of the leading elites and the substitution of merit for birth will proceed at an accelerating pace.' F. Bloch-Lainé, "La réforme de l'entreprise," *Esprit*, Mar. 1964, pp. 441–8.

24. It would be worth taking time to describe the feminine side of modernism and to show all that the life style today associated with the "new bourgeoisie" owes to the work of Françoise Giroud, first at *Elle*, where she worked with Hélène Gordon-Lazareff (who spent the war in the United States and was, according to Giroud, an "unconditional supporter of America"), and later at *L'Express*.
25. G. Boris, *Servir la République*, with an introduction by Pierre Mendès France (Paris: Julliard, 1956), p. 181.
26. In the 1920s the United States was considered by some Marxist intellectuals as a laboratory of capitalism, an avant-garde society (people had begun to speak of "neocapitalism") experimenting with new systems of production and modes of domination intended for export to the rest of the world. As is well known, America played a large part in shaping the thought of Henri de Man and some of the leading disciples, like André Philip.
27. The fundamentalists, who of course contributed more than any other group to shaping and publicizing the church's "social doctrine," referrerd to Liberal Catholics, who believed that the church should adapt to post-French Revolution society and to the "modern world" as it was, as "Americans." See D. Strauss, *Menace in the West: The Rise of Anti-Americanism in Modern Times* (Westport: Greenwood Press, 1978), p. 11.
28. Lucien Romier, *L'Homme nouveau: esquisse des conséquences du progrès* (Paris: Hachette, 1929). Lucien Romier, a writer for *Le Figaro*, had ties to Catholic Action. He later became an adviser to Marshal Pétain.
29. Alfred Fabre-Luce, *A quoi rêve le monde* (Paris: Grasset, 1931), the first section of which ("Crisis on Wall Street," pp. 9–11), repeats many of the clichés about American materialism and American civilization.
30. Concerning Franco-American conflicts between the two wars over

the debt, reparations, and disarmament, see R. Zahniser, *Uncertain Friendship: American-French Diplomatic Relations through the Cold War* (New York: Wiley, 1975), pp. 219–39.

31. See e.g. Charles Pomaret, *L'Amérique à la conquête de l'Europe* (Paris: Armand Colin, 1931). Pomaret, a businessman, differed from the "young right" in that he proposed combatting American imperialism by having European industry adopt the major innovations that had done so well for American capitalism.
32. On American investments in Europe between the two world wars, see M. Wilkins, *The Maturing of Multinational Enterprise: American Business Abroad from 1914 to 1970* (Cambridge, Mass.: Harvard University Press, 1974), esp. pp. 70ff. (on the electrical industry) and pp. 211ff. (on the petroleum industry).
33. Lucien Romier put it this way: "There are obvious similarities between the underlying tendencies of American civilization and the attempts by the Soviet Communists to create a would-be new society. In both countries there is the same all-out worship of applied science, of technology with a capital T, and the same effort, successful in America, still bogged down in Russia, to adapt all social forms to the needs not of the individual but of the human mass, enslaved to technology and machines." *L'homme nouveau*, p. 107.
34. See Robert Aron and Arnaud Dandieu, *Décadence de la nation française* (Paris: Rieder, 1931), and Robert Aron, *Le cancer américain* (Paris: Rieder, 1931).
35. America is merely the incarnation of a universal evil, "rationalism," so that "America is not an expanse of territory but a form of thought and action. America is a method, a technique, a malady of the spirit." Aron goes on to say that "the United States stands outside time as well as space" (*Le cancer americain*, pp. 80, 82).
36. Henri Massis, Tarde's collaborator (together they published, under the pseudonym Agathon, a pamphlet entitled *L'esprit de la nouvelle Sorbonne*, directed mainly against the Durkheimians), sought in his *Défense de l'Occident* (Paris: Plon, 1927) to defend the "Latin heritage" both against the "Asiatic peril" and its "barbarian" hordes, of which "bolshevism" was just one manifestation among others (pp. 71–5), and against the "materialism" of "modern civilization" by rediscovering "Christianity" and "returning to the Middle Ages" (pp. 253–68).
37. On the idea of "the masses" in conservative thought, see R. L. Geiger, "Democracy and the Crowd: The Social History of an Idea in France and Italy, 1890–1914," *Societas* 7(1)1977:47–71, and R. A. Nye's work on Le Bon, entitled *The Origins of Crowd Psychology: Gustave Le Bon and the Crisis of Mass Democracy in the Third Republic* (Beverly Hills: Sage Publications, 1975). Concerning the most recent manifestations of "crowds" and "masses" (in the 1960s), see P. Bourdieu and J.-C. Passeron, "Sociologues des mythologies ou mythologies des sociologues," *Temps modernes* 211, Dec. 1963, pp. 998–1921.

38. Hyacinthe Dubreuil spent fifteen months in the United States in the late 1920s, working in a large metal-working plant. When he returned to France he wrote a book very favorable to the new methods of rationalizing the labor process: *Standards: Le tavail américain vu par un ouvrier français*, with a preface by H. Le Chatelier (Paris: Grasset, 1929). Several years later he wrote a book on the New Deal: *Les codes de Roosevelt et les perspectives de la vie sociale* (Paris: Grasset, 1934). Dubreuil, who saw "scientific management as the indispensable tool of true socialism" (*Standards*, p. 422), regarded the National Recovery Act, which was "causing the creation of codes of legitimate competition," as a continuation of Taylor's work (*Les codes de Roosevelt*, pp. 58–60) and believed that the politics of "codes" was an "attempt to move from ... the old individualism ... to the coming forms of organized democracy" (p. 82).
39. Emile Schreiber published two reports on the United States: a youthful work, published in 1917, as "useful and powerful propaganda in favor of ideas that will be more pertinent than ever after the war," entitled *L'exemple américain. Le prix du temps aux Etats-Unis* (Paris: Plon, 1934), and a book on the New Deal and the National Recovery Act Administration, which Schreiber, too, believed ought to set an example for the ruling classes of Europe: in order "to build a new society," midway "between dying liberalism and out-and-out statism," there is no reason why Europe "should not once again look to the American example" (pp. 252–3).
40. Concerning the development of "technocratic revisionism" in the Socialist Party during the 1930s, a revisionism based on "the American example" and "the need for a revision of socialist policy in the light of changes in capitalism" and involving such names as J. Moch, B. Montagnon, and C. Spinasse, see A. Bergounioux, "Le néo-socialisme."
41. Georges Boris, *La révolution Roosevelt* (Paris: Gallimard, 1934). Berfore becoming a principal adviser to Pierre Mendès France, Georges Boris was a friend of Léon Blum and a Popular Front activist. His brother, Roland Boris, was president of the group X-crise (see A. Sauvy, *De Paul Reynaud*, pp. 55 and 63). Boris was probably one of the first in France to read Keynes. He introduced Pierre Mendès France to economics and thus played what François Fourquet has called "a discreet, but in my view decisive, role in our history" (*Les comptes de la puissance*, p. 21).
42. R. Marjolin, *Les expériences Roosevelt* (Paris: Librairie populaire, 1933).
43. Boris, *La révolution*, p. 181. The Roosevelt administration's policies were notable, as E. W. Hawley points out, mainly for reducing "the tension between the bureaucratization of industrial relations and the values associated with the liberal, democratic ethos." This was accomplished by developing new techniques of industrial management that required a minimum of state action and "governmental

coercion." So that even though business did not initiate the New Deal, it was "the major beneficiary of the innovations of the period." One of the effects of the New Deal was to reorganize the market, restoring competition while controlling its socially disastrous effects and quelling conflict within the business community and the bourgeoisie, thereby "moralizing economic life." See E. W. Hawley, "The New Deal and Business," in Braeman *et al.* (eds.), *The New Deal* (Columbus, Ohio: Ohio State University Press, 1975), vol. 1, pp. 50–82. In this respect, the New Deal was the inspiration for state economic planning as practiced in France in the 1950s and 1960s, i.e., planning based on "stimulus" and "cooperation." The earliest French observers of the "Roosevelt experiments" were struck by the possibility of overcoming the opposition between "liberalism" and "*dirigisme.*" Planning, they discovered, did not necessarily lead to "statism." Georges Boris put it this way: "What ideas are held up to the American citizen by those in whom he has placed his trust? Read the texts. For in them we find neither the old ideal of individualistic capitalism nor the socialist ideal but something in between the two, which takes its guiding principles from both left and right." (*La révolution*, pp. 190–1).

44. Bourdieu and Boltanski, "La production."
45. Pierre Bourdieu, "Structures sociales et structures de perception du monde social," *Actes de la recherche en sciences sociales* 2 March 1975, pp. 18–20.
46. Seymour M. Lipset, "The Changing Class Structure and Contemporary European Politics," *Daedalus*, winter 1964, pp. 271–303. These themes were popularized in France at about the same time by Michel Crozier. See, for example, his "Classes sans conscience ou préfiguration de la société sans classes," *Archives européennes de sociologie* 1(2)1960:233–47.
47. The distinction between the "old" and the "new" middle classes, which can be traced back to German Social Democracy and to the Bernstein–Kautsky debates, was taken up between the wars by academic sociologists in Germany. Little use was made of it in France, however, except in studies (mostly by Germanists, who took it from the untranslated work of Theodor Geiger) of the rise of national socialism in Germany. Henri de Man, who worked in Frankfurt and wrote in German, used it in his *Socialisme constructif* (Paris: Alcan, 1933), pp. 199–249: "Socialism and Fascist Nationalism." So did H. Laufenburger, who taught at the law faculty in Strasburg. See his "Classes moyennes et national-socialisme en Allemagne," *Revue politique et parlementaire* 40(461)1933:46–60. On the taxonomy of classes in Geiger, see his *On Social Order and Mass Society* (Chicago: The University of Chicago Press, 1969), pp. 10–11, and P. Ayçoberry, *La question nazie, les interprétations du national-socialisme 1922–1975* (Paris: Editions du Seuil, 1979), pp. 103–7.
48. P. Bleton, *Les hommes des temps qui viennent* (Paris: Editions ouvrières,

1956), p. 230.

49. On the role played by the CGPME in the advent of the Pinay government, the links between Gingembre and Laniel, and the hostility of the CGPME to Mendès France and planning officials, see G. Lavau, "La C.G.P.M.E." *Revue française de science politique* 5(2)1955:370–84.
50. See J. Touchard, "Bibliographie et chronologie du poujadisme," *Revue française de science politique* 6(1)1956:18–43.
51. Sapiens, *Mendès ou Pinay* (Paris: Grasset, 1953).
52. 'You seem surprised to hear me talking about economics. But it was to examine the political implications of economics – and economics is constantly mixed up in politics – that we founded *L'Express*. Look at the first issue. What was Mendès France at the time? A fellow who constantly kept saying, we've got to invest, we've got to reduce our unproductive expenditures – chief among which was the war in Indo-China – we've got to build housing, machinery, factories, and schools, we've got to create new jobs for those who are six, seven, or eight years old today and who will be entering the job market ten years from now. We've got to put an end to governments that go to Wasshington for their inauguration because we're living right now at the expense of the Americans. The mission of *L'Express*, then, was not at all what it became later on, during the war in Algeria, owing to the errors and the horrors of decolonization. Rather, it was to promote and implement a policy of economic recovery by providing French readers with accurate information so that they could see for themselves that that policy was the correct one. And now the magazine has returned to this initial mission.' F. Giroud, *op. cit.*, pp. 153–6.
53. R. Salmon, *L'information économique, clef de la prosperité* (Paris: Hachette, 1963), pp. 24–30.
54. This was one of the functions of company newspapers, the number of which increased from 20 in 1939 to 500 in 1962, with a readership of 1,500,000 (compared with 600,000 in 1952).
55. Cf. Michel Drancourt, *Les clefs du pouvoirs*, with an afterword by Louis Armand (Paris: Fayard, 1964), and Armand and Drancourt, *Plaidoyer pour l'avenir.*
56. M. Beaud, A. M. Lévy, and S. Liénard, *Dictionnaire des groupes industriels et financiers en France* (Paris: Editions du Seuil, 1978), p. 19. The industrial petite bourgeoisie had to accustom itself to company discipline, fixed hours, and to being treated, officially at any rate, as "workers like the rest." This seems to have caused tension up to the end of the war, at least among those cadres who came from previously independent segments of the bourgeoisie. For example, Pierre Alamigeon, who deplored the "proletarization" of "employers" ("employers whose companies have been taken from them have joined the ranks of workers"), painted a bleak picture in 1945 of the situation of cadres working for large companies: "It is normal for engineers and foremen to obey shop rules just like workers.... But is it really necessary for them to punch in four times a day, and when they arrive

late, often for work-related reasons, must they give interminable explanations to the guard who stands like a watchdog at the factory gate? Is it acceptable for the plant police to question them and make remarks within earshot of their workers and to search packages they take out of the plant to make sure that they are not removing company property from the premises? Is it really useful to make them wear photo-ID's and badges with their department number? ... In our view it is insulting and repellent to be treated as criminals when we fight all day long to defend the company's interest, to be watched like children when we strive at all times to shoulder our responsibilities like men." Alamigeon, *op. cit.*, p. 82.

57. In 1950 20,000 engineers and supervisors took night courses organized by the CNOF. See *Revue internationale du travail*, July 1950.
58. See "Le C.R.C., dix ans d'activités," *Direction du personnel* 76, Dec. 1963, pp. 15–17. The CRC was supposed to be a kind of "private university" (comparable to the American Committee for Economy and Development). Active in the early 1960s, when it supported "modernist" employers (against the CGPME in particular), its role has diminished since 1970. See Brizay, *op. cit.*, p. 268.
59. Cf. "Evolution de la formation à l'administration des entreprises," *Direction du personnel* 73, July 1963, pp. 17–24.
60. "L'institute des sciences sociales du travail," *Direction du personnel* 88, June 1964, pp. 38–40. The ISST, which had a budget for research, was, along with the Centre d'études sociologiques, one of the leading centers of labor sociology in the 1950s and 1960s. See M. Rose, *Servants of Post-Industrial Power? Sociologie du Travail in Modern France.* (London: Macmillan Press, 1979), pp. 45–9.
61. The managing board of "Humanisme et entreprise" included equal numbers of academics and big businessmen: "modern" executives of firms using advanced technology – always the same ones (Bleuste in-Blanchet, Demonque, Huvelin, Saint-Gobain, Pont-à-Mousson, Merlin-Gerin, Kodak-Pathé) and professors (Stoetzel, Daval, Mme Favez-Boutonnier) with "open minds" about the executives' concerns.
62. *Humanisme et entreprise*, 1963.
63. Until the 1950s economics had a very small place in the curricula of the engineering schools, with the possible exception of the Ecole des Mines in Paris, where Maurice Allais had been teaching since 1943. In this respect the Conservatoire national des arts et métiers served as a precursor: for instance, François Simiand began teaching there in 1923. Cf. P. Etner, "Note sur la formation économique des ingénieurs," paper read to the Creusot colloquim, October 1980.
64. The figure are taken from *Précis de l'enseignement, gestion* (Paris: Fondation nationale pour l'enseignement de la gestion des entreprises, 1972). See also P. Bourdieu, L. Boltanski, M. de Saint Martin, "Les stratégies de reconversion," *Information sur les sciences sociales* 12(5)1974:61–113. Comparison of the educational backgrounds of

executives in the 100 largest French firms in 1952, 1962, and 1972 reveals a marked rise in the level of educational achievement: the percentage of executives who do not mention their education (and who in all likelihood received no advanced degrees or graduated from less prestigious institutions) or who held no degree beyond the baccalaureate declined from 35% in 1952 to 16.5% in 1962 and to 12.5% in 1972. There was a corresponding diversification of types of curricula followed: the proportion of Polytechnique graduates declined (from 36% in 1952 to 33.5% in 1962 to 24.5% in 1972), but this was compensated mainly by an increase in the proportion of graduates of the Ecoles des hautes études commerciales and the Institut d'études politiques as well as the law schools (7% in 1952, 15.5% in 1962, 24.5% in 1972).

65. Cf. A. Moutet, "Les origines du système Taylor en France, le point de vue patronal, 1907–1914,' *Mouvement social* 93, Oct.–Dec. 1975, pp. 15–49. The development of scientific management owes much to the work of the syndicalist Albert Thomas, a graduate of the Ecole Normale, disciple of Lucien Herr, and a socialist and admirer of Bernstein, who was in charge of armaments production from 1914 to 1917. Director of the BIT after the war, he, like Hyacinthe Dubreuil after him, attempted to reconcile productivism, scientific management, and American-style reforms. See M. Rebérioux and P. Fridenson, "Albert Thomas, pivot du réforisme français," *Mouvement social* 87, April–June 1974, pp. 85–98. It was also during the war that de Fréminville, who offered his services to the armaments industry, was able to apply Taylorist techniques on a large scale. When the war was over, he, together with Le Chatelier and Fayol, founded the Comité national de l'organisation française, or CNOF. See L. Urwick and E. F. Brech, *The Making of Scientific Management* (London: Management Publication Trust, 1949), vol. 1, pp. 95 and 107–8.

66. In the early 1920s proponents of Fayol and Taylor clashed and established different networks and organizations. Most of Fayol's supporters were apparently either big businessmen or top civil servants, who disliked Taylor's overly "technical" papers and his interest in manual labor and workers. The Taylorists were mainly production engineers in direct contact with the labor force. Fayol and de Fréminville reconciled in 1925 at the second International Congress on the Organization of Labor in Brussels. As Judith A. Merkle, *Management and Ideology* (Berkeley: University of California Press, 1980), shows in her chapter on France (pp. 130–71), Fayol's influence on French scientific management was permanent and profound. Fayol emphasized not so much the technical division of labor as the administrative capacities of executives and the quality of "leaders" ("cadres"), and not so much the organization of production and appropriation of worker knowhow as the rationalization of administration and "leadership."

67. Auguste Detoeuf, a Polytechnique graduate not born into the world

of business, became head of a major company thanks to his talents and was thus a precursor of the "managerial" movement. Detoeuf was much influenced by the modernists and paid a great deal of attention to the "social question" (in 1937 he corresponded with Simone Weil; their letters have been published in Weil, *Les Nouveaux Cahiers*, pp. 245–65), to "American" ideas (O. L. Barenton, another polytechnician to whom Detoeuf paid tribute in a work published in 1938, established the Compagnie générale de la créme glacée after a trip to the United States), and to problems of organization. In May 1946, shortly before his death, Detoeuf gave a lecture at the Ecole normale supérieure (later published as a pamphlet by the CNOF) on "scientific management." In it he sang the praises of Taylorism, which "diminishes man's physical toil," and of "psychotechnics" and psychology: "I believe that the coming years will be the era of psychology, of research into what has been called the 'human factor.'" He ends his lecture by pointing to the example of "Swedish socialism" and to the "admirable social peace" of a country in which, despite "struggles between employers and employees," the president of the Worker's Confederation could state that the "majority of citizens today understands that improvement in the general standard of living is more a question of production than of distribution." But Detoeuf died before the productivity and "social relations" movements had developed to the full.

68. In the late 1920s Aimée Moutet counted some thirty-odd engineers who had received training in the area of organization. Many were associated with Henri Le Chatelier or Charles de Fréminville. It was the war that had caused them to take an interest in "organizational techniques." A few, employed mainly by electrical construction firms with close ties to American companies, had been sent by their employers to the United States for training. Two Americans named Thomson and Clark started the first management consulting firms in France in the 1920s. Bedaux himself worked in the United States. But these very small firms (with only a few employees) played only a minor role in French industry. See A. Moutet, "Ingénieurs et rationalisation en France de la guerre à la crise, 1914–1929," paper delivered to the Creusot colloquium on "Engineers and Society," 23 October 1980.
69. This information comes from two unpublished biographical notes, one written by Marie Coutrot-Toulouse, the other by Gilbert Bloch, an engineer who worked for CEGOS and former member of BICRA, as well as from various documents kindly made available to me by Mme Aline Coutrot.
70. B. Lussato has identified two main types of organization theories: a technicist or technocratic type, which from Taylor to Drucker has emphasized profit-seeking as the "goal of organizations" and which generally leads to the construction of formal models (using operations research, decision theory, etc.), and a pyschological, sociologi-

cal, and "humanistic" type, which was based originally on group dynamics and the industrial psychology of the 1930s and which has also taken inspiration from the work of March and Simon and of Barnard. See B. Lussato, *Introduction critique aux théories des organisations* (Paris: Dunod, 1972), pp. 57–70. One might also show that the psychological aspects of management interact with the technological and financial aspects. Had such techniques as budget forecasting, administrative controls, production planning, inventory control and standardization, and so forth not been developed, such social technologies as group psychology, human relations, etc. would probably not have been as influential as they were. Psychological techniques aimed at fostering independence in employees would be useless, for example, without administrative controls, which in their modern form make it possible to grant cadres a large measure of autonomy while monitoring their performance closely, though from a distance, using accounting techniques.

71. In the period 1945–50 some British and American manuals in human relations included chapters on psychiatry for the layman, which instructed personnel managers in how to identify the early symptoms of mental illness, how to distinguish between anxiety, hysteria, and obsession, and how to treat production-related neuroses. It was not enough for managers to know first aid for physical injuries; they must also be able to administer "mental first aid" and be skilled in counseling. See, for example, R. F. Tredgold, *Human Relations in Modern Industry* (London: Duckworth, 1949), pp. 117–52. The vocabulary of psychiatry was also used for evaluating employees. Personnel managers (like social workers: see J. Verdès-Leroux, *Le travail social*, Paris, Editions de Minuit, 1978) could discuss workers' personalities "scientifically" and "objectively," evaluating not their skills but their personalities and encouraging workers to freely discuss their problems, only to fire them on grounds of "neurotic behavior."
72. See, for example, R. Armand, R. Lattes, and J. Lesourne, *Matière grise, année zéro* (Paris: Denoël, 1970), p. 45.
73. CEGOS, "Les cadres et l'exercice du commandement," *Hommes et techniques*, January 1958.
74. Today, in part because of the economic crisis, management rhetoric has rediscovered the virtues of the "cadre as junior executive" (in contrast to the "cadre as bureaucrat"). Organization theorists advocate "breaking the chains of hierarchy" and establishing "autonomous" small companies within large corporations. Analysis is needed of the connections between this new image of the "ideal" and "efficient" organization and the rise of "Japanese-style management" to the detriment of the American model.
75. 'Ten years ago, training and self-improvement programs in industry were open almost exclusively to supervisory personnel: engineers, cadres, and foremen. It all began with the foremen. . . . Gradually, engineers and cadres were brought in . . . but cautiously, so as not to

affront their image of themselves as "leaders" and in many cases as graduates of a university or Grande Ecole. The need to rethink existing training programs then became acute... The present quality of adult-education programs, techniques, and methods of training owes much to the raising of standards that ensued.... By demanding more of what was offered to them, engineers and cadres performed an invaluable service, hastening the maturation of industrial training programs and those who taught them.' P. H. Giscard, "Le rôle des psychologues dans la société actuelle," *Psychologie française* 4(1966):318–32.

76. Interview with Noël Pouderoux in R. Priouret, *La France et le management* (Paris: Denoël, 1968), p. 397.
77. "Market research" was first promoted in France in the mid-1950s by management consulting firms. In 1956 the CNOF set up a committee to report on market research to the 11th International Congress on Scientific Management, whose members included representatives of the leading nationalized firms, INSEE, and CREDOC, and members of the Association française des conseils en organisation scientifique (AFCOS), CEGOS, the Organisation Paul Planus, the Comité d'action pour la productivité dans l'assurance, ETMAR, etc.
78. In this same period most major corporations, and especially American-based multinationals, set up their own sales training schools. Among the best known of these were the schools run by Philips, Nestlé, Olivetti, and especially IBM. Thomas Watson, the founder of the IBM dynasty, was in fact one of the inventors of modern sales techniques. On Watson and IBM see W. Rodgers, *L'Empire IBM* (Paris: Robert Laffont, 1971). Sales personnel today are tightly disciplined and supervised. Their heads are filled with selling precepts, often taught in the form of mnemonics, such as AIDA, a (French) mnemonic for attention, interest, desire, and purchasing, and SONCA, security, pride, novelty, comfort, and greed. The use of videotape training is an important recent innovation. The salesman is taped in a mock sales meeting, and his presentation is viewed and commented upon by the class. The teacher stops the tape at critical points in the interview and the image is frozen on the screen: "Look. See how right there you were aggressive." Without prejudging the virtues of the VCR as a sales training technique, one can in any case hypothesize that it fosters awareness of class markers (such as accent and body language) and tends to reinforce the norms and values imposed by the firm (and more generally by the environment), especially when used (as it often is) with employees from relatively modest backgrounds who are especially earnest and given to self-control.
79. Armand *et al.*, *Matière grise*, p. 206.
80. In 1967, 205 firms belonged to SYNTEC, representing some 400,000 employees, including 16,000 engineers and cadres. These 205 companies accounted formore than 4 billion francs of business in

1975, 30% of it abroad (source: brochure on the engineering professions published by SYNTEC in 1976).

81. "Les cabinets de conseil en recrutement de cadres," *Hommes et techniques* 325, Nov. 1971, pp. 841–76.
82. Similarly, Jean-Pierre Poitou shows that when group dyanamics was first invented in the United States in the 1930s it was used to train white-collar workers with backgrounds in the independent lower middle class to work in highly bureaucratized organizations. See Poitou, *La dynamique des groupes* (Marseille: Editions du CNRS, 1978), pp. 211–13.
83. Ehrmann, *op. cit.*, p. 387. Founded in 1946 by a group of Catholic Polytechnicians, some of whom were employed in the nationalized sector, ACADI represented reformist and progressive employers in the 1950s. See Bourdieu and Saint Martin, "Le patronat."
84. *Actions et problèmes*, p. 412.
85. Rather than the term "communication," which has impersonal, technicist connotations (as in "communications network"), employers often preferred the term "dialogue," which carries spiritualist, humanist connotations. See, for example, the paper read by philosopher Jean Lacroix to the convention of the National Association of Personnel Managers in 1964: "Nature et condition du dialogue."
86. In this chapter I have neglected sociology, and especially labor sociology, which developed in this period outside the influence of French intellectual traditions (mainly the Durkeimian school), generally by importing methods, research programs, and concepts from American sociology. I made this choice not only because an analysis of the work of other sociologists would have been perceived as polemical but also because few sociologists intervened directly in the field of industry and organization, with the exception of Michel Crozier, who, incidentally, began his career with a severe critique of human relations: "Human Engineering," *Temps modernes* 69, 1951, pp. 44–75. Unlike the psychosociologists, most sociologists had Marxist backgrounds, were critical of business, and often "workerist" in their orientation (sometimes confusing "field research" with "political organizing"). Even so, their work was often cited for purposes of legitimation by progressive civil servants and employers. On the origins of labor sociology in France, see Michael Rose, *op. cit.*, esp. pp. 161–5. In part 2 I shall consider the contribution of sociology to the definition and institutionalization of the cadre category.
87. Paul Fraisse, whose article in the special issue of the *Revue de psychologie appliquée* was deliberately technical and bibliographical, took his distance from the human relations school in an article published in *Esprit*, May 1953, in which he criticized the "pseudo-personalism" of the "human relations philosophy": "It claims to satisfy man's deepest longing by offering each individual a framework in which he can be seen as a human being and not as a source of energy or a machine. But this recognition, while obviously progressive, is also a sham to

the extent that it puts the individual in leading strings. Man does not achieve his destiny solely through satisfaction in his work but only by winning freedom from all the forces of alienation. But here he is placed in thrall, to the very depths of his soul, to the god of productivity." P. Fraisse and Y. Guibourg, "Human relations: progrès ou mystification," *Esprit*, May 1953, pp. 783–804.

88. Dr Lahy was one of the leading practitioners of "psychotechnics" in France. As early as 1910 he studied psychological aptitudes in various professions. He was also interested in labor conflict: cf. G. Ribeill, "Les débuts de l'ergonomie en France à la veille de la première guerre mondiale," *Mouvement social* 113, Oct.–Dec. 1980, pp. 3–37. In 1924 he established the first "psychotechnical laboratory" to help the transit company STCRP choose conductors. In 1933, along with Henri Laugier, he created the review *Le travail humain*, in which he published in 1936 in collaboration with Suzanne Pacaud the results of "experimental research into the psychological causes of industrial accidents." Close to the socialists, Lahy thought of psychotechnics as a tool for the emancipation of workers, Cf. J. Zurfluh, *Les tests mentaux* (Paris: Editions universitaires, 1976), p. 145.
89. B. Krief, *Le médecin chinois, pour une politique de santé de l'entreprise* (Paris: Presses de la Cité, 1979), p. 30.
90. Rural isolation and "disorientation" were regarded by organizational consultants and psychosociologists as a prerequisite for successful intervention; their work had to proceed without outside disturbance. Cf. R. Clayessen, "Sélection, orientation et formation des ingénieurs et cadres," *Cegos-hommes et entreprises*, Nov. 1959.
91. Cf. M. Pollak, "La planification des sciences sociales," *Actes de la recherche en sciences sociales* 2–3(1976):105–21 and idem., "Paul F. Lazarsfeld, fondateur d'une multinationale scientifique," *Actes de la recherche en sciences sociales* 25(1979):45–60. In the late 1950s big businessmen discovered "sociology," some enthusiastically. Paul Huvelin, vice-president and general manager of Kléber-Colombes praised sociology and cited Durkheim in doing so (*Cahiers du C.R.C.*., no. 3, 1958, pp. 3–38) and also called the industrial executive an "applied sociologist" (*Cahiers du C.R.C.*., no. 1, 1957, pp. 22–45).
92. As is well known, American overseas investments, which during the period 1930–50 of economic depression and war had gone mainly to Latin America, shifted in the late 1950s to Europe and the Common Market. Direct US investment in Europe went from 1,733 million dollars in 1950 to 4,151 million dollars in 1957, 8,930 million dollars in 1962, and 12,067 million dollars in 1964 (by conservative estimate). In 1962 45% of all foreign investment in France was American. C. Layton, *L'Europe et les investissements américains* (Paris: Gallimard, 1968), pp. 22–6.
93. O. Gélinier, *Morale de l'entreprise et destin de la nation* (Paris: Plon, 1965), p. 155.
94. On American multinationals' strategies for organizing national sub-

sidiaries, recruiting and training local cadres, personnel management, etc., see M. Z. Brooke and H. L. Remmers, *The Strategy of Multinational Enterprise* (London: Longman, 1970), especially part 1, chapters 2 and 5. Most of the strategies described are designed to standardize policies, organizations, and cadres' "habitus" as much as possible. The purpose is to ensure respect for the parent company, to inculcate company values, and to drive home the subordinate role of the subsidiary. For such a policy to succeed, however, the national susceptibilities of each country must be respected. Thus the parent company often instructs its missionaries to "go native," at least in little things: local folklore is allowed to influence organizational matters, values, and policies.

95. Beforehand, however, one needs a sociology of the nation (adumbrated by the Durkheimians, especially Marcel Mauss, *Œuvres* (Paris: Editions de Minuit, 1969), vol. 3, pp. 573–639, and one must overcome the ideological taboo that has rightly linked the idea of the nation to militarism and traditional right-wing chauvinism and tended to limit the concept of the study of newly independent states (no doubt because here nationalism and revolution are linked). Needless to say, I am not proposing a return to the dead end of "national character." I am proposing an analysis of the relations between culture dependency (which varies from field to field) and national structures of class domination. As anthropology has repeatedly shown, selective borrowing of culture schemes, taken out of context, imported from one country to another, and imposed on local life styles, are generally associated with the destruction of internalized systems of defense, products of local traditions and group solidarities that tend to strengthen the weak.
96. With, in particular, the opposition between segments linked mainly to the growth of the public sector, whose interests are "national" – or, as internationalists like to say, "local" – and segments linked mainly to big private firms, whose interests are in a clearer way "delocalized," that is, in simple terms, "multinationalized." See part 2, chapter 4 below.
97. See IFOP, "L'opinion française et les Etats-Unis," *Sondages* 15(2)1953:5–80.
98. From the late 1940s on, big business ceased to be totally hostile to planning and to some moderate form of *dirigisme*. For example, Henry Davezac, who as vice-president of the electrical construction industry association was a business leader (and an *éminence grise* of the CNPF), showed a positive attitude (in a course he gave in 1946–47 at the Institut d'études politiques on "Modern Industrial Economics") toward a "controlled economy" and "limited planning" in which "the government ... would set a small number of key economic goals." This idea, he said, came from "the so-called modernization and retooling plan developed by M. Jean Monnet" (mimeographed lecture notes, p. 208).

99. Gruson, *Programmer*, p. 92. Gruson sees Valéry Giscard d'Estaing as one of the principal artisans of this transformation: "For Valéry Giscard d'Estaing, it was a political choice that reflected a trend in public opinion. In this period, with the Common Market coming into its own, French companies found that they were not doing too badly in international competition. A new generation of executives arrived on the scene, executives with confidence in their own abilities. They were not altogether wrong; and the idea that management was a panacea spread among the young Turks, who learned it from their American counterparts or from colleagues who had been to Harvard Business School. They did not yet know that modern management requires a central agency, a system for producing an overall picture of the industrial environment, something rather similar to the French planning apparatus. This central agency took a different form in the United States than in France, however; in the United States it was less visible, less centralized, so that one had to know what logically necessary functions it performed in order to perceive it" (*ibid.*, p. 92).
100. Particularly in the 1950s in the following firms: SNCF, Renault, Air-France, Alsthom, Télémécanique, Electromécanique, SNECMA, Dunlop, and Esso Standard. See F. Jacquin, *Les cadres de l'industrie et du commerce en France* (Paris: Armand Colin, 1955), pp. 26–8.
101. See J. Tronson, *Le développement de la carrière des cadres dans la grande entreprise* (Paris: Librairie générale de droit et de jurisprudence, 1969), pp. 2–10.
102. "The system of sanctions," writes Octave Gélinier, "should help to bring rational order into business by ensuring that the fate of the efficient worker is different from that of the inefficient worker. Rewarding efficiency plays a major role in encouraging good management, in motivating men to manage themselves. While the principle is clear, its application is difficult. Indeed, if sanctions (positive and negative) are set in an arbitrary way, at the pleasure of management, they will fail of their intended purpose and destroy confidence and motivation. What is needed, therefore, is a *non-arbitrary* system of sanctions, determined by pre-established rules, rules worked out, if possible, with the help of those who will be subject to them." O. Gélinier, *Le secret des structures compétitives* (Paris: Hommes et techniques, 1966), pp. 222–3.
103. Organizational consultants' faith in the usefulness of career planning to enforce conformity was confirmed by American sociology, which provided statistical evidence that the most highly "professionalized" and "career-oriented" agents were also the best "integrated." Cf. for example H. L. Wilenski, "Orderly Careers and Social Participation: The Impact of Work History on Social Integration in the Middle Class," *American Sociological Review* 26(1961):521–39, which concludes that the "discriminating" power of the "traditional indicators of social class" has declined. This optimism would have been tempered had sociologists taken the trouble to compare in greater detail the social attributes of agents exhibiting stable career patterns with

the attributes of agents exhibiting erratic or declining patterns.

104. Personality tests are supposed to measure the subject's capacity for psychological investment. With them a firm is supposed to be able to predict the degree of a cadre's investment in the firm. In one career guide for young cadres we read the following: "In our society each of us performs many different functions. We must invest a greater or lesser part of ourselves in our professional lives as opposed to our private lives. Some jobs are perfectly compatible with varying levels of investment, provided the range of variation is not too large. Others can only be filled by individuals who are not only motivated but truly driven, even beyond their conscious awareness. The job in question is demanding enough that it can be offered only to a man who is perfectly adapted to its requirements." *Activités carrières, guide pratique de l'emploi* (Paris: Société d'études et de diffusion d'éditions techniques, n.d.), p. 118.
105. Tronson, *Le développement de la carrière des cadres*, p. 18.
106. See C. Lapierre, *L'évaluation des emplois* (Paris: Editions d'organization, 1959).
107. "Career rationalization" was widely used with cadres in the 1960s, but only in large firms. A poll carried out in 1964 by the National Association of Personnel Managers in 250 firms showed that 45% of the firms employing more than 500 persons rated engineers and cadres in some way, compared with only 14% of firms employing fewer than 500 persons: *Direction du personnel* 84, Oct. 1964. This was confirmed by a 1971 CEREQ study of firms employing more than 1,000 persons: *Note d'information* no. 9, 25 July 1972, cited and commented on by G. Genguigui and D. Montjardet, "La qualification du travail des cadres," *Sociologie du travail* 15(2)1973:176–88. Sixty-five percent of the firms analyzed employees' work and applied the results to 45% of their cadres (and to 76.5% of their workers), and the larger the firm, the more commonly such rating systems were used.
108. Starting in the 1950s higher-level cadres in major firms also received important bonuses and other perquisites. Accordingly, Jean Marchal and Jacques Lecaillon maintain that "higher-level cadres, though theoretically salaried employees, are increasingly like entrepreneurs. The various perquisites they receive are not so much a form of dependence as a sign of a change in the form of their remuneration, away from salary in the traditional sense and toward something rather like profit-sharing." See J. Marchal and J. Lecaillon, *La répartition du revenu national*, vol. 1: *Les salariés* (Paris: Editions Génin, 1958), p. 238.
109. See for example D. Vailland, "La hiérarchie s'affaisse progressivement depuis 1945," *Le Creuset*, November 1947.
110. See for example *Echo de l'USIC* 2, May 1947, p. 118.
111. Cf. Jacquin, *Les cadres de l'industrie*, p. 103.
112. For example, in the metals industry in the Paris region, the salary of a chief engineer was eight times that of a manual laborer in 1951, compared with six times in 1945 (see *ibid.*, p. 117)

113. Cf. M. Penouil, *Les cadres et leur revenu* (Paris: Editions Génin, 1956), pp. 213–14.
114. J. Lecaillon, "Tous les cadres ne sont pas victimes de l'écrasement de la hiérarchie," *Perspectives socialistes*, December 1957, and Marchal and Lecaillon, *La répartition*, pp. 427–8. Widening of the skill gap continued in the 1960s. For example, Carré, Dubois, and Malinvaud, *op. cit.*, p. 530, show that "since 1949 the monthly salary of cadres has increased more rapidly than the hourly earnings of workers: the gap between the two indices has grown by almost 25% between 1949 and the last quarter of 1967."
115. Marchal and Lecaillon, *La répartition*, p. 254.
116. See P. Durand, "Les équivoques de la redistribution du revenu par la Sécurité sociale," *Droit social* 16(5)1953:292–8.
117. For a detailed analysis of government expenditures and capital budgets in France, see C. André and R. Delorme, "L'évolution des dépenses publiques en longue période et le rôle de l'Etat en France," Paris, CEPREMAP, 1980, mimeographed.
118. See P. Bourdieu and A. Darbel, *L'amour de l'art, les musées et leur public* (Paris: Editions de Minuit, 1969).
119. See Luc Boltanski, "Les usages sociaux du corps," *Annales*, Jan.–Feb. 1971, no. 1, pp. 205–33.
120. Cf. Luc Boltanksi, "L'encombrement et la maîtrise des 'biens sans maître,'" *Actes de la recherche en sciences sociales* 2(1)1976:102–9.
121. Including, to some extent, guarantees against unemployment, especially with the founding in 1954 of the Association pour l'emploi des cadres (APEC), officially charged by the Ministry of Labor with finding jobs for and retraining of cadres.
122. Cf. H. Bertrand, "Le régime central d'accumulation de l'après-guerre et sa crise. Enseignements d'une étude en sections productives sur la France de 1950 à 1974," *Critiques de l'économie politique* 7/8, April–Sept. 1979, pp. 114–66.
123. See P. Bourdieu, L. Boltanski, and J. C. Chamboredon, "La banque et sa clientèle, introduction à une sociologie du crédit," Paris, CSE, 1964, mimeographed.
124. The percentage of indebted households increases as a function of the age of the head of household up to the 30–39-year-old age group (51.3%), and decreases steadily thereafter. Among the non-self-employed, "middle-level cadres" (51.5%) and "upper-level cadres" (47.5%) are the most likely to owe money. See A. Babeau and D. Strauss-Kahn, "La richesse des Français (Paris: Presses Universitaires de France, 1977), pp. 93 and 142.
125. Karl Marx, *Le capital* (Paris: Editions sociales, 1950), book I, vol. 1, p. 177 [here retranslated from the French – Trans.].
126. See Bourdieu, *La distinction.*
127. A full description of trends in consumption by different social classes in the period 1950–70 can be found in Darras, *Le partage des bénéfices* (Paris: Editions de Minuit, 1966), especially part 1, chap. 3 by J. P.

Pagé on the "uses of the products of growth" and chap. 4 by P. Bourdieu on "differences and distinctions."

128. See G. Lagneau, "Cadres publicitaires et publicité pour cadres," *Sociologie du travail* 10(3)1968:303–18.
129. After the war, two factions within the USIC vied for control of the organization. On one side were Catholic engineers who joined the CGC and supported "liberalism" and efforts to defend the interests of cadres. They were led by Roger Millot. On the other side were those who joined the CFTC – in the words of one informant, a more "ardent" group, more "faithful to the Catholic ethos," because, unlike the CGC members, who fought for their own interests, the CFTC members tried to "stand up for the worst off, whose interests they placed ahead of their own and those of the wealthy." The conflict between the CFTC (which had ties to Christian Democratic elements that grew out of the Resistance) and the CGC became quite bitter in the period 1945–50, when the CFTC accused the CGC of being "employer-inspired and not independent."
130. See G. Ville, *L'entreprise dans la nation, le rôle de l'ingénieur* (Paris: Editions de l'Entreprise moderne, 1956), p. 417.
131. J. Dubois, *Les cadres dans la société de consommation* (Paris: Editions du Cerf, 1969), pp. 17–19.
132. *Ibid.*, pp. 185 and 191. See also the series of articles that Dubois published in the Jesuit review *Projet*, especially "Le cadre consommateur" in the Feb.–Mar. 1968 issue.
133. For example, François Jacquin, speaking just after the war about the difficulties he encountered in trying to estimate the number of cadres in France, observed that the 1946 census was unusable, in the first place because it did not "distinguish clearly between higher-level cadres and owners" and above all because "cadres themselves were still relatively unfamiliar with the term cadre in 1946, so that it is difficult to rely on the individual declarations on which the census figures were based" (*Les cadres de l'industrie et du commerce en France*, p. 64). In other words, many people were cadres in 1946 without knowing it: they constituted a potential pool of new cadres, either as aspirants to the title unable to win recognition of their status or as individuals holding either titles that seemed to them to be worth more than the title of "cadre," so that they had no reason to adopt a new definition of their social role.
134. Thomas Hobbes, *Leviathan*; on the collective person in Hobbes, see M. Callon and B. Latour, "Unscrewing the Big Leviathan," in K. Knorr-Cetina and A. V. Cicourel (eds.), *Advances in Social Theory and Methodology* (Boston: Routledge and Kegan Paul, 1981), pp. 277–303.
135. A paradigmatic example of administrative discourse concerning the "middle classes" and "cadres" may be found in a work published in 1961 by authors all of whom were members of the Conseil d'Etat (S. Grévisse, N. Questiaux, M. Morisot, G. Guillaume, H. Roson, M. Gentot, with a preface and afterword by Pierre Laroque): *Succès et fai-*

blesses de l'effort social français (Paris: Armand Colin, 1961). The chapter on the "middle classes and cadres" raises the ritual question of the unity, cohesiveness, and "boundaries" of the group – but exclusively in the language of legal representation: Who represents the middle classes? Who is authorized to do so? Under what conditions can they be recognized?

136. See Luc Boltanski, "L'espace positionnel. Multiplicité des positions institutionelles et habitus de classe," *Revue française de sociologie* 14(1973):3–26.

3 The field of representations

1. See R. Mouriaux, "C.G.T. 1936–1948: structures syndicales et attitudes à l'égard des cadres," paper delivered to the Creusot colloquium on "Engineers and Society," 23 Oct. 1980. See also G. Grunberg and R. Mouriaux, *L'univers politique et syndical des cadres* (Paris: Presses de la Fondation nationale des sciences politiques, 1979), p. 81, and A. Bergounioux, *Force ouvrière* (Paris: Editions du Seuil, 1975), pp. 74–5.
2. The contradiction between the "common interest (say a "class interest") and "particular interests" comes out in unions in the form of conflicts between the national union executive and locals at the grassroots level. See, for example, N. W. Chamberlain, "Determinants of Collective Bargaining Structures," in A. R. Weber (ed.), *The Structure of Collective Bargaining* (New York: The Free Press, 1961).
3. Max Weber, *Economie et société* (Paris: Plon, 1971), p. 305.
4. In 1947 (shortly before the split in the union), a CGT official presenting the proposed metals industry contract to salaried employees (office workers, technicians, and cadres) answered union organizers' concerns that some special cases and local interests had not been provided for as follows: "This is the first time that we have tried to draft a classification at the national level that attempts to deal with all cases. Yesterday, my colleague spoke on technical questions concerning the rationalization of work. We are rationalists, not only in regards to work but also in regards to the organization of the union. In other words, we have tried to rationalize occupational terminology and definitions, so that if a draftsman in Marseilles is called 'manufacturing planner level two' he is called the same thing in Bordeaux. . . . In this we believe we are following the line that has been set for us, namely, to rationalize, to reduce the number of categories to a minimum so as not to leave the door open to arbitrary interpretations by employers" (source: archives of the CGT's Metals Industry Union).
5. Pollak, "La planification."
6. There is no better expression of "technocratic neo-evolutionism" than Pierre Bauchet's *La planification française* (Paris: Editions du Seuil, 1966): "In the past, history seemed to consist of a series of unrelated and interchangeable events. It was difficult to engage in

coordinated, deliberate action at a level transcending that of the event. Individuals did not know what they were working for or, worse, what direction they should be heading in. If the Classics abandoned the progress of the world to 'blind' economic and social mechanisms, the reason is that they were unable to predict the future. Today, thanks to convergent progress in the biological, historical, and natural sciences, we believe that there is a close connection between the past and the future. Everything seems to have some necessary connection with something that came before, as far back as one can go. This order of things is irreversible. Civilizations, men, and industries pass through stages of childhood and maturity. They are situated in history, dependent on the past, awaiting and working toward a future that they control. Concretely, what this means to the French people is that a future exists, and that it will come to pass thanks to their present efforts" (p. 24).

7. An analysis of the social representation developed by "neutral research teams" in the 1960s can be found in Bourdieu and Boltanski, "La production de l'idéologie dominante."
8. J. P. Bachy, *Les cadres en France* (Paris: Armand Colin, 1971).
9. See Pierre Bourdieu, "Le champ scientifique," *Actes de la recherche en sciences sociales* 2–3(1976):88–104.
10. See Boltanski, "L'espace positionnel."
11. Cf. N. Poulantzas, *Les classes sociales dans le capitalisme d'aujourd'hui* (Paris: Editions du Seuil, 1974), p. 246.
12. Bourdieu, "Le champ scientifique."
13. Specifically, this may involve publication in reviews that straddle the divide between the academic and political worlds (such as *Temps modernes*) or publication of similar material in different forms in scholarly journals and nonscholarly journals, which, though similar in conception, differ in the degree to which practical interests are concealed behind euphemistic language.
14. "Almost as far back as I can remember, we had to grapple with realities that forced us to *differentiate* and *individualize* ourselves. For many who joined the CFTC and its leaders, the point at that time was essentially to create an alternative to the CGT." Maurice Bouladoux in a debate with Jacques Julliard in *La C.F.D.T.* (Paris: Editions du Seuil, 1971), p. 146.
15. These were the most common positions. But since the ways of differentiating one position from another have no end, these could be combined with one another in a variety of ways to form still other variants.
16. Cf. M. Thorez, "Nouvelles données sur la paupérisation," *Cahiers du communisme*, July–Aug. 1955, pp. 803–26, and C. Quin, *Classes sociales et union du peuple de France* (Paris: Editions sociales, 1976).
17. The similarities between scholarly and political names for collective persons can be seen especially well in polls. Consider, for example, the following statements: "According to the SOFRES poll, cadres

prefer Giscard" (headline in *La Vie française-l'Opinion*, 18 Apr. 1974); "the cadres are abandoning Giscard" (*Le Point*, 28 June 1976, commentary on an IFOP poll); "Politics: cadres have no confidence, except in the CGC" (*Valeurs actuelles* 31 July–6 Aug. 1978, commenting on an IFOP "lightning poll"). Examples cited in Grunberg and Mouriaux, *L'univers politique*, p. 9.

18. On the stylization process and, more generally, on applications of gestalt psychology to the study of styles, see, for example, N. Goodman, *Languages of Art* (Indianapolis: Hackett, 1976), pp. 6–40.
19. On competition between different mobilizing factors, especially "class" and "nation," see Charles Tilly (ed.), *The Formation of National States in Western Europe* (Princeton: Princeton University Press, 1975), especially the editor's introduction. Tilly systematically reviews the factors that have mobilized large groups in Europe since the Middle Ages (such as religion, language, class, occupation, previous political status, etc.). This analysis also brings out the potential mobilizing factors that were not called upon in this period (such as color, kinship, age, sex, etc.). It can be shown that the groups in which sociology is interested and which it recognizes *qua* groups have mainly been groups constituted beforehand in the realm of social practice (note, for example, the interest of sociologists in women since the development of a women's movement).
20. Nationalist-type mobilization calls upon resolute and combative "patriots," defined by residence, by "blood and soil," and denies that "class" has the decisive influence ascribed to it by the internationalist tradition. As Zeev Sternhell (*op. cit.*) suggests, it is impossible to separate the rhetoric of "masses" from that of the "nation" (and the "army"), which itself makes sense only in relation to the rhetoric of class, union, and party. The theme of the "masses" (or the "crowd") has functioned as an instrument for the demobilization of the working class. Nationalist rhetoric counters the notion of class determinism by invoking the demobilizing image of "amorphous masses." The "proletariat," say the nationalists, does not exist as such. It is nothing but an "irrational mob" that explodes in riot, a "mass" governed by its urgent everyday needs. It becomes a "nation" or "people" when it becomes aware of its true nature, that is, when it develops "national consciousness." To say that the lower orders are mere "masses" is first of all to deny that they constitute, or are capable of constituting, a "class." It is thus to take a position opposed to class-based mobilization (and hence to the union and the party, its instruments) and instead to propose the notion of national mobilization based on the army, the principal means of disciplining the "masses."
21. For a critique of the notion of natural boundaries see G. de Greef, *Structure générale des sociétés* (Brussels, 1905), vol. 3: *Théorie générale des frontières et des classes*, pp. 393–4. On objectification resulting from the drawing of boundaries, or "cartographic reification," see O. Latti-

more, *Inner Asian Frontiers of China* (Boston: Beacon Press, 1962), esp. pp. 239–40, and P. Centlivres, "Groupes ethniques: de l'hétérogénéité d'un concept aux ambiguités de la representation. L'exemple afghan," pp. 25–35, in E. Ehlers (ed.), *Beîtrage zur Kulturgeographie des islamischen Orients* (Marburg: Lahn, 1979).

22. Cf. F. Lentacker, *La frontière franco-belge, étude géographique des effets d'une frontière internationale sur la vie de relations* (Lille: CCI, 1974), p. 9. Legal discourse tends to legitimate geography, especially physical geography, in the same way that sociology at times legitimates the economy: just as substantialist sociology constructs "typologies" that it claims are based on economic reality, so do the courts pretend that geography, and geographers, can establish a basis in nature for political divisions. Specialists in border issues have been forced to distinguish which aspects of "delimitation" and "demarcation" depend on geography as a descriptive science and which on law as a performative discipline (cf. the lexicon published as an appendix to H. Dorion, *La frontière Québec-Terre Neuve*, Quebec: Presses de l'université Laval, 1963).

23. Cf. H. Tajfel, "La catégorisation sociale," pp. 272–302, in S. Moscovici (ed.), *Introduction à la psychologie sociale*, vol. 1 (Paris: Larousse, 1972), and H. Tajfel *et al.*, "Social Categorization and Intergroup Behaviour," *European Journal of Social Psychology* 1(1971):149–78. The techniques employed by the experimentalist probably work in part because they have something in common with the objective social technologies that help to make and unmake groups in the realm of social practice. The experimentalist uses the power of his science to produce similarities (and differences), either by reinforcing and stylizing pre-existing properties or, in the case of the "minimum paradigm," by forming groups through random selection and then objectifying them by assigning a name. The educational system (to mention just one example) does this constantly.

24. A. Le Bayon, *Notion et statut juridique des cadres de l'entreprise privée* (Paris: Librairie générale de droit et de jurisprudence, 1971), pp. 17–19.

25. My italics.

26. Cf. e.g. J. Metzger, "Les cadres et le changement bureaucratique," *Cahiers du communisme* 50(9)1974:31–40, and, for an example of official union rhetoric, R. Le Guen, "Les cadres ne sont pas une troisième force," *Dire*, Dec. 1969, pp. 25–8. An idea of the difficulties faced by the CGT and PC in working out their new line on cadres can be gleaned from the following lines, written in 1954: "From this point of view, they [the cadres] cannot, notwithstanding the flattering illusions of "technocracy," play a role independent of the capitalists, whose vital interests it is their responsibility to protect. . . . They [the capitalists] often call upon the services of cadres, whose technical training is much less important than their training as agents of coercion assigned to impose a ferocious labor discipline," etc. See R.

Houet and P. Lévy, "Ingénieurs et cadres dans la France actuelle," *Economie et politique* 1(8)1954:56–63.

27. R. Linhart, *Lénine, les paysans, Taylor* (Paris: Editions du Seuil, 1976), p. 47.
28. *Ibid.*, p. 69.
29. Cf. M. Lewin, 'L'Etat et les classes sociales en U.R.S.S., 1929–1933," *Actes de la recherche en sciences sociales* 1(1976):2½31.
30. M. Bouvier-Ajam and G. Mury, *Les classes sociales en France* (Paris: Editions sociales, 1963), vol. 1. Maurice Bouvier-Ajam, then secretary of the Centre d'études et de recherches marxistes, was a leading Communist champion of the "bipolarization" thesis, which countered the "social-democratic deviation" that ended with the expulsion of Roger Garaudy from the party in the early 1970s: "Some writers have felt that by referring to 'well-paid' administrative and technical workers whose services are needed by employers they could talk about a 'new middle class.' Technically, these individuals are in no sense members of the middle strata: depending on what jobs they do, they are either exploited workers or else participate in bourgeois domination." M. Bouvier-Ajam, "Les couches sociales moyennes en France au temps du capitalisme monopoliste d'Etat," *Cahiers du Centre d'études et de recherches marxistes* 12(1963). The crudeness of Bouvier-Ajam's defense of Marxist orthodoxy is probably due to the tardiness of his conversion. Before the war and under Vichy Bouvier-Ajam was, of course, one of the most ardent propagandists of corporatist doctrine. See his *La doctrine corporative, op. cit.* This was a publication of the Institut d'études corporatives et sociales, which Bouvier-Ajam served as research director from its inception in 1934. Finally, in yet another of Bouvier-Ajam's books, *Histoire du travail en France* (Paris: Librairie générale de droit et de jurisprudence, 1969), pp. 346–52, there is a retrospective interpretation of the corporatist movement that is interesting for revealing the way in which the same set of social attitudes – a mixture of populism and fascination with order – can be invested in economic and political doctrines which, at a particular historical juncture, are situated at opposite ends of the political spectrum.
31. p. 61, my italics.
32. Almost identical remarks could be made about Nicos Poulantzas's *Classes sociales dans le capitalisme d'aujourd'hui* (Paris: Editions du Seuil, 1974), especially pp. 195–200, the "critique" of "occupational categories" and "bourgeois statistics," as well as pp. 212–26, on "productive and unproductive labor," and its application to the "class determination" of "low-level sales personnel," pp. 327–32. The reification inherent in the use of formal categories emerges with particular clarity where the legalism of the Marxist tradition meets the quantifying positivism of American sociology. American Marxists have attempted to "operationalize" Poulantzas's "theoretical" definitions. Thus Erik Wright, using Poulantzas's class-determination

criteria (especially the distinction between productive and unproductive workers), finds that the American working class accounts for only 20% of the population of the United States. Cf. E. Wright, "Class Boundaries in Advanced Capitalist States," *New Left Review* 98(1976):3–41. Accordingly, George Ross has called Poulantzas's work dangerous because his "boundary-setting principles" tend to increase the size of the petite bourgeoisie and to minimize the size of the working class. See Ross, "Marxism and the New Middle Classes: French Critiques," *Theory and Society* 5(2):163–90.

33. See James Burnham, *The New Managerial Revolution* (1941), and B. Rizzi, *La bureaucuratisation du monde* (Paris, pub. by the author, 1939).
34. A number of PSU factions were at odds in the 1960s, to the point of threatening the unity of the young party at its Alfortville Congress in January 1963. The primary bone of contention was the representation of the social structure. The "B faction" (which included Rocard, Mallet, Depreux, etc. and which finally won out) made the "new working class" part of its official doctrine. The leaders of this group believed that "socialist action" should be aimed first of all at conquering the "new groups of technicians – workers in high-technology industries, young cadres, engineers, technicians, and young farmers." Cf. Michel Rocard, *Le P.S.U.* (Paris: Editions du Seuil, 1969), pp. 26–7. "This observation," Rocard adds, "is connected with analyses developed elsewhere by Serge Mallet and Pierre Belleville, especially in regard to the new working class." See also pp. 65–70 for the debate between Jacques Julliard, Jean-Marie Domenach, and Michel Rocard on "the development of the middle classes of workers."
35. Here again it is impossible to separate the "theory" from its practical applications. As Jean-Daniel Reynaud has shown, the "new working class" thesis had all the earmarks of a self-fulfilling prophecy: "It played a part in a debate involving different factions of the union movement. The idea passed from the political left to the mouths of the actors themselves. Intended to be a description of new directions in trade-union action, it sometimes determined those new directions." See Reynaud, "La nouvelle classe ouvrière, la technologie et l'histoire," *Revue française de science politique* 22(3)1972:529–43.
36. My italics.
37. P. Belleville, *Une nouvelle classe ouvrière* (Paris: Julliard, 1963), p. 21.
38. *Ibid.*, pp. 169–70.
39. *Ibid.*, pp. 188–9.
40. *Ibid.*, pp. 193–4.
41. Cf. also, in the special 1962 issue of *Temps modernes* edited by André Gorz and devoted to the "workers' struggle," P. Belleville, "Perspective d'action syndicale," *Temps modernes*, Oct. 1962, pp. 548–82, and P. Belleville, "La sidérurgie lorraine et son prolétariat," *Temps modernes*, Apr. 1962, pp. 1492–535.
42. Serge Mallet, "Aspects nouveaux de l'industrie française, la Com-

pagnie des machines Bull," *Temps modernes*, Apr. 1959, pp. 1631–55.

43. Serge Mallet, *La nouvelle classe ouvrière* (Paris: Editions du Seuil, 1963), pp. 22, 85.

44. *Ibid.*, p. 196. 'Between the petroleum engineer in charge of controlling the refinery, a man who has often risen through the ranks, and the few technicians in white coats who work under him, the relationship is one of hierarchy within the same social group. The petroleum engineer has nothing in common with the old operating engineer (e.g., a pit manager for a coal company), who commanded an army of anonymous, semiskilled workers from whom he was separated by a class barrier' (*ibid.*, p. 85). Or again, in discussing the research department in a high-technology firm, Mallet has this to say: 'To make another simple comparison, the relations between the engineer and the small number of workers and technicians who work under him are like the relations between an airplane pilot and his crew. They have nothing in common with the classical relationship between the engineer-manager and the undifferentiated working masses, which rather resembles the relationship between the commander of an infantry battalion and his troops. The high level of technical competence required of the technicians and workers makes them culturally more similar to the engineer. Within the team there is a technical hierarchy but not a social hierarchy.'

45. Certain of the themes discussed here appeared in the late 1920s, during the period of prosperity and rapid growth that preceded the Depression. Repressed during the subsequent years of depression and war, they were *reinvented* in the 1950s. The theme of the bourgeoisification of the working class, for example, is already present in de Man (*Au-delà*), as David Lockwood notes in "The New Working Class," *Archives européennes de sociologie* 1(2)1960:248–59. It was introduced in France by André Philip in *Henri de Man* (esp. pp. 48ff.), in connection with a set of ideological themes, many of which would reappear in the 1960s (especially in PSU circles).

46. Cf. Mallet, *La nouvelle classe*, p. 85. The positions of the UGIC–CGT, says Mallet 'are much more "corporatist" than the positions of the CFDT cadres associated with the industrial federations. Its program includes campaigns against the "flattening of the salary hierarchy," against "raising the income tax rate," etc., and in this regard differs little from the program of the Confédération générale des cadres. In fact, recruitment of engineers and cadres draws on a very "new middle class" base, in keeping with "the action of the antimonopolistic forces." . . . In reality, the PCF, by keeping cadres "outside" the working class, merely confirms that it has in no way changed its fundamental point of view: namely, that it is inviting cadres to "support working-class positions" in the same way that it invites petits bourgeois, small merchants, and small industrialists. Its organizing strategy seeks more to flatter the cadres' sense of belonging to the bourgeoisie than to encourage those elements whose objective situ-

ation in the relations of production makes them a part of the modern working class.'

47. Cf. F. Bon and M. A. Burnier, *Les nouveaux intellectuels* (Paris: Cujas, 1966), especially the post-May '68 edition (Paris: Editions du Seuil, 1971) and, by the same authors, *Classe ouvrière et révolution* (Paris: Editions du Seuil, 1971).
48. Alain Touraine, *Le mouvement de mai ou le communisme utopique* (Paris: Editions du Seuil, 1968), esp. pp. 155–93.
49. Roger Garaudy, *Le grand tournant du socialisme* (Paris: Gallimard, 1969).
50. Julien Cheverny, *Les cadres, essai sur les nouveaux prolétaires* (Paris: Julliard, 1967). Julien Cheverny is the pseudonym of Alain Gourdon, a counselor at the Cour des comptes and lecturer at the Ecole des Sciences Politiques.
51. As in every instance of a successful ideology, the *corpus* is by definition almost limitless, since each agent (from the journalist to the student at Sciences-Po) who has internalized the "new working class" themes can reproduce a discourse that, however original, still conforms to the initial matrix. One could multiply citations indefinitely. My decision here to cite only certain canonical texts is intended simply to recall what was original in the idea of the new working class, whose popularity and widespread diffusion tend to obscure the difficulties that had to be overcome in the process of ideological invention that created it.
52. On the evolution of the "intellectual field" in the 1960s, see P. Bourdieu and J.-C. Passeron, "Sociology and Philosophy in France Since 1945," *Social Research* 34(1)1967:162–212, and J.-C. Passeron, "Changement et permanence dans le monde intellectuel," Paris, Centre de sociologie européenne, mimeographed, 1965.
53. A former technician, of Jewish descent and petit-bourgeois background, this "left-wing" cadre spent his entire career in the research department of a large electronics firm. An autodidact, with personal contacts in and aspirations toward the intellectual sphere, he embarked on a course of study at CNAM and then obtained a management position which he still occupies today. A revolutionary activist in his youth, he joined the Club Jean Moulin in 1965–7 and today belongs to the Socialist Party, having spent time along the way in the UGS (from which the PSU emerged) and in Jean-Paul Sartre's RDR.
54. Michel Crozier, "The Cultural Revolution: Notes on the Changes in the Intellectual Climate of France," *Daedalus*, winter 1964, pp. 514–42: "Optimism prevails in the economic and social spheres ... the French people in general seem to have regained confidence in a society and a world which, though imperfect, no longer seem impossible to improve. In this society, affluent and more confident in the future, intellectual life seems to have lost its fervor as well as its distinction." Changes in the mood of the "sociological community" are also evident in a note that François Isambert and Edgar Morin

published after the Colloque de la Société française de sociologie in October 1965. Isambert notes fascination with the American model, and Morin observes changes in the style (including the clothing style) of the "researchers": "The commentator on the first day, our friend [Henri] Mendras, spoke with the bow-tie of the American professor, in a phlegmatic Yankee drawl without gestures and a slight Harvard accent. He did not hand out the ritual compliments, did not cite everyone in the audience, and tried to pinpoint the significance of the problem. The Olympian who dominated this inaugural day was the Grand Master of National Planning. Our most dynamic sociologists dreamed of capturing his heart and mind." See F. A. Isambert and E. Morin, "Réflexions sur un colloque," *Revue française de sociologie* 7(1966):77-83. Finally, the effects of the intellectuals' discovery of money in the 1960s after years of comparative postwar poverty as well as their acquisition of hitherto forbidden goods and pleasures and their fascination with luxury and the monied bourgeoisie are scrutinized with remarkable lucidity by Georges Perec in his novel *Les choses* (Paris: Julliard, 1965).

55. The explanation in terms of individual interests becomes more convincing as one moves from the worst-off employees, those who had nothing to lose and everything to gain (or so they say) and hence could afford to join in collective action intended to bring about some change, to the better-off bourgeois employees, to whom at least the subjective possibility of altering their own fate through individual action remained open.
56. The first college comprised blue-collar workers and clerical personnel, the second college foremen and technicians as well as engineers and cadres if their total number was less than 25; the third college was reserved for engineers and cadres in larger firms.
57. In addition to interviews with union officials and a search of the union press and convention documents, I used the following sources: Grunberg and Mouriaux, *op. cit.*.; "Le syndicalisme en France," *Le Monde: Dossiers et documents* 39, Mar. 1977; G. Le Corre, "Cadres, les autres syndicats," *Usine nouvelle* 2, Jan. 1978; P. Meunier, *art. cit.*; Centre national des jeunes cadres (CNJC), *Les jeunes cadres et l'entreprise* (Paris: CNJC, 1974); *Les jeunes cadres et le syndicalisme* (Paris: CNJC, 1977); A. Andrieux and J. Lignon, *Le militant syndicaliste d'aujourd'hui* (Paris: Denoël-Gonthier, 1973); Confédération générale des cadres (CGC), *L'engagement syndical du personnel d'encadrement.* Special Report to the Twenty-third National Congress, Paris, undated; CGC, *André Malterre, op. cit.* And for the CFDT I used *Qui sont les cadres C.F.D.T.?*, a brochure published in 1977 by the UCC–CFDT.
58. These various attributes are obviously not independent. Thus, for example, the percentage of autodidacts among cadres decreases as one moves (1) from smaller firms to larger ones and from the consumer goods sector to the capital goods sector; (2) from the lower to the upper echelons; (3) from commercial functions to technical func-

tions, etc. Broadly speaking, the cadres with the most education are also those with the highest incomes and the most powerful positions. See chap. 5 below.

59. The study carried out in 1974 by Gérard Grunberg and René Mouriaux (*op. cit.*) showed, for example, that the percentage of cadres in favor of allowing different grades of workers into their unions was highest among R & D cadres (41%, versus 21% for manufacturing cadres), in the public and nationalized sectors (41%, versus 26% in the private sector), and in large firms (40% of cadres in firms with more than 2,000 workers, versus less than 30% in firms with fewer than 1,000 workers). In the sample analyzed by Grunberg and Mouriaux, 41% of cadres in the public and nationalized sectors (excluding civil servants) were unionized, compared with only 23% of cadres in the private sector. Furthermore, only 21% of cadres under age 34 were unionized, compared with 35% of those over 50 (pp. 93–102).
60. The larger the firm, the greater the influence of the unions, as is shown by the vote tallies in works' council elections. In firms employing 50–99 workers, non-union members received 60.8% of the votes in the second college, compared with only 2.2% in firms employing 1,000 or more workers. But the gap between the CGT and CGC was wider in small firms (7.6% and 11.7% respectively in firms employing 50–99 workers) than in large firms (25.7% and 26.1% in firms with more than 1,000 employees). See "Les élections aux comités d'entreprise en 1972," *Revue française des affaires sociales* 28(1)1974:213–34.
61. According to Paul Meunier, *art. cit.*, the tendency of lower-level supervisors to join the CGC increased after the events of May–June 1968, when this "personnel category" came to see the CGC as a means of defending its authority *vis-à-vis* the workers and workers' unions.
62. Confédération générale des cadres, *L'engagement*, pp. 7 and 8.
63. Clearly, under these conditions the upper echelons of cadres (and, through them, the employers) could no longer maintain control over the CGC merely by allowing individual interests to take their course, as in the days when cadres were fighting to defend their interests against a "left-wing" government (in 1945); an explicit policy was necessary. The CGC was always interested in maintaining and even expanding its influence among top-level cadres (to which end it entered into negotiations with the Centre national des jeunes cadres, most of whose members were graduates of the Grandes Ecoles). In some firms management attempted to influence relatively high-level cadres to join the CGC, primarily in order to counter moves by other unions.
64. "The cadre whose mission we are together going to consider is a man who usually has a command, generally takes the initiative, and always shoulders responsibility and who, moreover, is recognized as a leader by others, that is, as a man to whom people turn when it is

necessary to act. The cadre does intellectual work and does not change clothes when he leaves his office. Just a few years ago the company required him to be earnest, punctual, skilled, and loyal. Today it requires all that and more: the ability to adapt to new technologies, a heightened sense of responsibility, and above all a clear perception of his duties to his subordinates" (*Positions et propositions de la C.G.C.*, 1971).

65. These battles could be very fierce indeed, at least verbally, as is indicated by the following excerpt from an official CGC publication in regard to the Nasse affair: "This opposition, a small minority ... began using the classical methods of internal deviationism.... The technique was to create an internal faction in the guise of a study or discussion group" (p. 57). "These attempts at internal subversion ..." (p. 52). "Obstruction by a few trouble-makers" (p. 53). Maintain "unity by keeping 'polemics' from 'becoming known outside'" (p. 60). And so forth. See C.G.C., *André Malterre.*
66. The UCT never managed to establish itself sufficiently to compete with the other unions; the audience to which it addressed itself either had no interest in joining a union or had already been captured by the UGICT–CGT or the UCC–CFDT. The UCT therefore tried to rejoin the CGC and become its "advanced" wing.
67. The 1966 law established a new form of corporation administered and controlled by a "directorate," which exercised the powers normally exercised by both the board of directors and the chief executive officer under the control of a "board of overseers." The chief innovation was that nonstockholders could serve as members of the directorate: in practice these were mainly management cadres reporting to the firm's top management, and the directorate merely gave official status to the customary practice of a staff of vice-presidents reporting to the CEO [to put it into American terminology – Trans.]. As Alain Le Bayon, *op. cit.*, pp. 94–137, points out, the new law was inspired by the German *Vorstand* and introduced "the idea of technocratic management of corporations into French law" (p. 108). The aim of the new law, according to Le Bayon, was to "give legal recognition to the long-established *de facto* separation of ownership and management," partly under the influence of Bloch-Lainé's book, *Pour une réforme de l'entreprise.*
68. CGC spokesmen criticized "factional interests" in the UCT for succumbing to "the influence of certain technocratic ideas current in the civil and para-civil service" (p. 47) and for being manipulated by a coalition ranging from left-wing Gaullists to progressive employers and including elements of the PSU and graduates of the Ecole Nationale d'Administration. They also charged that the UCT favored "industrial reform" of the sort proposed by Bloch-Lainé and envisioned "a division of supervisory personnel into two groups: the rulers and the ruled" (p. 50). See CGC, *André Malterre.*
69. According to a study by the Centre national des jeunes cadres, the

position of the CGT was fairly strong among graduates of the type of technical school known as IUTs, or Instituts universitaires de technologie.

70. Cf. Andrieux and Lignon, *op. cit.*, pp. 172–82.
71. On the program of the UGICT, see, for example, A. Jaeglé, "Quel syndicalisme pour les cadres," *Options* 102, Dec. 1975, p. 31, and S. Monegare, "Remarques sur le rôle technique et social des ingénieurs," *Economie et politique*, Jan. 1969. Quite familiar today, this program was set forth in a series of brochures, reports, and other documents. On the PC's willingness to accept cadres after May 1968, see "Appel du parti communiste français aux ingénieurs, cadres techniciens," *Humanité*, 30 June 1969, and the articles by Joë Metzger, especially in *France nouvelle*, such as "Ingénieurs, cadres techniciens, trois évidences," *France nouvelle*, 2 Dec. 1968.
72. To use an expression coined by Marc Maurice, *La production de la hiérarchie dans l'entreprise*, CORDES, 1977.
73. The percentages given here are taken from a CFDT brochure giving the results of three studies conducted by the UCC–CFDT. One, involving 648 union activists, was carried out in 1977. Another, dating from 1976, looked at cadres employed by EDF–GDF. The third examined 346 cadres belonging to the union representing cadres in the chemical industry (Fédération unie de la chimie CFDT). I have used mainly figures from the first study. Obviously these are useful only as a rough index.
74. For example, a study carried out by the Association pour l'emploi des cadres in 1975 (based on the definition of cadres used by the cadres' retirement funds) showed that 7% of cadres are employed in research and development. These are mainly young cadres with advanced degrees (many jobs in R&D are entry level positions).
75. Andrieux and Lignon, *op. cit.*, pp. 204 and 224–8.
76. On the distinction between social art and social science, cf. Marcel Mauss: after stating that "sociology is closer than any other science to its corresponding practical art, politics," Mauss defines sociology as a "science of the social art." "This science is just beginning to establish itself: it simply involves using data, some of them already known, to determine how and by what political processes men act or believe they act upon one another, how they divide themselves into different groups, and how they react to other societies or to the natural environment." Marcel Mauss, "Divisions et proportions des divisions de la sociologie," *Œuvres* (Paris: Editions de Minuit, 1969), vol. 3, pp. 233–7.
77. For example, the CGC, which uses the broadest possible definition of the group (all those who exercise "responsibilities" in a firm are cadres) and in practice relies on the broad criterion of eligibility for membership in a cadres' retirement fund, has challenged both the INSEE definition and the definition used in the SOFRES–*Expansion* poll, the former for establishing an arbitrary division between *cadres*

moyens and *cadres supérieurs* and the latter for being too "Parisian, elitist, and selective."

78. On these different nomenclatures, the best source is probably the *Bible des statistiques sur l'emploi*, vol. 1: *Définitions et nomenclatures*, unpublished APEC document, 1977.
79. According to a poll conducted in the Nantes region, only 46% of those considered cadres according to the one-digit INSEE occupational classifications (a group that includes civil servants and teachers) contribute to a cadres' retirement fund. Conversely, 59% of those who do contribute are classified cadres by the INSEE. Cf. C. Thelot, "Les fils de cadres qui deviennent ouvriers," *Revue française de sociologie* 20 (1979): 409–30.
80. Other definitions of the cadre population are in current use, but none, to my knowledge, has been used as the basis of a statistical study. For example, the ROME system (ROME is an acronym for répertoire opérationnel des métiers et des emplois) is used by the ANPE. Cadres are grouped either under various functions or under the heading "*cadres intersecteurs*."

4 The university and business

1. Cf. A. Desrosières, J. Mairesse, and M. Volle, "Les temps forts de l'histoire de la statistique française," *Economie et statistique* 83(1976):19–28.
2. Boyer, "Les salaires."
3. Cf. Darras, *op. cit.* This work is interesting in that it contains not only a statistical overview of French society in the early 1960s but also a critical analysis of the then current interpretation of various statistical indicators (e.g., an analysis of the growth of consumption as a reflection of certain class differences, of cultural capital as a factor in reproduction, in which respect it differs from "human capital," and a critique of naïve formalist interpretations of the Cobb-Douglas function).
4. Cf. L. Thévenot, "Les catégories sociales en 1975: l'extension du salariat," *Economie et statistique* 91(1977):3–31. During the same period, the category of *cadres moyens administratifs*, until recently a group consisting mainly of people without college degrees, only doubled in size from 434,353 in 1954 to 970,180 in 1975. But this distinction, which is relatively clear-cut and quasi-institutionalized in the public sector, is quite ambiguous in the private sector (where the custom is to distinguish between *cadres* without further specification and *cadres de direction*, i.e., management). As we know, moreover, there is more than one definition of cadre, each definition reflecting the interests of different subgroups. Some definitions are broader than others, and this affects estimates of the growth rate as well as the size of the group.
5. *Code des catégories socio-professionnelles*, INSEE, 5th edition, 1969, p. 25.

Cf. also M. Cézard, "Un million de cadres supérieurs dénombrés au recensement de 1968," *Economie et statistique* 40(1972):51–4. Another index of "native practice": the periodic *Expansion* survey of cadres' salaries is based on a sample of applicants to major employment agencies; college graduates are automatically included in this sample, regardless of their salary or job, but non-graduates are included only if they have held "senior" positions and their most recent salary was in excess of a certain threshold, set in 1978 at about 120,000 francs.

6. The "neoliberal" ideologies that flourished in the late 1970s were first formulated in rough outline in the mid-1960s, as opponents of planning, Keynesianism, and democracy celebrated the "rebirth" of capitalism. P. de Calan's *Renaissance des libertés économiques et sociales* (Paris: Centre d'études politiques et civiques, 1964), which gives the traditional businessman's response to François Bloch-Lainé's proposals for "industrial reform," marks a milestone in this regard.
7. Cf. for example the report of the Commission on the Obstacles to Economic Expansion chaired by Jacques Rueff and Louis Armand (Paris: Imprimerie nationale, 1960). The commission included economists (like Pierre Massé and Alfred Sauvy), big businessmen (like Marcel Demonque), and top civil servants. "The present system is wasting the intellectual potential of our young people.... Such an effort to improve teaching, education, and culture would create a climate likely to make workers more aware of economic problems and would encourage upward mobility. This is an economic necessity, for it can help to meet the country's urgent need for more skilled workers, cadres, and professionals" (pp. 34–5).
8. In 1956 the UIMM, citing "the country's pressing need for scientific and technical cadres at various levels," surveyed firms in the metals industry to determine both "the current situation" and "immediate, short-term, medium-term, and long-term needs." The 1956 study focused on 500 firms and some 1,300 plants. Similar studies were carried out in 1962, 1970, and 1975.
9. Cf. for example P. Grimanelli, "Les obstacles humains à une expansion économique rapide," *Cahiers du C.R.C.*, 7(1962):5–38, and H. Desbruères (CEO of SNECMA) and A. Landucci (CEO of Kodak), "Les problèmes de la formation," *Cahiers du C.R.C.* 6(1961):5–34.
10. E. F. Denison, "La mesure de la contribution de l'enseignement et du facteur résiduel à la croissance économique," pp. 13–59, in Groupe d'étude sur les aspects économiques de l'enseignement, *Le facteur résiduel et le progrès économique* (Paris: Organization for Economic Cooperation and Development, 1964).
11. For example, a commission of industrialists, top civil servants, and teachers formed in 1961 with André Boulloche as chairman stated in its 1963 report to the prime minister that "all the information we have received confirms that there is a serious shortage of technicians that is hurting the French economy" and, further, that it favored a

"decrease in both the percentage and the absolute number of cadres who have received no formal training." See *Les conditions de développement, de fonctionnement et de localisation des grandes écoles en France* (Paris: Documentation française, 1964), pp. 20–5.

12. Cf. Desbruères and Landucci, "Les problèmes de la formation." The authors, who take the development of the educational system in Russia as an example, remark that the lower classes are not sufficiently sought out. A strict selection (as in Russia) should make it possible both to recruit elites and to democratize the educational system.
13. J. Boissonnat, writing in *Esprit* in 1964, said that the French educational system contributed to inflation because it was "unable to repair the shortage of skilled labor." See "L'économie française et la stabilité," *Esprit*, January 1964, pp. 122–34.
14. Cf. L. Lévy-Garboua, "Les demandes de l'étudiant ou les contradictions de l'université de masse," *Revue française de sociologie* 17(1975):53–80.
15. This corresponds to an increase in absolute value, because the percentage of cadres and engineers in the work force in this branch of industry increased steadily, from 3.5% in 1956 to 4.1% in 1962 to 5.5% in 1970 and 5.8% in 1975. Given that this study is based on a fairly narrow definition of cadres (that used in collective bargaining, which is narrower than the criteria used by, say, the retirement funds) and, further, that companies employing fewer than 100 workers, which employ many more autodidacts than the larger firms, are excluded, and, finally, that the study focused primarily on highly concentrated industries using advanced technology, such as the aviation industry (where 14.4% of all employees are supervisory personnel compared with only 3.1% in the steel industry, and cadres tend to be better educated than in more traditional sectors), it is reasonable to assume that the conclusions stated in the text are valid *a fortiori* for industry as a whole.
16. Between 1965 and 1975 many studies of the careers of recent graduates were carried out (most concentrating on a single university, discipline, or region). A list of such studies, and a description of each, may be found in G. Balazs *et al.*, "Bilan des travaux sur les jeunes et l'emploi," mimeographed, Paris: Centre d'études de l'emploi, 1977. The arguments developed here are based mainly on the results of three of the most comprehensive of these studies, detailed results of which may be found in APEC, *L'insertion des jeunes diplômés de l'enseignement supérieur dans la vie active* (Paris: APEC, 1975); P. Vrain, *Les débouchés professionels des étudiants* (Paris: PUF, 1975), cahiers du Centre d'études de l'emploi; A. Charlot *et al.*, *Les universités et le marché du travail* (Paris: Documentation française, 1977), CEREQ dossier no. 14.
17. Differences in activity rates seem to relate to the properties of the different studies (time between graduation and date of study, variations

in the number of students who went on to further studies, etc.).

18. Cf. for example F. Quilici, "La deuxième femme du cadre," *Vie des cadres* 4, Oct.–Nov. 1972. See also the testimony gathered by the CFDT, "La solitude particulière des secrétaires de direction," *Cadres C.F.D.T.* 282(1978):26–8.
19. There is a deeply internalized homology between the male/female opposition and the opposition of the cardinal points of social space: in the first place between the dominant and the lower classes, socially defined as "masculine" and attached to masculine values, and in the second place between two poles of the dominant class, one associated with business and economic power, in which masculine values are dominant, and the other associated with the intellect, with power over intellectual capital, which is socially defined as feminine.
20. For a critique of the market see O. W. Phelps, "A Structural Model of the US Labor Market," *Industrial and Labor Relations Reviews* 1(3)1957:402–23, and, more recently, the works of Michael Piore on segmentation of the job market, especially "Notes on a Theory of Labor Market Stratification," in R. C. Edwards *et al.* (eds.), *Labor Market Segmentation* (Lexington: Lexington Books, 1975).
21. Cf. P. Bourdieu, L. Boltanski, P. Maldidier, "La défense du corps," *Information sur les sciences sociales* 10(4)1971:45–86.
22. Cf. A. Desrosières and L. Thévenot, "Les mots et les chiffres: les nomenclatures socio-professionnelles," *Economie et statistique* 110(1979):49–75.
23. Bourdieu and Boltanski, "Le titre et le poste."
24. Cf. M. de Saint Martin, *Les fonctions sociales de l'enseignement scientifique* (Paris: Mouton, 1971), pp. 121–37.
25. The nomenclature used included 98 "positions" grouped under 19 major "functions": production, maintenance, marketing, advertising, personnel management, training, finance, administration, sales, technical sales, development, information processing, general management, and so forth. Each major function is associated with a number of positions of different hierarchical rank (for example, marketing director, group leader, product manager, assistant product manager, etc.) and different technical specialization. Professional diversity would be even clearer if the nomenclature allowed for intersectoral differences, which require different skills at least of personnel employed in production and development.
26. Cf. for example D. Porot, *Comment trouver une situation* (Paris: Editions d'organisation, 1976).
27. Weber, *Economie et société*, p. 225.
28. According to one career guide, this is how a young cadre should behave on his first job: "By using your powers of observation you will learn to understand the rules and customs of company life, which your coworkers have become accustomed to abiding by. No doubt you will have to unlearn certain habits that you acquired at school (camaraderie, a sharply critical attitude, flexible hours, etc.). By

being patient, carrying out assigned tasks, and listening to the good suggestions and advice that you will certainly receive, you will demonstrate your capacity to adapt." *Activités carrières*, *op. cit.*, p. 120.

29. The question was as follows: "Supposing that you had to accept a job in one of the following firms, which would you choose, assuming that all offered an attractive package of pay and benefits?" The firms listed were Crédit Lyonnais, EDF, IBM, Nestlé, Peugeot, the PTT, La Redoute, Shell, and the SNCF.
30. Cf. "Les cabinets de conseils en recrutement des cadres," *Hommes et techniques* 325(1971):841–76; SYNTEC, *Commission conseil en recrutement et gestion des ressources humaines: situation de la profession en France* (Paris: August 1975); APEC, *Développement, procédures et méthodes des cabinets conseils en recrutement* (Paris, 1976); J. Barry, "Les intermédiaires privés dans le domaine du recrutement," working document for preparation of the Seventh Plan, Employment Subcommittee of the Committee for Employment and Labor, Paris, February 1976.
31. Cf. J. Zurfluh, *op. cit.*, pp. 17–22. Another index of the importance of employment agencies is the recent emergence of job counselors offering advice to candidates. These counseling agencies, usually set up by the employment agencies themselves, sell to job-seeking cadres the skills necessary to meet the criteria established by the employment agencies. Appliclants pay about 2,000 francs to attend a "seminar" where they are taught, among other things, how to write a resumé.
32. There are at present twelve "headhunter" agencies operating in Paris, responsible for about 500 executive hirings annually. The headhunters, who came to France after the employment agencies, have rationalized traditional methods of selection through contacts and peer-group networks. Instead of consulting just friends and family, the headhunters systematically search the entire pool of potential applicants, which consists of approximately 15,000 cadres. Since the use of data banks for employment searches is illegal in France, headhunters resort to a technique known as "sourcing," which involves stationing in each branch of industry an agent who supplies the necessary information: "Nobody can stop us from having good memories and good contacts." They also use directories of graduates of the Grandes Ecoles and of members of the Rotary and Lion's Club. Last but not least, they assiduously attend receptions given by the Jockey Club, the Automobile Club de France, the Cercle interallié, and the American Chamber of Commerce.
33. Charlot *et al.*, *Les universités et la marché du travail*, p. 492, and Vrain, *Les dé bouchérs professionels des étudiants*, p. 115.
34. Cf. M. Cézard, "Les cadres et leurs diplômes," *Economie et statistique* 42(1973):25–40.
35. Among many examples see *Le plan Sauvy* (Paris: Calmann-Lévy, 1960), esp. pp. 118–20.
36. Cf. Bourdieu, Boltanski, and Maldidier, "La défense", *Information sur*

les sciences sociales.

37. Cf. M. C. Henry-Meininger, "La promotion interne dans l'administration française," *Annuaire international de la fonction publique 1975–76*," published by the Institut international d'administration publique, pp. 13–66.
38. Cf. C. Lalumière, "Les concours internes," *Revue du droit public et de la science politique*, May–June 1968, pp. 481–2.
39. Cf. P. Sadran, "Recrutement et sélection par concours dans l'administration française," *Revue française d'administration publique* 1(1977):53–107.
40. See Information Bulletin no. 78–03 published on 20 Jan. 1978 by the Service des échanges informatiques et statistiques of the Ministry of National Education.
41. Cf. J.-L. Bodiguel, "Sociologie des élèves de l'ENA," *Revue internationale des sciences administratives* 40(3)1974:230–44.
42. Bourdieu and de Saint Martin, *art. cit.*
43. The results of certain salary surveys, including the periodic CEGOS survey, are made known only to those who commissioned the study, generally large firms.
44. Cf. *L'expansion*, June 1977.
45. Cf. C. Baudelot and A. Lebeaupin, "Les salaires de 1950 à 1975," *Economie et statistique* 113(1979):15–22.
46. Any realistic analysis of rates of return on diplomas would obviously have to take account of differences in the pay received by people with similar diplomas but of different social background (cf. Darras, *op. cit.*, p. 347), as well as bonuses and benefits which, according to one recent estimate, may amount to as much as 50% of a person's salary. Cf. *Problèmes économiques* 1649, 28 Nov. 1979.
47. *Le monde de l'éducation*, 36 Feb. 1978.
48. P. Hardoin, "Les caractéristiques sociologiques du parti socialiste," *Revue française de science politique* 28(2)1978:220–56. The proportion of senior cadres among Socialist Party deputies rose from 18% in 1971 to 21% in 1973 (although senior cadres accounted for only 13% of socialist candidates in the 1973 elections). But most of these are senior cadres from the public sector. Cf. P. Bacot, *Les dirigeants du parti socialiste* (Lyon: Presses universitaires de Lyon, 1979), pp. 217–24.
49. Cf. D. Boy, "Origine sociale et comportement politique," *Revue française de sociologie* 19(1978):73–102.
50. Cf. G. Grunberg and E. Schewisguth, "Profession et vote: la poussée de la gauche," pp. 139–68, in J. Capdevielle *et al.*, *France de gauche, vote à droite* (Paris: Presses de la fondation nationale des sciences politiques, 1981).
51. Grunberg and Mouriaux, *op. cit.*
52. Bourdieu, *La distinction*, pp. 428–31.
53. COFREMCA, "Etude sur les jeunes cadres," Paris, 1978, mimeographed.
54. The differences analyzed here also appear, though in a different form,

in sectors where private and public interests are most intertwined. A senior cadre employed by a state-owned bank, a graduate of Sciences Po, contrasts the "spirit of public service" that one finds in the public sector with the "profit-seeking" of the private sector in the following terms: 'It was an unspoken rule here that the word "bank" was never mentioned, because we were not a bank. Contrary to what everyone thinks, money doesn't interest us. We are not a bank but a provider of service. We serve agriculture, local communities, everybody. That's the bank spirit, whereas the fellow who comes from advertising or marketing, from the private sector, is not looked upon with favor and his behavior is not approved. He's a soap peddler, disgusting. To win approval here you've got to be more or less humanistic, idealistic. So going to P . . . to make money, no, that's not our spirit.'

55. Cf. Grunberg and Mouriaux, *op. cit.*, p. 129.
56. Based on the Formation–Qualification–Profession survey of 1970 (unpublished figures).
57. Cf. Grunberg and Mouriaux, *op. cit.*, p. 130. See also Boy, "Origine sociale," *Revue française de sociologie*: given equivalent social backgrounds, graduate technicians employed in laboratories or corporate research departments voted "left" more often than technicians employed in manufacturing, many of whom are autodidacts who worked their way up through the ranks.
58. Cf. M. Maurice, R. Cornu, J. C. Garnier, "Les cadres en mai–juin 1968 dans la région d'Aix-Marseille," Aix-en-Provence, Laboratoire d'économie et de sociologie du travail, mimeographed, 1970. (This survey focused on a sample of 455 cadres in which cadres working for large public sector firms were greatly overrepresented. This fact explains the relatively high proportion of strikers among the cadres questioned.)
59. During and after the strikes of May–June 1968 two interview surveys (based on unscientifically selected samples) confirmed that a key role in what was sometimes called the "cadre movement" (suggesting a misleading analogy with the student movement) had been played by research engineers employed by large firms in high-technology sectors, especially nationalized firms. See A. Willener *et al.*, *Les cadres en mouvement* (Paris: Edition de l'Epi, 1969), and P. Dubois *et al.*, *Grèves revendicatives ou grèves politiques* (Paris: Anthropos, 1971).
60. Among many commentaries, cf. J. Boissonnat, "La France et son économie," *Esprit*, Feb. 1966, pp. 337–52.
61. "Faire l'université," *Esprit* 338, May–June 1964.
62. M. Drancourt, *Bilan économique de la Ve République* (Paris: Editions de l'entreprise moderne, 1961), p. 18.
63. *Le progrès scientifique* 103, Dec. 1966, p. 50.
64. "At the center of the original scene of the process, at Nanterre, an active minority of students repudiated their futures as cadres, as watchdogs of capital." A. Geismar, S. July, E. Morane, *Vers la guerre civile* (Paris: Editions et Publications premières, 1969), p. 178.

65. The question of social origins was a fundamental issue that had to be dealt with by those who attempted to mobilize students along the same lines as workers, in keeping with the revolutionary tradition. Not to recognize the influence on students of their social background was to break with the traditions of the workers' movement by denying that social class was the crucial determinant. But to see the diversity of student social backgrounds as an obstacle impossible to overcome was to refuse to see the uniqueness of the student group, and this was tantamount to abandoning all hope of student mobilization. The "sociological surveys" and "studies" carried out in 1963–5 by or under the influence of UNEF (such as the MNEF study of "student budgets") were designed to identify, by "objective" means, the unifying principles that bound students together, principles that it was assumed must derive automatically from "working conditions" or "life styles" (for example, the need to work part-time to pay for one's schooling).
66. In 1967 they would again join forces in the Mouvement d'action universitaire, which played a very active part in the student mobilization of May 1968.
67. Cf. M. Kravetz, "Naissance d'un syndicalisme étudiant," *Les temps modernes* 213(1964):1447–75. This article is the most sustained statement of the anti-technocratic ideology developed in UNEF circles in the period 1963–6. Cf. also A. Griset and M. Kravetz, "De l'Algérie à la réforme Fouchet: critique du syndicalisme étudiant," *Les temps modernes* 227(1965):1880–902 and 228(1965):2066–2090.
68. On the history of the UNEF between 1960 and 1970, cf. N. de Maupéou-Abboud, *Ouverture du ghetto étudiant* (Paris: Anthropos, 1974). Further information may be found in the introduction to A. Schnapp and P. Vidal-Naquet, *Journal de la commune étudiante* (Paris: Editions du Seuil, 1969), and, on the crisis in the UEC, the rebirth of the Trotskyite movement, and the emergence of Maoist groups, in D. Bensaïd and H. Weber, *Mai 1968: une répétition générale* (Paris: Maspero, 1968).
69. Cf., for example, the tract issued by the Mouvement d'actiion universitaire on 20 April 1967, cited in M. Perrot and M. Rebérioux, *La Sorbonne par elle-même* (Paris: Editions ouvrières, 1968), p. 20.
70. "The vast majority of university graduates . . . will be exposed to all the risks of full or partial unemployment and associated salary restrictions. After four to eight years of study, that is a powerful motive for rebellion. Not only are students aware that their future employment is insecure and unstable, they are also aware of the social function of that employment. . . . It is against the uncertainties of their professional future and against their impending role as watchdogs that large numbers of students are rising up." Bensaïd and Weber, *Mai 1968*, p. 29.
71. The interpretation of the "crisis of the universities" by UNREF spokesmen owed much to the writings of Serge Mallet and André Gorz,

the source of analyses of "neocapitalism" as an expression of the "interests of the most advanced segment of French capitalism." The contrast between the "liberal university" and the "technocratic university" was based on an analogy between "old-style capitalism" and "neocapitalism." See especially Mallet, "Gaullisme et néo-capitalisme," *Esprit*, Feb. 1960, pp. 205–28, and "Le deuxième âge du gaullisme," *Esprit*, June 1963, pp. 1041–57. The "new working class" thesis provided the theoretical underpinning needed to justify the allusions by student movement spokesmen to cadres as both victims and agents of neocapitalism.

72. Cf. Y. Delsaut, "Les opinions politiques dans le système des attitudes: les étudiants en lettres et la politique," *Revue française de sociologie* 11(1)1970:45–64. This questionnaire survey of a scientifically selected sample of 2,300 students in the faculties of letters and human sciences at various Parisian and provincial universities is one of the few empirical studies of the group among which student radicalism developed and to which it was addressed.
73. Compared with other academic disciplines in the mid-1960s, sociology attracted students of relatively high social class but relatively low scholastic level. This contrasts with both geography (low social class and low scholastic level) and classical letters (high social class and high scholastic level). Cf. Delsaut, "Les opinions."
74. Criticism of large lecture courses, for example, was almost always associated with descriptions of "crowded" lecture halls and student "anonymity." It was not so much the educational merits of lecture courses as such that led to student opposition as it was the discomfort that each student felt in the presence of so many others. Students felt "lost in the crowd," anonymous ciphers rather than members of a scholarly elite. This made attendance at large lecture courses a painful experience and revealed aspects of higher education that remained hidden so long as the universities were able to control the number and quality of their students. Cf. Bourdieu, Boltanski, and Maldidier, "La défense."
75. Cf. J. Chenevier, "La collaboration Université-Industrie," *Cahiers du C.R.C.*, 16(1970):25–55.
76. Since 1968, when the Report of the Working Group on Public Enterprises (Nora Report) was issued, a succession of French governments have implemented a variety of measures intended to apply private sector management principles to the civil service (including criteria of profitability, fiscal autonomy, limitation of employee guarantees, etc.). One effect of the May 1968 crisis was to heighten struggles over the autonomy of the public sector (with authoritarian "denationalization" measures in explicit pursuit of neoliberal aims replacing efforts to achieve an ideological compromise; another effect may have been to heighten opposition to "technocratic government," thereby delaying efforts under way in the mid-1960s to bring the public sector more into line with the private sector (including a reduction in the

number of persons employed in the civil service and nationalized industries). These efforts included the banking reform undertaken in 1966–7 by Michel Debré. Cf. J. Bouvier, *Un siècle de banque française* (Paris: Hachette, 1973), pp. 94–100.

77. Cf. Boyer, "Les salaires."
78. Of the 9,478 advertisements for cadre employment published in April, June, and September of 1977 and indicating the place of employment, 1,440 (15.3%) offered jobs in other countries, mostly in the Third World (24.5% in North Africa, 18.5% in the Middle East, 26% in Black Africa, 8% in Asia, and 8% in Latin America). The percentage of foreign jobs varied considerably with the nature of employment: 39% of the jobs for production cadres were abroad, compared with only 10% of the jobs in administration and 6% of the jobs in data processing (of which 53% and 77%, respectively, were located in Paris, whereas sales jobs were divided almost equally between Paris and the province). Based on the study by APEC, "Les offres de presse cadres et le lieu de travail," Paris, November 1977, mimeographed.
79. Maurice Clavel, "Attention! Cadres méchants," *Le nouvel observateur*, 17 Jan. 1972.
80. Cf. A. Cotta, *La France et l'impératif mondial* (Paris: Presses Universitaires de France, 1978), pp. 224–6.
81. Cf. F. Fröbel, J. Heinrichs, and O. Kreye, *The New International Division of Labour* (Cambridge–Paris: Editions de la Maison des Sciences de l'Homme/Cambridge University Press, 1980). As far as I know no similar data exist for France.
82. In any case it seems to me somewhat paradoxical to regard the territory of nations as open when it comes to the International economy but as closed when it is a question of dealing with relations between different social groups, as though the geographical reach of objective social relations (which may be different for different classes) were necessarily limited by legal boundaries.

5 Careers

1. On the ambiguity of the legal definition of a "company" and the difficulties encountered by statisticians in attempting to analyze "conglomerates," see especially B. Guibert *et al.*, *La mutation industrielle de la France*, INSEE collection, E. 31–32, vol. 1, p. 91. In a similar vein, Sylvain Wickham shows that the distinction between mere departments, which are not "moral persons" under the law but mere bookkeeping conveniences, and subsidiaries, which are independent legal persons and possess all the outward signs of independence, such as a board of directors, an executive committee, a works' council, and so forth, depends on factors other than the technical division of labor. According to Wickham, executives in large firms favor the proliferation of subsidiaries, which offers them material and intangible bene-

fits (such as titles, tax reductions, and comparative independence) normally available only to the heads of medium-sized firms. See S. Wickham, *Concentration et dimensions* (Paris: Flammarion, 1966), pp. 143–4.

2. Cf. for example A. Tiano, *Les traitements des fonctionnaires et leur détermination* (Paris: Editions Guénin, 1968), pp. 109ff. The question of parities, central to union efforts in the civil service (where certain types of workers play a "pilot" role, in that any wage increases they receive are immediately demanded by other types of workers), first arose after World War I. At that time there were 489 different salary scales in the civil service, and people in different types of jobs faced very different career prospects and were compensated at widely varying levels. But disparities between the sectors were not perceived as clearly as they are today, because the frame of reference consisted of a series of local markets, each with different hierarchies and rules of operation.
3. François Furet and Jacques Ozouf show, for example, that it proved all but impossible for the ministry of education to count the number of "teachers" in France in 1817, because without an official definition no one knew "who exactly could claim to be a teacher." See *Lire et écrire* (Paris: Editions de Minuit, 1977), pp. 118–20; English translation, Cambridge University Press, 1983. Construction of explicit social taxonomies grouping a set of well-defined categories in a hierarchy often begins with efforts to reform methods of tax collection. Cf. J. L. Perrot, "Rapports sociaux et villes au XVIIIe siècle," *Ordres et classes* (Paris: Mouton, 1973), pp. 141–66.
4. As Robert Boyer has shown, the concept of a competitive "labor market" is insufficient for interpreting the economic and social relations of labor because it takes no account of the "legislative, institutional, and social framework" that underlies the "strategies" of individual agents and groups. See Boyer, "Les transformations du rapport salarial dans la crise: une interprétation de ses aspects sociaux et économiques," *Critique de l'économie politique* 15–16(1981):185–228.
5. Cf. for example S. Spilerman, "Careers, Labor-Market Structure, and Socioeconomic Achievement," *American Journal of Sociology* 83(3)1976:551–92.
6. Cf. M. Vilette, "L'accès aux positions dominantes dans l'entreprise," *Actes de la recherche en sciences sociales* 4(1975):98–101.
7. One should be careful not to overestimate the effects of uncertainty due to complex organization and ambiguous terminology on the estimates of company size. In the APEC-sponsored study of cadre mobility, for example, some questions were concerned with "plants," others with "companies." It turns out that 77% of the cadres employed in plants with fewer than 50 workers worked for companies employing fewer than 200 workers. Similarly, 67% of cadres employed in plants with from 50 to 200 employees worked for firms

with fewer than 500 employees. And so on. Still, it seems likely that in many cases the cadres questioned were employed by small firms directly or indirectly controlled by large corporations, and in these cases there is no way of knowing whether the answers given refer to the subsidiary, the parent company, or some intermediate subsidiary. We may assume, however, that small plants are rarely the corporate headquarters of large corporations, because few of them show a high percentage of "cadres" on their payrolls. Hence self-taught cadres, who outnumber engineering school graduates in firms employing fewer than 50 workers by 50% to 23%, also outnumber them by 60% at 29% in firms with fewer than 10 cadres.

8. Cf. Bourdieu and de Saint Martin, "Le patronat."
9. Cf. J. P. Gorgé and A. Tandré, "Une étude du ministère de l'industrie sur la concentration industrielle entre 1970 et 1972," *Economie et statistique* 68(1975):39–58.
10. As Gorgé and Tandré indicate (*ibid.*), what is really going on is a concentration of productive capital; the statistical data, particularly data that focus on individual branches of industry, are not well suited to studying the concentration of finance capital. At present, the only "recognized statistical unit" is the 'firm." Gorgé and Tandré argue that "until the conglomerate in its various forms is seriously studied by economists and statisticians," it will be very difficult to get an accurate picture of the concentration of finance capital. The so-called dispersed sector actually includes the vast majority of firms: 1,350,000 small companies employing fewer than 20 workers account for 94% of all firms but for only 23% of all employed workers, and medium-sized firms (20–500 workers) account for 5% of all firms and 34% of all workers. Small- and medium-sized firms are found mainly in the service sector and the consumer goods sector. On the other hand, large firms (more than 500 workers) account for only 1% of all firms but for 43% of all employed workers; they are especially prominent in the intermediate and producers' goods sectors. Cf. R. Brocard and J. M. Gandois, "Grandes entreprises et P.M.E.," *Economie et statistique* 96(1978):25–41.
11. As François Eymard-Duvernay, "Segmentation du marché du travail: premier examen," unpublished INSEE document, Paris, 1980, remarks, "defining these spaces in terms of size is probably the best one can do with the usual statistical sources, but it would be useful to allow for firms that subcontract to or are subsidiaries of larger companies. The gap between small- and medium-sized firms and large firms is of fundamental importance. It represents not so much a difference in 'technology' as in positions in the power structure."
12. The cultural capital accumulated by a firm or branch of industry, as capital embodied in individuals and objectified in machines, is often considered in studies of industry but usually in an unsystematic fashion. For example, Christian Sautter, "L'efficacité et la rentabilité de l'industrie française de 1954 à 1975," *Economie et statistique*

68(1975):5–22, discusses "machinery that embodies a considerable amount of technological progress." Despite the scarcity of work on the relation between characteristics of firms and the attributes of their employees, the statistical literature does contain information on span of control and skill levels as a function of branch and size of firm. See D. Deberdt and E. Messeca, "L'incidence de la recherche sur les entreprises industrielles," *Economie et statistique* 95(1977):43–53; M. Gaspard, "Comment se déterminent les structures d'emploi des établissements industriels?" *Economie et statistique* 67((975):34–57; A. Azouvi, "Caractéristiques d'entreprises, structures d'emploi et de salaires," *Economie et statistique* 92(1977):17–27. Furthermore, a characteristic such as span of control does not have the same significance in medium-sized firms in traditional branches of industry, where cadres are mainly self-taught, as in large firms in advanced sectors where many cadres are graduates of prestigious schools. In each case one must allow for the existence of research departments, internal training departments, etc.

13. Cf. A. Desrosières, "Un découpage de l'industrie en trois secteurs," *Economie et statistique* 40, December 1972.
14. Pierre Rivard, Jean-Marie Saussois, and Pierre Tripier, "L'espace de qualification des cadres," Paris, Groupe de sociologie du travail université de Paris VII, 1979, mimeographed, p. 104, analyzed the relation between industrial firms and engineering schools and showed that the cadre job market is not structured by variables such as "technology" (e.g., continuous process versus short-run or long-run batch processing) or "branch of industry." Rather, they found that the key "explanatory" variables were labor intensity and above all the importance of "research" and the presence of a large research department.
15. In 1975 the UIMM carried out a study of rather limited scope, in that it was confined to a highly concentrated branch of industry, it excluded firms employing fewer than 100 workers, and it used the definition of cadres set forth by collective bargaining agreements rather than the retirement fund criterion. Nevertheless, this study shows clear differentiation according to size of firm: the percentage of cadres who were self-taught ranged from 59% in firms employing 100–250 workers to 31% in firms employing 5,000–10,000 workers (it was slightly higher in firms employing more than 10,000 workers, which were labor-intensive and employed many cadres who had come up through the ranks). The percentage of graduate engineers varies conversely, from 32% to 60%. See UIMM, *Ingénieurs et cadres* (Paris, 1977).
16. Research and development (financed largely by public funds, 30.7% coming from the defense ministry alone) is done mainly in the most concentrated zones of the capital goods sector, such as aeronautics, electronics, nuclear energy, computers, etc. (and to a lesser extent in the chemicals industry) and in the largest firms in these branches (in

1974, 20 companies accounted for 49% of all domestic expenditure on research, 100 companies accounted for 79.4%, and 603 companies for 96%). Eighty percent of the workers employed by firms doing research worked for companies with more than 2,000 workers on the payroll. In 1974 89% of public research funds went to 20 companies in the "key sectors of advanced technology." Cf. Deberdt and Messeca, "L'incidence de la recherche sur les entreprises industrielles."

17. Major corporations play a comparatively less important role in the consumer goods sector than in either the producer's goods sector or the intermediate goods sector. See R. de Vannoise, "Etude économique et financière de 18 groupes industriels français en 1972," *Economie et statistique* 87 (1977):11–27.

18. The relationship between the degree of concentration in a given sector and the average age of workers reverses as one moves from cadres to blue-collar workers, and for the same reasons: young workers are cheaper and less demanding than older workers, less unionized, and less stable. Small firms in dispersed sectors producing consumer goods are more likely to hire young workers (who can be paid the minimum wage) than are large, capital-intensive firms. In firms employing fewer than 50 workers 9.7% of all workers are under age 20, compared with only 5.8% in firms employing more than 1,000 workers. It takes longer, moreover, 'for skills to be recognized in smaller firms, and the transition from semi-skilled to skilled status is a much more rapid process in a large company." See F. Eymard-Duvernay, "Segmentation du marché du travail: premier examen," unpublished INSEE note, Paris, 1980.

19. Michel Cézard shows that senior cadres, who are generally less well educated than engineers, are present in small firms in greater numbers; 22.8% are sons of owners of businesses, compared with only 15.2% of the engineers, but 30.3% are sons of senior cadres, compared with 40.4% of engineers. What is more, only 11% of those who were sons of owners of businesses held advanced degrees, compared with 24.7% of those who were sons of senior cadres. See Michel Cézard, "Les cadres et leur origine scolaire et sociale," unpublished INSEE note, 1978. Similarly, the percentage of senior cadres and engineers whose fathers were self-employed or employers ranges from 21.2% for those employed in firms with fewer than 500 workers, to 26.6% of those employed in firms with 100–500 workers, to 32% of those employed in firms with fewer than 100 workers, to 44.6% of those employed in firms with fewer than 20 workers (source: Formation–Qualification–Profession survey, 1970).

20. The existence of a number of more or less distinct cadre job markets helps to interpret systematic differences between the image of cadres in the *Expansion*–SOFRES study and their image in other studies based on different principles, such as the APEC-sponsored studies. The cadres in the *Expansion*–SOFRES sample filled out questionnaires distributed by the major Paris employment agencies. They

were participating in the central job market and best fit the prevalent social image of the cadre. Not only were they generally well educated, but a high proportion worked in marketing and advertising (11%, compared with only 2% of the cadres in the APEC study). On the other hand, far fewer of them worked in production-related jobs (14.2%, compared with 19.5% of those in the APEC study, 25% of those in the UIMM study, and 42% of those in the 1970 Formation–Qualification–Profession survey). An additional 14% worked in "engineering" and consulting agencies and various service organizations.

21. Cf. A. Sales, "Des pratiques de rémunération aux politiques d'emploi. Tendances à la rationalisation de la rémunération des cadres," *Sociologie du travail* 10(3)1968:291–302.
22. The study carried out by APEC in 1975 of a sample of 3,000 new members of a cadres' retirement fund provides information about cadre job mobility, which is very different for university graduates and autodidacts. The questionnaire did not cover the full career trajectory. It concentrated instead on the characteristics of the new and previous employers as well as on characteristics of the individual, such as age, education, etc. Unfortunately, social background was not ascertained. The individuals in the sample were at different stages in their careers, and their answers obviously depended in large part on their age, or, rather, on their age in relation to their other characteristics.
23. A study carried out by the Centre national des jeunes cadres shows similarly that 40% of the cadres hired by small and medium firms owed their jobs to contacts. Cited in AISEC, *Etudiants en sciences économiques et commerciales et cadre de vie professionelle, étude nationale 1975–1976*, CEREQ, 1978.
24. An appointed officer can be fired at any time by the board of directors without being entitled to compensation, whereas the salaried employee enjoys certain benefits guaranteed by labor legislation (such as severance pay). In case of bankruptcy, moreover, corporate officers may be liable for company debts, but employees may not. Holding more than one job means having more than one status and hence receiving more than one kind of compensation. As for the tax aspect, "remuneration received by corporate officers by virtue of performing salaried work for the firm is considered to be salary and as such is deductible from taxable capital gains, as is the compensation paid to said officers for discharge of their fiduciary responsibilities." See Le Bayon, *op. cit.*, p. 125.
25. According to a 1973 SOFRES study of small and medium firms, in one out of two such firms one or more cadres are related to the firm's owners. See M. Herblay, "La vérité sur les P.M.E.," *L'expansion*, October 1973, pp. 119–29.
26. Cf. Bourdieu, Boltanski, and de Saint Martin, "Les stratégies."
27. This independence is never complete, primarily because the cadre's

rank in the firm he is leaving, the number of subordinates he supervised, and above all the importance and prestige of the firm all affect the level of the job he may hope to attain and the share in the profits of the new firm he may hope to claim.

28. One cadre employed by a relative who owns a small business says that "there are fewer than three dozen cadres in our outfit. In a small company you don't plan to make your career by replacing somebody above you in the hierarchy. Your best chance is for the company to grow, and you along with it. Over the past four years my company has grown at an average rate of 25% annually. The chief of manufacturing and the comptroller and I myself, along with the other fellow who shares responsibility with me for sales, all had to face problems of a new order of magnitude. One took on an assistant, another a secretary, another a group of new salesmen. The chief of manufacturing and the comptroller didn't change their titles, but their jobs did change, and their pay increased. In short, their careers moved forward.... So for a young cadre first starting out with a new company, it seems to me that the important things to worry about are the company's sales and its plans more than the age of its executives, which doesn't necessarily have anthing to do with their energy."
29. On the integration of large corporations, in which compartmentalization is coupled with centralized financial controls, see for example M. Beaud, P. Danjou, and J. David, *Une multinationale française, Péchiney-Ugine-Kuhlmann* (Paris: Editions du Seuil, 1975), esp. pp. 167–90.
30. This is the purpose of "internal auditing," a practice that has become increasingly common since the early 1970s and that is designed to coordinate activities of far-flung production units with plans laid down by corporate headquarters. Internal auditors are always college graduates. Twenty-seven percent have attended one of the Grandes Ecoles or business schools. They do not supervise operations directly but gather figures in order to "estimate and evaluate the efficacy of other controls." See APEC, "L'audit interne," in the Dossiers Emploi series, 1976.
31. Cf. A. Wei Djao, "Dependent Development and Social Control: Labour-Intensive Industrialization in Hong Kong," *Social Praxis* 5(3–4)1979:275–93.
32. Cf. Bourdieu and de Saint Martin, "Le patronat."
33. One of the objective (and sometimes explicit) purposes of business reorganizations is to disrupt union organizations based on the firm's previous structure. This strategy can be very effective, moreover, because employers can move very quickly, not to say instantaneously, when all that is involved is a change in a firm's legal status, for example, whereas the reorganization of the union local, say, requires a lengthy, and costly, reunification effort and a reconstruction of the "common interest."
34. A concise formulation of these new strategies may be found in the last work of Octave Gélinier, *Nouvelle direction de l'entreprise* (Paris:

Editions d'Organisation, 1979). Gélinier advises his executive readers to "divide the firm into small production units, plants, or subsidiaries; keep stockpiles outside the factories; concentrate on major operations (such as research and sales or production and service); and subcontract the rest.... Grow by franchising or licensing in the developed countries and by management contracts in the developing countries. Go to many different countries in the developed world for marketing, research, and services and in the underdeveloped world for production" (p. 38):

35. J. Magaud, "L'éclatement juridique de la communauté de travail," *Droit social*, December 1975, pp. 525–30.
36. Cf. for example J. Broda, "L'emploi et le travail temporaire dans la zone de Fos," *Sociologie du Sud-Est* 7–8(1976):2–42.
37. Cf. R. Linhart, "Evolution du procès de travail et luttes de classes," *Critique communiste* 23(1978):105–29.
38. Cf. B. Bennin and E. de Banville, "Procès de production et changement social," Sainte-Etienne, CRESAL (CORDES research), July1975, mimeographed.
39. We must be careful not to make a natural entity out of the "tertiary sector," which, like the cadre category, is a statistical and economic artifact that carries with it an implicit representation of social space and is therefore an issue in social struggles that figures in many different strategies. To take just one example, the growth of the tertiary sector in the 1970s is not unrelated to the increasing reliance on subcontracting. Small service firms in the tertiary sector perform the maintenance tasks once carried out by manufacturing personnel employed by large firms (and hence employed in the secondary sector).
40. Cf. Bertrand, *art. cit.*
41. Cf. Bourdieu, Boltanski, and de Saint Martin, "Les stratégies," and Bourdieu and de Saint Martin, "Le patronat."
42. The title "cadre" is increasingly being used by engineers, including engineering school graduates. This fact helps to explain why the ratio of engineers to cadres has been decreasing. The number of engineers has been growing at a slower rate than the number of senior cadres since 1962 (cf. Thévenot, "Les catégories sociales en 1975"). This is partly due to the emergence of new professions on the borderline between production and management (such as data processing and information management) and partly to the growth in the number of graduate engineers taking jobs in sales, administration, and management. Perhaps related to this, perhaps not, many engineers find it more gratifying to call themselves cadres. Both FASFID and INSEE publish censuses of engineers; the numbers counted are roughly the same (235,000 and 256,000), but only about half of the two groups overlap. In fact, 25% of the engineers in the INSEE survey are categorized as "industrialists" and 25% as "senior cadres," while 50% are "in-house engineers" who did not graduate from engineering

school. Cf. "6e enquête socio-économique sur la situation des ingénieurs diplômés," special issue of *I.D.* 71, Oct. 1977.

43. Cf. J. Daguze, "Les cadres autodidactes et la formation permanente," thesis, Paris, 1977, mimeographed, p. 45.
44. As was stated in almost explicit terms by Georges Villiers, spokesman for business, on "productivity day," 8 May 1952, in Marseilles: "Cadres will not do their jobs unless we restore their prestige and authority. This difficult decision warrants special care. Steady promotion through the ranks is indispensable, because it fosters competition between the autodidact and the engineer who graduates from a prestigious school, competition that is healthy for the general climate and for the country as a whole." Cited in *Actions et problèmes, op. cit.*, p. 77.
45. In France the fundamental change in status in industry is the promotion to cadre, which "implies a fundamental shift in the unions allegiance to the firm." By contrast, in German firms the "status distinction" between different levels of the hierarchy is much less marked, and there is a continuum of positions ranging from the executive levels down to the workers. The highly discontinuous nature of the cadre/non-cadre opposition may be part of the reason why the numbers of the cadres have grown so dramatically; there are more cadres in French firms than there are people in corresponding positions in German firms. Cf. Maurice, *op. cit.*, pp. 770–1.
46. See Nicolas Dubost's excellent analysis of working-class mobility in *Flins sans fin* (Paris: Maspero, 1979), esp. pp. 159–80.
47. Daguze, "Les cadres autodidactes," pp. 32–3.
48. Cf. Le Bayon, *op. cit.*, pp. 76–80. "Joining a cadres' retirement fund is more a sign than a decisive criterion." Among the many criteria that may be considered by the courts are "salary coefficient, registration by the employer in a cadres' retirement and insurance fund, employee's diploma and credentials," and above all "the express or tacit recognition of the employee as a cadre by the employer."
49. Cf. Lawrence Stone, "The Inflation of Honors 1558–1641," *Past and Present* 14(1958):45–70. And on the analogy between the inflation of noble titles and the inflation of scholastic titles, see Pierre Bourdieu, "Classement, déclassement, reclassement," *Actes de la recherche en sciences sociales* 24(1978):2–22.
50. As Rivard *et al., op. cit.*, pp. 156ff, have shown, the main job of manufacturing engineers (60% of whom are autodidacts) is to manage workers. They are "down in the mines," as the authors say, and directly supervise the work force, unlike graduates of the Grandes Ecoles, who usually try to avoid this kind of job in favor of positions in administration and finance. Manufacturing cadres often have large numbers of "subordinates" (in one case, a self-taught shop manager supervised 1,350 workers, 70% of them semiskilled), but few of these subordinates are themselves cadres (except for beginners being given a "tryout' on the shop floor).

51. Cézard, *Les cadres et leur origine.*
52. FASFID, "Enquête socio-économique sur la situation des ingénieurs et cadres," special issue of *I.D.*, March 1969.
53. Cf. M. Calviac, "Combien gagne un ingénieur," *Economie et statistique* 99(1978):45–53.
54. M. Praderie and R. Salais, "Une enquête sur la formation et la qualification des Français,' *Etudes et conjoncture* 22(2)1967:3–110. On shifts by graduate engineers after age 35 from technical jobs to positions in finance, management, and administration, see also Calviac, "Combien gagne un ingénieur."
55. Cf. R. Perrucci and R. A. Rothman, "Obsolescence of Knowledge and the Professional Career," in R. Perrucci and J. E. Gerstl (eds.), *The Engineers and the Social System* (New York: John Wiley, 1969), pp. 247–76.
56. The pairing of an agent and a job, the position occupied and actually worked at (as opposed to the position formally defined in the organization chart but in fact "vacant"), or what might be called the *tenure*, is comparable in every way to a "couple," a supra-individual entity that is greater than the sum of its parts. The occupation of the post, which is like a marriage, creates value and power (as does the joining of two families in marriage), because it joins together in a productive unit agents (who in general are powerless to realize their social capital outside the institutions in which the positions they hold are objectified) and positions (which, no matter how high they stand in the formal organization and no matter how much potential power they imply, always owe much of their real importance to the personal attributes of the agents who fill them).
57. See Bourdieu and de Saint Martin, "Le patronat," for a description of a day in the life of "Roger Martin, a man with contacts." According to a poll conducted by the magazine *Entreprise* in 1963 (no. 403), more than 70% of the working time of senior cadres is taken up with meetings, receiving visitors, telephone calls (15%), outside calls, and so on, compared with only 5% devoted to the study of important decisions.
58. Cf. C. Sofer, *Men in Mid-Career: A Study of British Managers and Technical Specialists* (Cambridge, England: Cambridge University Press, 1970), pp. 345–6.
59. Pierre Rivard, Jean-Michel Saussois, and Pierre Tripier, *op. cit.*, p. 46, show, for example, that recruitment of Grande Ecole graduates is highly uneven. In their sample, recruitment was maximal in firms "adopting an offensive research and development strategy." Other firms hired graduates of these prestigious institutions "to use the contacts that go along with their degrees." The "competence" of these engineers is then defined in terms of their ability to mobilize actors both outside and inside the firm. In one firm, Glissoire, what mattered was their ability "to negotiate with clients' research departments, largely staffed by graduate engineers." In another firm,

Mecanod, what mattered was their ability to carry on negotiations between "corporate headquarters, where there were many college graduates, and the production plants."

60. APEC, *Le marketing et le chef de produit* (Paris, 1977), p. 63.
61. Octave Gélinier, *Fonctions et tâches de direction générale* (Paris: Editions Hommes et techniques, 1969), p. 375.
62. A 1976 APEC-sponsored survey of 300 firms ranging in size from fewer than 200 employees (11.7%) to more than 10,000 employees (6.3%) showed that "small and medium firms adopted a parasitic policy, in that they preferred and actively sought to hire middle-level cadres who had gained experience of the industry and the job through a previous position.... This was particularly true of production and sales cadres, for in these kinds of jobs experience is particularly valuable." See APEC, *Politique et pratique de l'emploi des cadres* (Paris, 1977), p. 49.
63. The salary level at which the risks of changing jobs outweigh the advantages is much lower for autodidacts than for college-trained cadres: the percentage of cadres who claim to be earning more in their new jobs than in their old ones varies: among college graduates, 90% of those earning less than 30,000 francs before the change were earning more after, as were 47% of those earning more than 90,000 francs before; for autodidacts the corresponding figures are 80% and 10%.
64. As was suggested, for example, by the conclusions of the commission chaired by Mr Sirinelli: cf. Commission sur les formations supérieures, "Document de travail no. 1," Imprimerie nationale, April 1971.
65. Although the unemployment level for cadres remained lower than that for other categories, the number of cadres and related workers on the job market has increased steadily, especially since 1968: 7,170 in 1965, 16,900 in 1968, 28,800 in 1972, 41,500 in 1974, 81,000 in 1975, 100,000 in 1976. See B. Seys and P. Laulhé, *Enquête sur l'emploi de 1976*, INSEE collections, series D, no. 48, Nov. 1976. In 1976, 19,511 cadres were registered with APEC, 11,276 of whom were unemployed cadres, 1,824 employed cadres, and 6,411 recent graduates. See *L'Expansion* 108, June 1977, p. 208.
66. French firms participated in 2,202 "concentration operations" between 1963 and 1973, with peaks in 1964 (265), 1966 (249), and 1972 (249). See Guibert *et al.*, *op. cit.*, vol. 1, p. 95. Many of these were "internal reorganizations" rather than mergers, however. See Y. Citoleux *et. al.*, "Les groupes de sociétés en 1974: une méthode d'analyse," *Economie et statistique* 87(1977):55–63.
67. From 1968 to 1977 10,000–15,000 business bankruptcies were recorded, most involving small businesses. See J. Albert and L. Violet, "Les défaillances d'entreprises depuis dix ans: un tournant en 1974," *Economie et statistique* 95(1977):23–32.
68. According to an Ires-Marketing survey in 1971, 41% of self-taught

cadres think of going into business for themselves some day, compared with only 32% of college graduates. *Entreprise* 850, December 1971.

69. Cf. F. H. Gouldner, "Demotion in Industrial Management," *American Sociological Review* 30(1965):714–24.
70. In at least one-third of the cases, "resignation" is a camouflaged form of dismissal, as is suggested by the APEC survey result that 34% of cadres who resigned did so before signing a contract with a new employer. More than half of this group did not subsequently find a job at an equivalent salary level. Note, too, that self-taught cadres most commonly cite problems with their superiors as reasons for resignation (39%), whereas engineering school graduates most commonly cite lack of opportunities for advancement (37%). Another indicator: the UNEDIC survey of unemployed cadres shows that the percentage of those who state that leaving their jobs came as a "psychological shock" is roughly the same for those who "resigned" (26%) as for those who were dismissed.
71. The law of 13 July 1973 states that dismissal must be for "real and sufficient cause," and any firm that fails to meet this test may be required to pay indemnities to the dismissed employee. One way to get around the law (which does not define "real and sufficient cause") is to invoke "loss of confidence." Cf. *Option* 116, April 1977.
72. Cf. for example F. Bourricaud, "Contre le sociologisme: une critique et des propositions," *Revue française de sociologie* 16, 1975 supplement, pp. 583–604, or R. Boudon, "La logique de la frustratiion relative," *Archives européennes de sociologie* 18(1)197:3–26.
73. Gélinier, *Fonctions et tâches*, pp. 377–8.
74. A firm is a finite space; the number of positions in it cannot be multiplied indefinitely. In order to hire new employees with new skills and put them to the test, jobs have to be freed up. One function of upward mobility is precisely to create what Harrisson C. White calls "chains of opportunity," which he compares to musical chairs: freeing up certain posts creates "vacancy chains." In contrast to mobility models, which always assume that agents feel a "desire" or "need" to move up, White puts forward the hypothesis that under certain conditions mobility may be a structural component of the system, in which "job controllers" (those who occupy the dominant positions) manage investments in vacant positions created by forces that may have nothing to do with the mobility process itself. Cf. H. C. White, *Chains of Opportunity* (Cambridge, Mass.: Harvard University Press, 1970).
75. Concerning the various forms that "cooling out" mechanisms may take, see E. Goffman, "On Cooling the Mark Out: Some Adaptations to Failure," *Psychiatry* 15(1952):451–63. Cf. also N. H. Martin and A. L. Strauss, "Consequences of Failures in Organization," in B. G. Glaser (ed.), *Organizational Careers* (Chicago: Aldine, 1968), pp. 263–6; on techniques of divestiture aimed at making cooling out acceptable, see B. R. Clark, "The Cooling-Out Function in Higher

Education," *American Journal of Sociology* 65(6)1960:569–76.

76. Knowledge of financial, family, and friendship networks that link management of different firms in unofficial and sometimes clandestine ways is indispensable to a cadre's survival. Without such knowledge, a sales cadre tends to defend the interests of his own firm, regardless of the partner with whom he is negotiating and regardless of the interests of those who exert power over the firm, which need not coincide with the firm's interests *per se*. If things go wrong, he can be disavowed and removed from the negotiations, which can then be continued "on friendly terms" between owners.
77. A pamphlet issued to managers in one large American-based multinational contains the following: 'You will meet your supervisor at least once a year. At that time he will present you with an evaluation of your performance and together with you will work out a self-improvement program for the following year and set the goals that you must meet.... Everyone wants to know what his supervisor thinks of his work. It is reassuring to know that at least once a year you will receive a thorough evaluation of your work over the preceding year.... When your superior informs you that he has scheduled an Evaluation and Professional Counseling Interview with you, he will give you a brochure that will help you prepare for the meeting. This document includes a form on which you can write down the subjects you plan to bring up during the interview.... The interview itself is in five stages.... You will begin by discussing your work-related problems and concerns for the future.... Then you will discuss with your supervisor the work goals he has set for you for the coming year.... This procedure will ensure that all your concerns are fully dealt with.'
78. The case analyzed here, as well as those that follow, is described in the UIMM's *Cahiers techniques*, a confidential publication that the organization makes available to its members to inform them of new techniques of organization and personnel management.
79. Cf. P. Fritsch, *L'éducation des adultes* (Paris: Mouton, 1971), pp. 45–55.
80. Cf. Bourdieu and Boltanski, "Le titre et le poste."
81. Negotiation of the agreement on adult education provoked conflicts among business leaders. The owners of small and medium businesses were hostile to the accord, for they felt that it would impose a permanent additional cost on business. There was also opposition from certain big businessmen, most notably members of the association Entreprise et progrès, who already had their own independent and flexible training systems in place. See Brizay, *op. cit.*, pp. 152–6.
82. See for example Chenevier, "La collaboration": "In a system of adult education the universities cannot hold a monopoly on education."
83. Cf. R. Pohl, C. Thélot, and M. F. Jousset, "L'enquête formation qualification professionnelle de 1970," Paris, INSEE collections, series D(32), May 1974, pp. 143 and 175.
84. Cf. APEC, *Politique et pratique*, pp. 66–7. It should be noted, however,

that if adult education does not automatically lead to advancement, it does tend to limit "deskilling." Almost no salary decreases were noted among those who engaged in further studies after graduation. This is not an insignificant result, especially for workers in lower-level positions (technicians, clerical personnel, etc.), whose bonuses tend to stagnate quite early, particularly when related to technical knowledge bound up with the current state of the art in the branch in which they are employed (to take only the most obvious example, think of the changes in the computing industry). Cf. Pohl, Thélot, and Jousset, "L'enquête," p. 143.

85. Cf. C. de Montlibert, "L'éducation permanente et la promotion des classes moyennes," *Sociologie du travail* 19(3)1977:243–65.
86. The survey of readers of *Science et vie* (abbreviated SV in the text) was conducted with the help of Pascale Maldidier, using a questionnaire of about 80 questions inserted into the January 1974 issue of the magazine. We received 6,000 responses (the circulation of SV in May 1974 was 207,811). In addition to the statistics thus obtained, we made use of a large number of letters and thirty in-depth interviews. The results of this survey are analyzed in detail in Boltanski and Maldidier, "La vulgarisation scientifique et son public," Paris, Centre de Sociologie de l'Education, mimeographed, 1977.
87. The population analyzed here is comparable to the students of the Instituts de promotion supérieure du travail (IPST) analyzed by Philippe Fritsch, who shows that the chance of success in an IPST program is still a function of cultural background (i.e., of social and educational background). See Fritsch, *Les élèves des instituts de promotion supérieure du travail* (Nancy: INFA, 1970).
88. Every issue of SV carries an advertisement or two for gymnastic equipment designed to restore a person's physical and psychological balance. The apparatus is supposed to be an "economical" and "efficient" way to relax: "With Slendertone [a sort of vibromassage machine] do your exercises while reading Balzac."
89. Claude Grignon studied another group of rising autodidacts: engineering students at the Conservatoire national des arts et métiers (65% of them technicians, two-thirds with degrees lower than the baccalaureate). Their whole private life tends to be organized around the need to make up for deficiencies in their education: "Evening school students tend to lead solitary lives, to give up consuming or at least defer their purchases, and in short to sacrifice the present for the sake of the future." See Grignon, "L'art et le métier: école parallèle et petite bourgeoise," *Actes de la recherche en sciences sociales* 4(1976):21–46.
90. Cf. E. M. Lemert, "Paranoia and the Dynamics of Exclusion," *Sociometry* 25(1962):2–20, republished in *Social Problems and Social Control* (Englewood Cliffs, NJ: Prentice Hall, 1967), pp. 197–211.
91. Except, to my knowledge, in France.
92. Cf. J. Ruesch *et al.*, *Duodenal Ulcer* (Berkeley: University of California Press, 1948).

93. Cf. A. Zaleznik, M. F. Kets de Vries, and J. Howard, "Stress Reactions in Organizations: Syndromes, Causes, and Consequences," *Behavioral Science* 22(3)1977:151–62.
94. Cf. P. Castelnuovo-Tedesco, "Emotion Antecedents of Perforation of Ulcers of the Stomach and Duodenum," *Psychosomatic Medicine* 24(1962):398–416.
95. A full bibliography of the many German, British, and American studies on social factors in heart disease may be found in J. Siegrist and M. J. Halhuber, *Myocardial Infarction and Psychosocial Risks* (Berlin–New York: Springer Verlag, 1981).

Conclusion: the cohesion of a fluid group

1. Cf. P. Bourdieu, *Le sens pratique* (Paris: Editions de Minuit, 1980).
2. Cf. E. Rosch, "On the Internal Structure of Perceptual and Semantic Categories," in T. E. Moore (ed.), *Cognitive Development and the Acquisition of Language* (New York: Academic Press, 1973), pp. 111–14; E. Rosch, "Classification of Real-World Objects: Origins and Representations in Cognition," in P. N. Johnson-Laird and P. C. Wason (eds.), *Thinking: Readings in Cognitive Science* (Cambridge, England: Cambridge University Press, 1977), pp. 212–22. Cf. also the recent collection edited by E. Rosch and B. B. Lloyd, *Cognition and Categorization* (New York: Erlbaum, 1978).
3. On the effects of schematic (or cartographic) objectification see J. Goody, *La raison graphique* (Paris: Editions de Minuit, 1978).
4. Cf. for example W. H. Goodenough, "Componential Analysis and the Study of Meaning," *Language* 32(1956):195–216, and A. Kimball Romney and R. Goodwin D'Andrade, "Cognitive Aspects of English Kin Terms," *American Anthropologist* 66(1964):146–70. Many other examples may be found in S. Tyler (ed.), *Cognitive Anthropology* (New York: Holt, Rinehart, and Winston 1969). Rosch's work originated with a critique of "componentialist" thinking. In substance, Rosch argues that current anthropological thinking about common classification, including componential analysis, seeks to discover the minimal basic attributes in terms of which popular usage of terms in a particular domain can be formally ordered, which leads to focusing exclusively on the boundaries between terms and pretending that the boundaries between categories are always well defined.
5. Where Rosch's work links up with that of Brent Berlin, P. Kay, and C. McDaniel. See Berlin and Kay, *Basic Color Terms: Their Universality and Evolution* (Berkeley, University of California Press, 1969); and P. Kay and C. McDaniel, "The Linguistic Significance of the Meanings of Basic Color Terms," *Language* 54(3):610–43.
6. Cf. A. Margalit, "Vagueness in Vogue," *Synthèse* 33(1976)211–21: "The discrete approach, according to which the question whether a natural species belongs to a given class can be answered 'yes' or 'no', is false.... Since we form our categories without clear-cut bound-

aries and criteria to cover borderline cases, we work with the central members of the category.... When logical inferences are made in natural languages, it is usually the clear (central) cases that are invoked." Rosch and her collaborators implicitly accept the view of Wittgenstein, that words have no rigorous definition.

7. The incomplete data used here come from an ongoing research project conducted by Laurent Thévenot and the author, the purpose of which is to explore empirically the ordinary social orientation and competence of individual social agents (implicit taxonomies, processes of categorization, recognition of social membership, etc.). To date, 135 persons (in groups of 15 or so) have been asked to select "good examples" of members of different social categories (including cadres), which gives an exemplary sample of around 400 cadres. Since the collection of data is not yet complete, I shall here confine myself to comparing the responses given by four different groups: a group of well-educated cadres employed by a large nationalized firm; a group of unemployed individuals enrolled in a training course and consisting mainly of self-taught cadres; a group of salesmen, for the most part not college graduates, employed by a multinational corporation; and a group of retired teachers (elementary and secondary school teachers). The analyses and results described here are incomplete and superficial. Nevertheless, it seemed worthwhile, given the aims of this book, to put forward certain hypotheses concerning the historical origins of mental categories associated with the words used to designate social groups, rather than wait until this research, the results of which will be published separately, has been completed.
8. Cf. Kay and McDaniel, "Linguistic Significance."
9. Cf. T. C. Schelling, *The Strategy of Conflict* (New York: Oxford University Press, 1960), pp. 53–81. Schelling develops the theory of tacit cooperation in his chapter on "limited war" (how to halt nuclear escalation), which, he says, requires boundaries and allows no explicit negotiation of those boundaries. Schelling takes his inspiration from game theory as well as from Goffman, who was himself a reader of von Neumann and Morgenstern. The works of Schelling and Goffman intersect: Goffman treats individual relations as though they were relations between collective persons (states, unions, parties, and so forth), while Schelling treats collective relations as though they were relations between individuals (with bluffing, bad faith, saving face, and so on). On the relations between Schelling and Goffman, see M. Daubry, "Note sur la théorie de l'interaction stratégique," *Annuaire ARES*, 1(1978):43–64.
10. Cf. Mauss, "La cohésion sociale dans les sociétés polysegmentaires," pp. 11–27.
11. Margalit, "Vagueness in Vogue," shows that the word "vague" is sometimes used to mean "indefinite," as when one says "there are no definite boundaries" between mountain and valley, and sometimes to mean "indeterminate," as in distinguishing between mountains

and hills.

12. In some versions the theme of "proletarization of cadres" seems to reflect a defensive reaction on the part of highly educated cadres. In a study of "young cadres and trade unionism" carried out by the Centre national des jeunes cadres, for example, with a sample of which 88% consisted of cadres who had graduated from the Grandes Ecoles, "the slow disappearance of the distinction between cadre and white-collar employee was cited by more than a third of those questioned." The commentators on this survey remark that "if there is to be a levelling, it should involve upward reclassification rather than downward. Downward reclassification means fragmenting cadres' tasks and responsibilities, making them little more than *bureaucracy's semiskilled intellectual laborers*." See CNJC, *Les jeunes cadres et le syndicalisme*, pp. 12–13.
13. Georg Lukačs, *History and Class Consciousness* (Cambridge, Mass.: MIT Press, 1971), p. 51.
14. "By relating consciousness to the whole of society it becomes possible to infer the thoughts and feelings which men would have in a particular situation if they were *able* to assess both it [i.e., the particular situation] and the interests arising from it in their impact on immediate action and on the whole structure of society. That is to say, it would be possible to infer the thoughts and feelings appropriate to their objective situation. The number of such situations is not unlimited in any society. However much detailed researches are able to refine social typologies there will always be a number of clearly distinguished basic types whose characteristics are determined by the types of position available in the process of production. Now class consciousness consists in fact of the appropriate and rational reactions 'imputed' [*zugerechnet*] to a particular typical position in the process of production." Ibid., p. 51.

Epilogue: the car in the garage

1. On the background of Erving Goffman's first book, *The Representation of Self in Everyday Life*, see my "Erving Goffman et le temps du soupçon," *Informations sur les sciences sociales* 12(3)1973, pp. 127–47.

Principal statistical sources

Statistical information about the cadre population was gleaned primarily from seven surveys conducted during the past ten years. The results of the first three have been subjected to further analysis.

The seven surveys are as follows:

1. INSEE: 1970 Formation–Qualification–Profession Survey.

A full account of the results of this survey may be found in R. Pohl, C. Thélot, M.-F. Jousset, *L'enquête formation-qualification professionelle de 1970*, vol. 32, series D, INSEE, May 1974. The analysis focused on a sample of engineers and senior cadres who belonged to a cadre retirement fund. The correlations among the following variables were examined: function in the firm, educational level, age at graduation, age at entry into working life, father's income and status, first job held, age, branch of industry (eight were considered), and size of firm.

2. APEC: Enquête sur la mobilité professionelle des cadres.

A 1975 study conducted by APEC on a sample of new members of a cadres' retirement fund (AGIRC). The sample included 2,920 individuals, distributed as follows: "beginners" (17%, n = 500) who obtained a cadre-level position as their first employment; individuals "promoted" to cadre-level positions (32%, n = 920), 13% of whom were promoted after changing employers, 12% by the same employer, and 4% after moving from the public to the private sector); and "veteran cadres" (51%, n = 1,500), who changed employer and retirement plan, after either dismissal (18%) or resignation. These subgroups were analyzed separately.

3. *Expansion*–SOFRES: Les salaires des cadres.

The *Expansion*–SOFRES survey of cadre salaries has been carried out every year since 1970. I have subjected the results of the 1976 survey to further analysis. The statistical sample was compiled from 5,396 detailed questionnaires filled out by cadres at eleven of the most important hiring consultants' offices. These questionnaires contained information about job description, educational background, additional training, salary, benefits, branch of industry, firm's total sales, number of persons supervised, age, and sex. Various correlations were determined from these data. Conclusions were checked against the data for all the other surveys through 1978.

4. Survey by the Union des industries métallurgiques et minières of the situation of engineers and senior cadres, and forecast of the metal industry's need for cadres.

This survey, carried out by a business association, was conducted on four occasions, in 1956, 1962, 1970, and 1977. Though limited to a single branch of industry, these studies provide important information about the evolution of the cadre population. In 1977 the questionnaire was sent to all firms in the metals industries employing more than 100 workers, and to all corporate headquarters. The unit of analysis was the corporation, with all its various plants and subsidiaries. In all, 635 companies responded, representing 962,783 workers, 51,467 of whom were engineers and cadres under the terms of collective bargaining agreements. The results of each of the four surveys have been published in detail.

5. Study of cadres by the Centre d'études de la vie politique française.

Carried out in 1975 by Gérard Grunberg and René Mouriaux, this survey examined a sample of 1,481 cadres (engineers, senior cadres, middle-level cadres, and technicians as defined by INSEE). The questionnaire included about 100 questions, bearing mainly on political opinions and attitudes toward unions, but also covering characteristics of firms such as size, status, existence of subsidiaries, and so forth, and attributes of individuals such as educational and social background, position in the firm, etc. This study is one of the most complete sources of statistical information about cadres currently available. Some of the results have been published in Grunberg and Mouriaux, *L'univers politique et syndical des cadres* (Paris: Presses de la Fondation nationale des sciences politiques, 1979).

6. Study of cadres' attitudes toward security carried out by the Centre d'études et de recherches sur l'aménagement urbain.

This study was carried out in 1972–73 by Agnès Pitrou at the behest of the Caisse interprofessionnelle de prévoyance des cadres. Questionnaires were sent to 1,200 subscribers of the CIPC. The results have been published in Pitrou, *Les attitudes des cadres envers la sécurité* (Paris: CIPC, 1974), and J. Mauduit and A. Constantin, *Les cadres et la sécurité* (Paris: CIPC, n.d.).

7. Surveys by the Fédération des associations et sociétés françaises d'ingénieurs diplômes.

The FASFID conducted six "socioeconomic surveys of the situation of graduate engineers" in 1958, 1963, 1967, 1971, 1974, and 1977. In 1977 questionnaires were sent to 112,000 engineers by 66 different associations. Of these, 21,480 were returned and analyzed by FASFID in collaboration with INSEE and the Laboratoire d'économie et de sociologie du travail d'Aix-en-Provence. The questionnaire dealt mainly with education, postgraduate studies, age, position in the firm, characteristics of the firm, etc. The main results of the 1977 study were published in a special issue of the review *ID*, October 1977.

Index